TO THE ENDS OF THE EARTH

To the Ends of the Earth

Romans and the Mission of God

JEFF ROPER

WIPF & STOCK · Eugene, Oregon

TO THE ENDS OF THE EARTH
Romans and the Mission of God

Wipf & Stock
An Imprint of Wipf and Stock Publishers
199 W. 8th Ave., Suite 3
Eugene, OR 97401

www.wipfandstock.com

PAPERBACK ISBN: 979-8-3852-6393-6
HARDCOVER ISBN: 979-8-3852-6394-3
EBOOK ISBN: 979-8-3852-6395-0

VERSION NUMBER 04/10/26

To Dr. Jim Scott
Mentor, Friend

Contents

Acknowledgments

I AM DEEPLY GRATEFUL to the many people who have walked with me through the long and demanding journey of writing this book. Although the work bears my name, it has been sustained at every stage by the patience, wisdom, and generosity of others.

First and foremost, I thank my wife Debbie Roper. Thank you for your patience, understanding, and grace during the many seasons when I disappeared into my dissertation—and later into the demanding work of turning that dissertation into a book. Thank you for bearing with me during countless moments when my body was present but my mind was elsewhere, occupied by this work. Your steady love made this project possible.

This book began as my PhD dissertation, and I am profoundly grateful to Dr. Sam Ahn for his wise and patient guidance throughout my doctoral studies. I had little sense at the outset of how much work it would take to transform a dissertation into a book; it proved to be far more demanding than I ever imagined. I am also thankful to Brandon Brazee, Steve Overman, and Bud Stanley for reading the original dissertation and offering thoughtful and constructive feedback that helped shape it for a wider audience.

To my children and grandchildren: You continually remind me of the joy, richness, and grounding power of family. You teach me, often without words, what truly matters.

I am deeply thankful for my ministry team—Brandon and Marcie Brazee, Steve and Kim Cecil, Gary and Joy Peiss, and Tim and Dhana Wimberly. You have carried the weight of our shared ministry with faithfulness and generosity, offered invaluable insight and honest feedback, and provided a safe harbor of friendship along the way. I am a better follower of Jesus because of you.

I also extend my gratitude to Foursquare President Randy Remington, Vice President of Global Operations Ted Vail, Foursquare Missions International Director Paul Greer, and to the broader leadership of The Foursquare Church and Foursquare Missions International. Thank you for the privilege of serving this global family and for the trust extended to me in that service.

To the friends and family who contributed to my GoFundMe campaign, thank you for helping bridge the financial gap during this process. Your support was both practical and deeply encouraging.

Finally, I wish to express my deepest thanks to Dr. Jim Scott. It was an honor to serve under your leadership during your tenure as director of Foursquare Missions International. More than a supervisor, you have been a mentor and a friend. For more than a decade, you were the steady and persistent voice encouraging me to pursue Romans as a PhD topic and, eventually, as a book for a broader audience. I am grateful for your confidence in me and for your persistence. This work is dedicated to you.

Introduction: Romans and the Mission of God

THIS BOOK EMERGED FROM a long personal journey, years in the making, that began with hope and gradually gave way to disillusionment. It took shape through decades of cross-cultural ministry and global mission leadership within the Foursquare movement, where I first sensed an invitation to take my place in the ongoing story of God's mission. That invitation, however, was tested by lived experience.

By 2012, after extended ministry in Europe and the former Soviet Union, I found myself increasingly disturbed by the widening gap between churches in the United States and the global mission they claimed to embody. The divide was formed in theology and imagination, not simply in structures. As a result, mission no longer animated the church's life but hovered at its margins.

Within my own denomination, a church could be recognized as fully compliant with denominational expectations by contributing as little as one dollar per year to global missions. The problem was not the dollar itself, but what it signified. It functioned as a theological signal, revealing how mission had been reduced to an optional acknowledgment rather than a shared vocation. Over time, this arrangement normalized a vision of faithfulness in which global mission could be affirmed without being meaningfully embraced. The message, though rarely spoken aloud, was unmistakable: local priorities came first.[1]

As these patterns accumulated, my frustration hardened into judgment. I began to interpret the growing distance between churches and mission not only as a structural weakness, but as a theological failure. Yet

1. Thankfully, this practice was ended during the final stages of writing this book. The bylaws of The Foursquare Church required congregations to provide monthly support to Foursquare Missions International.

I also understood the pressures pastors faced. Having served as a senior pastor for more than two decades, I knew the demands of sustaining congregational life amid competing priorities and limited resources. Still, beneath these realities, I sensed a deeper distortion. When institutional survival becomes the church's primary concern, participation in the mission of God inevitably recedes, and the church begins to exist for itself rather than as a community sent into the world.

It was during this season of disillusionment that a remark by Luke Timothy Johnson disrupted my settled assumptions. While lecturing on the apostle Paul, he observed that Paul's letter to the Romans is, at its core, a missionary appeal letter. I had written many missionary appeal letters, yet nothing like Romans. That observation stopped me short. It felt as though a familiar text had turned and faced me, refusing to be read as I had always read it. The sentence lingered, unsettling and persistent, until it exposed what I had been unwilling to name: Beneath my frustration lay not simply disappointment with the church, but a diminished vision of the church's vocation within the mission of God.

What emerged through this journey became both a personal and scholarly effort to understand why Paul wrote Romans as he did if its primary purpose was, in fact, missionary. That question carried me through nearly fifteen years of research and culminated in doctoral work; the results of that journey are contained in these pages. What emerged was not only a fresh reading of Romans, but a clearer vision of how theology, mission, and communal life belong together and are, in fact, inseparable.

I had been trained to read Romans primarily as a systematic exposition of Christian doctrine. Returning to the letter amid personal and vocational strain, however, I encountered it differently—not as an abstract theological treatise, but as a pastoral and apostolic summons. Romans is addressed to a real community, shaped and in significant ways distorted by its surrounding culture. Paul's theology is not detached speculation; it is deliberately deployed to form a people capable of embodying the gospel together. The letter seeks to cultivate a shared life that can sustain faithful witness across cultural, social, and geographic boundaries.

The Roman congregations to whom Paul wrote were deeply fractured. Jewish and gentile believers were divided by history, theology, and practice. Economic disparities further shaped communal life, as some Christians inhabited wealthy households and networks of patronage while others lived as enslaved persons, freed laborers, or migrants on the margins of Roman society. Within a culture ordered by honor, status, and power, the church was continually tempted to reproduce imperial hierarchies rather than live the cruciform pattern of Christ. For Paul, these divisions were not peripheral concerns; they threatened the church's ability to participate faithfully in the mission of God.

It is in this context that Paul summons the Roman believers to mutual welcome, shared obedience, and participation in his westward mission to Spain. What is at stake is not merely institutional harmony, but the formation of a reconciled people whose common life makes the gospel visible. Romans functions as a carefully constructed apostolic strategy aimed at shaping a new humanity—one in which social, cultural, and theological divisions are not ignored or managed but overcome in Christ. Only such a community can bear credible witness together and serve as a launching point for the gospel's advance into new frontiers.

Reading Romans through this missiological lens reshaped my understanding of Scripture and church leadership. I came to see that there are challenges the church will never overcome apart from renewed participation in the mission of God, and mission frontiers that will never be reached without deeper partnership with the church. Romans did not simply reorient my ministry; it saved it.

This book grows out of my encounter with Romans. Now, I am inviting you to share in this journey. We begin by reading Romans as a pastoral and missionary intervention, attending to Paul's argument within its historical and communal setting. On that foundation, we trace the missiological logic that emerges from the letter, showing how spiritual formation, reconciled communal life, and mission are inseparable in the life of the church. The final sections bring this vision into conversation with lived practice through a series of case studies.

While these case studies draw from the experience of The Foursquare Church and its global mission partnerships, they are offered not as denominational prescriptions but as illustrative material. The Foursquare movement functions here as a bounded ecclesial ecosystem through which broader theological, missiological, and organizational dynamics can be examined with clarity. Readers from diverse traditions are invited to look beyond denominational distinctives and attend to our shared calling: to become communities formed by the Spirit, reconciled in Christ, and sent into the world for the sake of the nations. Thank you for taking this journey with me.

PART 1

Background Matters on the Letter to the Romans

THIS SECTION UNFOLDS IN several movements. We begin with areas of scholarly consensus regarding authorship, date, and occasion, before turning to the interpretive questions that have shaped the reading of Romans. The focus then widens from the text to its world, examining the social, political, and religious environment of the Roman Empire and the concrete realities of life within the Roman congregations. Attending to this context is essential, for Paul's letter emerged from cultural and religious dynamics that shaped both his mission and the situation of the churches in Rome. Set within a world marked by imperial power, religious plurality, and entrenched social divisions, these communities navigated honor–shame values and Jewish–gentile tensions that threatened not only their internal life and public witness in the imperial capital, but also their capacity to participate in Paul's envisioned mission to Spain.

1

Areas of Consensus and Debate

ROMANS STANDS AMONG THE most theologically influential texts in the New Testament and, in several respects, rests on unusually stable scholarly ground.[1] Paul's authorship is virtually undisputed, and both author and audience are explicitly identified in the letter's opening (Rom 1:1–15). Although its precise dating cannot be established with certainty, broad scholarly consensus places the composition of Romans during Paul's stay in Corinth, most likely between 55 and 58 CE.[2] The letter's occasion is likewise clear: Paul writes in anticipation of a visit to Rome near the conclusion of his eastern mission and shortly before his journey to Jerusalem (Rom 15:23–29).

WHY DID PAUL WRITE ROMANS?

Few New Testament writings have generated as wide a range of interpretations as Paul's Letter to the Romans. Across the history of the church, it has been read as a doctrinal compendium, a theological manifesto, a pastoral intervention, and a missionary strategy.[3] This diversity is not a sign of confusion but a measure of the letter's depth and generative power. As Joseph Fitzmyer observed, much of the history of Christian

1. Dunn, *Romans 1–8*, xlv.

2. Schreiner, *Romans*, 3. Jewett, drawing on a careful analysis of internal and external factors, argues with a high degree of probability that Romans was composed in the winter of 56–57 CE or in the early spring of 57. Jewett, *Romans*, 18. See also deSilva, *Introduction*, 598–601; Dunn, *Romans 1–8*, xxxix.

3. Beker, *Paul*, 59.

theology can be traced by attending to how Romans has been read across time and place.[4]

This diversity of interpretations arises from the wide range of purposes scholars have attributed to Paul's writing of Romans. Leon Morris famously catalogued twelve distinct explanations for the letter, and subsequent collections, such as *The Romans Debate*, have only expanded that range.[5] The scale of disagreement reflects not interpretive failure but the complexity of a letter that resists reduction to a single abstract aim. This interpretive richness is further evident in the multivolume series *Romans Through History and Culture*, which traces how the letter has been received and reread across eras, cultures, and traditions.[6] Early Christian interpreters emphasized salvation and grace;[7] Augustine, Luther, and Calvin foregrounded justification by faith in ways that shaped the Reformation;[8] and contemporary liberation, feminist, and postcolonial readings attend to questions of justice, inclusion, and resistance to domination.[9] Romans has endured, not because it offers a static theological system but because it continues to speak to the concrete concerns of communities seeking faithfulness amid changing historical circumstances.

Further complicating questions of purpose and audience are longstanding textual debates surrounding Romans 16.[10] While Paul's authorship of the letter is not disputed, the integrity of its conclusion has been the subject of sustained scholarly discussion. Manuscript evidence reveals significant variation in the placement of the doxology (Rom 16:25–27),

4. Fitzmyer, *Roman*, xiii.

5. Morris, *Romans*, 8–17. For representative views, see interpretations of Romans as a theological compendium or mature summation of Paul's thought (Shedd, *Romans*; Nygren, *Romans*; Barclay, *Romans*); as a missionally oriented letter shaped by Paul's plans for Spain and support from Rome (Leenhardt, *Romans*; Donfried, *Romans Debate*); and as a pastoral or ecclesial response to tensions within the Roman churches, particularly between Jewish and gentile believers (Käsemann, *Romans*; Longenecker, *Romans*). Many conclude that Romans integrates these concerns, functioning as theological preparation for Paul's hoped-for visit and missionary partnership (Morris, *Romans*). Donfried, *Romans Debate*.

6. Patte and Grenholm, *Romans Through History and Culture*.

7. Gaca and Welborn, *Early Patristic Readings of Romans*.

8. Ehrensperger and Holder, *Reformation Readings of Romans*; Gaca and Welborn, *Early Patristic Readings of Romans*.

9. Patte and Grenholm, *Modern Interpretations of Romans*. Grenholm and Patte, *Gender, Tradition, and Romans*.

10. Jewett is convinced that Romans 16:17–20, 25–27 were inserted into Romans "after the death of Paul to advocate aggressive methods of conflict management that contrast with the tolerant realism in the original letter." Jewett, *Romans*, 214.

which appears at the end of chapters 14, 15, or 16 in different witnesses and is omitted entirely in some. The earliest extant fragment places the doxology at the end of chapter 15.[11] These variations have prompted proposals that Romans circulated in more than one form, or that chapter 16, in whole or in part, may represent a separate letter later appended to the Roman correspondence, possibly originally addressed to another community such as Ephesus.[12]

Such hypotheses are often linked to the density of personal greetings in Romans 16 and to questions about how Paul could have known so many believers in a city he had not yet visited.[13] While these proposals remain debated, they clarify an important interpretive issue: how one understands the integrity of Romans 16 shapes whether the letter is read primarily as a generalized theological treatise or as a carefully situated apostolic appeal. If chapter 16 belongs integrally to the letter, its relational texture underscores Paul's engagement with a specific network of communities whose unity and cooperation were essential to his projected mission to Spain. If portions of the chapter reflect later adaptation or reuse, this suggests that the letter's missionary logic was sufficiently robust to be received, extended, and repurposed beyond its initial setting.

In either case, the textual history of Romans ultimately strengthens rather than weakens the argument advanced in this study. Whether read as a unified correspondence or as a letter whose conclusion reflects a complex process of transmission, Romans emerges not as abstract theology for its own sake but as a strategic apostolic intervention. Paul writes to form a reconciled community whose shared life embodies the gospel and whose unity in Christ enables participation in the unfolding mission of God.

ENCYCLICAL OR SITUATIONAL?

Closely related to these questions is the debate over the nature of Romans itself. Some scholars have argued that the letter functions as an encyclical

11. The Greek manuscript P46 is one of the New Testament's earliest and most significant papyri, dating to around 175 to 225 CE. It contains portions of several Pauline epistles, including Romans, 1–2 Corinthians, Galatians, Ephesians, Philippians, Colossians, and 1 Thessalonians, as well as parts of Hebrews, which was often associated with Paul's writings in the early church.

12. Witherington, *Romans*, 4.

13. Witherington, *Romans*, 4.

or theological manifesto intended for broad circulation.[14] The structure of the letter resembles a carefully crafted argument, almost like a public address or theological essay.[15] The letter's introduction (Rom 1:1–15) and conclusion (Rom 15:14—16:27) frame the letter in a way that suggests it could serve as a general manifesto of Paul's gospel, intended to introduce his teaching to those who had not yet met him personally. Paul's extensive use of Scripture (e.g., Romans 4, 9–11) and his theological reasoning align with a didactic purpose, aiming to instruct a broad audience in the implications of the gospel.[16] Its extensive use of Scripture and sustained rhetorical structure support the view that Paul intended the letter to have wide relevance beyond Rome alone.

Others, however, caution against detaching Romans from its epistolary character. As Ernst Käsemann famously insisted, all of Paul's letters are situational, shaped by concrete historical and missionary circumstances.[17] From this vantage point, Romans reflects both Paul's vocational horizon and the internal dynamics of the Roman congregations.[18] Its theology emerges not in abstraction but in response to lived realities.[19]

These two perspectives need not be opposed. Romans can be both theologically expansive and situationally grounded. The task of interpretation is not to choose between theology and context, but to recognize how Paul's most profound theological reflections emerged in service of concrete pastoral aims and a clear missionary purpose.[20]

ROMANS AS PASTORAL THEOLOGY IN MISSIONAL SERVICE

Romans is an apostolic letter written to form a community. Paul addresses believers living in the heart of the empire, negotiating ethnic difference, social inequality, and competing claims of allegiance. His theological argument aims to reconcile divided believers, reorient their identity around God's mercy, and shape a communal life capable of sustaining

14. deSilva, *Introduction*, 598.

15. Witherington, *Romans*, 16–23.

16. Hays, *Echoes of Scripture*, 34–83.

17. Käsemann, *Romans*, 3–4.

18. Green, *Christianity in Ancient Rome*, 28–29.

19. Beker, *Paul*, 59.

20. Beker, *Paul*, 71.

unity and bearing credible witness. Romans is pastoral because it addresses real fractures within the community. It is missional because those fractures threaten the church's capacity to participate in God's purposes beyond itself.

With these debates in view, we are now prepared to widen our lens. To understand how Paul's theological vision takes shape, we must attend to the social, political, and religious world in which the Roman believers lived. The Letter to the Romans did not emerge in a vacuum. It was written into a city shaped by imperial power, religious pluralism, and entrenched social hierarchies. It is to this historical and cultural context that we now turn.

2

The Historical and Cultural Context

If Paul's theology is inseparable from his pastoral and missionary purpose, then Romans must be read within the concrete world that shaped both the apostle and the communities he addressed.[1] The letter arose within the political, social, and religious realities of first-century Rome, a contested space where the gospel was proclaimed as an embodied alternative. As the political and cultural center of the Mediterranean world, Rome concentrated imperial power, religious plurality, entrenched social hierarchies, and ethnic diversity. In such a setting, claims about lordship, justice, peace, and salvation functioned as public assertions of allegiance. To announce the gospel in Rome was to confront a world that sacralized power and normalized hierarchy, a context that gives Paul's message both its urgency and its carefully measured tone.

Founded in the eighth century BCE as a small settlement along the Tiber River, Rome expanded by absorbing neighboring Sabine and Etruscan populations and eventually emerged as the political, economic, and administrative hub of a vast empire. By the first century CE, when Paul wrote to the Roman churches, imperial rule stretched across southern Europe, North Africa, and the Near East, binding diverse regions together through military force, economic extraction, and bureaucratic control.[2] With a population approaching one million, Rome was among the largest and most socially complex cities of the ancient world. Citizens and non-citizens, elites and the urban poor, enslaved and formerly

1. Beker, *Paul*, 8–12.

2. Hall, "Rome (Place)," 5:830.

enslaved persons, and migrants from across the empire lived in close proximity within a sharply stratified society. Wealth and status were concentrated among a small elite and sustained through systems of patronage and exploitation, conditions that shaped the daily realities of the earliest Christian communities.

Although Roman tradition explained the city's origins through legend,[3] it was Rome's political development rather than its myths that forged the social and institutional world Paul encountered. From its earliest periods, public authority and religious life were tightly intertwined. Civic cults, political institutions, and shared urban spaces reinforced assumptions about honor, hierarchy, and the legitimacy of power. These patterns persisted through the republic and into the empire, forming the cultural grammar within which the gospel was heard, contested, and embodied by the Roman churches.

REPUBLICAN PERIOD

The Roman Republic emerged around 509 BCE after the expulsion of the last king, Tarquinius Superbus. What followed was nearly five centuries of oligarchic rule dominated by elite families. Roman society was formally divided between patricians, the aristocratic class, and plebeians, the broader population. Although plebeian rights expanded gradually, political power remained concentrated among a narrow elite, and tensions between these groups shaped the republic's life.[4]

By the mid-fourth century BCE, Rome had consolidated control over the Italian peninsula and turned outward in sustained expansion. Contact with Greek colonies introduced Roman elites to Greek language, art, and philosophy, while Rome's distinctive policy of incorporating conquered peoples through citizenship and alliances produced a flexible, integrative imperial structure.[5] These networks of roads, cities, and social ties would later facilitate the rapid spread of Christianity.[6]

Military power was central to Rome's rise.[7] Universal conscription produced a formidable army, while extensive road networks and

3. Gladigow, "Roman Religion," 810–1163; Fitzmyer, *Romans*, 25.
4. Hall, "Rome (Place)," 5:830–31.
5. Saller, "Culture and Religion."
6. Keown, *Romans*, 9.
7. Kauffman, *At Home in the Universe*, 71–92.

aqueducts bound distant regions to the capital. Rome's defeat of Carthage in the Punic Wars (264–146 BCE) marked a decisive turning point. From the Punic world, Rome inherited vast slave-worked plantations and brutal methods of social control, including crucifixion. These developments intensified social inequality and entrenched systems of domination that shaped daily life across the empire.

As territories expanded, Rome organized them into provinces governed by Roman officials responsible for taxation and order, alongside semi-autonomous client kingdoms such as Herodian Judea.[8] Imperial wealth poured into the capital, transforming Rome into a cosmopolitan center and drawing migrants, veterans, and laborers in search of opportunity.[9] Rapid urban growth produced severe housing shortages, forcing much of the population into overcrowded, poorly constructed tenements marked by constant risk from fire and collapse, conditions that later shaped the social world of Roman Christians.[10]

Economic and political tensions intensified as wealth concentrated in elite hands.[11] Small landholders were displaced by large estates, while an expanding urban population grew dependent on patronage and state subsidies. Late republican politics was characterized by factionalism, bribery, and rivalry between the *Populares*, who claimed to represent the interests of the people, and the *Optimates*, defenders of aristocratic privilege. At the same time, military reforms created a professional army increasingly loyal to individual commanders rather than to the republic itself. As a result, military power became deeply entangled with political ambition.[12]

The final century of the republic was marked by recurring civil conflict and the gradual collapse of collective governance. Military leaders such as Pompey and Julius Caesar expanded Rome's frontiers while simultaneously concentrating authority in their own hands. Pompey's eastern campaigns brought Judea firmly under Roman control, embedding Jewish life within imperial structures that would later shape the world of early Christianity.[13] Caesar's assassination in 44 BCE did not restore the republic but exposed its fragility, plunging Rome into renewed turmoil that would only be resolved through the rise of a new political order.

8. Green, *Christianity*, 6–11.
9. Keown, *Romans*, 9–10.
10. Jeffers, *Greco-Roman World*, 48–69.
11. Hall, "Rome (Place)," 5:831.
12. Hall, "Rome (Place)," 5:831–33.
13. Green, *Christianity*, 4–6.

That resolution came with Octavian's victory over Antony and Cleopatra at Actium in 31 BCE.[14] In 27 BCE, Octavian received the title Imperator Caesar Augustus, conferring near-divine prestige[15] and inaugurating a form of rule that preserved the language and institutions of the republic while emptying them of real power.[16] Authority over the military, finances, and key provinces was consolidated in the hands of a single ruler, even as the Senate and magistracies remained as symbols of continuity. The republic, in effect, survived in name while imperial rule took hold in practice. This transformation marked a decisive shift in Roman political imagination, from shared civic responsibility to centralized authority presented as the guarantor of peace and order. It was into this reconfigured world that Jesus was born, and within which Paul later proclaimed the gospel.

THE ROMAN EMPIRE

The Roman Empire formally emerged in 27 BCE and endured in the west until 476 CE, with its eastern counterpart continuing for nearly a millennium.[17] From the outset, imperial power was sustained not only through military force and administrative control but through a carefully constructed narrative that presented Roman rule as divinely favored and universally beneficial. This vision found its most enduring expression in the *Pax Romana*, a period of relative stability that promised peace, prosperity, and order under imperial authority.

Augustus played a central role in shaping Rome's imperial imagination. His claim to have "found Rome built of brick and left it made of marble" signaled both the ambition and meaning of his reign. Monumental building projects reshaped the city's public and religious landscape—temples, forums, civic buildings, and imperial residences—embedding imperial presence into everyday life. Architecture became theology in stone, presenting Rome's peace and prosperity as gifts flowing from the emperor's favor with the gods and his mediation of cosmic order. Religion and political legitimacy were thus bound together, forming a world

14. Le Glay et al., *History of Rome*, 107–121, 157.
15. Hall, "Rome (Place)," 5:831–33.
16. Green, *Christianity*, 6–7.
17. Kaldellis, *New Roman Empire*.

in which claims about lordship, peace, and salvation were already densely charged before Paul ever addressed the Roman churches.[18]

Following Augustus's death (14 CE), power passed to the Julio-Claudian emperors—Tiberius, Caligula, Claudius, and Nero. Despite the instability and excesses associated with some of these rulers, the empire continued to enjoy relative peace, territorial expansion, and sustained urban development. Public baths, theaters, aqueducts, and monumental civic spaces reshaped cities across the empire, reinforcing Rome's image as the source of order, abundance, and civilization.[19]

By the time Paul wrote his Letter to the Romans, the city stood as the political and cultural center of the Mediterranean world. Governed in part by influential administrators such as Burrus and Seneca during the early years of Nero's reign, Rome housed the emperor, Senate, military leadership, and priestly elites.[20] A cosmopolitan aristocracy drawn from across the empire populated the city, while public benefactions, grain distributions, and spectacles helped secure popular loyalty. Rome also flourished as a center of literature, philosophy, and the arts, projecting an image of cultural superiority alongside its political dominance.[21]

This imperial context forms a critical background for understanding Paul's message. Claims about peace, lordship, justice, and salvation were not abstract theological ideas but were already saturated with imperial meaning. To proclaim the gospel of Jesus Christ in Rome was therefore to announce an alternative vision of power and allegiance, one that challenged imperial narratives even as it spoke into the social realities shaped by them.[22]

Religion in Rome

In the ancient world, religion permeated every aspect of life; the notion of a secular sphere was virtually inconceivable.[23] Rome's civic and religious geography reflected this integration. The Capitoline Hill was dominated by the temple of Jupiter Optimus Maximus, while the Forum

18 Wells, "Roman Empire," 5:801.

19. Gladigow, "Roman Religion," 810–1163.

20. deSilva, *Introduction*, 636.

21. Wells, "Roman Empire," 5:802–3.

22. Bryan, *Preface to Romans*.

23. Le Glay et al., *History of Rome*, 184.

and Palatine complex were filled with shrines, altars, and sacred spaces. Even private homes contained household shrines honoring ancestors and domestic gods.

Religion was inseparable from the state. Priests advised emperors and the Senate, regulated sacred calendars, oversaw rituals, and interpreted omens and sacred texts. Participation in public ritual was therefore not optional. It was understood as a civic responsibility essential to maintaining divine favor and social order.[24]

Religious identity was largely inherited or socially embedded rather than chosen. Guilds and associations were often organized around patron deities, with membership reflecting occupation or ethnicity.[25] While foreign cults could be introduced with Senate approval, suspicion toward unregulated religious movements persisted, particularly after the violent suppression of the Bacchic cult in 186 BCE. From that point forward, religious groups perceived as socially disruptive or insufficiently loyal to Rome were restricted, monitored, or forcibly opposed.[26] This civic orientation helps illuminate Paul's engagement with moral law (Rom 2:14–16), Torah (Rom 3:21; 10:4), and governing authorities (Rom 13:1–7). Within this integrated religious world, the most powerful and consequential expression of Roman piety was the civic cult surrounding the emperor himself.

The Civic Cult

The civic cult occupied the theological center of imperial power. Imperial ideology, especially under Augustus, shaped the conceptual world Paul addressed.[27] Early forms of ruler veneration focused on the *Genius Populi Romani*, the divine guardian spirit of the Roman people, before gradually transferring sacred significance to the emperor himself. Augustus cast his reign in overtly theological terms, presenting himself as the "son of the divine" and as the restorer of Roman virtue in the aftermath of Actium.[28] Through disciplined and pervasive propaganda, autocratic rule was reframed as the renewal of republican ideals.

24. Gladigow, "Roman Religion," 809–815.
25. Aune, "Religions, Greco-Roman," 789.
26. Gladigow, "Roman Religion," 814.
27. Heilig, "Roman Context," 68–109.
28. Jewett, *Romans*, 48.

Augustus's cultivated modesty as *pontifex maximus* and guardian of Roman piety set a template followed by successors such as Claudius and Nero.[29] Civic rituals, festivals, and public benefactions reinforced the association between imperial authority and divine favor. Peace, prosperity, and order were credited to the emperor's virtuous rule.

Paul's letter quietly but decisively subverts this vision. His critique of idolatry (Rom 1:18, 25) and insistence that righteousness cannot be achieved through human virtue or power (Rom 3:19–20) undermine Roman claims to moral superiority and divine sanction.[30] By appropriating and inverting imperial language, Romans contrasts the violent foundations of Roman peace with the cruciform reign of Christ. Jesus, not Caesar, is proclaimed as Lord, and reconciliation, not domination, marks the true shape of God's rule.[31]

A Culture of Honor and Shame

Roman society was structured around honor and shame, a system in which public recognition determined worth, status, and identity.[32] Honor was the highest social value, gained through lineage, patronage, public achievement, and displays of power. Shame, by contrast, was not primarily an internal emotion but a social condition involving loss of status, exclusion, or public disapproval. This system shaped social interactions, political competition, and moral imagination throughout the empire.

The empire was governed by a small elite relying on force, propaganda, and patronage, upheld by cultural values of honor and pride.[33] These values fostered loyalty and respect, shaping relationships defined by mutual respect rather than mere obedience. At the apex stood the emperor, who amassed honors while feigning humility. Intense competition for status permeated public life.[34] Military victories, political success, and public benefactions generated *gloria*, commemorated through monuments, inscriptions, and ceremonies.[35] Augustus exemplified this

29. Jones, "Roman Imperial Cult," 5:806.
30. Keown, *Romans*, 12–13.
31. Longenecker, *Romans*, 724–25.
32. deSilva, *Honor*, 17–93.
33. Lendon, *Empire*, 13.
34. Lendon, *Empire*, 75.
35. Jewett, *Romans*, 49–51.

system, carefully curating his image while consolidating power. His *Res Gestae*[36] celebrated virtues such as clemency, justice, and piety, terms Paul reappropriates and redefines in Romans to expose the distortion of Roman ideals.[37]

Slaves and Barbarians

Slavery was integral to Roman society, with enslaved persons comprising as much as one-third of the population.[38] Although Paul does not directly call for the abolition of slavery, he radically reframes it theologically. In Romans 1:1, Paul identifies himself as a "slave" of Christ, aligning the lowest social status with apostolic vocation. In Romans 6:15–23, he insists that all people are enslaved either to sin or to righteousness, thereby offering hope and purpose beyond social status and grounding identity in allegiance to God.[39]

Similarly, the term "barbarian" functioned as a label for non-Greco-Roman peoples, marking them as culturally inferior and viewed with disdain.[40] In Romans 1:14, Paul declares his obligation to both Greeks and barbarians, signaling a mission that crosses ethnic identity, cultural boundaries, and social status.[41] This inclusive vision directly challenges Roman assumptions about civilization, worth, and belonging.

Judaism and Christianity in Rome

Judaism had a long and complex history in Rome. Jews first appeared in the city in significant numbers in the second century BCE, and after Pompey's conquest of Judea in 63 BCE, many Jewish captives were brought to Rome, some later gaining freedom. Over time, a substantial Jewish population emerged, supported by strong trans-Mediterranean connections.

36. *Res Gestae Divi Augusti* ("The Deeds of the Divine Augustus") is an account written by Augustus detailing his military victories, public works, and contributions to the Roman state. It served as both propaganda and a legacy document. See Cooley, *Res Gestae Divi Augusti.*

37. Lendon, *Empire*, 131; MacMullen, *Roman Social Relations*, 105–107.

38. Bartchy, "Slavery: New Testament," 6:65–66.

39. Longenecker, *Romans*, 619–21.

40. Jewett, *Romans*, 114.

41. Keown, *Romans*, 70.

Under Julius Caesar and Augustus, Judaism received legal recognition.[42] Jews were permitted to observe the Sabbath, maintain dietary laws, gather in synagogues, and celebrate major festivals.[43] Augustus ensured that Jews received their share of public food distributions, reflecting both their poverty and, in some cases, their Roman citizenship.[44] Archaeological evidence indicates the presence of ten to thirteen synagogues in Rome by the first century CE, suggesting a Jewish population of roughly forty to sixty thousand.[45]

Despite these protections, Jews were frequently viewed with suspicion. Roman anxiety about Jewish distinctiveness and proselytism led to periodic expulsions from the city, including actions in 139 BCE and 19 CE.[46] In 31 CE, Tiberius reaffirmed Jewish rights, allowing many to return.[47] By 38 CE, Philo observed that a large district across the Tiber was populated by Jews, many of whom held Roman citizenship.[48]

By the time of Claudius, tensions had resurfaced. In 41 CE, Claudius revoked Jews' right to assemble due to their large population in Rome.[49] The literature of this period reflected strong anti-Jewish sentiment. Cicero called Judaism a "barbaric superstition" opposed to Roman values, while Seneca referred to Jews as an "accursed race." Tacitus expressed particularly harsh views, claiming, "The Jews, who are so abominable to the human race, despise our gods and regard as profane all that we hold sacred; they permit all that we abhor."[50]

These sentiments hardened into action in 49 CE, when Claudius expelled Jews from Rome following disturbances "at the instigation of Chrestus," a reference widely understood as disputes over Christ (Christos). While the precise nature of these disturbances remains debated, both Suetonius and Acts 18:1–2 indicate that conflicts within Jewish communities concerning Jesus as Messiah had become sufficiently public to attract imperial attention. The edict forced Jewish believers to leave the city, including figures such as Prisca and Aquila, whom Paul would later

42. Green, *Christianity*, 2–7.

43. Penna, *Judaism in Rome*, 1074.

44. Green, *Christianity*, 10.

45. Lampe, *Paul*, 84.

46. Carroll, "Tacitus (Person)," 6:306.

47. Penna, *Judaism in Rome*, 1075.

48. Green, *Christianity*, 19–20.

49. Green, *Christianity*, 24.

50. Tacitus, *Annals and Histories*, 567.

encounter in Corinth, an absence that would have lasting consequences for the shape and tensions of the Roman church.

These events are crucial for understanding both the composition of the Roman-Christian communities and the tensions that shaped them. Christianity emerged within Judaism and initially spread through synagogues, but disputes over Jesus as Messiah soon generated conflict within Jewish communities and attracted the attention of Roman authorities. When Claudius expelled Jews from Rome, Jewish believers were absent from the city for approximately five years. During this period, the Christian communities in Rome became predominantly, if not exclusively, gentile.[51] In the absence of Torah-observant members, communal life was necessarily reshaped. Practices tied to Jewish identity such as dietary observance, sacred days, and ritual rhythms ceased to function as points of negotiation, while leadership patterns, worship habits, and shared assumptions about discipleship developed without sustained Jewish participation. What had once been a mixed community learning to live with difference became a gentile-majority church whose identity was formed in the prolonged absence of Jewish voices.

After Claudius's death in 54 CE, the edict lapsed, allowing Jews, and likely Jewish Christians such as Prisca and Aquila (Rom 16:3), to return to Rome. Their return reintroduced divergent practices and convictions into communities that had already adapted to gentile norms. This historical disruption provides a concrete social backdrop for Paul's appeal in Romans 14–15, where disputes over food, sacred days, and mutual recognition threaten communal unity. Paul's exhortation to welcome one another, refrain from judgment, and bear with the "weak" and the "strong" reflects not abstract ethical reflection but the lived reality of a church struggling to integrate Jewish and gentile believers after a prolonged period of separation.

When Paul wrote Romans, Nero's administration still appeared stable and competent, despite his personal excesses.[52] For ordinary citizens, and for the Christian communities in Rome, life under Nero involved a daily tension between public order and private contradiction. It is within this unsettled space that Paul's call to respect governing authorities (Rom 13:1–7) should be heard, not as uncritical endorsement of imperial power but as pastoral counsel for faithful living under a regime that

51. Longenecker, *Romans*, 950–52; Lateiner, "Historiography," 3:217; Fitzmyer, *Romans*, 31.

52. deSilva, *Introduction*, 636.

preserved civic stability while revealing the fragility and inconsistency of human rule.[53]

FROM CONTEXT TO COMMUNITY

Taken together, the political, religious, and social realities of first-century Rome form more than background information for Paul's letter; they constitute the contested space into which the gospel was proclaimed and embodied. Empire promised peace secured through power, honor gained through status, and belonging defined by ethnicity, citizenship, and social hierarchy. Religious life reinforced civic loyalty, while systems of patronage, slavery, and exclusion structured everyday relationships. These forces shaped not only public life in Rome, but also the assumptions, loyalties, and tensions carried into the emerging Christian communities.

Yet Romans is not addressed to Rome in the abstract, nor to imperial ideology as such, but to concrete assemblies of believers living within this world. Paul writes to people whose lives were already marked by these dynamics—Jewish and gentile believers negotiating identity, allegiance, and belonging under imperial rule; households shaped by hierarchy and dependency; communities learning to live the gospel amid suspicion, marginalization, and cultural pressure. The historical and cultural context clarifies the stakes of Paul's argument, but it does not tell the whole story.

To understand how Paul's theological vision takes flesh, we must now turn from the world that surrounded the Roman Christians to the communities themselves. Chapter 3 examines the origins, composition, and lived realities of the church in Rome, tracing how these believers emerged, organized, and struggled within the complex environment described above. Only by attending to the church as a concrete social body can we fully grasp the pastoral urgency and missional imagination that animate Paul's letter.

53. Jewett, *Romans*, 785–801.

3

The Church in Rome

The precise origins of Christianity in Rome remain elusive, yet the contours of its emergence can be traced with reasonable confidence. Unlike churches founded through direct apostolic initiative, the Roman-Christian community appears to have developed organically through the movement of people within the Jewish diaspora and the social networks of the empire.[1] The fourth-century commentator Ambrosiaster suggests that the Christian movement in Rome initially took root within the context of the synagogue, a claim that aligns well with what is known of early Christian expansion patterns.[2] When read alongside Acts 2:10, which notes the presence of Jews from Rome among the pilgrims gathered in Jerusalem at Pentecost, it is plausible that some of these individuals encountered the gospel there, embraced Jesus as Messiah, and returned to Rome bearing this new confession into their existing synagogue communities.[3]

If so, the earliest Christian gatherings in Rome were likely composed primarily of Jewish and God-fearing gentile believers who continued to participate in synagogue life while confessing Jesus as the fulfillment of Israel's hopes. As elsewhere in the Mediterranean world, the proclamation of the gospel would have unfolded first within Jewish communal spaces, framed by Israel's Scriptures and shaped by messianic expectation. Over time, gentiles attracted to synagogue worship or connected

1. Fitzmeyer, *Romans*, 30–31.
2. Jewett, *Romans*, 60.
3. deSilva, *Introduction*, 599.

through household and commercial networks would have joined these gatherings, gradually contributing to the growing diversity of the Roman church. From the beginning, then, the Christian community in Rome appears to have been marked by plurality, mobility, and porous boundaries rather than centralized leadership or uniform practice.

Additional texture is provided by Paul's brief but revealing encounter with believers in Puteoli, the bustling port city through which ships entered Italy (Acts 28:13–14). Paul notes that he and his companions were invited to stay with believers there for seven days, suggesting an established Christian presence prior to his arrival in Rome. While little is known about the origins of this community, some scholars have suggested that Christianity may have reached Rome through Jewish slaves and freedpersons attached to Roman households, particularly those connected to imperial or elite estates.[4] Enslaved persons often moved between regions of the empire and served as conduits for ideas, practices, and beliefs. Taken together, the Pentecost account and the Puteoli episode offer complementary windows into how the gospel made its way to the capital, not through official channels or apostolic planning but through the ordinary movement of people whose lives were already embedded in Rome's social and economic networks.

From its earliest days, the Roman church was a mixed Jewish–gentile community whose fragile balance was disrupted by the Claudian expulsion and reshaped during the prolonged absence of Jewish believers. This disruption provides essential background for understanding Paul's appeal in Romans 14–15. The disputes he addresses over food, holy days, and mutual judgment are not abstract theological disagreements but the lived consequences of communal rupture and return. Paul understands how easily the gentile majority might assume its practices had become normative, just as he recognizes the vulnerability of returning Jewish believers who could feel displaced or marginalized within communities they once helped form.

Paul writes into this moment with pastoral and apostolic restraint. Rather than resolving the conflict by privileging one group's practices over another's, he reframes the dispute around belonging in Christ. Those he calls "strong," likely gentile believers who felt free from Jewish dietary restrictions, are urged toward humility and accommodation. Those deemed "weak," likely Jewish believers who continued to observe

4. Lampe, *Paul*, 7–10.

these practices, are affirmed in the integrity of their faithfulness. Paul's aim is not assimilation or uniformity, but mutual welcome: "Accept one another, just as Christ accepted you, for the glory of God" (Rom 15:7).

The stakes of this appeal are explicitly missional. A divided church in the imperial capital would compromise the credibility of the gospel and weaken support for Paul's westward mission to Spain. A reconciled, hospitable, cross-cultural community, by contrast, would embody the reconciling power of the gospel itself. Unity, for Paul, is not an abstract ideal but a missional necessity. The church's shared life is meant to make visible the new reality inaugurated in Christ, a community no longer defined by ethnicity or tradition, but by participation in God's redemptive work.

Romans 16 offers a glimpse into this diverse and interconnected community. Paul's greetings reveal a network of relationships forged across cities, regions, and social strata. Many of the individuals he names were likely encountered during their exile from Rome and returned after Claudius's death.[5] Prisca and Aquila stand as prominent examples, hosting a house church and serving as trusted co-laborers in Paul's mission (Rom 16:3–5). Others, such as Andronicus and Junia, are described as Paul's "kinsmen" and as apostles whose faith preceded his own, suggesting deep roots in the earliest Christian movement.

Paul's greetings unveil a richly textured community in which women and men, Jews and gentiles, wealthy patrons and household servants stand side by side in Christ.[6] Some figures, such as Phoebe, appear to have possessed considerable resources. Described as a *diakonos* of the church in Cenchreae and a patron to many, including Paul himself (Rom 16:1–2), Phoebe was likely affluent enough to fund travel and support missionary work. Others, such as Herodion (v. 11) or those associated with the households of Aristobulus and Narcissus (vv. 10–11), may have been enslaved or freedpersons connected to elite estates.[7] The juxtaposition of such figures within a single letter underscores the radical social reconfiguration underway within the Roman church.

Ethnic diversity is evident throughout the list. Jewish believers such as Andronicus and Junia are named alongside gentile Christians like Rufus (v. 13). Women appear prominently, not as peripheral supporters but as leaders, patrons, and coworkers in the gospel. Together,

5. deSilva, *Introduction*, 598–601.

6. Mounce, *Romans*, 274.

7. Lampe, "Herodion (Person)," 3:176.

these greetings depict a community in which conventional boundaries of ethnicity, gender, and status are being reconfigured around shared allegiance to Christ.

Taken as a whole, Paul's list offers a living portrait of the new-creation order coming into view. Wealthy patrons and manual laborers, women who lead and teach, and Jews and gentiles learning to worship together are all drawn into a shared life shaped by participation in Christ and mutual service in love. Identity and belonging are no longer grounded in status or ethnicity, but in the transforming reality of the gospel at work within the community.[8]

Paul's repeated references to house churches further illuminate the structure of the Roman-Christian community. The church met not as a single congregation but as a constellation of small gatherings in homes and tenements scattered across the city. Paul greets the church in the house of Prisca and Aquila (v. 5), as well as those associated with the households of Aristobulus and Narcissus. Such decentralization was likely shaped by practical realities, restrictions on large assemblies, the size of urban dwellings, but it also fostered a participatory ecclesial life.[9] Many believers are described as co-laborers, suggesting that ministry was widely shared rather than concentrated in a clerical elite.

These greetings also reveal the depth of relational bonds within the early Christian movement. Paul recalls Epaenetus as "the first convert in Asia" (v. 5) and honors Rufus's mother as one who "has been a mother to me also" (v. 13). Such language discloses a community sustained through long memory, practiced care, and mutual dependence. The church in Rome existed as a living network of households, bound together by faith, hospitality, and a shared participation in God's mission.

This portrait of the Roman church reveals a community that is ethnically and socially diverse, decentralized in structure, and actively engaged in ministry amid ongoing tension and transformation.[10] Its life had been shaped by displacement and return, by negotiation and reconciliation, and by the challenge of living faithfully under imperial rule. Paul writes not to impose uniformity but to cultivate a shared identity capable of sustaining unity and advancing the mission of God. In doing so, the church in Rome becomes a concrete expression of the gospel's

8. Green, *Christianity*, 31.

9. Dunn, *Romans 1–8*, liii.

10. Dunn, *Romans 9–16*, 887–89.

power to form a new people, one whose common life bears witness to the reconciling work of Christ in the heart of the empire.

THE SIZE OF THE CHRISTIAN COMMUNITY IN ROME

The actual size of the Christian community in Rome has long been a matter of scholarly debate, in part because the available evidence is fragmentary and indirect. Some estimates have been relatively modest. Peter Lampe, for example, suggested a community of roughly two hundred believers distributed across "at least seven separate islands,"[11] while Rodney Stark proposed that by 50 CE the total number of Christians throughout the Empire may have been as low as fourteen hundred, with only a few hundred residing in Rome.[12]

Evidence from Roman historians complicates minimal estimates of the early Christian presence in Rome and points instead to a movement that was both visible and growing. Tacitus reports that following the Great Fire of Rome in 64 CE, Nero's persecution swept up a "huge crowd" of Christians.[13] While his language may reflect rhetorical exaggeration, it is difficult to reconcile this description with the notion of a tiny or insignificant sect. Other sources reinforce this impression. First Clement, written only a few decades later, presumes a sizeable and organized Roman church capable of sustained correspondence and collective action. In addition, both Tacitus and Suetonius record imperial measures involving Christians or Jewish Christians in 41 and 49 CE, indicating a level of public visibility sufficient to draw official attention. Movements that remained truly marginal rarely provoked such responses.[14]

Taken together, these data suggest that by the time Paul wrote Romans, the city likely hosted multiple Christian congregations dispersed across different neighborhoods. While the exact number of believers cannot be determined with precision, the evidence points to a community that was no longer negligible. The Roman church was large enough to be socially disruptive, internally diverse, and missiologically significant, yet still vulnerable enough to lack institutional protection or public

11. Lampe, *Paul*, 359.

12. Stark, *Rise of Christianity*, 7.

13. Fitzmeyer, *Romans*, 35.

14. Fitzmeyer, *Romans*, 35; Green, *Christianity*, 28.

legitimacy. This combination of growth and social vulnerability helps explain both the urgency and the careful tone of Paul's letter.

THE LOCATION OF CONGREGATIONS IN ROME

The social geography of early Christianity in Rome further illuminates the character of these communities. Most scholars agree that the earliest Christian congregations were concentrated in the city's poorer districts, where dense populations, high mobility, and economic instability created fertile ground for new movements.[15] Many believers lived in overcrowded tenements characterized by precarious housing conditions, shared facilities, and constant exposure to fire, disease, and eviction. These were the neighborhoods in which the gospel first took root.

Two areas in particular emerge as likely centers of early Christian activity: Trastevere and the region near Porta Capena along the Appian Way.[16] Trastevere, located across the Tiber River, was a working-class district populated by laborers, sailors, artisans, and a substantial Jewish community. Its narrow streets and crowded tenements reflect the low-income conditions under which many early Christians lived. Notably, Trastevere was largely spared during the Great Fire of 64 CE, a fact that may have contributed to suspicions that Christians were implicated in the disaster and thus intensified Nero's subsequent scapegoating of the movement.[17]

Porta Capena, a low-lying and often damp area near a major entryway into the city, was another hub for migrants, traders, and transport workers. Archaeological and literary evidence suggests that both Jews and Christians in this district occupied similarly modest positions within Rome's social hierarchy.[18] These neighborhoods were marked by constant movement, economic vulnerability, and ethnic diversity, conditions that shaped both the challenges and the opportunities of Christian communal life.

The personal names listed in Romans 16 reinforce this picture. A significant majority of those greeted bear Greek names, pointing to a predominantly immigrant and Hellenistic constituency. Several individuals

15. Burton, "By Any Means Necessary," 246.

16. Lampe, *Paul*, 51–52.

17. Penna, "Judaism in Rome," 3:1074.

18. Lampe, *Paul*, 50.

appear to have been enslaved or formerly enslaved, suggesting that many believers occupied the lower rungs of Roman society. Roman Christians were largely people whose daily lives were shaped by insecurity, dependence, and limited social power, meeting in small tenement churches scattered throughout the city's working-class neighborhoods.

At the same time, the community was not socially uniform. A smaller number of believers likely belonged to higher social strata and resided in more affluent neighborhoods, such as the Aventine Hill, where Prisca and Aquila may have resided.[19] Prisca and Aquila appear to have had sufficient means to host a house church and to travel in support of Paul's mission. These wealthier households played a crucial role in sustaining the movement by providing meeting spaces, material resources, and a measure of stability within an otherwise precarious social environment.

This combination of poverty and patronage, marginality and mobility, shaped the life of the Roman church. Congregations were small, dispersed, and socially mixed, dependent upon relationships rather than institutions. Unity could not be imposed through hierarchy or proximity; it had to be cultivated through trust, hospitality, and shared allegiance to Christ. Paul's emphasis on mutual obligation, humility, and the honoring of one another across difference takes on particular force within this context. The church's social geography helps explain why Romans is so deeply concerned with forming a community capable of sustaining unity and witness amid inequality and dispersion.

THE SOCIAL STRUCTURE OF HOUSE AND TENEMENT CHURCHES IN ROME

Within this urban environment, the household functioned as the primary unit of social organization, economic survival, and communal identity. As a result, the earliest Christian gatherings took shape in ordinary domestic spaces—both cramped tenement apartments and, in some cases, the homes of wealthier patrons.[20] These settings brought people of differing status into close proximity, shaping patterns of leadership, hospitality, and participation while also intensifying the social tensions that Paul addresses in Romans.[21] Whether meeting in a villa's dining room, a shop-

19. Lampe, *Paul*, 62–63.

20. Green, *Christianity*, 17–25.

21. Jewett, *Romans*, 835–59.

front, or a modest apartment, these communities worshiped together, shared meals, taught the faith, and supported one another materially and spiritually.[22] The physical and social architecture of these households was not incidental—the "church" was not a separate sacred structure but the household itself, a space where authority was negotiated, unity was tested, and daily life and devotion were inseparably intertwined. This proximity between faith and ordinary existence gave early Christian communities a deeply embodied character and allowed the gospel to take root within the rhythms of work, family, and neighborhood life.

These intimate settings fostered belonging, mutual care, and resilience, qualities essential for a movement that lacked public legitimacy and was often regarded with suspicion. Gathering in small, relationally dense groups enabled believers to form bonds of trust, practice hospitality, and sustain one another amid social vulnerability and external pressure. At the same time, the household setting meant that leadership, authority, and participation were shaped not only by theological commitments but also by the social realities of the space in which the church met.

The earliest Roman house churches reflected a striking diversity in structure and leadership. Some congregations were patron-led, supported by wealthier members who possessed the resources to host gatherings and provide financial support.[23] This arrangement mirrored familiar Roman patterns of patronage, in which benefactors exercised influence and offered protection in exchange for loyalty and honor. Hosts of such gatherings, including figures like Prisca and Aquila (Rom 16:3–5), played significant roles in sustaining the life of the church by providing meeting spaces, facilitating travel, and connecting disparate groups across the city.[24]

Yet patronage did not define all Christian gatherings. Many communities, particularly those composed primarily of enslaved or formerly enslaved persons, operated without the support of a wealthy patron. Groups such as "those belonging to Aristobulus" and "those belonging to Narcissus" likely consisted of enslaved and formerly enslaved believers who met in modest, often crowded spaces within Rome's tenement districts.[25] These communities took root in economically strained neigh-

22. Jewett, *Romans*, 835–59.

23. Jewett, *Romans*, 64–65.

24. Longenecker, *Romans*, 1066–67.

25. Jewett, *Romans*, 972.

borhoods, gathering in rooms that reflected the hard realities of their daily lives.[26]

Despite limited material resources, tenement churches played a crucial role in the spread of Christianity. They formed dense, grassroots networks through which the faith moved naturally from household to household and street to street.[27] Their survival depended upon mutual aid, shared meals, and collective forms of leadership, with responsibility distributed across the community rather than concentrated in a single patron.[28]

Set alongside house churches associated with wealthier believers, whose larger, more private settings allowed for extended teaching and hospitality, tenement churches reveal the full social breadth of early Christianity in Rome. Far from hindering the movement's growth, the conditions of economic vulnerability fostered resilient communities whose shared life became a powerful vehicle for the gospel's expansion.

This mingling of classes within the Christian movement was both a strength and a source of tension.[29] Roman society was structured to keep social groups apart, reinforcing hierarchy through spatial separation and cultural expectation. In contrast, Christian gatherings brought together individuals who would rarely have shared social space in ordinary Roman life. Enslaved persons, freedpeople, artisans, merchants, and patrons found themselves eating together, praying together, and addressing one another as brothers and sisters in Christ. Such practices subverted prevailing honor–shame norms and challenged deeply ingrained assumptions about status and worth.

Navigating these tensions required continual discernment. Wealthy hosts exercised influence simply by virtue of controlling meeting spaces, while poorer believers risked marginalization even within communities committed to mutuality. Paul's repeated exhortations to humility, mutual service, and the honoring of one another take on particular force within this context. His vision of the church as a body in which each member is indispensable (Rom 12:3–8) addresses not an abstract ecclesial ideal but the concrete challenge of sustaining unity amid inequality.

These social realities illuminate the pastoral urgency of Paul's exhortations in Romans 12–15. In a community marked by inequality,

26. Jeffers, *Greco-Roman World*, 131–33.

27. Jewett, *Romans*, 950–53.

28. Jewett, *Romans*, 66.

29. Jewett, *Romans*, 23.

cultural difference, and contested practices, unity could not be sustained by shared belief alone. It had to be embodied in shared life. Paul therefore places particular emphasis on mutual welcome, restraint, and responsibility, urging believers to receive one another "just as Christ has welcomed you" (Rom 15:7).

Nowhere is this vision more concrete than in the shared meal. Communal gatherings, likely including love feasts connected to the Eucharist, functioned as sites where difference was either intensified or reconciled. Around the table, questions of food, status, and belonging came to the fore. Paul's counsel in Romans 14–15 addresses precisely this setting, calling believers to forgo the assertion of freedom for the sake of love and to prioritize the building up of the community over the display of individual conviction.[30] In doing so, he articulates a vision of the church as a love-shaped community, ordered not by dominance or patronage but by mutual responsibility and self-giving love.[31]

This vision stands in deliberate contrast to the hierarchical logic of Roman society. Whereas patronage systems reinforced dependency and honor competition, Paul imagines a community defined by radical inclusion, where believers welcome one another as Christ has welcomed them. This "radical welcome" transcends tolerance. Tolerance keeps its distance; radical welcome draws near and embraces, it bears with the other. In the house and tenement churches of Rome, such welcome required intentional practices of humility, patience, and mutual accommodation.

These communities are to become more than sociological curiosities. They are to function as laboratories of ecclesial formation, spaces where the gospel's reconciling power is placed under strain and tested in practice. By calling believers across class, ethnic, and cultural divides into shared life, Paul summons the Roman churches toward a unity they have not yet fully achieved. Their communal life is presented not as an accomplished ideal, but as a concrete vocation: to bear witness to a new social reality in Christ, one capable of sustaining difference without fragmentation and of forming a people shaped by love rather than status.

The web of house and tenement churches in Rome reveals a dynamic and adaptable form of Christian community capable of thriving across the full spectrum of the city's social landscape. These small, scattered gatherings were not signs of weakness or disorganization but expressions

30. Jewett, *Romans*, 833–36.

31. Jewett, *Romans*, 66, 971–72.

of a resilient and relational ecclesiology. In these domestic spaces, the gospel began to form a new kind of community, one in which belonging was no longer secured by status, wealth, or lineage, but by shared participation in Christ. Within the deeply stratified world of the Roman Empire, the household churches of Rome were called to bear witness to the reconciling work of the gospel and its capacity to reconfigure social life from the ground up.

THE ETHNIC IDENTITY OF PAUL'S AUDIENCE

While there is broad agreement regarding the authorship, date, and general occasion of Romans, the ethnic composition of Paul's audience has long been a matter of scholarly debate.[32] Earlier interpreters often assumed a predominantly Jewish-Christian readership, given Paul's extensive engagement with the law, Israel's Scriptures, and covenantal themes. By the late nineteenth century, however, many scholars began to argue that Paul was addressing a primarily gentile audience, pointing to passages in which he explicitly identifies his addressees as gentiles (Rom 1:5, 13; 11:13) and to his self-understanding as apostle to the nations (Rom 15:14–19).

Others have emphasized the letter's "double character," noting Paul's sustained attention to both Jewish and gentile concerns. He repeatedly addresses "Jew and Greek" together (Rom 1:16; 2:9–10), engages deeply with Israel's story and the Mosaic law (Rom 2:17–29; 7:1–25; 9–11), and assumes a community shaped by Jewish Scripture even as it includes large numbers of gentile believers.[33] A third position seeks to hold these perspectives together, suggesting that while gentiles likely formed the numerical majority of the Roman church, Paul's Jewish theological framework was essential for grounding gentile believers in Israel's covenantal heritage and clarifying Israel's ongoing role in God's redemptive purposes.[34]

Taken together, the evidence points toward a mixed community in which gentile believers were prominent, while Jewish identity remained central and contested. Paul's sustained attention to both groups (Rom 3:9; 9:24; 10:12), alongside his affirmation of Israel's enduring privileges

32. Longenecker, *Romans*, 4–5.

33. Mathis, "Romans."

34. Elliott, *Paul Against the Nations*, 10.

and calling (Rom 9:4–5; 11:18), reveals a pastoral strategy rather than a sociological inventory. Paul addresses his audience as a people in the making. His aim is the formation of one reconciled community whose identity is neither erased nor secured by ethnicity, but reconstituted in Christ.

This mixed social and cultural landscape created real and persistent tensions within the Roman church.[35] Jewish believers carried long-standing commitments to Torah-shaped practices, formed through generations of covenantal faithfulness. Gentile believers were learning how to inhabit a movement whose theological roots were unmistakably Jewish. The resulting community wrestled with questions of belonging, authority, and the meaning of covenant identity in everyday life.[36] Who set the norms? Whose practices counted as faithful? And how were differences to be negotiated without fracturing the body?

Paul's letter reflects a keen awareness of these pressures.[37] He challenges Jewish believers who might assume moral or theological superiority on the basis of the law, insisting that possession of Torah does not guarantee righteousness (Rom 2:17–24). At the same time, he rebukes gentile believers who might regard Israel's story as obsolete or irrelevant, warning them against arrogance and reminding them that they are grafted into a story not their own (Rom 11:17–21). By emphasizing the universality of sin and the shared ground of justification by faith, Paul dismantles the ethnic and religious hierarchies that threatened to take root within the church. Identity, for Paul, is no longer secured by cultural inheritance or religious performance, but by participation in Christ.

These tensions surface most clearly in Paul's extended discussion of the "weak" and the "strong" in Romans 14:1—15:13.[38] The issues at stake—food laws and the observance of sacred days—are not mere matters of personal preference but embodied expressions of deeply held convictions. The "weak," likely Jewish believers or gentiles strongly influenced by Jewish practice, maintained stricter observances out of concern for purity, faithfulness, and loyalty to God. The "strong," likely gentile believers confident in their freedom in Christ, felt no obligation to observe such restrictions.[39] Mutual suspicion followed. The strong were tempted

35. Esler, *Conflict*, 19–39.

36. Esler, *Conflict*, 40–76.

37. Jeffers, *Conflict at Rome*.

38. Longenecker, *Romans*, 1063.

39. Longenecker, *Romans*, 1012–13.

to view the weak as rigid or backward; the weak were inclined to see the strong as careless or unfaithful.

Paul refuses to allow these disagreements to become defining markers of belonging.[40] Rather than adjudicating the dispute by declaring one position correct and the other mistaken, he reframes the conflict theologically and relationally. Judgment belongs to God, not to the community (Rom 14:10–12). Freedom in Christ is real, but it is never absolute; it is constrained by love and responsibility for the other (Rom 14:13–15). The question Paul presses upon the community is not simply which practices are permissible, but how believers are to honor God while honoring one another amid difference.

In Romans 15:1–7, Paul gathers these threads into a climactic vision of ecclesial unity grounded in the gospel itself. If all stand before God on the same basis, grace received through faith, no one may elevate or diminish another on the basis of custom, practice, or cultural background. The command is mutual welcome: "Accept one another, just as Christ has welcomed you, for the glory of God" (Rom 15:7). Unity, in this vision, does not require sameness. It requires a shared orientation toward Christ that makes space for difference without allowing difference to fracture the body.[41]

Beneath these social and ethnic tensions lies a deeper unity shaped by the Spirit. Implicit throughout the letter is a charismatic and apocalyptic spirituality characteristic of the early Christian movement.[42] Paul's frequent use of the language of Spirit (*pneuma*) and spiritual life (*pneumatikos*), appearing more than thirty times in Romans, reflects his conviction that the church is a Spirit-animated community participating in God's new creation. Whatever their differences in background, practice, or conviction, Roman believers were united by the shared experience of God's transformative presence and by the hope that God was actively reshaping their lives in light of the coming new creation.

The ethnic identity of Paul's audience is not a problem to be solved but a reality to be transformed. Romans does not aim to erase Jewish distinctiveness or subsume gentile diversity into a new monoculture. Instead, Paul envisions a reconciled community in which difference is held within the larger story of God's faithfulness, mercy, and mission to the nations. The Roman church thus becomes a living testimony to the

40. deSilva, *Introduction*, 599–642.

41. Longenecker, *Romans*, 1014.

42. Morris, *Romans*, 156–77.

gospel's power to form a people whose shared life bears witness to God's reconciling work in the world.

LIFE UNDER IMPERIAL AUTHORITY AND THE WITNESS OF THE CHURCH

Any account of the Roman church would be incomplete without attending to the political reality under which it lived. The believers addressed in Romans were not only navigating ethnic and cultural tensions within the church; they were also learning how to live faithfully under an imperial regime that claimed ultimate authority, demanded public loyalty, and sacralized its power through religious and civic ritual. Paul's teaching in Romans 13:1–7 must be read within this lived context, not as an abstract political theology but as pastoral counsel to a vulnerable community seeking to embody the gospel within the heart of empire.

Although Paul wrote Romans at a moment of relative administrative stability under Nero, the memory of imperial intervention in Jewish and Christian life was still close at hand. The Claudian expulsion of Jews in 49 CE had demonstrated how quickly religious disputes could attract state attention. Believers knew that their gatherings, practices, and speech were visible, and that suspicion could turn into repression with little warning. In such a setting, the question of how to relate to governing authorities was not theoretical. It was existential.

Romans 13 must therefore be read alongside the broader argument of the letter. Paul has already undermined imperial claims to moral superiority by exposing the universal reach of sin (Rom 1–3). He has relativized ethnic privilege and redefined righteousness apart from law or status. He has announced a lordship that belongs not to Caesar but to Jesus Christ. Yet having done all this, Paul does not call the Roman believers to political withdrawal or revolutionary defiance. Instead, he offers a way of faithful presence shaped by discernment, humility, and missional wisdom.

Paul's exhortation to "be subject to the governing authorities" (Rom 13:1) is grounded, not in the intrinsic righteousness of the empire but in God's sovereign ordering of history. Authority exists because God permits it, not because it embodies God's justice. This distinction is crucial. Paul does not sacralize Rome. Nor does he portray the state as the agent of salvation. Rather, he recognizes governing authority as a provisional structure through which God restrains chaos and preserves social order in a fallen world. Submission is pragmatic and theological, not ideological.

At the same time, Paul's language subtly resists imperial absolutism. By insisting that rulers are accountable to God and limited in scope, Paul denies them ultimate authority. Allegiance to Christ relativizes all other claims. The call to obedience is framed within a larger ethic of love, which Paul identifies as the fulfillment of the law (Rom 13:8–10). Love, not fear, is the defining mark of Christian life. Where obedience to the state conflicts with fidelity to God, the gospel's claims take precedence, even if Paul does not explicitly articulate that boundary here.[43]

Paul's instruction regarding taxes and public obligations (Rom 13:6–7) likewise reflects pastoral realism. Taxation in Rome was often exploitative and resented, particularly among Jews and the poor. Tacitus records public unrest over indirect taxes during Nero's reign, and uncertainty surrounding tax obligations may have contributed to anxiety among Roman believers.[44] Paul's counsel to continue paying taxes functions as a protective strategy. It minimizes unnecessary attention, reduces suspicion, and allows the church to pursue its mission without provoking avoidable conflict.[45] Faithfulness, in Paul's vision, is not performative resistance but embodied integrity.

This political posture is inseparable from Paul's vision of communal life. A church fractured by internal judgment and cultural rivalry would be ill-equipped to bear witness in such a context. Romans 12–15 presents an alternative social imagination rooted in humility, mutual service, and sacrificial love. The refusal to repay evil for evil, the commitment to peace insofar as it depends on the community, and the call to overcome evil with good (Rom 12:17–21) all shape how believers inhabit public life. These are not private virtues. They are practices that form a distinctive public presence within the empire.

43. While Paul exhorts respect for governing authorities (Rom 13:1–7), the wider canonical witness places clear limits on such obedience. Scripture consistently affirms that allegiance to God takes precedence when human authority contradicts divine command (Exod 1:17; Dan 3:16–18; 6:10; Acts 4:19–20; 5:29), a principle reinforced by Jesus' relativizing of political power (Matt 22:21; John 19:11). Early Christian theology thus understood submission to the state as contingent rather than absolute, a reading confirmed by Paul's own suffering for the gospel (2 Cor 11:23–28).

44. Jewett, *Romans*, 800.

45. Dunn, *Romans 9–16*, 768–69.

Romans 13 does not stand apart from Paul's teaching on ethnic reconciliation or communal unity. Rather, it presupposes it. A community capable of honoring governing authorities without idolizing them is one that has already learned to relativize power, status, and cultural dominance within its own life. A church formed by mutual welcome and shared witness is better positioned to resist both assimilation and antagonism. Its witness lies, not in seizing control but in embodying a different way of being human under God.

Paul's political ethic is therefore deeply missional. He is concerned not only with the survival of the Roman church but with its credibility as a community shaped by the gospel. Public order is not an end in itself but a context within which the church lives out its calling. By encouraging submission without servility, obedience without idolatry, and peace without compromise, Paul equips the Roman believers to inhabit the imperial world without being formed by it.

This posture anticipates the costly faithfulness that many Roman Christians would later face. Paul does not promise safety or success. What he offers instead is a way of life anchored in hope, grounded in love, and oriented toward God's coming reign. The church in Rome is called to live between the times, honoring the structures of the present age while bearing witness to the age to come.

A COMMUNITY FORMED IN TENSION AND HOPE

The portrait that emerges of the church in Rome is one of remarkable diversity, vulnerability, and possibility. Situated at the heart of the empire, these early Christian communities were shaped by overlapping pressures: imperial power, ethnic division, economic inequality, and cultural suspicion. They gathered in homes and tenements scattered across the city, forming small, interconnected networks of faith within a vast and stratified metropolis. Jews and gentiles, enslaved and free, women and men found themselves bound together by a shared confession that Jesus, not Caesar, is Lord.

This diversity was both a gift and a challenge. The five-year absence of Jewish believers during the Claudian expulsion altered the rhythms, leadership, and practices of the Roman churches in lasting ways. Their return reintroduced questions about law, custom, and belonging that touched daily life at the table and in worship. These tensions were not peripheral. They struck at the heart of what it meant to be the people of God in a city defined by hierarchy, honor, and exclusion.

Paul writes into this complexity not as a distant theologian but as a pastor and missionary attentive to lived realities. His concern is not simply to resolve disputes or clarify doctrine, but to form a community capable of bearing faithful witness in the center of empire. The Roman churches are called to embody a new social reality, one in which identity is rooted in Christ rather than ethnicity, status, or cultural practice, and in which freedom is shaped by love and responsibility for one another. Unity, in Paul's vision, is not achieved through uniformity or control but through mutual welcome and shared participation in God's reconciling work.

At the same time, these communities lived under the shadow of imperial authority, navigating the demands of civic loyalty without surrendering ultimate allegiance to the gospel. Paul's counsel regarding governing authorities reflects a posture of discerning faithfulness rather than ideological alignment or rebellion. The church is to live peaceably, act with integrity, and resist the temptation to define itself through fear or antagonism. In doing so, it offers a quiet yet profound alternative to Rome's claims of power and peace.

The church in Rome, then, stands as a living laboratory of the gospel's capacity to form a people amid difference, uncertainty, and pressure. Its struggles and hopes illuminate the concrete stakes of Paul's message and underscore the inseparability of theology and communal life. The letter to the Romans emerges from this context, not as an abstract treatise but as a pastoral and missional intervention addressed to real communities learning how to live together under the lordship of Christ.

Yet one dimension of the Roman church's life still requires focused attention. Throughout this chapter, enslaved and formerly enslaved persons have appeared repeatedly, within households, tenement churches, and the social networks named in Romans 16, yet largely in the background of the narrative. This reflects, not their insignificance but the nature of the sources themselves, which often obscure the labor and agency of those who occupied the lowest social positions in Roman society. To read Romans attentively, however, requires more than acknowledging the presence of enslaved believers; it requires reckoning with their formative role in the transmission, embodiment, and expansion of the gospel. Paul's theology of enslavement to Christ, suffering with Christ, and participation in God's mission cannot be abstracted from the lived realities of those whose bodies bore the daily weight of coercion and constraint. In the story of enslaved Christians, we see a quiet yet decisive example of how God confounds the wise and the powerful by choosing what the world calls weak and foolish. They emerge, not as marginal figures in the early church but as indispensable agents through whom the gospel took root and moved outward from the heart of the empire.

ENSLAVED WITNESSES, ROMANS, AND THE HIDDEN LABOR OF THE GOSPEL

Romans offers a missiological vision in which the gospel advances through embodied faithfulness rather than social power. Paul identifies himself as a *doulos* of Christ Jesus (Rom 1:1), deliberately adopting a term that carried the full social weight of enslavement in the Roman world. Throughout Romans 6, freedom in Christ is paradoxically redefined as a transfer of enslavement, from sin to righteousness (Rom 6:16–22). This is not metaphorical excess, but theological realism: Allegiance to Christ reorders every other claim of ownership, status, and honor.

This Pauline framework clarifies why enslaved persons played a decisive role in the spread of early Christianity. As Candida Moss has demonstrated, much of the labor that sustained, transmitted, and embodied the Christian movement was performed by people whose names rarely appear in surviving texts.[46] Enslaved believers occupied liminal social locations that allowed the gospel to move across boundaries of household, ethnicity, and region. They were present in elite homes, commercial networks, and domestic spaces inaccessible to formal missionaries, making them indispensable agents in the gospel's expansion.

Romans also provides a theological grammar for understanding the relationship between suffering and mission. Paul insists that suffering is not an anomaly to be explained away, but a participatory reality that conforms believers to Christ (Rom 8:17). Enslaved Christians lived this reality daily. Their witness demonstrates that mission does not proceed despite weakness but often *through* it. As Moss notes, the early Christian movement depended on precisely this kind of hidden, embodied labor. It was faithfulness enacted in ordinary, often coercive circumstances rather than in public displays of authority.[47]

46. Moss, *God's Ghostwriters*, 1–12.

47. Moss, *God's Ghostwriters*, 63–92.

Historical examples underscore this pattern. Blandina, an enslaved woman martyred in Lyons in the late second century, was remembered by contemporaries as a central figure whose endurance strengthened the church and emboldened others to confess Christ.[48] Her body became a site of witness, echoing Paul's claim that God's power is revealed in weakness (cf. Rom 8:36).

A later example is Patrick, who was captured and enslaved in Ireland before eventually returning as a missionary bishop. In his *Confession*, Patrick interprets his enslavement as formative for his vocation and as an arena in which God was at work long before his formal ministry began.[49] His story reflects Paul's conviction that God's purposes unfold through suffering, displacement, and apparent loss (Rom 8:28).

More radical still are accounts from late antiquity of Christians who willingly accepted extreme vulnerability, including forms of bonded labor, in order to remain with family members or bear witness within non-Christian households. Such actions must never be romanticized. Moss rightly cautions against turning coerced suffering into a theological ideal.[50] Yet within a Romans-shaped framework, these decisions can be understood as expressions of cruciform obedience rather than endorsements of the systems that produced them. Paul's ethic of self-giving love (Rom 12:9–21; 15:1–3) locates mission, not in self-preservation but in costly solidarity patterned after Christ.

Romans also decisively resists any theological legitimation of slavery itself. Paul's eschatological vision anticipates the liberation of all creation from bondage to decay (Rom 8:21), while his communal ethic destabilizes honor-based hierarchies that sustained enslavement in the Roman world (Rom 12:3–16). The gospel advanced through enslaved persons, not because slavery was redemptive but because God's righteousness is revealed precisely where human systems of domination fail.

The spread of the gospel has advanced through forms of power distinct from visibility, control, and institutional authority. As Romans and the witness of enslaved believers together reveal, God's mission has taken shape through hidden labor, constrained bodies, and lives the world deemed expendable. Enslaved believers functioned as the gospel's ghostwriters, to use Moss's term, composing its story through faithfulness,

48. Eusebius, *Church History* 5.1–2 (*NPNF*^{2} 1:211–18); Moss, *God's Ghostwriters*, 141–46.

49. Patrick, *Confession of St. Patrick*, §§1–6; cf. Moss, *God's Ghostwriters*, 187–90.

50. Moss, *God's Ghostwriters*, 9–10, 213–15.

suffering, and hope as Christ became known among the nations. Recovering their witness brings into focus a social and theological reality that shaped how the gospel was embodied, transmitted, and received, a reality that must guide our reading as we turn to the form, rhetoric, and missional logic of Paul's letter itself.

4

The Genre of Romans

BIBLICAL INTERPRETATION REQUIRES MORE than careful attention to historical, cultural, and linguistic contexts; it also demands attentiveness to genre. Genre identifies the kind of text we are reading and, in doing so, governs how its message is heard, its arguments weighed, and its claims embodied. Narrative, poetry, prophecy, and epistle cultivate different habits of reading and invite distinct modes of response.[1] Genre therefore functions as a hermeneutical key. It shapes interpretive expectations, directs theological reasoning, and determines how Scripture addresses the life of the church. When genre is misidentified, a text's voice is muffled, its aims misconstrued, and its message pressed into service for purposes it was never written to fulfill. The question before us, then, is decisive: What kind of text is Romans?

AGAINST ROMANS AS SYSTEMATIC THEOLOGY

Romans has often been read as a comprehensive theological system, a kind of proto–systematic theology arranged around core doctrines such as sin, justification, law, and grace. This approach has deep roots in Christian interpretation and gained particular influence in the post-Reformation period, following Philip Melanchthon's influential description of the letter as a summary of Christian doctrine.[2] Such readings rightly

1. Kugler and Hartin, *Introduction to the Bible*, xvii.

2. Some of the many commentaries in this category include Luther, *Commentary on Romans*; Calvin, *Epistles of Paul to the Romans and Thessalonians*; Piper, *Future of*

recognize the theological depth and coherence of Romans. Yet when Romans is approached primarily as an abstract system, it is detached from the historical, communal, and missional realities that gave it life.

This mode of reading privileges logical structure over pastoral intent and doctrinal coherence over rhetorical purpose. Themes are extracted from the letter and organized according to later theological frameworks, while the epistolary, situational, and missionary character of the text recedes into the background. The result is a Romans that feels timeless and universal but also flattened, reduced to a repository of propositions rather than a dynamic act of apostolic address.

Romans itself resists this abstraction. Paul writes with concrete aims in view: to explain his long delay in visiting Rome (Rom 1:13), to prepare the churches for his arrival (Rom 15:22–23), to secure their partnership in his projected mission to Spain (Rom 15:24), and to enlist their prayers as he journeys to Jerusalem and hopes to arrive in Rome "in joy" (Rom 15:30–32). These stated purposes anchor the letter firmly in the life of a real community whose internal relationships and external witness mattered deeply to Paul's vocation.

The argument of Romans unfolds rhetorically rather than schematically. Paul revisits themes, reframes them, and deepens them across the letter, responding to anticipated objections and pastoral concerns as he goes. This repetition reflects intentional formation rather than disorder. Paul is not constructing a system in the abstract; he is shaping a community over time through persuasion, exhortation, and theological reorientation.

When Romans is treated primarily as a universal blueprint detached from its audience, its communal and missional dimensions are muted.[3] The gospel becomes individualized, salvation narrowed to private experience, and theology severed from the formation of a reconciled people called to participate together in God's redemptive purposes for the world.

ROMANS PROCLAIMS THE GOSPEL, IT IS NOT A GOSPEL

A related but equally significant misreading emerges when Romans is treated as a Gospel in itself. In some Christian traditions, the letter has been elevated as the definitive articulation of the gospel and employed

Justification; Naselli, *Romans*. A popular example is Sproul, *Gospel of God*.

3. Green, *Christianity*, 28–29.

as a universal template for evangelistic proclamation. The influence of this approach is evident in the widespread use of Romans within tracts and evangelistic methods, at times granting it functional priority over the four canonical Gospels. Such a reading, however, calls for careful reconsideration.

The early church understood "the gospel" as the proclamation of the incarnation, life, death, resurrection, and exaltation of Jesus Christ as the fulfillment of God's redemptive purposes.[4] This story is told canonically in the four Gospels. While Romans undeniably proclaims the gospel, it does not narrate it. It presupposes the gospel rather than retelling it. Paul assumes a shared apostolic narrative already known within the Christian communities and explores its implications for a divided church living under imperial power.[5]

When Paul does summarize the gospel explicitly, as in 1 Corinthians 15:1–8, he does so narratively and concisely. In Romans, by contrast, he is not attempting to rehearse the story of Jesus but to unfold its meaning for a specific community wrestling with questions of identity, allegiance, and communal life. He is concerned not only with what God has done in Christ, but with what kind of people this good news creates.

The Gospel as Encounter, Event, and Power

For Paul, the gospel is not a set of ideas to be understood. It is an encounter with the living God. He presents the gospel as the unveiling (*apokalypsis*) of God's righteousness in Christ (Rom 1:17). This revelation is both event and proclamation. It is the proclamation of what God has done in Christ and the dynamic reality of Christ himself as the content of the gospel. The gospel confronts every human system of self-exaltation, whether expressed through Jewish legalism or gentile idolatry, and calls humanity into reconciled relationship with God and with one another. It is not an intellectual ascent to correct propositions about Christ and his resurrection. It is an existential encounter with the living God that transforms allegiance, reorders life, and refuses to be reduced to doctrinal statements or a worldview.

For this reason, every attempt to tame the gospel must be resisted. The gospel is not static truth to be managed, preserved, or deployed as a

4. Carson and Moo, *Introduction to the New Testament*, 112–15.

5. Carson and Moo, *Introduction to the New Testament*, 402.

slogan. It is living power that breaks in, unsettles, and transforms those who receive it. Paul proclaims the gospel not as a system to be mastered or a culture to be defended, but as God's decisive action in history to confront sin, death, and human self-reliance. The gospel calls for a response that goes beyond belief understood narrowly as agreement. It demands participation. It is the inbreaking of divine grace that liberates, renews, and reshapes the way people live, see the world, and relate to one another.

Central to Paul's vision is the gospel as event rather than abstraction. The gospel names what God has done and is doing. When Paul declares it "the power of God for salvation," he signals this active reality. Salvation is not merely a change of status but participation in God's reconciling work. God's righteousness appears not as an attribute to be admired but as an action that sets the world right. Sin emerges not simply as moral failure but as a power that enslaves. Justification is not merely a declarative verdict that leaves reality intact, but an act of liberation that transfers people into a new realm of life. Life in the Spirit is not an optional enhancement to faith but the defining mark of participation in the new creation.

This apocalyptic vision, however, is never detached from pastoral concern. Paul's proclamation of universal sin dismantles ethnic, moral, and religious hierarchies within the church. Justification by faith levels the ground at the foot of the cross. The promise of life in the Spirit empowers a fractured community to live differently in the present age. Theology is mobilized not to win arguments but to heal divisions, sustain hope, and form a people capable of faithful witness.

Paul seeks to awaken the believers in Rome to this reality. He calls them to live as the people of God, fully immersed in the life of the gospel and animated by the Spirit within their own cultural setting. The movement of Romans 1:18–16:27 is not toward abstraction but embodiment. Paul interprets their context, confronts their divisions, and summons them into a renewed way of life shaped by grace. The gospel, as Paul proclaims it, is not simply to be believed. It is to be lived, together, as the living expression of God's reconciling love in a world marked by fragmentation and alienation.

ROMANS AS AN APOSTOLIC LETTER

Romans belongs to the epistolary genre common in the ancient Mediterranean world. Letters were situational, rhetorical, and purposive, written to persuade, exhort, correct, and coordinate action. Paul's letters share these characteristics while displaying an unusual depth of theological reflection. For Paul, theology is never detached speculation. Rather, theology serves discipleship and exists for the sake of the church's life and mission.

Read as an apostolic letter, Romans functions as a sustained act of pastoral formation addressed to a particular community, at a particular moment, in service of a particular mission.[6] Paul writes to a community he did not found, composed of Jewish and gentile believers navigating deep tensions over identity, practice, and belonging. He writes in order to form a people capable of embodying the gospel faithfully within the heart of the empire and of partnering with him in its advance toward new horizons.

This genre-sensitive reading reframes the letter's theological argument. Paul's sustained engagement with sin, righteousness, justification, and life in the Spirit serves concrete pastoral ends: healing division, relativizing claims of moral or ethnic superiority, and grounding communal life in God's mercy. In Romans, theology functions as formation, doctrine serves discipleship, and argument serves reconciliation. Genre carries theological weight, because it shapes how the gospel is heard, lived, and proclaimed.

RHETORIC AND MISSIONAL FORMATION

Recognizing Romans as an apostolic letter also draws attention to its rhetorical shape. Paul employs diatribe, anticipates objections, and addresses imagined interlocutors throughout the letter.[7] These rhetorical moves reflect the realities of oral communication and communal reading in the ancient world. Romans was not read silently by individuals but proclaimed aloud to gathered communities.

Paul's argument unfolds in discernible movements rather than discrete doctrinal units. He moves from the universal problem of sin (Rom 1–3) to the faithfulness of God revealed in Christ (Rom 3–5), from life under sin to life in the Spirit (Rom 6–8), from Israel's place in God's purposes (Rom 9–11) to the concrete shape of transformed communal life (Rom 12–15). These movements are formative. They invite

6. Käsemann, *Romans*, 3–4.

7. See Jewett, *Romans*; and Witherington, *Romans*.

the community to journey together from division to reconciliation, from fear to hope, from self-assertion to mutual service.

Genre awareness helps prevent selective reading. Romans 1–3 cannot be isolated from Romans 12–15. Justification cannot be severed from communal ethics. Faith cannot be detached from embodied love. Paul's theology resists fragmentation precisely because it is written for a living community.

ROMANS AND MISSIONAL COORDINATION

Romans is also distinctive among Paul's letters for its role in missional coordination. Paul writes not only to address internal tensions within the Roman churches but to invite them into partnership in his apostolic mission. His desire to visit Rome, to be "helped on [his] way" to Spain, and to enjoy mutual encouragement underscores the letter's strategic dimension.

This missional purpose situates Romans within the dynamic relationship between local congregations and translocal apostolic movements.[8] Paul neither imagines mission apart from the church nor envisions the church as self-contained. The gospel advances through partnership, mutual support, and shared discernment across communities. Romans functions as a mediating text that holds these dimensions together, aligning theology, identity, and practice so that the Roman churches may participate faithfully in God's mission beyond their own setting.[9]

Genre matters here because apostolic letters are uniquely suited to this mediating role. They are neither purely local nor abstractly universal. They speak from within mission to communities called into mission. Romans exemplifies this dynamic at an unparalleled scale.

TRADITION AS LIVING TRANSMISSION

Another implication of Romans as an apostolic letter concerns how the gospel is handed on and lived out over time within the body of Christ, what the church has historically meant by *tradition*.[10] In the New Testament,

8. Tennent, *Invitation to World Missions*, 441–43.

9. Winter, "Two Structures," 121–39.

10. The New Testament regularly uses "tradition" (*paradosis*) in a positive sense to describe the faithful transmission of the apostolic gospel through teaching, practice,

tradition does not primarily denote a fixed body of ideas preserved in abstraction, but the faithful transmission of the apostolic gospel as it is received, practiced, and embodied in community under the guidance of the Spirit. Because Romans is an apostolic letter, Paul presents tradition not as something merely stored or defended, but as the gospel actively at work among real people, shaping worship, ethics, and shared life as communities learn to live faithfully amid changing circumstances.

Paul writes as a missionary theologian addressing a concrete situation. He is neither preserving doctrine for its own sake nor assembling a theological archive. Rather, he interprets the gospel in light of lived realities and summons a divided community into obedient participation in God's redemptive work. Tradition does not stand alongside Scripture as a competing authority, nor does it function as a repository of settled conclusions. It names the ongoing process by which the apostolic gospel is handed on through teaching, worship, ethical formation, and communal practice as the Spirit forms the church across time.

Tradition is not the preservation of conclusions but the transmission of faithfulness. It is Scripture rightly received and enacted, tested in new contexts, and embodied in the life of God's people. Paul's letter itself exemplifies tradition in motion—the gospel once proclaimed is now interpreted, applied, and entrusted to others so that it may continue to bear fruit.

The gospel Paul proclaims is rooted in Israel's Scriptures, centered on Christ, and animated by the Spirit, yet continually translated into new cultural and social settings as God's mission advances. Paul does not fear contextual engagement because he trusts the gospel's power to remain faithful even as it takes new forms. Tradition, for Paul, is therefore not static or fossilized. It lives in faithful interpretation and embodied practice as communities are reshaped by the gospel in changing circumstances.

This dynamic vision reframes Christian tradition itself. Tradition is not a museum of immutable dogmas or a mechanism for preserving religious identity. It is a living transmission grounded in the apocalyptic event of Christ and sustained by God's ongoing action in history. Faith

---

and communal life. Paul commends churches for maintaining the traditions he handed on (1 Cor 11:2) and urges believers to hold fast to what they received orally and in writing (2 Thess 2:15; see also 3:6). This pattern is evident in his summary of the resurrection tradition (1 Cor 15:1–3) and his instruction to entrust what has been received to others for continued transmission (2 Tim 2:2). Tradition does not function as a competing authority alongside Scripture, but as Scripture faithfully received, embodied, and handed on within a Spirit-formed community (see also Acts 2:42; Phil 4:9).

is not the defense of what once was but an ongoing awakening to God's living presence, a journey that resists reducing revelation to static formulations or closed systems.[11]

READING ROMANS FAITHFULLY

To read Romans faithfully is to read it as it was written: an apostolic letter shaped by mission, addressed to a concrete and diverse community, and animated by a living gospel that forms a reconciled people. Attention to genre guards against reductionism, whether doctrinal, moral, or political, by reminding readers that Romans is not a quarry for isolated propositions but a sustained call into a shared way of life. Faithful reading requires entering the letter's movement rather than abstracting its conclusions.

Romans does not invite mastery of its arguments so much as participation in the life it proclaims. It summons its hearers into a way of life shaped by God's mercy, formed through humility, and oriented toward God's purposes among the nations. Its theology cannot be separated from its aim, and its aim cannot be detached from the kind of community it seeks to bring into being. To read Romans rightly, then, is not merely to understand its claims, but to be drawn into the transforming vision of the gospel it announces.

ROMANS AS MISSIONAL INTERVENTION

Reading Romans through this missional and epistolary lens brings into focus dimensions of the letter that are easily obscured when it is treated primarily as an abstract theological system. Paul's sustained concern with reconciliation across theological, ethnic, social, and political boundaries comes into sharper relief, as does his vision of the gospel as God's power for all peoples. Romans emerges, not simply as a treatise on salvation but as a summons to become one new humanity in Christ, formed together by grace and called into shared participation in God's redemptive work.

This perspective also clarifies why Romans continues to speak with urgency to the contemporary church. Paul addresses a community fractured by competing identities, contested loyalties, and unexamined claims to superiority. His theological argument does not evade these

11. Hart, *Tradition and Apocalypse*, 49–50, 60.

tensions; it confronts them directly. By dismantling every human basis for boasting and re-centering identity in God's mercy, Paul calls the church into a form of life capable of resisting division and bearing faithful witness amid cultural and political pressure. Unity, in Romans, is not achieved by suppressing difference or enforcing conformity, but by learning to live together under the lordship of Christ.

To grasp Romans as such a missional intervention, it is essential to enter the world in which it was written. The Roman congregations lived in the shadow of imperial power and bore the legacy of a volatile political history marked by displacement, exclusion, and return. Questions of belonging, authority, and cultural superiority were not abstract concerns but lived realities. These tensions threatened not only the church's internal cohesion but also its capacity to participate in Paul's missionary horizon, including his desire to extend the gospel westward into regions Rome regarded as marginal and uncivilized.

It is into this contested environment that Paul crafted his most expansive theological argument. Romans does not abstract believers from their world; it re-forms them within it. By exposing the limits of human righteousness and proclaiming God's reconciling action in Christ, Paul seeks to forge a community capable of embodying the gospel across difference and of advancing God's mission beyond its own context. Genre is not only a literary classification. It is the key to recognizing Romans as a living apostolic act, one aimed at shaping a people whose shared life bears witness to the power of the gospel in the midst of empire.

PREPARING TO READ ROMANS AS MISSION

Having attended to the historical context of Rome, the social realities of the Roman church, and the genre of Paul's letter, we are now positioned to read Romans on its own terms. Context and genre do not determine meaning, but they establish the conditions under which meaning can be responsibly discerned. They enable us to hear Paul's argument as it was intended to be heard, addressed to real communities, shaped by concrete pressures, and oriented toward God's mission in the world.

The chapters that follow turn directly to the structure and theological movement of Romans itself. Rather than extracting doctrines in isolation, we will trace how Paul's argument unfolds as a formative process, how its claims function within the life of the community, and how its vision shapes a people capable of faithful participation in the mission of God among the nations. Romans will be read, not as a theological system to be mastered but as a missional text designed to form the life and witness of the church.

5

A Summary of Romans

ROMANS UNFOLDS AS A sustained theological, pastoral, and missional argument aimed at forming a reconciled community capable of participating in God's redemptive purposes among the nations. Romans is written to shape a people whose shared life embodies the gospel in a world ordered by hierarchy, power, and exclusion.

The community Paul addresses is diverse in ways that exceed ethnic difference alone. Jewish and gentile believers worship side by side, but so do the wealthy and the poor, patrons and clients, enslaved and free, long-established residents and recent arrivals, the socially visible and the largely invisible. These believers do not gather on neutral ground. They meet within a city structured by honor and shame, economic inequality, and imperial power, where difference is typically managed through domination rather than reconciliation.

Romans is written to form a community capable of living truthfully within such tensions. Paul seeks to reconfigure identity, allegiance, and belonging so that a fractured and vulnerable church might become a credible witness to the gospel. The letter's theological claims are inseparable from this pastoral aim: to cultivate a shared life grounded in God's mercy rather than status, achievement, or power, and thus to prepare the Roman believers to participate faithfully in God's mission beyond their own context.

ROMANS 1–4 LEVELS THE GROUND BENEATH EVERY HUMAN DISTINCTION

The Gospel's Purpose and Power (Romans 1:1–17)

Romans opens with Paul situating himself and his message within the long arc of God's redemptive purposes. He introduces himself as a servant and apostle, set apart for the gospel promised beforehand through the prophets and now revealed in Jesus Christ, the risen Son of God (Rom 1:1–4). This gospel defines Paul's vocation and animates his mission: to bring about the obedience of faith among all the nations (Rom 1:5). From the outset, Paul frames the gospel, not only as information to be believed but as a summons that reshapes allegiance, identity, and communal life.

Paul expresses gratitude for the Roman believers, whose faith is known throughout the world, and shares his longing to visit them so that they might be mutually encouraged in their shared calling (Rom 1:8–12). Though he has not yet reached Rome, Paul understands himself as indebted to proclaim the gospel to all people, Greeks and non-Greeks, wise and foolish alike (Rom 1:13–15). This sense of obligation reflects the universal scope of the gospel and anticipates the letter's sustained concern for the inclusion of all peoples within God's saving purposes.

The theological center of the letter is announced in Romans 1:16–17. Paul declares that he is not ashamed of the gospel because it is the power of God for salvation to everyone who believes. In the gospel, God's righteousness is revealed "from faith to faith," grounding salvation not in ethnic identity, moral achievement, or social status, but in trusting response to God's action in Christ. These verses establish the letter's central conviction: the gospel dismantles every human hierarchy, creates a people defined by faith rather than privilege, and propels the church into God's mission to the nations.

God's Righteousness and the Overthrow of Human Honor (Romans 1:18—4:25)

Having announced the gospel as God's saving power, Paul turns to expose the universal human condition that makes such salvation necessary. In Romans 1:18–4:25, he systematically dismantles every claim to righteousness rooted in human achievement, cultural superiority, or religious status. Both gentiles and Jews, though differently positioned within God's story, stand equally in need of God's redeeming action.

Paul begins with the gentile world, describing how humanity has suppressed the truth about God that is evident in creation (Rom 1:18–20). Rather than honoring God as Creator, gentiles exchange God's glory for idols, worshiping created things instead of the One who made them (Rom 1:21–23). This refusal to honor God results in disordered desires and practices, as God "gives them over" to the consequences of their rebellion (Rom 1:24–32). What appears as cultural sophistication or moral autonomy is exposed as a movement from honor to shame, marked by relational breakdown and moral distortion.

Paul then turns to Israel, confronting the assumption that possession of the law guarantees righteousness (Rom 2:1–3:8). Though Israel was entrusted with the Torah, Paul insists that the law cannot confer righteousness apart from faithful obedience. Boasting in religious identity while failing to live in covenant faithfulness brings dishonor rather than honor to God's name (Rom 2:17–24). The law exposes sin, but it cannot heal it. As a result, Paul concludes that both Jews and gentiles stand under sin's power: "There is no one righteous, not even one. . . . All have sinned and fall short of the glory of God" (Rom 3:10, 23). Every human strategy for securing righteousness collapses, leaving humanity dependent upon God's grace.

Against this backdrop of universal failure, Paul announces the heart of the gospel. God's righteousness has been revealed apart from the law, though it is witnessed by the law and the prophets (Rom 3:21). This righteousness comes through faith in Jesus Christ and is available to all, without distinction (Rom 3:22). It is a gift of grace, grounded in God's faithfulness rather than human performance, and it removes every basis for boasting (Rom 3:27). Justification restores honor not by elevating one group over another, but by reconciling all to God on the same terms.

To show that this has always been God's way, Paul appeals to Abraham. Long before the giving of the law, Abraham was declared righteous because he trusted God's promise (Rom 4:3). His righteousness was not earned through works but credited through faith. In Abraham, Paul finds the prototype of a faith-based righteousness that precedes ethnic boundary markers and extends to all who share his trust in God. Romans 1–4 thus levels the ground beneath every human distinction, clearing space for a community whose identity rests not in honor claimed, but in grace received.

ROMANS 5–8 ANNOUNCES THE CREATION OF A NEW HUMANITY IN CHRIST

Having exposed the failure of every human claim to righteousness, Paul turns in Romans 5–8 to announce what God has accomplished in Christ. This section moves from diagnosis to deliverance, from exposure of sin's power to the emergence of a new humanity formed by grace and animated by the Spirit. Paul frames Christ's work as both the solution to individual guilt and as the inauguration of a new way of being human.

Paul begins by placing Christ within a sweeping redemptive contrast. Adam's disobedience introduced sin and death into the human story, subjecting humanity to corruption and alienation (Rom 5:12–14). Christ, by contrast, embodies faithful obedience, through which righteousness and life now flow to many (Rom 5:15–21). Where Adam's act unleashed death's reign, Christ's act establishes the reign of grace. The issue at stake is not simply moral failure, but dominion: Who or what exercises authority over human life. In Christ, believers are transferred from the realm of sin and death into the realm of grace and life.

This transfer is not abstract. In Romans 6, Paul grounds it in participation. Through baptism into Christ, believers are joined to his death and resurrection, sharing in both the death of the old self and the emergence of new life (Rom 6:3–5).[1] Sin no longer holds rightful authority. Believers are no longer captive to its power, but are freed to live as those who belong to God. Paul insists that this freedom is not merely a change in legal status but a transformation of allegiance and practice. Those who have died with Christ are called to present themselves as "instruments of righteousness," living in a way that reflects their new identity (Rom 6:12–14).[2]

Paul then turns to the law, addressing a tension central to both Jewish and gentile believers. The law, though holy and good, lacks the power to liberate humanity from sin's grip (Rom 7:7–12). Instead, sin exploits the law, twisting its good intentions into instruments of condemnation and death. Romans 7 articulates the tragedy of human willing without human power: the desire to do good without the capacity to carry it out. Paul's anguished cry—"Who will rescue me from this body of death?" (Rom 7:24)—captures the experience of life under sin's dominion and prepares the way for the decisive answer that follows.[3]

1. Jewett, *Romans*, 396–98.
2. Holland, *Contours of Pauline Theology*, 152.
3. Interpreting Romans 7 presents significant challenges due to its complex theological

That answer arrives in Romans 8. What the law could not do, God has done through the gift of the Spirit. Paul opens with a declaration that signals a new reality: "There is now no condemnation for those who are in Christ Jesus" (Rom 8:1). Liberation from sin and death is no longer theoretical. Through the Spirit, believers are empowered to live in accordance with God's purposes. Life in the Spirit is not an optional enhancement to faith but the defining mark of participation in the new creation.

The Spirit confirms believers' identity as God's children, enabling them to cry out "Abba, Father" and to live not in fear but in trust (Rom 8:15–16). Adoption establishes believers as heirs and participants in both Christ's sufferings and his future glory (Rom 8:17). Paul does not deny the reality of suffering; rather, he situates it within the hope of redemption. Creation itself groans for liberation, and believers groan with it, sustained by the Spirit's intercession when words fail (Rom 8:18–27).

Paul assures the community that God is actively at work within this tension-filled present. God's purposes are not thwarted by suffering or weakness. All things are being woven toward redemption for those who love God and are called according to his purpose (Rom 8:28). The chapter culminates in a hymn-like affirmation of God's unbreakable love. No power, whether hardship, persecution, or cosmic force, can sever believers from the love of God revealed in Christ Jesus (Rom 8:31–39).

Romans 5–8 thus announces more than personal assurance. It proclaims the emergence of a new humanity, freed from sin's dominion, indwelt by the Spirit, and sustained by hope. This Spirit-formed community embodies the future of God's creation in the present, bearing witness to a gospel that both forgives and transforms.

---

and rhetorical structure, as well as debates over its autobiographical nature. Scholars have long wrestled with whether Paul's description of the internal struggle with sin refers to his own experience, a generic depiction of human nature, or the plight of Israel under the law. Additionally, the chapter's oscillation between first-person singular ("I") and broader theological implications complicates its interpretation. Understanding Paul's view of the law, whether he critiques it as inherently negative or affirms its divine purpose, further adds to the difficulty. These challenges highlight the need to carefully situate Romans 7 within its broader literary and theological context, particularly its connections to chapters 6 and 8, which frame the passage in terms of liberation from sin and life in the Spirit.

ROMANS 9–11 CONFRONTS THE QUESTION OF ISRAEL'S PLACE WITHIN GOD'S REDEMPTIVE PLAN

Romans 9–11 stands among the most theologically demanding and pastorally charged sections of Paul's letter. Across the centuries, these chapters have provoked sustained reflection and disagreement as readers have grappled with Paul's treatment of divine sovereignty, Israel's vocation, and the inclusion of the nations. Yet for Paul, the questions addressed here are not abstract puzzles. They are fundamentally missional. The credibility of the gospel itself is at stake, for if God has abandoned Israel, then God's promises cannot be trusted, and the church's mission to the nations rests on uncertain ground.

Paul therefore frames the central issue with stark clarity: Has God's word failed? (Rom 9:6). His answer is unequivocal. The gospel does not represent a departure from God's covenantal purposes but their fulfillment. God's faithfulness to Israel remains intact, even as the nations are drawn into the scope of God's mercy. Romans 9–11 thus functions as a theological safeguard, ensuring that the church's mission is grounded in the reliability of God's promises rather than in cultural triumphalism or ethnic replacement.

Paul begins with an expression of profound anguish for his fellow Israelites (Rom 9:1–3). His sorrow underscores that what follows is not detached speculation but covenantal grief. Israel, he reminds his readers, remains the people to whom belong the covenants, the law, the worship, and the promises, and from whom the Messiah himself comes (Rom 9:4–5). Yet Paul insists that God's saving purpose has never been reducible to ethnic descent alone.[4] From the beginning, God's election has operated through promise rather than lineage, through mercy rather than entitlement. The stories of Isaac and Ishmael, Jacob and Esau, demonstrate that God's faithfulness unfolds through divine initiative rather than human claim (Rom 9:6–13).

Anticipating objections, Paul defends the justice of God's freedom in election (Rom 9:14–29). Drawing on prophetic imagery and Israel's own Scriptures, he shows that God's mercy and hardening alike serve a larger redemptive purpose: the revelation of God's glory and the extension of mercy to all peoples. The inclusion of gentiles is not an afterthought or deviation, but the outworking of God's long-standing promise to bless

4. Longenecker, *Romans*, 825.

the nations through Abraham.[5] In this way, Romans 9 reframes election not as exclusionary privilege, but as a means through which God advances redemption in the world.

In Romans 10, Paul turns from divine purpose to human response. He affirms the universal availability of salvation: "There is no distinction between Jew and gentile; the same Lord is Lord of all" (Rom 10:12). Yet this openness intensifies, rather than diminishes, the urgency of proclamation. Faith comes by hearing, and hearing requires messengers who are sent (Rom 10:14–17). Israel's present unbelief, Paul argues, does not signal divine abandonment but reflects a tragic mismatch between zeal and understanding. Even so, God's covenantal commitment endures, preserved through a faithful remnant within Israel.

Romans 11 brings Paul's argument to its theological and pastoral climax. He emphatically rejects the idea that God has rejected Israel (Rom 11:1). A remnant remains, sustained by grace, bearing witness to God's ongoing work within Israel (Rom 11:5). Israel's partial hardening, Paul explains, serves a redemptive purpose—it opens space for the inclusion of the nations and ultimately aims at Israel's own restoration (Rom 11:11–12).

The olive tree metaphor captures this vision with striking clarity. Gentiles are not a replacement people but wild branches grafted into Israel's covenantal root (Rom 11:17–24). The tree remains one. Gentile believers live by grace drawn from promises not originally their own, and this reality demands humility rather than boasting. Paul warns the gentile majority in Rome against presumption, reminding them that their inclusion depends entirely on God's mercy.

Paul looks ahead to a future act of divine reconciliation in which Israel, too, will be gathered into the fullness of God's saving purpose: "And so all Israel will be saved" (Rom 11:26). However one interprets the timing or mechanics of this hope, its theological weight is unmistakable. God's mercy will have the final word. Jew and gentile alike are bound together within a single story of grace. This reconciliation highlights God's faithfulness to his promises and his goal of uniting all things in Christ.[6] Paul concludes with a doxology that acknowledges the mystery of God's ways and celebrates the depth of divine wisdom and faithfulness (Rom 11:33–36).

Romans 9–11 thus offers more than doctrinal clarification. It provides a missional framework rooted in covenantal faithfulness. The church

5. Jewett, *Romans*, 652.

6. Dunn, *Romans 9–16*, 690–97.

does not replace Israel; it participates in the expansion of God's covenantal purposes to include the nations without negating Israel's ongoing vocation. The church is summoned to participate in God's unfolding covenantal plan, inviting all peoples to share in the blessings promised to Abraham and fulfilled in Christ. This vision calls the church to humility, gratitude, and perseverance in mission. Sustained by hope in God's irrevocable promises, the church is summoned to participate in God's unfolding redemptive plan, bearing witness to a mercy that embraces all peoples and remains faithful to the promises through which it was first made known.

ROMANS 12–16 PORTRAYS THE CHURCH AS THE LIVING EMBODIMENT OF THE GOSPEL

In Romans 12–16, Paul turns from theological exposition to embodied response. Yet this shift is not a move from doctrine to ethics, as though belief now gives way to behavior. Rather, Paul shows that the gospel, rightly received, necessarily takes visible form in the life of a community shaped by God's mercy.[7] The exhortations that follow are not add-ons to the gospel; they are its lived expression.

Paul begins by calling believers to present their bodies as "living sacrifices," a response grounded explicitly in God's mercy rather than in obligation or fear (Rom 12:1–2). This self-offering signals a reorientation of life itself, no longer conformed to the patterns of the age, but transformed by renewed perception and allegiance. Such transformation reshapes how believers see themselves and one another. Paul insists that humility replaces self-exaltation, and that gifts are exercised not for status but for mutual service within the body (Rom 12:3–8). Love, sincere and self-giving, becomes the defining mark of the community (Rom 12:9–21).

This ethic of love extends beyond the boundaries of the church and into the public world. Paul addresses the community's posture toward governing authorities (Rom 13:1–7) and reframes obedience not as passive submission but as a witness shaped by conscience and hope. At the heart of this public ethic stands love, which Paul describes as the fulfillment of the law (Rom 13:8–10). Love is not sentiment but a concrete practice that resists harm, transcends social division, and binds the community together across difference.

7. deSilva, *Honor*, 299.

The most sustained application of this gospel-shaped life appears in Romans 14:1—15:13, where Paul confronts tensions between the "strong" and the "weak." These divisions, likely reflecting gentile freedom and Jewish faithfulness to ancestral practices, threatened the unity of the Roman churches.[8] Paul refuses to resolve the conflict by privileging one group over the other. Instead, he calls both to mutual welcome, insisting that belonging in Christ precedes agreement on disputable matters (Rom 14:1; 15:7).[9] In a culture governed by honor and shame, this mutual acceptance represents a radical redefinition of honor, one grounded not in dominance or conformity but in self-giving love.[10]

Paul reminds the community that all believers stand accountable to God rather than to one another's judgments (Rom 14:1–12). Freedom is exercised with care, guided by love and concern for the flourishing of others (Rom 14:13–23). The goal is shared faithfulness, not uniformity. As believers bear with one another's differences, the church becomes a living sign of the gospel's reconciling power. This unity extends beyond the community itself. Paul explicitly links it to mission, envisioning a reconciled Roman church capable of supporting and participating in his westward mission to Spain (Rom 15:14–24).

Throughout these chapters, the Roman believers are portrayed as living in a liminal space, no longer defined by Jewish or gentile identity, yet not fully at home within the Roman world. This in-between existence is not a weakness to be resolved but a vocation to be embraced.[11] Paul calls the church to inhabit this liminality faithfully, embodying the gospel as a bridge across cultural, ethnic, and social divides. In doing so, the Roman churches are positioned to bear witness to the inbreaking kingdom of God, offering a foretaste of the reconciled humanity God is bringing into being through Christ.

CONCLUSION

Taken as a whole, Romans narrates the formation of a people grounded in God's righteousness, transformed by the Spirit, reconciled across difference, and oriented toward God's mission in the world. Paul's theology is

8. Jewett, *Romans*, 833–52.

9. McKnight, *Reading Romans Backwards*, 22–23.

10. Flemming, *Contextualization in the New Testament*, 127.

11. Jennings, *Acts*, 121–22.

never detached from lived reality. It serves pastoral formation; its ethical exhortations arise from mercy; its vision of unity fuels mission.[12] What unfolds across the letter is not a system of ideas but a communal reordering of life under the lordship of Christ.[13] The gospel is simultaneously theological foundation and social critique, calling believers to embody God's indiscriminate grace in their shared life.[14]

Romans enacts the gospel it proclaims. Addressing communities shaped by honor and shame, social hierarchy, ethnic division, and imperial pressure, Paul announces a gospel that dismantles claims to superiority and re-centers identity in God's reconciling grace.[15] Justification by faith functions as the means by which God creates a new humanity, capable of mutual welcome and shared allegiance in the midst of empire.

Paul writes not simply to correct belief but to form a people. The unity of the Roman churches is not an end in itself but a living testimony to the power of the gospel and a necessary condition for faithful participation in God's mission beyond their own context. The church that Romans envisions is neither inward-turned nor self-sustaining. It exists as a community caught up in God's redemptive movement among the nations.[16]

Romans thus reveals an integrated vision of church and mission. Paul does not separate pastoral care from missionary calling.[17] The gospel that creates the church also commissions it. The church cannot understand itself apart from its participation in God's mission, just as mission cannot flourish apart from communities formed by the gospel. Paul's own apostolic ministry embodies this unity: He nurtures churches, not as static institutions but as missional communities caught up in God's redemptive movement toward the nations.[18]

This integrated vision of church and mission now presses a further question: If the gospel creates such a people, how does Paul understand their place within God's mission to the world? It is to this question that we now turn.

12. Jewett, *Romans*, 75.

13. Beker, *Paul*, 19.

14. Roper, *Following Wisdom, Leading Wisely*, 224–29.

15. Jewett, *Romans*, 50.

16. Jewett, *Romans*, 926.

17. Thomassen, *Liminality and the Modern*.

18. Van Engen, *God's Missionary People*.

PART 2

Romans as Missiology for the Nations

PAUL'S LETTER TO THE Romans is a missiological text written at a moment when the gospel was crossing cultural, linguistic, and social boundaries at unprecedented speed. As the message of Jesus moved beyond its Jewish origins into the wider Greco-Roman world, fundamental questions emerged about identity, belonging, Scripture, and faithfulness. Romans addresses these questions in the concrete context of a diverse community situated at the center of the empire.

We explore how Paul articulates the gospel in continuity with Israel's Scriptures while orienting it toward the nations, and how translation of language, concepts, and communal identity becomes an essential feature of faithful witness. Mission in Romans is not a later application of doctrine but integral to the gospel itself, shaping how Paul understands apostleship, community, and the scope of God's redemptive purposes.

6

The Rapid Spread of Christianity and Its Cross-Cultural Challenges

EARLY CHRISTIANITY SPREAD WITH remarkable speed across the cultural, linguistic, and social boundaries of the Roman world. What began as a Jewish messianic movement in Jerusalem quickly extended into the Jewish diaspora and, soon after, into gentile communities throughout the empire.[1] This expansion carried theological and missiological weight, raising fundamental questions about how a gospel rooted in Israel's Scriptures could be faithfully proclaimed and embodied within a Greco-Roman world shaped by different languages, assumptions, and religious imaginations.

The challenge was not simply one of communication but of translation in the fullest sense. Israel's Scriptures had formed a theological worldview in which covenant, worship, ethics, and communal life were inseparably bound together.[2] As the gospel moved beyond its Jewish matrix, these deeply embedded convictions had to be articulated within cultural frameworks that did not share the same narrative memory or moral imagination. Early Christian mission required sustained discernment: how to speak faithfully without distortion and how to adapt without surrendering the gospel's center.

1. Bruce, *Spreading Flame*, 13–23, illustrates the cultural diversity of the early Christian movement in Corinth, where a visitor from Rome, a rabbi from Tarsus, a scholar from Alexandria, and visitors from Palestine converged in this principle Greek city.

2. See for example the discussion on Hebrew and Greek thought in Bruce, *Spreading Flame*, 242–44.

LINGUISTIC DIFFICULTIES

One of the most immediate challenges confronting early Christian proclamation was linguistic. Hebrew and Greek differ not only in vocabulary but in conceptual orientation. Hebrew discourse tends toward concrete, relational expressions grounded in lived experience and covenantal history, whereas Greek discourse often privileges abstraction, categorization, and analytical precision.[3] This divergence complicated the translation of key biblical concepts whose meanings were carried through narrative, practice, and communal memory.

Terms such as *ḥesed* (steadfast covenantal love) and *shalom* (peace understood as holistic well-being and relational wholeness) resist simple equivalence. Greek approximations could convey aspects of their meaning but rarely their full theological density. Translating these concepts into Greek therefore involved unavoidable compromises, as the latter language lacked exact semantic counterparts. For example, *ḥesed* might be rendered as *eleos* (mercy) or *charis* (grace), yet neither term fully captures the covenantal loyalty, relational durability, and ethical obligation embedded in the Hebrew concept.[4] Translation, then, was never a neutral or mechanical exercise. It required interpretive judgment about how Israel's story and God's covenantal faithfulness could be rendered intelligible within a different conceptual world. From the outset, the transmission of the gospel involved theological interpretation shaped by cultural context.

At the same time, the Greek language proved indispensable to early Christianity. By the first century CE, Greek functioned as the lingua franca of the eastern Mediterranean, enabling communication across ethnic and regional boundaries and providing a shared medium for theological articulation. The Septuagint (LXX), a Greek translation of the Hebrew Scriptures produced during the Hellenistic period (primarily the third to second centuries BCE), supplied early Christians with a common scriptural vocabulary and exerted a decisive influence on New Testament language and thought.[5] Paul, though trained in Hebrew Scripture,[6] appears to have relied primarily on the LXX or related Greek traditions,

3. Betz, "Hellenism," 127–30.

4. Harris, "698 חסד,"305–7; Quell and Stauffer, "Ἀγαπάω, Ἀγάπη, Ἀγαπητός," 21–35.

5. Altaweel and Squitieri, "Spread of Common Languages," 231–39.

6. Paul, a "Hebrew of the Hebrews" (Phil 3:5) educated under Gamaliel (Acts 22:3), likely spoke and read Hebrew. Acts 21:40; 22:2; and 26:14 indicate he spoke Hebrew, though scholars debate whether this refers to biblical Hebrew or Aramaic. Cho and Park suggest it could be either but argue in favor of Hebrew. Cho and Park, *Acts*, 161.

sometimes translating independently or citing from memory, which may account for variations in his scriptural quotations.[7]

The existence of multiple Greek textual traditions, later documented in Origen's *Hexapla*, further underscores the interpretive complexity of translation.[8] No single Greek version of the First Testament[9] functioned as universally authoritative.[10] These variations sharpen the challenge faced by early Christian theologians, particularly with conceptually dense terms such as *dikaiosynē* ("righteousness" / "justice"), whose semantic range in Greek does not map neatly onto its Hebrew counterpart *ṣĕdāqâ* ("righteousness" / "justice").[11] Such linguistic slippage shaped how the gospel was heard, understood, and lived. Translation thus emerged as one of the earliest and most enduring sites of missiological discernment.

WORLDVIEW DIFFERENCES

The Greco-Roman world, shaped by Greek philosophy and Roman pragmatism, often approached reality through a dualistic lens, separating the spiritual and material realms. In contrast, Hebrew thought is holistic, integrating the physical, spiritual, and communal dimensions of life.[12] This difference posed challenges when conveying concepts like resurrection, covenant, or God's lordship over all creation. For example, the bodily

7. Jobes and Silva, *Invitation to the Septuagint*, 13–32.

8. The *Hexapla* was a critical edition of the First Testament compiled by Origen in the third century CE. Its name, meaning "sixfold," reflects its structure of six parallel columns presenting various versions of the Scriptures: the Hebrew text, a Greek transliteration of the Hebrew, the Greek translations of Aquila, Symmachus, and Theodotion, and the Septuagint.

9. The title "Old Testament" was coined by Melito of Sardis around 170 CE. The word "testament" refers to "covenant." The New Testament, from the perspective of Christians, contains books of the new covenant, while the earlier Scriptures (i.e., the Hebrew Bible) contain the old covenant. Though he did not intend it, the term can imply "old and outdated." Following John Goldingay, I will primarily refer to what is traditionally called the Old Testament as the First Testament, while also occasionally using the terms Hebrew Bible or Tanak. The term "Old Testament" is problematic, as it suggests something outdated or inferior. "Hebrew Bible," though widely used, is not entirely accurate due to its Aramaic content and its separation from the "New Testament." "Tanak," the Hebrew acronym for "Torah, Prophets, and Writings," is more precise, but as the Jewish counterpart to "Old Testament," it carries a confessional tone that can feel unfamiliar in Christian contexts. See Goldingay, *Israel's Gospel*, 15.

10. Turner, "Paul and the Old Testament," 132.

11. Balz and Schneider, *Exegetical Dictionary*, 1:325–30.

12. Droge, "Apologetics, NT," 1:305–7.

resurrection central to Christian theology clashed sharply with prevailing Greek assumptions that regarded the physical body as inferior, or even a hindrance, to the soul. This tension is evident in Paul's address at the Areopagus (Acts 17:16–34), where his proclamation of resurrection moved his audience from curiosity to mockery and hesitation, revealing the deep cultural resistance to a gospel that affirmed God's redemptive purposes for embodied life itself.

RELIGIOUS DIFFERENCES

Hebrew theology is deeply covenantal, centered on God's promises to Israel and the ethical implications of those promises.[13] In the Greco-Roman context, gods were often impersonal, distant, or capricious, and religious devotion was primarily transactional.[14] Communicating the personal, faithful nature of the God of Israel as revealed in Jesus required reframing monotheism and covenantal ethics in ways that resonated with Greek philosophical categories.

Greco-Roman culture valued honor, status, and power, whereas Hebrew concepts often subverted these values. Communicating ideas such as the crucified Messiah or the call to love enemies challenged cultural norms, requiring early missionaries like Paul to contextualize the gospel without diluting its essence.[15] The challenge of contextualizing the gospel was made even more complex by the multicultural environment of the first-century Mediterranean world, where "each group defined honorable and dishonorable conduct according to its own distinctive set of values and beliefs."[16]

OPPORTUNITIES CREATED BY THE GRECO-ROMAN WORLD

At the same time, the Roman imperial system created conditions that facilitated the gospel's spread.[17] The widespread use of Greek as a com-

13. Goldingay, *Israel's Gospel*, 369–70.
14. Gladigow, "Roman Religion," 5:809–15.
15. deSilva, *Honor*, 17–93.
16. deSilva, *Honor*, 37.
17. Lipka, "Conclusions," 187–94.

mon language enabled communication across regions.[18] Roman roads, trade routes, and urban centers allowed missionaries to travel, maintain contact with communities, and sustain networks of correspondence.[19] Diaspora synagogues provided initial points of engagement, while household networks carried the gospel into everyday social spaces.

These imperial structures functioned ambivalently. They enabled the movement of the gospel even as they embodied rival claims to authority, peace, and belonging. Early Christian mission unfolded within this tension, advancing through the very systems that sustained empire while quietly subverting its ideological foundations. The gospel neither withdrew from this world nor simply accommodated to it; it took root within it, reshaping identity and allegiance from the inside.

TOWARD PAUL AND ROMANS

It is within this complex cross-cultural environment that Paul's apostolic vocation must be understood. As a Jew formed by Israel's Scriptures and an apostle to the nations, Paul stands at the intersection of worlds. His calling required him to proclaim a gospel that could cross cultural boundaries without losing its theological center. The Letter to the Romans reflects this tension with particular clarity, not as a theoretical exercise, but as a practical engagement with communities already navigating the pressures of translation, identity, and belonging.

Before Paul articulates his apostolic identity, ministry, message, or method, he writes from within a world marked by linguistic negotiation, cultural contestation, and imperial constraint. Chapter 6 has traced the contours of that world. The chapters that follow turn directly to Paul himself, beginning with his self-identification in Romans 1:1–7. To understand Paul's apostolic identity, we must first recognize the missiological complexity of the world into which he was sent, and the extraordinary task the gospel had already begun to accomplish within it.

18. Jevons, "Hellenism and Christianity," 169–88.

19. Harper, "Why Did Christianity Conquer the Roman Empire?," 478.

7

Paul's Apostolic Identity, Romans 1:1–7

Paul's greeting in Romans 1:1–7 consists of a single, extended sentence whose length and density immediately signal the letter's theological weight.[1] In contrast to the brief and formulaic greetings typical of Greco-Roman correspondence, this opening functions as a deliberate act of theological self-positioning.[2] Romans 1:1–7 serves as a compressed prologue in which Paul locates himself within Israel's story, articulates the source and scope of his authority, and signals the missional horizon that governs the letter as a whole. These verses establish the identity from which the argument of Romans unfolds. Before addressing the Roman churches' practices, tensions, or future participation in mission, Paul clarifies who he is and why he writes.[3]

This ordering is itself instructive. In Romans, mission does not begin with strategy or method, but with identity. Paul does not present his apostleship as a functional role or institutional office, but as a vocation received and sustained within the purposes of God. His authority is derivative rather than inherent, grounded not in rhetorical skill, ecclesial appointment, or personal charisma, but in divine summons and fidelity to the gospel. Read missiologically, Romans 1:1–7 reveals that apostolic identity is the foundational condition for apostolic mission.

Though compact in form, Romans 1:1–7 is among Paul's most theologically dense and rhetorically charged passages. This passage has

1. Schreiner, *Romans*, 31–32.
2. Fitzmyer, *Romans*, 227.
3. Longenecker, *Romans*, 47.

attracted more attention than any other New Testament text in recent years, highlighting its significance not only for understanding the letter to the Romans but also for grasping Paul's broader theological and missiological vision.[4] Within these seven verses, Paul compresses key dimensions of his gospel, including Christology, eschatology, ecclesiology, and mission, into a carefully crafted introduction that both anchors the letter in Israel's scriptural story and projects its scope onto the global stage.

These opening verses set the tone for the entire epistle, revealing Paul's intent to engage the Roman believers with clarity, apostolic authority, and a compelling vision of their place within God's redemptive purposes. Far from offering a casual greeting, Paul constructs a theological prelude that anticipates the letter's major themes: the universal scope of the gospel, the reconciliation of Jews and gentiles within a single people of God, and the formation of a community whose identity is shaped by "the obedience of faith" among all nations. His careful blending of covenantal language with Hellenistic forms signals both continuity with Israel's Scriptures and attentiveness to the cultural realities of his audience.

By framing his apostleship as a divine calling undertaken "for the sake of his name among all the nations" (Rom 1:5), Paul situates the Roman churches within a larger missional narrative. They are not passive recipients of theological instruction but active participants in the unfolding mission of God. Romans 1:1–7 thus functions, not only as a theological overture to the letter but as a missiological summons, preparing the Roman community to embrace its role within a gospel movement that transcends cultural, ethnic, and geographic boundaries.

PAUL, A SERVANT OF CHRIST JESUS

Paul, a Greek name meaning "small" or "little," was likely his Roman name, while his Hebrew name was Saul, after Israel's first Benjamite king (Phil 3:5). As a Roman citizen he would have had three names, though only *Paulus* is recorded.[5] Retaining a Greek name was common among Roman citizens, and Paul's choice likely reflects his mission to a gentile audience.[6]

4. Longenecker, *Romans*, 47.
5. Acts 16:37–38; 25:10–12.
6. Longenecker, *Romans*, 48.

In Romans 1:1, Paul introduces himself with an unusually expansive self-description: "servant of Christ Jesus," "called to be an apostle," and "set apart for the gospel of God." In contrast to the briefer openings of several other letters (e.g., 1 Cor 1:1; Phil 1:1; Titus 1:1), this elaborated greeting signals Paul's intent to establish both his identity and authority for a Roman audience he has not yet visited.[7] Each designation contributes to a layered presentation of vocation rather than a mere accumulation of titles.

The phrase "servant of Christ Jesus" carries a range of connotations. At a basic level, it aligns Paul with the broader identity of believers as those who belong wholly to God (Rom 6:22). More fundamentally, however, it expresses Paul's total submission and exclusive allegiance to Christ as Lord. In Romans 6:16–22, Paul frames slavery, not as a metaphor of humility alone but as a reality of ownership: one belongs either to sin or to obedience, to death or to righteousness.[8] By identifying himself first as Christ's servant, Paul presents his apostleship as grounded in obedience rather than status and in belonging rather than self-authorization.

Some scholars have further suggested that this language may carry an implicit political resonance for a Roman audience. The designation "servant of Christ Jesus" stands in contrast to the imperial title *servi Caesaris*, members of the imperial household, whose identity and loyalty were bound to the emperor.[9] Paul's self-identification signals a competing allegiance and a reordered hierarchy of lordship. His life, authority, and mission derive not from Rome's structures of power, but from exclusive fidelity to the crucified and risen Christ.

More importantly, the phrase likely signals Paul's prophetic self-understanding.[10] In the First Testament, "Servant of Yahweh" is an honorific title for: (1) Israel as a nation; (2) its leaders (e.g., Moses, Joshua, David); (3) prophets; and (4) the "Servant of the Lord" in Isaiah's Servant Songs.[11] This biblical designation would resonate with the Roman church, Jewish and gentile Christians alike, who were well-versed in Scripture.

Paul's prophetic identity as "servant of Christ Jesus" reappears in Galatians 1:10 and Philippians 1:1. It is also used in distinctly Jewish-Christian writings (Jas 1:1; 2 Pet 1:1; Jude 1). Notably, Paul and these authors replace

7. Schreiner, *Romans*, 97–113.

8. Longenecker, *Romans*, 50.

9. Schreiner, *Romans*, 100.

10. Longenecker, *Romans*, 51–52.

11. Longenecker, *Romans*, 51.

"Yahweh" with "Christ Jesus," "Jesus Christ," or simply "Christ," a striking affirmation of Jesus' divine lordship. For Paul, *Christos* (Christ) retains its messianic connotations.[12] This is particularly evident in Romans, where *ho Christos* ("the Christ") signifies Israel's Messiah (9:5) and appears in exhortations addressing unity between "the strong" and "the weak" (15:3, 7). Thus, Paul's choice of titles reflects both theological precision and a contextually relevant emphasis on Christ's authority and mission.[13]

To grasp Paul's understanding of himself, we begin where his journey began: his encounter with the risen Lord on the road to Damascus.[14] This revelation of God's Son was a transformative moment. Paul was converted, called, and commissioned to preach to the gentiles. From that point, Paul's life was defined by this divine appointment, which he pursued with unwavering determination. The Damascus road event transformed Paul so completely that he regarded his life before it as "rubbish" (Phil 3:8).

The Damascus Road Event

Paul's dramatic encounter with the risen Christ on the Damascus road marks a pivotal moment in salvation history.[15] Initially a zealous persecutor of Christians, Paul was struck by a blinding light, fell to the ground, and heard Jesus ask, "Why are you persecuting me?" (Acts 9:4). Led to Damascus, he remained blind until Ananias, following God's command, restored his sight and baptized him, commissioning him as a "chosen instrument" to proclaim Christ to gentiles, kings, and Israel (Acts 9:15).

Paul recounts this event differently depending on his audience. In Acts 22:3–21, speaking before a hostile Jewish crowd, he emphasizes his Jewish heritage, education under Gamaliel, and obedience to the divine vision. He highlights Ananias as a devout Jew who confirmed his mission, framing his calling as part of Israel's prophetic tradition. In Acts 26:12–18, addressing King Agrippa, Paul highlights his specific commission to the gentiles, describing his vision as a divine appointment to open their eyes, turn them from darkness to light, and bring them forgiveness.[16]

12. Silva, *New International Dictionary*, 688–96.

13. Dunn, *Romans 1–8*, 7–8.

14. Acts 9:1–19; 22:3–21; 26:12–18.

15. Recorded three times in Acts 9:1–19; 22:3–21; 26:12–18.

16. Marshall, *Acts*, 415.

Beyond a personal conversion, this event established Paul's apostolic authority. In Galatians 1:11–12, he insists that his gospel came not from human teaching but directly from Christ.[17] This revelation was not only his calling but also the content of his message: Christ himself as the fulfillment of God's redemptive plan.[18] Käsemann said it well: "Christ is not the author of the gospel; he is its decisive content."[19] Paul consistently frames his transformation as God's sovereign initiative, redirecting his life to preach the gospel to the nations (Gal 1:16; Rom 1:5).[20] His Damascus road encounter serves as both the foundation of his mission and the validation of his apostolic authority.

CALLED TO BE AN APOSTLE

Paul's identification as an apostle is grounded in the biblical logic of divine commissioning. Within Israel's Scriptures, call narratives mark moments of divine interruption, in which God summons individuals for purposes that exceed personal ambition or self-selection. Prophets do not appoint themselves; they are summoned. This framework clarifies the force of Paul's claim to apostleship as a vocation initiated by God rather than a role constructed by the church or the self.

The Greek verb *apostellō* ("to send") and its cognate noun *apostolos* ("one who is sent") underscore both mission and delegated authority. Sending implies not only movement but representation—the apostle acts on behalf of another and derives authority from the sender.[21] In the Septuagint, *apostellō* frequently renders the Hebrew *šālaḥ*, a verb commonly used to describe God's sending of messengers to carry divine words and enact divine purposes.[22] This linguistic continuity situates Paul's apostleship within Israel's long-standing tradition of commissioned agents. Paul's authority is neither autonomous nor institutional; it is derivative, grounded in divine initiative and sustained by faithful obedience to the mission entrusted to him.[23]

17. See also 1 Cor 15:8; Acts 9:17; 26:16.

18. Arichea and Nida, *Handbook on Paul's Letter to the Galatians*, 18.

19. Käsemann, *Romans*, 10.

20. See also Gal 2:7; Rom 15:15–16.

21. Silva, *New International Dictionary*, 365–75.

22. Rengstorf, "Ἀποστέλλω (πέμπω), Ἐξαποστέλλω, Ἀπόστολος, Ψευδαπόστολος, Ἀποστολή." 1:398–400.

23. Hultgren, "Paul's Christology," 115–27.

While *apostolos* originally referred to naval expeditions in classical Greek, it later came to denote envoys or messengers with a specific mandate.[24] The New Testament redefines the term to describe those commissioned by Christ to proclaim the gospel and establish the church.[25] Jesus chose twelve apostles to represent him and continue his mission (Matt 10:1–4; Mark 3:13–19; Luke 6:12–16), and after Judas's death, Matthias was selected (Acts 1:23–26).[26]

24. Silva, *New International Dictionary*, 366.

25. In the New Testament, ἀποστέλλω appears around 135 times, primarily in the Gospels and Acts, often describing divine commissioning. It is used alongside πέμπω, which sometimes overlaps in meaning, particularly in Luke-Acts. However, ἀποστέλλω generally carries a stronger emphasis on the commission and authority of the sender, particularly when referring to God. The gospel of John frequently uses both ἀποστέλλω and πέμπω to describe Jesus' relationship with the Father. Ἀποστέλλω emphasizes Jesus' divine commission, portraying him as the ultimate emissary sent to fulfill God's will. For example, John highlights the unity of purpose and action between the Father and the Son, with ἀποστέλλω underscoring the divine authority behind Jesus' mission (e.g., John 3:17, 20:21). The term ἐξαποστέλλω, used thirteen times in the New Testament, primarily in Luke-Acts and Paul's writings, reinforces this idea. While the prefix ἐξ- adds intensity to the act of sending, the theological implications remain consistent with ἀποστέλλω, emphasizing divine commission and purpose (e.g., Gal 4:4).

26. While the twelve apostles are the most prominent, the term "apostle" is also used more broadly in the New Testament to describe others who were commissioned for specific purposes within the early church. These individuals carried out distinct roles in spreading the gospel and advancing the mission of the church. Paul identifies himself as an apostle, commissioned directly by the risen Christ (Acts 9:15; Gal 1:1, 15–16; Rom 1:1). Paul's apostleship was uniquely focused on taking the gospel to the gentiles. Barnabas is explicitly called an apostle alongside Paul during their missionary journeys (Acts 14:4, 14). James, the brother of Jesus, is regarded as an apostle, particularly in his leadership role in the early Jerusalem church (Gal 1:19; 1 Cor 15:7). While Apollos is not explicitly called an apostle, his ministry aligns with apostolic functions, and some scholars suggest his apostolic activity in Corinth (1 Cor 3:6, 4:6–9). Silas and Timothy are closely associated with Paul and share in his apostolic work, although they are not formally called apostles as frequently. "We [Paul, Silas, and Timothy] might have made demands as apostles of Christ" (1 Thess 1:1; 2:6). Paul mentions Andronicus and Junia as being "prominent among the apostles" (Rom 16:7), suggesting they were highly regarded within the apostolic circle. Epaphroditus is referred to as an ἀπόστολος (messenger) of the Philippian church, though here the term is used in a functional, missionary sense (Phil 2:25). Paul refers to individuals sent by churches as "apostles" in the sense of messengers or missionaries entrusted with special tasks (2 Cor 8:23). Paul warns against individuals who falsely claim apostolic authority, distorting the gospel for their own gain: "For such men are false apostles, deceitful workmen" (2 Cor 11:13). In Hebrews 3:1, Jesus is described as an ἀπόστολος, the supreme envoy sent by God. This title highlights his unique role as the divine mediator who flawlessly embodies and executes God's will, uniting word and deed in the fulfillment of God's redemptive plan. As the ultimate apostle, Christ sets the standard for all who are sent in his name. See also, Longenecker, *Romans*, 54.

Paul, though not among the original twelve, was directly commissioned by the risen Christ with a distinct mission to the gentiles.[27] In fact, he stands out in his repeated emphasis on being an apostle to the gentiles (Rom 1:5; 15:15–16; Gal 2:7). Paul knew his apostleship was foundational to the church's expansion beyond Israel and was rooted in his divine calling rather than human appointment (Gal 1:11–12).

Paul's commission aligns with First Testament prophetic callings, echoing figures like Jeremiah (Jer 1:5), Isaiah (Isa 49:6), and Moses (Exod 3:1–22).[28] However, Paul never explicitly calls himself a prophet, distinguishing his role as one who proclaims the fulfillment of God's promises rather than one who anticipates them.[29] His calling represents both continuity with Israel's prophetic tradition and a decisive shift in salvation history,[30] as he proclaims Christ's fulfillment of God's redemptive plan foretold by the prophets (Gen 12:1–4; Gal 3:7–9).[31]

Paul understands his apostolic vocation as an extension of Isaiah's vision of the Servant of the Lord who would bring salvation to the nations (Isa 49:6).[32] Yet he does not present himself as the Servant; rather, he conceives his ministry as patterned after, and participating in, the Servant's mission, now fulfilled in Christ and carried to the nations through his apostleship.[33][34] His declaration in Romans 1:1 makes explicit the divine origin, universal scope, and ultimate purpose of his calling to bring salvation to all peoples for the glory of Christ's name.[35]

By situating his calling within this salvation-historical framework, Paul highlighted his unique role as the apostle to the nations and emphasized the global scope of God's redemptive mission. He saw the inclusion of the nations as central to God's covenantal plan,[36] not as a later devel-

27. E.g. Acts 9:15; 13:46–48; Rom 1:5, 13; 15:16; Gal 1:16; Eph 3:1, 6, 8; 2 Tim 4:17.
28. Dunn, "Paul's Conversion: A Light to the Disputes," 341–59.
29. Schreiner, *Romans*, 452–53.
30. Sandnes, "Prophet-Like Apostle," 550–64.
31. Keown, *Romans*, 53.
32. Hays, *Echoes*, 63–73.
33. Longenecker, *Romans*, 50–53; Kim, "Paul as an Eschatological Herald," 9–24.
34. Longenecker, *Romans*, 50–53.
35. Fitzmyer, *Romans*, 232–33.
36. Keown, *Romans*, 57.

opment but as a fulfillment of the promise to bless all nations through Abraham (Gal 3:8). His apostolic identity, grounded in divine revelation (Gal 1:11–17), reinforced the universality of the gospel, breaking ethnic and cultural barriers to bring salvation to all people.[37]

SET APART FOR THE GOSPEL OF GOD

Paul understood his apostleship as a calling to serve, not for personal gain,[38] but as an instrument of God's revelation.[39] His authority was not self-derived but given by God, as he states in Romans 1:1 and Galatians 1:15, emphasizing that he was "set apart for the gospel of God." The Greek term *aphorizō* ("set apart") signifies a divine act, marking Paul for a sacred mission.[40] This language echoes Jeremiah 1:5 and Isaiah 49:1, where God's calling occurs before birth, reinforcing Paul's conviction that his mission to the gentiles was part of God's eternal plan.[41]

Like Jeremiah, who faced opposition from false prophets (Jer 23:18–22), Paul's apostleship was frequently challenged (1 Cor 4:9–13; 2 Cor 11:12–15, 23–27). Yet, his legitimacy rested on his direct encounter with Christ and the gospel he received from God.[42] Like Jeremiah, Paul understood that his calling came from standing in the "council of the Lord." He had encountered the risen Christ, who gave him not only his commission but also the gospel he was to proclaim. Paul situates his calling within the prophetic tradition, aligning his mission with God's redemptive work through the prophets and the Servant of the Lord.

THE GOSPEL WAS FORETOLD IN SCRIPTURE AND FULFILLED IN CHRIST, ROMANS 1:2–4

In Romans 1:2–4, Paul establishes the continuity between the gospel and God's promises in the Hebrew Scriptures.[43] He presents Christ, not as a

37. Wagner, *Heralds of the Good News*, 272.

38. Wright, *Paul and the Faithfulness of God*, 812–14.

39. Mounce, "Preaching, Kerygma," 735.

40. Schnabel, *Paul the Missionary*, 437–38.

41. Arndt et al., *Greek-English Lexicon*, 158.

42. This could be reflected in the Pauline statement "my gospel" (see Rom 2:16; 16:25–27; 2 Thess 2:14; 2 Tim 2:8).

43. Witherington, *Romans*, 32.

rupture within Israel's story but as its climactic fulfillment, affirming that the gospel emerges from within God's long-standing redemptive purposes. By stating that the gospel was "promised beforehand through his prophets in the holy Scriptures" (Rom 1:2), Paul deliberately anchors the message in God's covenantal faithfulness rather than in novelty or innovation.[44]

This scriptural grounding reveals that mission originates not in human initiative but in God's own movement toward creation.[45] The Scriptures bear witness to a God who acts, sends, and redeems, whose purposes unfold across history in faithful continuity. The gospel is not merely a message to be believed or a command to be obeyed; it is an invitation to participate in the ongoing mission of God.[46] As David Bosch famously articulated, "Mission is not primarily an activity of the church, but an attribute of God."[47] Paul's framing of the gospel in Romans 1:2–4 reflects precisely this conviction: mission flows from God's initiative and precedes the church's response.

The Hebrew Scriptures anticipated a messiah who would bring salvation and renewal.[48] Key prophetic texts such as Isaiah 53 (the Suffering Servant) and Jeremiah 31:31–34 (the new covenant) pointed toward Christ.[49] Paul later asserts that the gospel is "made known through the prophetic writings by the command of the eternal God" (Rom 16:26) and that "the law and the prophets" testify to the righteousness revealed in Christ (Rom 3:21).[50] This thematic unity[51] undergirds Paul's argument: The gospel fulfills, rather than replaces Israel's Scriptures.[52]

Romans is a richly intertextual composition that reflects Paul's sustained and sophisticated engagement with the Hebrew Scriptures,

44. Paul often refers to the First Testament as "the Scriptures" (e.g., Rom 4:3; 9:17; 10:11; 11:2; 15:4; 16:26; 1 Cor 15:3–4; Gal 3:8, 22; 4:30; 1 Tim 5:18; 2 Tim 3:16), but in Romans 1:2 he uniquely calls them "the holy Scriptures," likely to underscore their authority and the significance of the gospel they promised.

See also, Longenecker, *Romans*, 62. An example of this is can also be seen in 1 Corinthians 15:3–4, where Paul explicitly links Christ's death and resurrection to the Scriptures, showing that God's redemptive plan was foretold. See Kruse, *Romans*, 41.

45. Wright, *Mission of God*, 51.

46. Tennent, *Invitation to World Missions*, 61.

47. Bosch, *Transforming Mission*, 390.

48. Porter and Stanley, *As It Is Written*.

49. Wagner, *Heralds*, 334–40.

50. Punt, "Paul, Hermeneutics and the Scriptures of Israel," 377.

51. Porter, *Romans*, 43–44.

52. Schreiner, *Romans*, 103.

integrating them into the letter's theological argumentation.[53] Paul's use of the First Testament in Romans is extensive, with references to Genesis, Deuteronomy, Psalms, Ezekiel, Hosea, Joel, Habakkuk, and especially Isaiah, shaping his theological framework.[54]

PAUL'S USE OF ISAIAH IN ROMANS

Paul's engagement with Isaiah in Romans is extensive, with references appearing throughout his argument.[55] Nearly half of his scriptural citations in Romans come from Isaiah, demonstrating the prophet's significance in shaping Paul's theology. Isaiah's words often function as a second voice alongside Paul, reinforcing God's redemptive plan for both Israel and the nations.[56] Paul draws upon Isaiah to articulate the universal scope of salvation, the righteousness of God, and the inclusion of gentiles in covenant promises. Paul does not attempt to impose his authority over Scripture but instead works to justify his claim about what God has done in Christ while remaining faithful to the biblical narrative.[57]

Isaiah and Paul's Vision of Redemption

Paul's frequent allusions to Isaiah highlight how deeply the prophet's vision informs his understanding of God's faithfulness. Isaiah's eschatological theme of God's salvation extending beyond Israel serve as a scriptural foundation for Paul's gospel and his redefinition of Israel's identity in light of Christ. Romans 8 exemplifies how Paul weaves Isaiah's eschatological vision into his broader theological framework, integrating Scripture seamlessly into his vision of life in the Spirit. Paul's depiction of creation groaning for redemption (Rom 8:19–22) mirrors Isaiah's vision of a new heaven and new earth (Isa 65:17; 66:22). Paul integrates

53. Turner, "Paul and the Old Testament," 128–41.

54. See Romans 1:17; 4:3, 7–9, 16–17, 22; 9:25–26; 10:6–8, 11, 13; 11:26–27; 15:9–12. This pattern extends to his other letters as well (see 1 Cor 2:9; 15:27, 54–55; 2 Cor 6:2, 16–18; Gal 3:6, 8, 11, 13, 16; 4:27–28; Eph 4:7–8).

55. Paul's use of Isaiah in Romans is so extensive that it is hard to count the number of references to the prophet. These references include direct quotations and subtle allusions, making up almost half of Paul's scriptural appeals in Romans. See Wagner, *Heralds*, 1–2.

56. Wagner, *Heralds*, 1–2.

57. Hays, *Echoes*, 158–59.

Isaiah's prophetic hope into his argument for Spirit-led transformation, inaugurated by Christ's resurrection. Isaiah's eschatology provides Paul with a framework for expressing the believer's hope in future glory. The restoration of creation is inseparable from the redemption of humanity, reinforcing Paul's view that the gospel brings about cosmic renewal.[58]

The Inclusion of the Gentiles in Paul's Gospel

Isaiah's vision of gentiles participating in Israel's salvation is central to Paul's argument in Romans. Nowhere is this clearer than in Romans 9–11, where Paul reflects on Israel's election and the place of the nations in God's plan. Paul employs Isaiah to validate gentile inclusion without negating God's promises to Israel.[59] In Romans 9:27–29, Paul cites Isaiah 10:22–23 and Isaiah 1:9 to support the remnant principle, God always preserves a faithful remnant despite widespread unbelief.[60] Paul stresses that Israel's salvation has always depended on God's sovereign will rather than human effort.[61]

In Romans 10:15, Paul references Isaiah 52:7, emphasizing the need to spread the gospel.[62] This passage reinforces that salvation is not exclusive to Israel but is offered to all who believe. In Romans 10:16–21, Paul quotes Isaiah 53:1, highlighting Israel's rejection of the gospel.[63] He demonstrates that Israel's unbelief was neither unexpected nor unprecedented but a fulfillment of prophetic warnings.[64]

In Romans 10:20, Paul cites Isaiah 65:1—"I was found by those who did not seek me; I revealed myself to those who did not ask for me." This passage illustrates God's initiative in saving the gentiles, reflecting Isaiah's depiction of a God who reaches beyond Israel.[65] Equally, in Romans 11:8, Paul references Isaiah 29:10 to explain Israel's temporary hardening, paving the way for gentile inclusion and, ultimately, Israel's future restoration.

58. Hays, *Echoes*, 71.
59. Wagner, *Heralds*, 43–305.
60. Wagner, *Heralds*, 92–94.
61. Fitzmyer, *Romans*, 567–605.
62. Käsemann, *Romans*, 294.
63. Wagner, *Heralds*, 178–84.
64. Schreiner, *Romans*, 533.
65. Wagner, *Heralds*, 187–90.

Paul's Typological Approach to Isaiah

Paul reads Isaiah typologically, interpreting Israel's past as a foreshadowing of present realities.[66] Israel's rejection and the gentiles' inclusion were not deviations but prefigured in Isaiah's prophecies. Wagner likens Romans 9–11 to a theological symphony, where multiple scriptural voices blend to address God's faithfulness to Israel, a question heightened by his own mission to the gentiles. Among these voices, Isaiah stands out, sometimes solo (9:20, 33; 10:15–16; 11:26–27), other times in harmony with Hosea (9:25–29), Moses (10:19–21; 11:8–10), the psalmist (10:18), Joel (10:5–13), David (11:8–10), and Job (11:34–35). Under Paul's direction, Isaiah's words resonate within this rich interplay, culminating in a unified proclamation of God's redemptive purpose of bringing Jews and gentiles together in Christ.[67]

Isaiah's Influence on Paul's View of Mission

Paul's extensive use of Isaiah demonstrates the missional nature of Scripture. The prophet's vision of God's salvation extending to the nations aligns with Paul's conviction that the gospel is for both Jews and gentiles. Mission is not an optional church activity but is woven into the fabric of God's redemptive plan.[68] Isaiah provides a biblical foundation for Paul's understanding of mission, demonstrating that the spread of the gospel is the fulfillment of God's covenantal promises.[69]

Paul's Use of Isaiah and the Integrity of Scripture

Paul's interweaving of Isaiah's words into his argument reinforces his belief that Scripture speaks in harmony with the gospel. Paul does not merely cite Isaiah for validation, he engages Isaiah as a theological partner, shaping his understanding of God's righteousness, covenant faithfulness, and the universal scope of salvation.

66. Hays, *Echoes*, 33.
67. Wagner, *Heralds*, 305.
68. Schreiner, *Romans*, 28–29.
69. Fitzmyer, *Romans*, 233–37.

Isaiah's influence on Paul extends beyond eschatology and mission, it also shapes his view of Jesus' identity.[70] Paul affirms Jesus as the Davidic Messiah,[71] the fulfillment of Isaiah's Servant figure, and the one who inaugurates God's final act of redemption.[72] In Romans 1:3, Paul declares that Jesus was "descended from David according to the flesh," linking him to the messianic promises of 2 Samuel 7:12–16 and Isaiah 11:1. Jesus is the rightful heir of Israel's hope, the king who reigns eternally.

However, Paul goes further in Romans 1:4, stating that Jesus "was declared to be the Son of God in power . . . by his resurrection from the dead." The resurrection is the climactic event in redemptive history, vindicating Jesus' identity and inaugurating his reign. The title "Son of God" signifies more than divine sonship; it denotes Jesus' universal lordship over creation. In Paul's theology, the resurrection is not only the fulfillment of prophecy but also the foundation of Christian hope.[73]

Isaiah's Lasting Influence on Paul's Theology

Paul's use of Isaiah throughout Romans demonstrates his deep engagement with the Hebrew Scriptures. Isaiah serves not just as a proof-text but as a theological cornerstone in Paul's proclamation of the gospel. Through Isaiah, Paul articulates the righteousness of God, the inclusion of gentiles, the faithfulness of God to Israel, and the hope of new creation. His intertextual dialogue with the prophet reveals a theological vision in which prophecy and gospel harmonize to proclaim the fulfillment of God's promises in Christ. Paul's use of Isaiah also highlights the essential role of Scripture in mission. The gospel is not a human invention but the culmination of God's redemptive plan, foretold in the prophets and realized in Jesus. As Paul weaves Isaiah into Romans, he invites his readers, both Jews and gentiles, to see the gospel as the climactic moment in salvation history, bringing all nations under Christ's reign.

70. Longenecker, *Romans*, 76.

71. Dunn, *Romans* 1–8, 13–14.

72. Schreiner, *Romans*, 110–16.

73. Wright, *Paul and the Faithfulness of God*, 1192–94.

PAUL'S APOSTOLIC CALLING TO THE NATIONS, ROMANS 1:5–7

In Romans 1:5–7, Paul outlines key aspects of his apostolic calling, linking his mission to the nations to the divine authority and purposes of the mission of God. These verses provide a succinct summary of the theological foundation of Paul's ministry, his identity as an apostle, and the scope of his mission. By examining these verses, we gain insight into how Paul understood his calling, not only as an individual but as part of God's broader plan for the salvation of the world. Through the christological focus of these verses, Paul reveals the centrality of Jesus Christ in his apostolic identity and the global scope of the gospel he was called to preach.

Paul begins by grounding his apostleship in the resurrection of Jesus Christ, "through whom we have received grace and apostleship" (Rom 1:5a). The resurrection of Jesus, brought about by the power of the Spirit, is the pivotal event that declares his divine sonship and authority, providing the foundation for Paul's apostolic mission.[74] For Paul, Jesus' resurrection by the power of the Spirit was not only a proof of his divine identity but also a confirmation of the authority with which Paul was sent to proclaim the gospel.

In Romans 1:5b, Paul explains that he received grace and apostleship "to bring about the obedience of faith among all the nations for his name's sake." This verse highlights two crucial aspects of Paul's apostolic mission: grace and the goal of bringing the nations to the obedience of faith. The grace Paul speaks of is not only the unmerited favor of God that enabled him to be an apostle but also the divine empowerment necessary for him to fulfill his mission. The purpose of this grace is explicitly stated: "To bring about the obedience of faith for the sake of his name among all the nations, including you who are called to belong to Jesus Christ" (Rom 1:5–6). This statement encapsulates Paul's mission, emphasizing its purpose—the "obedience of faith"—its scope—"among all the nations"—and its ultimate goal—"for the sake of his name."

In Romans 15:18–19, Paul returns to the themes of the power of the Spirit and the obedience that results from faith. He reflects on his ministry to the nations, emphasizing that it is through the power of the Holy Spirit that he has been able to accomplish his work, which includes both proclaiming the gospel and leading people to obedience. Paul asserts that his ministry has been marked by "word and deed," as well as

74. Rom 1:4. See also 2 Cor 13:4; Eph 1:19, 20; Phil 3:10; Acts 10:38; 26:23.

"signs and wonders," all of which are indicators of the Spirit's empowering presence.[75]

The phrase "obedience of faith" appears again in Romans 16:26, thus framing the entire letter. While interpretations of this phrase may vary, it likely refers to two interconnected ideas: first, "faith's obedience," meaning that obedience is rooted in faith, and second, obedience that flows from faith, reflecting the believer's total response to the gospel.[76] This includes both the initial act of conversion and the ongoing conduct that results from a life of faith. The phrase captures the holistic nature of Christian discipleship as faith that leads to obedience and obedience that is continually shaped by faith. The phrase links faith and obedience in a way that underlines the transformative power of the gospel. For Paul, faith is not intellectual assent; it is a response to God's revelation that leads to a life of obedience to God's will. This faith which leads to obedience is the means by which the nations can be reconciled to God. The phrase "for the sake of his name" (1:5) reinforces that this mission is not for Paul's own glory but for the glory of Jesus Christ, whose name represents the very essence of the gospel Paul is called to proclaim.[77]

Importantly, while Paul was a Jew by birth, his mission was primarily to those outside the covenantal promises made to Israel, reflecting the universal scope of the gospel.[78] This shift is central to the New Testament's understanding of the gospel as a message not just for the Jewish people but for the entire world.[79] In Romans, Paul frequently emphasizes that the gospel has broken down the dividing wall between Jews and gentiles, making it available to all people regardless of ethnicity or background (Rom 3:27–4:25; see also Rom 1:16; 6:4; 7:4; Eph 2:14).[80]

Regarding Gentiles and Nations as Options for *Ethnē*

At this point, it is necessary to pause and consider an issue that may initially appear to be a minor translational concern but which proves essential for engaging Romans as a missiological document. The Greek

75. Tennent, *Invitation to World Missions*, 409–31.

76. Longenecker, *Romans*, 79–82. See also, Dunn, *Romans 1–8*, 17–18; and Fitzmyer, *Romans*, 237–38.

77. Fitzmyer, *Romans*, 238.

78. Mounce, *Romans*, 62–63.

79. Osborne, *Romans*, 33.

80. Calvert, "Abraham," 6.

term *ethnē* can refer both to "gentiles" (non-Jews) and to "nations," depending on context.[81] In Paul's letters, it often designates non-Jews as the primary audience of his apostolic mission (Rom 1:5; Gal 2:7), yet in other instances it clearly carries the broader sense of "all peoples" or "the nations" (Rom 15:11; Gal 3:8).[82] Paul's usage is not arbitrary. It is rooted in Israel's Scriptures and shaped by his conviction that the gospel fulfills God's covenantal promises to the nations.[83] His apostolic calling aligns with Isaiah's vision of salvation extending beyond Israel (Isa 49:6), reinforcing that the gospel is intended for all humanity within the scope of God's redemptive plan.

Understanding Paul's language requires attention to the conceptual world of the Hebrew Scriptures. In the Hebrew Bible, *gôy* (plural *gôyim*) fundamentally means "nation" or "people," a designation that applies not only to foreign peoples but at times to Israel itself, even as a "holy nation." In "Paul and the Invention of the Gentiles," Ishay Rosen-Zvi and Adi Ophir argue that the category "gentile" (*gôy* / *ethnē*) as a generalized, individualized, and binary counterpart to "Jew," did not exist in the Hebrew Bible or Second Temple Judaism in the form often assumed by modern scholarship.[84]

The authors trace a genealogy of the term *gôy*, showing that in the Hebrew Bible it simply means "nation," a designation that applies to Israel as well as to other peoples. While Israel is distinguished by election and covenant, the biblical texts do not produce a unified or comprehensive category encompassing all non-Israelites. Instead, Scripture maintains a plurality of peoples and differentiated relationships (e.g., nations of

81. Balz and Schneider, *Exegetical Dictionary*, 1:381–82. In the Bible, ἔθνη (*ethnē*) is often translated as "nations" in a broad sense (Gen 12:7; Isa 40:7; Matt 24:14; Mark 13:10), while in the New Testament, it frequently refers specifically to gentiles, distinguishing them from Jews or Christians (Matt 6:32; Eph 2:12; 1 Cor 1:23). In Romans, *ethnē* appears twenty-nine times—Rom 1:5, 13; 2:14, 24; 3:29; 4:17, 18; 9:24, 30; 10:19; 11:11, 12, 13, 25; 15:9, 10, 11, 12, 16, 18, 27; 16:4, 26. Some uses of *ethnē* denote gentile believers (Rom 11:13; Eph 3:1), while other passages highlight the church's distinct identity from the gentiles (1 Cor 5:1; 1 Thess 4:5; 1 Pet 2:12).

82. Bertram and Schmidt, "Ἔθνος, Ἐθνικός," 2:364–72.

83. Douglas, "Call to Law."

84. Rosen-Zvi and Ophir, "Paul and the Invention of the Gentiles." Rosen-Zvi and Ophir argue that Paul plays a decisive role in consolidating *ethnē* as a generalized, individualized category opposed to "Jew," rather than simply inheriting a fixed binary from Israel's Scriptures or Second Temple Judaism. While this study rightly draws attention to the fluidity and historical development of the category "gentile," its more radical claim that Paul effectively "invents" the gentile risks overstating discontinuity with Israel's scriptural and prophetic traditions.

Canaan, neighboring peoples, resident aliens). Even terms such as *nokhri* ("foreigner") and *ger* ("resident alien") do not amount to a universalized, binary classification of humanity into Jew and non-Jew.

During the Hellenistic period, the Septuagint introduces a partial conceptual shift by consistently translating *gôyim* as *ethnē* and reserving *laos* for Israel. This linguistic move sharpens the distinction between Israel and the nations, but it still does not produce a fully individualized category of "the gentile." The nations remain plural, political, and geographically situated rather than a single abstract class.

This scriptural background is decisive for how *ethnē* should be heard in Romans. When Paul draws on the language and narratives of Israel's Scriptures, he inherits a vision in which God's purposes are oriented toward the nations as nations, not merely toward non-Jewish individuals abstracted from their peoples. Translating *ethnē* as "nations" therefore resonates more closely with the conceptual world Paul presupposes and reinterprets. It preserves the corporate and covenantal horizon of his argument, in which God's faithfulness to Israel is expressed through the inclusion and renewal of the nations in Christ.[85]

The English translation of *ethnē* as either "gentiles" or "nations" can subtly redirect interpretation. "Gentiles" often sounds like a narrow religious label, as though it referred to a technical category of people outside Judaism. Yet the Latin root *gentilis* simply means "nations." What began as a broad designation of peoples has come, over time, to sound like a specialized theological term. This shift risks shrinking Paul's expansive vision.

In the New Testament, the issue was never abstract. The early church wrestled with the concrete question of how the nations could be grafted into God's covenant promises to Israel. Paul's argument in Romans is missional, addressing the staggering reality that Israel's covenant God was now extending blessing to the nations through the Messiah. Translating *ethnē* as "nations" helps keep this reality in view, reminding readers that Paul is articulating God's redemptive purpose for all peoples within the wider family of nations.

For this reason, translating *ethnē* consistently as "gentiles" deserves renewed scrutiny. While English translations reflect generations of careful scholarship, this choice often reframes Paul's argument in individualistic or oppositional terms. In many contexts, Paul does not employ *ethnē* as a rigid ethnic or religious contrast to "Jews" but in its more common

85. Magda, "Ἐθνῶν ἀπόστολος."

Hebrew and Hellenistic sense of "nations" or "peoples." Rendering the term as "gentiles" risks importing later theological and sociological assumptions, particularly notions of fixed religious identities, that were not yet fully formed in the first century.[86]

This issue is therefore not merely semantic but theological. Paul frames much of Romans in terms of the relationship between Israel and the nations as two corporate actors within God's covenantal economy. Translating *ethnē* as "gentiles" can reduce this symmetry to a simplified Jew–non-Jew dichotomy, obscuring Paul's central concern: the inclusion of the nations alongside Israel in the unfolding purposes of God. As studies of Romans 11 have shown, the "fullness of the nations" belongs within Israel's eschatological restoration, not as a replacement for Israel but as part of God's design to bring both Israel and the nations to salvation.[87]

Paul's rhetorical strategy also benefits from preserving this distinction. In certain contexts, such as when he identifies himself as "apostle to the Gentiles" (Rom 11:13), the translation "gentiles" may rightly highlight his mission to non-Jews. Yet elsewhere, collapsing *ethnē* into "gentiles" can mislead readers about Paul's aim. Translating Romans 11:25 as "the fullness of the Gentiles," for example, can foster supersessionist interpretations, whereas "the fullness of the nations" better reflects Paul's insistence on God's ongoing fidelity to Israel and the nations' inclusion within that fidelity.[88]

Translation, then, is never neutral. The choice between "gentiles" and "nations" shapes whether Romans is heard primarily as a letter about individual salvation across ethnic boundaries or as a missionary text oriented toward the reconciliation and renewal of the nations under the lordship of Jesus Christ. It influences how the Abrahamic promise is received, whether as the inheritance of "many nations" (Rom 4:17–18) or merely as a Jew–gentile contrast, and it carries ethical weight for

86. In Romans, the term ἔθνος / ἔθνη appears twenty-three times (Rom 1:5, 13; 2:14, 24; 3:29; 4:17–18; 9:24, 30; 10:19; 11:11–13, 25; 15:9–12, 16, 18, 27; 16:4, 26). The NRSVue translates it as "Gentiles" in twenty cases, "nations" twice (4:17–18), and "nation" once (10:19). The ESV renders the term "Gentiles" eighteen times but preserves "nations" in key theological or Abrahamic contexts (1:5; 4:17–18; 16:26) and "nation" once (10:19). The NIV uses "Gentiles" twenty-one times and opts for "nation(s)" three times (4:17–18; 10:19). The NASB2020 follows a similar pattern, predominantly translating the word as "Gentiles," with "nation(s)" reserved for Old Testament quotations or contexts highlighting the Abrahamic promise (4:17–18; 10:19; 15:11).

87. Ábel, "Role of Israel Concerning the Gentiles."

88. Nanos, *Reading Romans Within Judaism*, 200–213.

Christian–Jewish relations, particularly in a post-Holocaust context, since certain translations can unintentionally perpetuate supersessionist readings of Paul.

For these reasons, it seems preferable to translate *ethnos / ethnē*) in Romans as "nations" whenever covenantal, eschatological, or universal dimensions are in view, especially in texts such as Romans 1:5; 4:17–18; 11:25–26; 15:9–12; and 16:26. The translation "gentiles" should be reserved for passages where Paul explicitly foregrounds the Jew–non-Jew distinction at the level of persons or assemblies (e.g., Rom 2:14; 11:13). Adopting this practice aligns more closely with Paul's lexical environment and preserves the theological breadth of his vision, safeguarding both the universal horizon of mission and the enduring place of Israel in God's purposes.[89]

ADDRESSING THE CALLED IN ROME

Paul's self-identification in Romans 1:1–7 culminates in his address to the Roman believers as those who are themselves "called." They are "called to belong to Jesus Christ" and "called to be saints." This repetition of calling language establishes a deliberate theological symmetry between apostle and community. Both Paul and the Roman churches are constituted by divine initiative rather than ethnic identity, moral achievement, or social status.

This symmetry has missiological implications. Paul does not approach the Roman churches as passive recipients of instruction or merely as instruments for his own mission. They are participants in the same divine calling that grounds his apostleship. His authority exists not to eclipse their vocation but to cultivate it. In Romans, apostolic leadership functions to form apostolic communities capable of faithful participation in the mission of God.

The greeting concludes with the familiar blessing of grace and peace, drawing together Greek and Jewish conventions. Even here, Paul models integration rather than replacement. The community he addresses is already hybrid, already shaped by translation and cultural overlap, and already implicated in the mission he will articulate more fully throughout the letter.

89. Magda, "'Εθνῶν ἀπόστολος."

APOSTOLIC IDENTITY AS MISSIOLOGICAL FOUNDATION

Romans 1:1–7 establishes apostolic identity as the foundation for everything that follows. Before Paul argues, exhorts, or plans, he names who he is in relation to God, Christ, Scripture, and the nations. This identity is not static or abstract but vocational, oriented toward obedience, formation, and mission.

These verses reveal a pattern that governs the letter as a whole. Mission flows from identity. Authority flows from calling. Proclamation flows from allegiance. Paul's apostleship is not defined by technique, strategy, or expansion, but by faithfulness to the gospel of God revealed in Jesus Christ.

Crucially, this identity does not belong to Paul alone. Romans 1:6–7 clarifies that the calling extends to the Roman believers themselves: "including you who are called to belong to Jesus Christ." Paul's apostolic vocation to the nations places him "under obligation both to Greeks and to barbarians, both to the wise and to the foolish" (Rom 1:14), underscoring the universal scope of the gospel.[90] This obligation is not driven by personal familiarity or institutional responsibility. Although Paul has not yet visited Rome and knows the churches there only through indirect relationships, he understands his responsibility toward them as arising directly from his calling in Christ.[91]

Here again, identity precedes action. Paul's sense of obligation is not pragmatic but theological. His calling to the nations binds him to the Roman believers, situating them within the same missional horizon that defines his own apostleship. The gospel he bears is intended for all peoples, across cultural, intellectual, and social boundaries, and the Roman churches are already embedded within that divine purpose.

CONCLUSION

Paul's opening in Romans thus establishes the foundation of his apostolic identity, authority, and calling. By weaving together language from Israel's Scriptures, Greco-Roman conventions, and his own encounter with the risen Christ, Paul presents himself as a servant and apostle set apart

90. Schreiner, *Romans*, 130–132; Fitzmyer, *Romans*, 238.

91. Witherington, *Romans*, 44–45.

for the gospel and commissioned to embody and proclaim it among the nations. His identity is inseparable from his mission: to make known the faithfulness of God fulfilled in Christ and extended to all peoples.

Yet this self-description is not an end in itself. Identity gives way to action, and apostolic authority takes the form of apostolic labor. Having traced how Paul defines who he is and why he has been called, the letter now turns toward expression. The next section moves from identity to practice, exploring how Paul's vocation is lived out through prayer, relationship, and partnership with the Roman churches (Rom 1:8–15). Apostolic identity, once named, now begins to act.

8

Paul's Apostolic Ministry, Romans 1:8–15

PAUL'S APOSTOLIC VOCATION WAS decisively oriented toward the nations. He understood himself as having been entrusted with the task of carrying the gospel beyond the boundaries of Israel into the wider Greco-Roman world. This calling surfaces repeatedly across his letters and finds particularly clear expression in Romans, where Paul speaks of his ambition to proclaim Christ "where Christ has not been named" (Rom 15:20) and describes himself as a "minister of Christ Jesus to the nations" (Rom 15:16). His missionary horizons stretched from the eastern provinces of the Roman Empire to its western limits, culminating in his hope of reaching Spain (Rom 15:24, 28).[1]

Yet Paul's expansive missionary vision never eclipsed his concern for the concrete communities that emerged from the proclamation of the gospel.[2] His mission to the nations and his pastoral care for the church were not parallel tracks but interwoven dimensions of a single apostolic calling.[3] Paul did not conceive of evangelization apart from community formation, nor did he imagine the church as an end in itself detached from God's mission to the world.[4] For Paul, the advance of the gospel and the vitality of the church belonged together, each sustaining and reinforcing the other.[5]

1. Schnabel, *Paul the Missionary*, 39–122.
2. Thompson, "Paul as Missionary Pastor," 25–36.
3. Witherington, *Romans*, 45.
4. Allen, *Missionary Methods*.
5. Schnabel, *Paul the Missionary*, 231–55.

MINISTRY TO THE CHURCH: GRATITUDE, PRAYER, AND MUTUAL ENCOURAGEMENT, ROMANS 1:8–15

Romans 1:8–15 offers an early and revealing window into Paul's integrated vision of apostolic ministry. Before unfolding the theological argument of the letter, Paul discloses how his apostolic identity takes concrete shape through gratitude, persistent prayer, relational longing, and a deep sense of obligation to both believers and the wider world. His opening thanksgiving and prayer are not mere formalities; they express genuine pastoral concern for the Roman church and situate that concern within his broader mission to the nations.[6] These verses show that Paul's ministry cannot be reduced to itinerant preaching or abstract theological reflection. His apostleship is simultaneously pastoral, relational, and missional.

In this opening section, Paul names his gratitude for the Roman believers, affirms his continual intercession on their behalf, and articulates his desire to be present with them, not as a distant authority, but for the sake of mutual encouragement in the shared life of faith.[7] His longing to visit Rome is bound to his sense of apostolic obligation, revealing a ministry oriented toward the formation of communities capable of faithful participation in God's redemptive purposes. Examining Romans 1:8–15 clarifies Paul's vision for the church and underscores the central role of prayer, gratitude, and relational reciprocity in sustaining both mission and fellowship.[8]

Paul's Thanksgiving for the Roman Church

Paul begins by expressing gratitude for the faith of the Roman believers, which he says is "proclaimed in all the world" (Rom 1:8). Some view this as hyperbolic language.[9] However, news about the Christian community in Rome would have naturally spread throughout the empire due to the city's political and cultural significance.[10] Regardless of how far their reputation had reached, Paul's emphasis is not on the extent of their fame but on the very existence of a thriving church in the heart of the Roman

6. Barran, "Pauline Mission as Salvific Intentionality," 234–46.
7. Schubert, *Pauline Thanksgivings*.
8. Longenecker, *Romans*, 100–101.
9. Similar to 1 Thessalonians 1:8 and 2 Corinthians 2:14, see Fitzmyer, *Romans*, 244.
10. Schreiner, *Romans*, 120.

Empire.[11] This reality fills him with joy and gratitude, as it signifies the spread of the gospel into the world's most influential city.

Paul's thanksgiving reflects his conviction that faith itself is a gift from God.[12] By thanking God rather than the believers themselves, Paul emphasizes God's activity in bringing people to faith. He also makes it clear that this thanksgiving is offered "through Jesus Christ," highlighting Christ's mediatorial role in the believer's relationship with God.

Paul's Unceasing Prayer and Longing to Visit Rome

Paul transitions from gratitude to his persistent prayer for the Romans, "For God is my witness, whom I serve with my spirit in the gospel of his Son, that without ceasing I mention you always in my prayers" (Rom 1:9). Paul's unceasing prayer for the Roman church reflects his pastoral commitment. He does not merely offer general prayers; he intercedes specifically and continuously for their faith and well-being. This persistent prayer illustrates Paul's conviction that mission depends on divine empowerment. In Romans 1:10, Paul expresses his longing to visit Rome, praying that by God's will, he may finally succeed in coming to them. His desire to visit Rome is more than a personal ambition, it is an apostolic calling aligned with God's purpose. However, Paul recognizes that his plans are subject to God's sovereignty, a theme he reiterates in Romans 15:22–32.

The importance of prayer in mission. Paul's commitment to prayer reflects his broader understanding of the relationship between prayer and mission.[13] Throughout his letters, Paul emphasizes that prayer is not an optional religious activity but an essential aspect of God's work in the world (1 Thess 5:17; Col 4:2).[14] Prayer ensures that mission is not reduced to human effort and strategy but remains dependent on God's guidance and power.[15] Paul recognizes that proclaiming the gospel involves spiritual warfare,[16] requiring divine intervention (Eph 6:10–18).[17] The opposition he faced from imprisonment to persecution demonstrates

11. Longenecker, *Romans*, 107.
12. Kruse, *Romans*, 58–60.
13. Carson, *Praying with Paul*, 45–58.
14. Wright, *Mission of God*, 346–347.
15. Carson, *Praying with Paul*, 183–201.
16. Lincoln, *Ephesians*, 452.
17. O'Brien, *Ephesians*, 460–490. See also, Barth, *Ephesians on Chapters 4–6*, 759–808.

that gospel proclamation often encounters spiritual and earthly resistance (Acts 16:16–40; 2 Cor 11:23–27).[18]

In the book of Acts, we see how prayer overcame barriers to mission.[19] In Acts 12, when Peter was imprisoned, the church prayed fervently, and God miraculously delivered him. Similarly, Paul and Silas, while imprisoned in Philippi, prayed and worshiped, resulting in their release and the jailer's conversion (Acts 16:25–34). These examples highlight that mission is not only about human effort but about spiritual breakthroughs that come through prayer.[20]

Paul's desire for mutual encouragement. In Romans 1:11–12, Paul elaborates on his reason for wanting to visit Rome: "For I long to see you so that I may share with you some spiritual gift so that you may be strengthened—or rather so that we may be mutually encouraged by each other's faith, both yours and mine." Paul desires to strengthen the faith of the Roman believers while also receiving encouragement from them. This reciprocal relationship highlights Paul's humility and recognition of the interdependence of believers. Even as an apostle, Paul acknowledges his need for spiritual nourishment from fellow believers. This mutual encouragement is a central theme in Paul's understanding of Christian community. The church is a living body, where believers build up one another (Rom 12:3–8; 1 Cor 12:12–27).

Paul's obligation to preach to all people. In Romans 1:13–15, Paul clarifies that his intention to visit Rome is part of his broader apostolic mission: "I do not want you to be unaware, brothers and sisters, that I have often intended to come to you (but have been prevented until now) in order that I may reap some harvest among you, as I have among the rest of the Gentiles" (Rom 1:13). Paul's use of agricultural imagery ("reap some harvest") suggests that he sees his ministry in Rome as part of a greater mission to gather more people into the faith. His delayed visit was not due to lack of desire but due to various obstacles, likely related to other mission priorities (Rom 15:22–24). He then expresses his universal obligation to preach the gospel: "I am under obligation both to Greeks and to barbarians, both to the wise and to the foolish" (Rom 1:14).[21]

Paul's sense of duty is not based on social, intellectual, or ethnic distinctions. The terms "Greeks" and "barbarians" refer to cultural and

18. O'Brien, *Gospel and Mission*, 119–25.

19. Martin, "Creed," 192.

20. Clowney, "Biblical Theology of Prayer," 136–73.

21. Schreiner, *Romans*, 132.

linguistic divisions, while "wise" and "foolish" highlight intellectual differences. Paul's mission transcends human categories, reinforcing that the gospel is for all people.[22] His eagerness to preach in Rome (Rom 1:15) stems from this global vision.[23] Though Rome already has a Christian community, Paul sees his visit as an opportunity to mobilize believers for further mission. His goal is to gain support for his planned journey to Spain (Rom 15:24, 28). Paul's use of "Greeks and barbarians" is particularly significant in light of his mission to Spain. The Spaniards were regarded as both barbaric and uneducated, falling outside the boundaries of honor in the Roman worldview.[24] By directing his efforts toward them, Paul demonstrates the radical inclusivity of the gospel and his obligation to reach all nations.

RECONCILING ROMANS 1:13–15 WITH ROMANS 15:18–21

At first glance, Paul's desire to preach the gospel in Rome may seem to contradict his statement in Romans 15:18–21, where he says his ambition is to preach where Christ has not been named.[25] Further investigation will show these statements are complementary rather than contradictory.[26] Romans 1:13–15 expresses his desire to strengthen existing believers and partner with them in mission,[27] while Romans 15:18–21 highlights his commitment to expanding the gospel to unreached areas.[28] Paul is not coming to Rome to plant new churches but to mobilize the existing churches for further mission, particularly toward Spain, which represents the westernmost edge of his mission field.[29]

CONCLUSION

Romans 1:8–15 presents a rich portrait of Paul's apostolic ministry. From gratitude and prayer to longing, mutual encouragement, and universal

22. Fitzmyer, *Romans*, 250–51.
23. Schreiner, *Romans*, 911–17.
24. Schreiner, *Romans*, 131.
25. Dunn, *Romans 1–8*, 31–36.
26. Dunn, *Romans 1–8*, 31–36.
27. Longenecker, *Romans*, 142.
28. Longenecker, *Romans*, 138–41.
29. Schreiner, *Romans*, 703–1010.

obligation, Paul embodies a form of leadership in which mission flows from identity and community. The church is both the fruit of the gospel and its primary vehicle. Paul's concern for the Roman believers reflects his conviction that strong, faithful communities are essential for the ongoing advance of God's redemptive work among the nations.

Here, the integration of mission and church life becomes unmistakable. Paul does not separate proclamation from formation, nor does he imagine mission apart from community. The vitality of the church and the expansion of the gospel belong together. Romans 1:8–15 thus prepares the reader to encounter a letter in which theology, mission, and communal life are woven into a single, coherent vision of God's purposes in Christ.

9

Paul's Apostolic Message, Romans 1:16–17

At the heart of Paul's letter to the Romans stands a brief but densely packed declaration that has shaped Christian theology for centuries. Romans 1:16–17 functions as more than a thematic summary or inspirational confession; it articulates the controlling vision that governs everything that follows. Here Paul names the gospel as God's active power, announces its universal scope, and frames it as the revelation of God's righteousness, a righteousness that gives life and calls forth faith.

These verses are often quoted, debated, and systematized, yet they resist reduction to a single formula or doctrinal abstraction. For Paul, the gospel is not only a message about salvation but the means by which God is presently at work in the world, fulfilling ancient promises and inaugurating a new reality in Christ. It is public, disruptive, and deeply relational, addressing not only individual guilt but the restoration of broken relationships between God, humanity, and creation itself.

In Romans 1:16–17, Paul draws together Israel's Scriptures, the scandal of the cross, and the hope of new creation into a single proclamation. The gospel announces that God's righteousness is being revealed not as a distant attribute, but as a saving action unfolding in history. This universal scope is made explicit in Paul's declaration that the gospel is "the power of God for salvation to everyone who believes, to the Jew first and also to the Greek." Drawing on Isaiah's vision of God as both Israel's redeemer and a light to the nations (Isa 49:6), Paul presents the gospel as the fulfillment of the prophetic hope for new creation inaugurated through Jesus Christ.

For this reason, there is near-universal agreement among interpreters that Romans 1:16–17 presents the central theme or thesis of the letter.[1] To understand the argument of Romans, it is therefore essential to pause here, allowing Paul's definitions of gospel, power, salvation, faith, and righteousness to shape our reading before he turns to the darker realities the gospel confronts. The confession that follows is the lens through which the entire letter must be read:

> For I am not ashamed of the gospel, for it is the power of God for salvation to everyone who believes, to the Jew first and also to the Greek. For in it the righteousness of God is revealed from faith for faith, as it is written, "The righteous shall live by faith."

I AM NOT ASHAMED

Paul's declaration in Romans 1:16, "For I am not ashamed of the gospel," is an affirmation of his unwavering confidence in the message of salvation through Jesus Christ.[2] This assertion is significant in the context of his time, as the gospel's core of a crucified Messiah was scandalous.[3] In 1 Corinthians 1:23, Paul acknowledges this challenge, stating, "We preach Christ crucified, a stumbling block to Jews and foolishness to Gentiles." Despite these cultural and religious objections, Paul refuses to shy away from proclaiming the gospel, which he identifies as "the power of God for salvation to everyone who believes" (Rom 1:16).

Paul's lack of shame concerning the gospel is closely tied to his understanding of the cross.[4] In Greco-Roman society, crucifixion was a humiliating and degrading form of execution, symbolizing weakness and defeat. In Jewish thought, crucifixion was viewed as a sign of divine curse, for "cursed is everyone who hangs on a tree" (Deut. 21:23). Yet, Paul not only embraces the cross but places it at the very heart of his theology.[5] In Galatians 6:14, he declares, "May I never boast except in

1. Schreiner, *Romans*, 135.

2. Kruse, *Romans*, 58–60. See also Fitzmyer, *Romans*, 255–56. Longenecker, *Romans*, 157–63.

3. McGrath, "Cross," 193.

4. Dunn, *Theology of Paul*, 22–23.

5. McGrath, "Cross," 192–93.

the cross of our Lord Jesus Christ." For Paul, the cross is not a symbol of shame but of God's ultimate wisdom and power. In 1 Corinthians 1:18, he writes, "For the message of the cross is foolishness to those who are perishing, but to us who are being saved it is the power of God."

Paul's unashamed proclamation of the gospel is rooted in his conviction that it reveals the righteousness of God and brings salvation to all people. This universality further emphasizes why he is not ashamed. Paul sees the gospel as God's ultimate act of love and justice, made available to humanity through Christ's death.[6] The transformative power of the gospel emboldens him, even in the face of persecution, ridicule, and suffering.

By refusing to be ashamed of the gospel or the cross, Paul challenges the prevailing values of his time, redefining concepts of honor and shame in light of God's redemptive work through Christ.[7] His courage serves as a model of faith, demonstrating that the apparent foolishness of the cross is, in fact, the ultimate expression of God's power and wisdom. Paul's steadfast commitment to this message, despite its countercultural implications, testifies to his trust in the gospel's transformative and salvific power.

Paul's statement echoes Isaiah 28:16—"Therefore thus says the Lord God, 'See, I am laying in Zion a foundation stone, a tested stone, a precious cornerstone, a sure foundation: "One who trusts will not panic"'" (NRSVue). This verse is later directly quoted in Romans 9:33 and 10:11. In these passages, Paul weaves Isaiah's prophecy into his argument about faith and the righteousness of God, identifying Christ as the fulfillment of the "cornerstone." By doing so, Paul demonstrates the continuity between the gospel and the Hebrew Scriptures, presenting faith in Christ as the ultimate expression of reliance on God's promises. This thematic connection reinforces Paul's broader theological claim that the gospel is rooted in and fulfills the prophetic witness of the First Testament.[8]

We can hear echoes of Isaiah 50:7–8 in Romans 1:16. Like Isaiah, Paul could affirm, "And the Lord God has become a helper to me; for this reason I was not ashamed, but I set my face like a solid rock, and I knew that I would surely not be ashamed. Because the one who justifies me is approaching."[9] Paul's confidence in the gospel stems from its role

6. Crisler, *Reading Romans as Lament*, 57–61.

7. Schreiner, *Romans*, 137.

8. Harvey, *Romans*, 29.

9. Brannan et al., *Lexham English Septuagint*, Isa 50:7–9.

as God's eschatological vindication of those who trust in him, thereby demonstrating God's own faithfulness. Notably, Paul modifies Isaiah's emphatic future negation—"I shall not be ashamed"—into a present one: "I am not ashamed." This shift to the present tense aligns with Paul's declarations that both the righteousness and wrath of God are currently being revealed (Rom 1:17–18). Through this transformation, Isaiah's future hope resounds in Paul's proclamation, redefined within the temporal framework of God's already accomplished act of eschatological deliverance in Christ.[10]

"I am not ashamed of the gospel" is often dismissed as a mere rhetorical flourish, but such a reading overlooks the honor–shame dynamics embedded in the statement.[11] In ancient rhetorical conventions, declarations of being "unashamed" commonly signaled engagement with a socially sensitive or potentially discrediting subject. For Paul, the sensitive issue was the gospel itself. Centered on a crucified and resurrected Messiah, the message confronted deeply ingrained cultural expectations and carried the weight of shame within both Jewish and Greco-Roman worlds.

Although Romans does not dwell explicitly on the cross, Paul's gospel is anchored in "Jesus Christ and him crucified" (1 Cor 2:2). The gospel is proclaimed as a decisive event, bound to Paul's calling as an apostle and bearer of an eschatological message. Its substance is "the word of the cross" (1 Cor 1:18), a proclamation that unsettled Jewish expectations and exposed the fragility of Greco-Roman visions of honor and power. The figure of a crucified redeemer stood in sharp tension with deeply held assumptions about divine action and human worth.[12]

Yet it is precisely this scandal that reveals the gospel's subversive power. Addressed to the despised and the powerless, the proclamation of Christ crucified inverted prevailing social hierarchies and exposed the fragility of human claims to wisdom and strength. As Paul insists, "God chose what is foolish in the world to shame the wise . . . what is weak in the world to shame the strong" (1 Cor 1:27–29). Paul's refusal to experience shame is therefore not rhetorical bravado but a theological conviction. The gospel inaugurates a new divine order that overturns dominant systems of honor and redefines power, wisdom, and belonging in light of the crucified Messiah.[13]

10. Hays, *Echoes*, 39.

11. Schreiner, *Romans*, 136–37.

12. Schreiner, *Romans*, 137.

13. Schreiner, *Romans*, 136–37.

"I am not ashamed" may also reflect an early Christian confessional formula. This phrase resonates with other New Testament texts, such as Mark 8:38, Luke 9:26, and 2 Timothy 1:8, where the theme of not being ashamed of Christ or the gospel plays a significant role in early Christian identity and proclamation, emphasizing the believer's public and unwavering affirmation of faith in Christ.[14]

This interpretation situates Paul's declaration within the broader framework of early Christian witness and community practice, where allegiance to Christ was both a theological commitment and a public testimony, often in the face of social stigma or persecution. The use of "I am not ashamed" highlights not only Paul's personal conviction but also his alignment with a shared confessional tradition.[15]

THE GOSPEL

Paul's use of the term "gospel" (*euangelion*) serves to emphasize its centrality in his theology. He introduces himself in Romans as "set apart for the gospel of God" (Rom 1:1), highlighting his commitment to proclaiming it, especially to the gentiles (Rom 1:15; 11:13). For Paul, the gospel is "the power of God for salvation to everyone who believes" (Rom 1:16), forming the foundation of his mission.[16] The gospel is not a new concept but the fulfillment of God's redemptive plan, revealing his faithfulness and culminating in Christ.

The Gospel in the First Testament

The roots of the gospel lie in the First Testament (LXX), where the verbal form *euangelizomai* ("to proclaim good news") appears frequently, especially in Isaiah. Passages like Isaiah 52:7 and 61:1–2 depict the announcement of salvation, liberation, and divine restoration. Paul draws from these prophetic traditions, reinterpreting them in light of Christ's life, death, and resurrection. In Isaiah 61, the proclamation of good news to the poor and freedom for captives prefigures Jesus' mission (Luke 4:18–19) and, by extension, Paul's gospel proclamation.

14. Fitzmyer, *Romans*, 255–57.

15. Dunn, *Romans 1–8*, 38.

16. Colenso, *Romans*, 41–46.

For Paul, the gospel is not a departure from Israel's Scriptures but their fulfillment. He asserts that it was "promised beforehand through [God's] prophets in the holy scriptures" (Rom 1:2). By referencing Abraham's faith (Gen 15:6) and Habakkuk's declaration that "the righteous shall live by faith" (Hab 2:4), Paul roots the gospel in the covenantal history of Israel. His engagement with Scripture is dynamic, rather than rigidly quoting texts,[17] he reinterprets them in light of Christ.[18] This method, common in Jewish and Greco-Roman traditions, reflects Paul's conviction that the Scriptures point forward to Christ and his redemptive work.[19]

The Gospel as the Fulfillment of God's Redemptive Plan

Paul's understanding of the gospel is multifaceted. It is deeply grounded in Scripture yet radically transformed by Christ's work. It upholds divine justice while proclaiming God's grace. Paul presents the gospel as a paradox: power revealed in weakness, life emerging from death, and divine wisdom displayed in what the world considers foolishness (1 Cor 1:18–25). The gospel is not just doctrine but the very heart of God's redemptive activity, bringing life and transformation to all who believe. The gospel reveals God's faithfulness, justice, and mercy, offering salvation to both Jews and gentiles. It is not a static theological concept but a living reality that reshapes human history. For Paul, it is the means by which God reconciles the world to himself and brings about a new creation in Christ (2 Cor 5:17–19).

The Gospel in the Greco-Roman World

Paul's use of *euangelion* also interacts with the language of the Roman Empire.[20] In Greco-Roman culture, the term was associated with imperial proclamations such as announcements of a ruler's birth, victories, or ascension to power.[21] In Homer's *Odyssey*, *euangelion* refers to a re-

17. Wright, *Paul and the Faithfulness of God*, 1495.

18. Stanley, *Paul and the Language of Scripture*, 267–73, 292–337.

19. Dunn, *Theology of Paul*, 19–20, 181–553.

20. Friedrich, "Εὐαγγελίζομαι, Εὐαγγέλιον, Προευαγγελίζομαι, Εὐαγγελιστής," 2:707–35.

21. Dittenberger, *Orientis Graeci Inscriptiones Selectae*, 1:13, 20.

ward for good tidings (xiv.152), while in Jewish-Hellenistic literature, it conveys messages of salvation and divine intervention. Josephus, for example, uses *euangelion* to describe the proclamation of Caesar's rule.[22]

The Priene inscription, dating to the first century BCE, provides a striking parallel. It declares the birth of Augustus as "good news" (*euangelia*), heralding the beginning of a new era of peace and prosperity. Such proclamations positioned the emperor as a divine figure whose reign brought salvation to the world.[23] The New Testament writers, particularly Paul, adopt this term but redefine it.[24] Instead of referring to a human ruler, the gospel proclaims the reign of Jesus Christ as the true Lord and Savior.

The Gospel as a Radical Alternative to Imperial Claims

Scholars such as Adolf Deissmann argue that Paul's use of *euangelion* is a deliberate counterclaim against Roman imperial ideology.[25] While the emperor's rule was presented as "good news" for the empire, Paul proclaims a greater and universal gospel: the salvation accomplished through Jesus Christ. However, others, such as Ernst Käsemann, caution against overemphasizing the connection between the gospel and imperial rhetoric, arguing that the New Testament's use of *euangelion* primarily arises from Jewish eschatological traditions rather than direct opposition to Rome.[26] Peter Stuhlmacher further argues that while Paul and other early Christians were aware of the imperial connotations of euangelion, these did not fundamentally shape their understanding of the gospel. Instead, their proclamation was rooted in Israel's Scriptures and the eschatological expectation of God's reign breaking into history through Jesus Christ.[27]

22. Josephus, *Works of Josephus*, 695–96.

23. Balz and Schneider, *Exegetical Dictionary*, 1:71.

24. Balz and Schneider, *Exegetical Dictionary*, 1:71.

25. Deissmann, *Light from the Ancient East*, 366–67.

26. Käsemann, *Romans*, 7.

27. Stuhlmacher, *Romans*, 25.

The Gospel as the Christ-Event

For Paul, the gospel is the proclamation of God's saving work in Christ. It encompasses Jesus' life, death, resurrection, and exaltation.[28] The gospel is both the message of salvation and the power that brings it about (Rom 1:16). It is not a human philosophy or religious system but a divine intervention that transforms individuals and communities.

Paul's gospel is eschatological, it announces that through Christ's resurrection, the new age has begun. The old world, marked by sin and death, is passing away, and a new reality is emerging in Christ (2 Cor 5:17). This is why the gospel demands not just intellectual assent but a response of faith and obedience. It is an invitation to participate in God's redemptive work.

The Transformative Power of the Gospel

The gospel is not a collection of metaphysical truths or a cultural construct. It is a dynamic and transformative proclamation of God's decisive action in Jesus Christ, breaking into human history to confront the deepest realities of sin, death, and the search for meaning.[29] Far from being a static set of doctrines, a religious system, or a philosophical worldview, the gospel transcends cultural, political, philosophical, and scientific frameworks. It directly addresses individuals, calling for a personal response of faith and trust in God's redemptive work.[30] The gospel communicates a message of salvation, liberating individuals and communities from the limitations of human systems and ideologies. It is a living and active event, summoning both personal and communal transformation through an encounter with the living God. A theology that hardens itself into a closed system is always dangerous. When faith becomes a structure rather than a living encounter, it risks mistaking its own formulations for the truth they seek to express. Systematized thought can serve understanding, but when it becomes self-enclosed, it imprisons within the walls of abstraction the very reality it was meant to reveal. Theology must

28. Kim, "Jesus," 489.

29. Käsemann, *Romans*, 21–25.

30. Wright, "New Tübingen School?" 12–13.

remain porous to mystery, open to the God who continually exceeds our categories and refuses to be contained by them.[31]

Rather than being a locked theological system, the gospel is centered on a personal, reciprocal relationship with God, one that involves both knowing God and being known by him, alongside engaging in love and communication with others. At its deepest, this relationship is one of intimate communion: I know as I am known (1 Cor 13:12; see also Ps 139:1–2; Jer 31:34; 1 John 3:2). The gospel is grounded in a dynamic of revelation, where God takes the initiative and invites a human response of faith and love. God's involvement calls for our active participation. The theological journey, then, presupposes that the one sought has already come and is present with us: God, who first loved us and sent his Son (1 John 4:19).

The gospel reveals God's lordship breaking into history, resisting any attempts to domesticate it into a human system or worldview. We should be wary of the gospel being co-opted by cultural, national, or political agendas.[32] For the gospel is a proclamation of God's sovereign reign inaugurated in Christ, one that challenges and relativizes all human claims to ultimate truth.

THE COMMUNAL AND MISSIONAL NATURE OF THE GOSPEL

Paul insists that the gospel is not an individualistic message but one that creates and sustains a community. The gospel forms a body of believers united in Christ. This community is called to embody the gospel in its life and witness, demonstrating the reconciliation and transformation it proclaims. Moreover, the gospel is inherently missional. It is not a private truth but a public proclamation that must be shared with all nations. Paul's apostolic mission reflects this urgency, he is "under obligation both to Greeks and to barbarians" (Rom 1:14). The gospel is for all people, breaking down cultural, social, and ethnic barriers (Gal 3:28).

For Paul, the gospel is the central reality of God's redemptive work. It is not a human philosophy, religious ritual, or political ideology but the power of God that brings salvation to all who believe (Rom 1:16). The gospel fulfills the promises of Scripture, challenges worldly powers,

31. Lossky, *Orthodox Theology*, 15.

32. Käsemann, *On Being a Disciple*, 280–319.

transforms lives, and creates a new human community. The gospel is the announcement of God's faithfulness, revealed in Christ, and the invitation to participate in his kingdom. The gospel demands a response. It calls for faith, obedience, and a willingness to be shaped by its reality. It is not static but dynamic, continuing to unfold in history as God's purposes are realized in Christ. Paul's commitment to the gospel reflects his conviction that it is the only true hope for humanity, a message of divine power, grace, and transformation.

The Power of God for Salvation

At the heart of the thesis in Romans 1:16–17 lies a paradox of power: The seemingly shameful gospel, which appears weak and unimpressive, is, in fact, the revelation of God's power. This power, Paul asserts, is the divine means of salvation, echoing his statement in 1 Corinthians 1:18 that "the word of the cross is the power of God for those being saved."

Jewish tradition frequently associates God's power with pivotal events and symbols, such as the "strength" of his hand in the exodus (Exod 15:6; 32:11; Deut 9:26, 29; 26:8). In contrast, Roman culture celebrated power in priestly, military, and administrative forms, often framing the emperor's activities as salvific. The imperial cult proclaimed the emperor as a divine savior whose "gospel" brought peace and order.[33]

Paul's message directly challenges the imperial ideology of his time. While Roman triumphs and civic cults celebrated the emperor as the embodiment of divine power and the source of salvation, Paul proclaims that true salvation is found only through the gospel of Christ crucified and resurrected. The phrase *eis sōtērian* ("for salvation") draws attention to the transformative power of the gospel, which Paul presents as both a present reality and a future hope. Salvation, as Paul describes it, entails deliverance from divine wrath, the restoration of wholeness, and ultimate redemption, standing in stark contrast to the hollow promises of Roman authority.

The power of the gospel is most clearly demonstrated in the seemingly powerless communities of faith that bear its witness. In direct opposition to the Roman social order, which prioritized strength, status, and education, Paul proclaims a radical inversion: Divine power uplifts the weak, the marginalized, and the dishonored, granting them a new

33. Schreiner, *Romans*, 138.

honor rooted in God's righteousness. This reordering of societal values overturns the Roman constructs of shame and honor, affirming that all who place their faith in the gospel are justified and brought into right relationship with God.[34]

In this way, the thesis of Romans undermines the Roman Empire's claims to power and salvation, revealing instead the triumph of divine righteousness through the gospel. By transforming the system by which honor and shame are distributed, Paul's message fundamentally reshapes the social and spiritual order, offering a vision of salvation that transcends human constructs of power and privilege.[35]

Salvation is a broad term that signifies deliverance in various contexts, encompassing physical, spiritual, and ultimate forms of rescue.[36] Paul uses terms related to salvation extensively, more than any other New Testament author. For instance, he employs *sōzō* ("to save") twenty-nine times, *sōtēr* ("savior") twelve times, and *sōtēria* ("salvation") eighteen times. He also uses *rhuomai* ("to rescue") eleven times. This frequency brings into focus the centrality of salvation in Paul's theology.

Salvation in the Pauline writings encompasses various dimensions, but it consistently emphasizes God's initiative and the central role of Christ in delivering humanity from sin and its consequences. In the Pastoral Letters, references to "God our Savior" (1 Tim 1:1; 2:3; Tit 1:3; 2:10; 3:4) and "Christ our Savior" (2 Tim 1:10; Tit 1:4; 2:13; 3:6) make clear the unified action of the Father and the Son in salvation, as seen in Paul's teaching that "God was in Christ reconciling the world to himself" (2 Cor 5:19). Salvation is not earned by human effort but is a gift from God, initiated by his grace (2 Tim 1:9). It involves both present experience and future fulfillment, with believers saved "in Christ" through his life, death, and resurrection, which secure their salvation and bring new life.

Salvation is the core purpose of Christ's incarnation: "Christ Jesus came into the world to save sinners" (1 Tim 1:15). Paul focuses on salvation as the great saving act of Christ for those enslaved to sin. Yet, salvation is far more than the forgiveness of sin: Salvation is a dynamic process of transformation and restoration rooted in the redemptive work of God in Christ.[37] It is a comprehensive term that encompasses God's act of rescuing humanity from the desperate condition brought about by

34. Schreiner, *Romans*, 298.

35. Schreiner, *Romans*, 137–39.

36. Balz and Schneider, *Exegetical Dictionary*, 3:327–29.

37. We will explore sin and the wrath of God more thoroughly in the next chapter.

sin, offering restoration, renewal, and eternal life through Christ.[38] Salvation, in Paul's theology, encapsulates the transformative and redemptive work of God, revealing the heart of the Christian message. At its heart is the call for humanity to partake in the divine life, reflecting the image and likeness of God and experiencing a restored relationship with him. Salvation is a holistic reality encompassing personal transformation, communal life, and the ultimate renewal of all creation.

Paul consistently emphasizes the believer's union with Christ as the heart of salvation (Phil 3:8–11). In passages such as 2 Corinthians 5:17 and Galatians 2:20, salvation appears as a transformative reality in which believers become new creations and share in Christ's own life. This union unfolds through participation, as those who are in Christ grow into his likeness and embody his righteousness and love. Salvation thus involves a dynamic sharing in divine life, marked by ongoing renewal rather than static status.

Paul also frames salvation in terms of reconciliation and restoration. In Romans 5:10–11, he depicts salvation as the healing of a broken relationship between humanity and God through Christ. Sin appears as a condition that produces death and alienation, while salvation brings restoration, culminating in life and peace with God (Rom 8:6). This vision highlights salvation as a divine act that restores what was fractured and brings creation toward wholeness.[39]

For Paul, the life, death, and resurrection of Christ form the foundation of salvation. In Philippians 2:6–11, Paul presents Christ's incarnation as the ultimate act of humility and obedience, through which salvation is made possible. His death on the cross serves as the decisive moment of atonement, while the resurrection signifies victory over sin and death (1 Cor 15:20–22). This holistic view of salvation encompasses not only forgiveness but the transformation of humanity and all creation into the fullness of life in Christ.[40]

Paul's vision of salvation extends beyond the individual to the communal and cosmic dimensions. The church, as the body of Christ, is the locus of salvation, where believers are united in faith and love (1 Cor 12:12–27). Moreover, salvation encompasses all creation, as seen in Romans 8:19–23, where Paul describes the ultimate renewal of the cosmos.

38. Dunn, *Theology of Paul*, 486–87.

39. Wenham, *Paul*, 18–23.

40. Royster, *Romans*, 33–34.

This communal and cosmic perspective reveals salvation as a reality that transcends personal transformation, calling humanity to participate in God's plan for the redemption of the entire world.

Salvation is both a present reality and a future hope. Believers are already justified and reconciled through faith (Rom 5:1), but the fullness of salvation will be realized in the eschaton, the resurrection of the dead and the renewal of all things (1 Cor 15:50–57). This tension between the "already" and the "not yet" shapes Paul's understanding of salvation as an ongoing journey toward ultimate glorification with Christ (Rom 8:30).

Salvation is a comprehensive and transformative process. It involves personal reconciliation with God, growth in holiness, participation in Christ's life, and the renewal of the entire cosmos. Grounded in Christ's life, death, and resurrection, salvation is both a divine gift and a human calling, inviting individuals and communities into the unbounded reality of God's redemptive work.[41] This transformative vision compels believers to live out their faith and share the message of salvation with the world.

Although the noun "faith" (*pistis*) appears three times in the introduction (Rom 1:5, 8, 12), its verbal expression in the participle in Romans 1:16—"to the one who believes" (*tō pisteuonti*)—highlights the identity of those who experience salvation. The use of the present participle emphasizes faith as an ongoing orientation rather than a one-time act.[42] "Believing" and "faith" involve a positive response to the gospel, accepting its proclamation and placing trust in its content—Jesus Christ—and reliance on the one who provides it—God. These are the essential human responses to what God has graciously provided in the person and work of Jesus Christ. Faith is about receiving, trusting, and relying entirely on God. Faith excludes all grounds for human boasting, emphasizing instead God's unmerited grace.[43]

The adjective *panti*, ("all," "everyone") with the substantival participle *tō pisteuonti* ("the one who believes") makes explicit the universal scope of the gospel as "the power of God" effective "for salvation" to everyone who responds positively, without exception or distinction. This universal scope of salvation is a recurring theme in Romans, appearing over seventy-five times in the letter.[44] This inclusiveness is introduced in 1:5 ("for the obedience of faith among all the Gentiles"), emphasized

41. Oden, *Classic Christianity*, 562.

42. Schreiner, *Romans*, 139–40. See also Harvey, *Exegetical Guide*, 29–30.

43. Longenecker, *Romans*, 165.

44. Schreiner, *Romans*, 139–40. See also Harvey, *Exegetical Guide*, 29–30.

immediately in 1:16 and reiterated in 2:9–10 ("to the Jew first and also to the Greek"), and reinforced throughout Romans in passages such as 3:22–24; 4:16; 5:18; 8:32; 10:4, 11–13; 11:32; and 15:10–11.[45]

This emphasis on inclusion addresses divisions among Roman house and tenement churches. Paul's phrase "to the Jew first and also to the Greek" counters claims of superiority among gentile-oriented groups, affirming the precedence of Jews in salvation history while maintaining the equal access of all to salvation through faith. Paul's use of "Greek" rather than "gentile" likely reflects a rhetorical choice to avoid alienating the Greco-Roman majority dominating the Christian movement in Rome.[46]

This inclusive vision overturns both Jewish exclusivism and Roman claims of cultural and political superiority. This contrasts with Roman claims that the emperor and Roman people held a "monopoly" on *fides* (faith, faithfulness), a virtue said to please the gods and justify their imperial dominance.[47] Paul counters all claims of cultural superiority by asserting that God's saving power transforms all who respond in faith to the gospel of Christ crucified. Paul asserts that salvation is achieved through the gospel's persuasive power, uniting believers across cultural divides. This theme culminates in Romans 16, where Paul exhorts competing groups to welcome one another as members of the same family in Christ.[48]

The Righteousness of God is Revealed in the Gospel

The gospel reveals God's righteousness, a righteousness that is not static or distant but living and active. It is the power by which God keeps his promises, rescues humanity from sin, and restores what has been broken between us and him, and among ourselves. This righteousness is not something we earn or achieve; it is something God gives and does.

In classical Greek usage, righteousness (*dikaiosynē*) commonly referred to legal justice, the observance of law, and the fulfillment of civic or moral duty, often carrying a retributive dimension tied to judicial outcomes. This understanding continued into the broader Greco-Roman

45. Longenecker, *Romans*, 166.

46. Witherington, *Romans*, 51.

47. Schreiner, *Romans*, 140.

48. Schreiner, *Romans*, 139–41.

world, where *dikaiosynē* remained closely associated with forensic justice, social order, and the proper functioning of legal institutions.[49]

In early Christian contexts, particularly through the Latin reception of the New Testament, *dikaiosynē theou* was rendered as *iustitia Dei* ("the justice of God"). This translation reinforced a primarily juridical interpretation, emphasizing God's absolute justice expressed both in divine character and in acts of judgment. While not incorrect, this framing tended to privilege legal categories and would later shape Western theological trajectories, often foregrounding divine retribution over relational restoration.

The Hebrew Bible emphasizes righteousness as a covenantal and relational reality. Unlike the Greek concept of justice, which often centers on equitable distribution, the Hebrew term *tzedakah* primarily reflects Yahweh's faithfulness to his covenant and his saving acts. This understanding portrays righteousness not as an abstract quality but as God's character expressed through his restorative actions.[50] For Israel, Yahweh was not merely a lawgiver but the covenant-keeping God whose righteousness was displayed in acts of deliverance and provision. For instance, God's liberation of Israel from Egypt and his promises to the patriarchs exemplify this relational and redemptive righteousness (Exod 6:6–8; Gen 12:1–3).

God's righteousness is often tied to his saving actions for his covenant people, delivering them from enemies and alienation. It is closely associated with terms like "steadfast love" and "faithfulness" (e.g., Isa 11:5; Ps 89:14), which at times are synonymous with "righteousness" and "salvation" (e.g., Ps 85:7–13). This concept of righteousness, understood as God's saving deeds or relation-restoring love, forms the backdrop for Paul's usage. Paul describes "unrighteousness" as disobedience, both of individuals and God's people, who reject God's covenant (Rom 1:28, 3:3–5).

The righteousness of God also emphasizes his commitment to partnership with humanity in the work of restoration, encapsulated in the Jewish concept of *tikkun olam* ("repairing the world").[51] This is evident in the Sinai covenant, where Israel is called to be "a kingdom of priests and a holy nation" (Exod 19:6). Here, God's righteousness reflects his desire for a just and flourishing world, with humanity as active participants in this mission. Additionally, *tzedakah* is frequently paired with *mishpat*

49. Onesti and Brauch, "Righteousness, Righteousness of God," 829.

50. Onesti and Brauch, "Righteousness, Righteousness of God," 827–37.

51. Sacks, *To Heal a Fractured World*, 73.

("justice"), which refers to fairness and equity in societal relationships (e.g., Gen 18:19; Amos 5:24). Together, these terms call for a society that mirrors God's justice and compassion, particularly in its care for the vulnerable, especially widows, orphans, and strangers (Deut 10:18).

The relational nature of God's righteousness is further emphasized in the prophetic literature, where it is often tied to God's steadfast love (*ḥesed*) and willingness to forgive. For example, Isaiah 46:13 portrays God's righteousness as his promise to bring salvation, reflecting his commitment to redeem his people despite their failures.[52] This relational understanding of righteousness imposes a reciprocal responsibility on humanity: Just as God remains faithful to his covenant, humanity is called to uphold justice, compassion, and fidelity in their relationships with God, one another, and creation.[53] This will inform Paul's later arguments in Romans.

God's righteousness is not an abstract moral attribute but a dynamic quality that manifests in God's faithfulness to covenantal commitments.[54] This faithfulness is expressed through acts of deliverance, provision, and justice, particularly on behalf of the marginalized and oppressed. We see this concept of righteousness within the broader framework of the prophetic tradition, where righteousness is inextricably linked to justice (*mishpat*) and steadfast love (*ḥesed*).[55] The prophets frequently portray God's righteousness as a driving force behind divine intervention in history, especially in moments of crisis and covenantal failure. For instance, in Isaiah, the righteousness of God is associated with the restoration of Zion and the renewal of the covenant community: "I bring near my righteousness; it is not far off, and my salvation will not delay" (Isa 46:13). Here, righteousness signifies God's commitment to set things right, bringing salvation to a wayward people and confronting systems of injustice.[56]

The righteousness of God calls for a human response that mirrors divine faithfulness.[57] This response entails covenantal obedience, care for the vulnerable, and the pursuit of justice within the community. The righteousness of God is not only a divine initiative but also an invitation to communal participation. Psalms exemplifies this dynamic interplay, as

52. Brueggemann, *Isaiah 40–66*, 46.

53. Goldingay, *Isaiah for Everyone*, 178–79. See also Paul, *Isaiah 40–66*, 194–95.

54. Brueggemann, *Theology of the Old Testament*, 130–35.

55. Brueggemann, *Prophetic Imagination*, 7–9.

56. Brueggemann, *Isaiah 40–66*, 90–91.

57. Brueggemann, *Theology of the Old Testament*, 83–84.

they often celebrate God's righteousness while simultaneously calling for its realization in the life of the covenant community (e.g., Ps 72:1–4).[58]

God's righteousness is fundamentally about God's commitment to restoring the created order and fulfilling the divine mission of renewal.[59] Righteousness is God's "doing right" in a way that aligns with divine purposes for creation, reflecting both God's character and actions in history.[60] The righteousness of God operates within a restorative framework.[61] This restorative dimension is evident in the narratives of exile and return, where God's righteousness is revealed through acts of mercy and deliverance. For example, in the book of Jeremiah, God's righteousness is expressed in the promise to restore Israel after judgment: "The Lord our Righteousness" (Jer 23:6) becomes a title for the anticipated Davidic king who will embody God's justice and covenantal faithfulness.[62]

In addition to its restorative aspect, there are missional implications of God's righteousness.[63] God's righteousness is not confined to Israel but extends to the nations. This universal dimension is particularly prominent in texts like Isaiah 42:6, where the servant of the Lord is called to be "a light to the nations."[64] The righteousness of God encompasses not only the renewal of Israel but also the reconciliation of all peoples and the establishment of peace and justice on a global scale.

We should also pay attention to the eschatological dimension of God's righteousness. The full realization of God's righteousness involves a future hope in which God's justice will be perfectly established, and all creation will be restored to its intended harmony.[65] This eschatological vision ties God's righteousness to the overarching narrative of Scripture, in which God's actions in history point toward a consummated future.[66]

By grounding our understanding in the First Testament, we can avoid reducing God's righteousness to a static attribute or theological abstraction.[67] Instead, we affirm its dynamic, active nature as God's ongo-

58. Brueggemann, *Theology of the Old Testament*, 422–24.

59. Goldingay, *Israel's Gospel*, 91–92.

60. Goldingay, *Israel's Faith*, 673.

61. Goldingay, *Israel's Life*, 502–3.

62. Brueggemann, *Jeremiah*, 209.

63. Goldingay, *Israel's Life*, 339–41.

64. Goldingay, *Israel's Life*, 557–59.

65. Goldingay, *Israel's Faith*, 553.

66. Goldingay, *Israel's Faith*, 832.

67. Davies, "Theodicy," 815.

ing work of justice, mercy, and restoration in the world. This perspective challenges Latin-Augustinian-Reformation theological paradigms and highlights the importance of understanding righteousness as relational and transformative rather than merely a legal or moral standard.[68]

Paul describes this righteousness as the very heart of the good news (Rom 1:17).[69] It is God's faithfulness on display, his unwavering commitment to set things right. We see it in the cross, where justice and mercy meet, and in the resurrection, where life triumphs over death (Rom 3:5, 3:21–22, 25–26; 10:3). It is God's gracious action on our behalf, a righteousness that makes us new and draws us into right relationship with him, with others, and with the world he loves. To grasp this truth is not merely to understand a doctrine but to encounter the God who makes wrong things right and calls us to live as people shaped by that same grace.

Paul's message is deeply rooted in the Hebrew Scriptures, particularly in his description of the gospel as the revelation of the "righteousness of God" (Rom 1:17).[70] This language is shaped decisively by Isaiah's portrayal of God's covenant faithfulness and saving justice. Isaiah's proclamations of God's righteous acts on behalf of Israel inform Paul's understanding of righteousness as both a divine attribute and a gracious gift bestowed upon believers. In this way, Paul echoes Isaiah's vision of God's redemptive intervention in history, in which divine faithfulness is enacted through saving action for God's people and, ultimately, for the nations (Isa 45:21–25).[71]

Paul's use of Isaiah 52:7 in Romans 10:15 further connects the gospel with the heralding of God's righteousness. The imagery of the messenger bringing "good news" of salvation and proclaiming, "Your God reigns!" (Isa 52:7), aligns with Paul's proclamation of the gospel as the fulfillment of God's redemptive purposes. Paul's adaptation of this Isaianic imagery highlights the continuity between Israel's Scriptures and the Christ-event, portraying the gospel as the realization of God's promised deliverance.[72]

68. Brueggemann, *Theology of the Old Testament*, 199. See also Stendahl, "Apostle Paul and the Introspective Conscience of the West," 78–96; Sanders, *Paul and Palestinian Judaism*.

69. See Longenecker, *Romans*, 168–76; see also Longenecker, *Introducing Romans*, 388–400.

70. Ropes, "'Righteousness' and 'The Righteousness of God,'" 211–27.

71. Wagner, *Heralds*, 120–21.

72. Hays, *Echoes*, 36–41.

Paul interprets and proclaims this relational and restorative righteousness through the lens of the Christ-event. For Paul, the righteousness of God is most fully revealed in the life, death, and resurrection of Jesus Christ. In Romans 1:16–17, Paul declares that the gospel reveals the righteousness of God. This righteousness is not merely a legal declaration but a dynamic act of reconciliation and renewal.[73] It restores the broken relationship between humanity and God, addressing the alienation caused by sin.[74] Paul's understanding of justification by faith (Rom 3:22; 5:1) emphasizes the transformative power of God's righteousness, which reconciles those enslaved to sin and brings them into the covenant community.

Paul's theology also aligns with the Hebrew Bible's vision of righteousness as a social and communal reality.[75] In 2 Corinthians 5:18–21, Paul describes believers as ambassadors of reconciliation entrusted with the message of God's righteousness. This ministry reflects the church's calling to embody God's justice and mercy in a fractured world. For Paul, the church is a living demonstration of God's righteousness, transcending divisions of ethnicity, class, and culture (Gal 3:28; Rom 15:7). The unity and love displayed within the covenant community are signs of God's restorative work in the world.[76]

For Paul, God's righteousness is not an abstract attribute but a concrete, historical act of salvation through Jesus Christ (Rom 1:16–17, 3:21–26). Righteousness is the restoration of relationships. In Christ, God reconciles humanity to himself, offering restored fellowship to a fractured world. It is God's faithfulness to his covenant promises, revealed through Christ. This divine act restores the broken relationship between God and humanity, which had been marred by sin. God's righteousness, in this sense, is not a judicial act. It is God's forgiving love and redemptive intervention in the world, manifest in Christ's death. This act is a gift that is received by faith and leads to justification and the restoration of the divine–human relationship.

This righteousness is dynamic and missional, as God actively works to reconcile all things to himself.[77] Paul highlights this in 2 Corinthians 5:17–21, showing that believers are entrusted with the ministry of

73. Schreiner, *Romans*, 115–56.

74. Tarazi, *Romans*, 47.

75. Goldingay, *Israel's Gospel*, 56.

76. Goldingay, *Israel's Faith*, 341.

77. Goldingay, *Israel's Faith*, 553.

reconciliation. Ultimately, Paul's vision of God's righteousness is cosmic, encompassing the restoration of creation itself, as described in Romans 8. For Paul, the righteousness of God is the foundation of his mission to participate in God's redemptive work among the nations.[78] His apostolic calling centers on proclaiming the righteousness of God and inviting others into this reconciled relationship. He also viewed the church as a living testimony of God's righteousness (Gal 3:28; Rom 15:7).

God's righteousness encompasses both who God is and what God does. God is holy and just, yet also merciful and compassionate, faithful to covenant promises even in the face of human unfaithfulness. Divine justice is neither cold nor abstract but is expressed through steadfast love. In God's righteousness, judgment is not the final word; redemption is.[79] Through Jesus Christ, God's justice and mercy converge. The cross bears witness to a God who remains true to divine holiness while graciously opening the way to forgiveness, reconciliation, and restored relationship.

The righteousness of God names God's active, redemptive purpose to restore right relationships between himself and humanity and the whole of creation. This theological vision animates Paul's apostolic ministry and shapes the substance of his gospel proclamation, his approach to forming churches, and his relentless commitment to "present everyone mature in Christ" (Col 1:28).

Romans 1:16–17 places the gospel at the living center of Paul's theology and mission. The gospel is the power of God at work for salvation, revealing a righteousness grounded not in human achievement but in God's covenant faithfulness. This righteousness is God's decisive commitment to set things right—healing broken relationships, renewing communities, and reclaiming creation through the Christ-event.

By grounding the gospel in Israel's Scriptures while proclaiming its fulfillment in Jesus Christ, Paul refuses both novelty and nostalgia. The gospel is ancient in promise and radically new in fulfillment. It confronts entrenched systems of power, reconfigures honor and shame, and summons faith as a sustained posture of trust and allegiance. Salvation, in this vision, exceeds individual forgiveness; it encompasses reconciliation, transformation, and active participation in God's ongoing work of renewal. This is why Paul is not ashamed of the gospel.

78. Schreiner, *Romans*, 535–36.

79. McGrath, *Historical Theology*, 71–73.

10

Paul's Apostolic Method, Romans 15:14–33

ROMANS 15:14–33 DRAWS THE reader into the lived reality of Paul's apostolic life and the unfolding movement of the gospel. Having laid out his theological vision, Paul now speaks personally, situating himself and the Roman believers within a shared missionary story. He recounts how the grace given to him has shaped his ministry among the nations, describes the path the gospel has already taken from Jerusalem to the eastern reaches of the empire, and casts his eyes westward toward Rome and Spain. Along the way, Paul weaves together theology, geography, and relationship, presenting mission not as a solitary endeavor but as a communal vocation. The collection for Jerusalem becomes a concrete expression of reconciled Jewish–gentile unity, while his appeal for prayer underscores dependence on the Spirit rather than human strategy. In this passage, Paul invites the Roman churches to see themselves not as passive recipients of his letter but as active partners in God's mission, drawn into the ongoing movement of the gospel toward the ends of the earth.

PAUL'S PRIESTLY SERVICE TO THE NATIONS

Paul describes his ministry as a "priestly service of the gospel of God" (Rom 15:16), an image that evokes the Jewish priesthood yet reorients it around the new covenant in Christ.[1] His role is not merely to proclaim

1. Gibson, "Paul the Missionary," 51–62.

the gospel but to present the nations as a sanctified offering to God, shaped by the transforming work of the Holy Spirit. This reflects Paul's understanding of mission as more than evangelism; it is about forming a holy community that glorifies God.[2]

He makes it clear that the success of his mission is not due to his own ability but to what Christ has accomplished through him: "I will not venture to speak of anything except what Christ has accomplished through me" (15:18). This humility reflects Paul's belief that mission is ultimately God's work, carried out through human vessels.[3] Paul does not claim personal credit but attributes all fruitfulness to Christ's power working through him.

OBEDIENCE OF FAITH AND THE POWER OF THE SPIRIT

Paul describes his ministry as drawing the nations into the "obedience of faith" (15:18), a phrase that binds belief and transformation into a single reality. Faith, for Paul, is never mere assent to ideas. It is a decisive reorientation of life brought about by an encounter with the risen Christ, one that reshapes allegiance, practice, and purpose.[4] To believe the gospel is to be drawn into a life of obedience, a life increasingly ordered by the will of God.

This vision of faith is embodied in the way Paul understands his own ministry. He insists that his work among the nations has not been carried out by words alone but "by word and deed, by the power of signs and wonders, by the power of the Spirit of God" (15:18–19). Proclamation and embodiment belong together. The gospel is spoken, but it is also enacted, made visible through Spirit-empowered lives and, at times, through signs that testify to the inbreaking reign of God.[5] At every point, Paul locates the effectiveness of mission not in human ability but in the active presence of the Spirit, who empowers both the messenger and the message.[6]

From Jerusalem to Illyricum, Paul can say that he has "fulfilled the ministry of the gospel of Christ" (15:19). This claim is not one of

2. Rosner, "Glory of God," 158–68.
3. Tennent, *Invitation to World Missions*, 53–101.
4. Käsemann, *Romans*, 393.
5. Reymond, *Paul Missionary Theologian*, 385–420.
6. Warrington, *Pentecostal Theology*, 59, 127.

completion in a statistical sense, as though every person had heard, but of faithfulness to a pioneering calling. Paul's vocation has been to push the gospel into new territory, laying foundations in strategic centers and establishing communities of faith where Christ had not yet been named. His ministry traces a widening arc across the eastern Mediterranean, a testament to a mission driven not by personal ambition but by a desire to see the gospel take root among the nations.

PAUL'S AMBITION TO REACH THE UNREACHED

Paul's ambition is "to preach the gospel, not where Christ has already been named, lest I build on someone else's foundation" (15:20). This reveals his priority of reaching the unreached. Paul does not seek to establish himself in already evangelized regions but instead pushes the boundaries of the mission field.[7] His work aligns with Isaiah's prophecy: "Those who have never been told of him will see, and those who have never heard will understand" (15:21). Paul sees his mission as the fulfillment of God's promise to extend salvation to the nations.[8] His priority had been establishing churches in new regions, but now, having completed that phase, he turns his attention to Spain via Rome (15:22–29).

PAUL'S DESIRE TO VISIT ROME

Paul explains that his long delay in visiting Rome has not been due to neglect but to vocation. "This is the reason why I have so often been hindered from coming to you" (15:22), he tells them, as he traces the demands of a ministry focused on pioneering work where Christ had not yet been named. Now, however, with his work in the eastern regions complete and his obligations in Jerusalem nearly fulfilled, Paul looks westward. He hopes to visit Rome on his way to Spain, not simply for fellowship but to enlist the Roman churches as partners in his ongoing apostolic mission.[9] "I hope to see you in passing . . . and to be helped on my journey there by you" (15:24), a phrase that assumes practical support

7. Gaventa, "Mission of God," 69–72.
8. Wright, *Paul and the Faithfulness of God*, 812–14.
9. Little, *Mission in the Way of Paul.*

and shared responsibility, much as Antioch had once provided for his earlier missionary endeavors.[10]

Paul anticipates arriving in Rome "in the fullness of the blessing of Christ" (15:29), expecting an encounter marked by mutual encouragement and spiritual enrichment.[11] Yet even as he plans this visit, he underscores that mission advances through more than travel and strategy alone.[12] He urges the Roman believers to "strive together with me in your prayers to God on my behalf" (15:30), framing intercessory prayer as an essential act of partnership in the work of the gospel. For Paul, mission is a shared vocation, empowered by the Spirit and sustained through the faithful solidarity of the churches.[13] His appeal insists that the gospel does more than reconcile individuals—it forges a unified, interdependent people mobilized for God's redemptive mission among the nations.[14]

THE COLLECTION FOR JERUSALEM: A SIGN OF UNITY

However, before turning west toward Spain through Rome, Paul sets his course eastward to Jerusalem, carrying with him a financial offering gathered from gentile churches for the poor among the Jewish believers there (15:25–26). This collection is far more than an act of charity. For Paul, it is a concrete, embodied expression of the gospel itself. What God has accomplished in Christ has bound Jews and gentiles into a single people, and the sharing of material resources becomes a visible sign of that new reality.[15] Those from the nations, having received Israel's spiritual heritage, now respond by meeting the material needs of the Jerusalem church (15:27). In this exchange, Paul envisions the church as one body, sustained by mutual dependence and marked by the crossing of ethnic and cultural boundaries in Christ.[16]

Yet Paul approaches Jerusalem with clear-eyed realism. He knows the journey carries risk and anticipates resistance, both from those

10. Kruse, *Romans*, 544.
11. Dunn, *Theology of Paul*, 731–32.
12. Downs, *Offering*, 146–57.
13. Schreiner, *Romans*, 930–31.
14. Schnabel, *Paul the Missionary*, 401–4.
15. Downs, *Offering*, 3–8.
16. Downs, *Offering*, 9–14.

outside the church and from those who remain suspicious of his mission. For this reason, he appeals to the Roman believers to "strive together with me in your prayers to God on my behalf" (15:30). Mission, in Paul's telling, advances not through strategy or courage alone but through shared struggle before God. Intercessory prayer becomes an essential form of participation in the mission, underscoring that the work of the gospel requires embodied action and sustained spiritual solidarity alike.

PAUL'S MISSION STRATEGY

Following his encounter with the risen Jesus on the road to Damascus (Acts 9:1–25), Paul's life and vocation were decisively reoriented. He soon traveled to Jerusalem, where he met with the apostles, particularly Peter and James (Acts 9:26–32). Though initial suspicion surrounded him, these encounters marked the beginning of the church's eventual recognition of his calling as a fellow apostle. That calling was later publicly affirmed by the Spirit-led community in Antioch, who, through prayer and the laying on of hands, sent Paul and Barnabas into missionary service (Acts 13:1–3). From this point forward, Paul understood himself as one called and set apart by the will of God to be an apostle of Christ Jesus to the nations (Rom 1:1–6; 1 Cor 1:1). This conviction was central to his identity. Throughout his letters, Paul speaks with clarity and confidence about the authority entrusted to him and the particular regions and peoples assigned to his care.[17]

Paul's apostolic practice reflected both theological conviction and cultural adaptability. In city after city, he began by entering the local synagogue, engaging Jews and God-fearing gentiles from the Scriptures he knew so well as a former Pharisee.[18] Yet his ministry extended far beyond synagogue walls. He reasoned in marketplaces (Acts 17:17), taught in lecture halls (Acts 19:9), worked in workshops (Acts 18:3), and proclaimed the gospel in private homes (Acts 16:14–15, 32–34; 18:8; 1 Cor 1:16; 16:15).[19] Wherever people gathered, Paul met them. As communities of faith emerged, he established local churches, appointed leaders, provided instruction, and maintained ongoing pastoral and theological engagement through letters, many of which would later be received as Scripture.

17. Beker, *Paul*, 5.

18. See Acts 13:5, 14; 14:1; 16:12–13; 17:1, 10; 17:17; 18:1, 4, 19; 19:8.

19. Schnabel, *Paul the Missionary*, 287–306.

Paul's commitment to the gospel was also expressed through his willingness to support himself financially through tentmaking. Though tentmaking was associated with a lower social class, Paul, an educated Roman citizen, embraced it as a form of missional flexibility and accommodation. More than a practical choice, his manual labor embodied a deeper theological posture. By relinquishing his rights and working with his hands, Paul enacted a form of self-enslavement for the sake of the gospel.[20]

The book of Acts presents Paul's ministry as unfolding through a recognizable pattern, one that aligns with Jesus's programmatic vision of witness "in Jerusalem, and in all Judea and Samaria, and to the ends of the earth" (Acts 1:8).[21] Beginning with the Jewish people, the gospel took root through proclamation, Spirit-empowered signs, the formation of disciplined communities, and the multiplication of leaders and churches.[22] In Jerusalem, thousands responded to the apostles' preaching, devoting themselves to teaching, fellowship, the breaking of bread, and prayer (Acts 2:42–47; 4:4). Even moments of internal crisis did not halt the movement; the church continued to grow so that "more and more men and women believed in the Lord and were added to their number" (Acts 5:14). Within a short time, vibrant communities of faith spread throughout Judea and Galilee (Acts 9:31), forming a national movement among the Jewish people.

From there, the gospel crossed long-standing boundaries. It spread among the Samaritans, whose reception of the message prompted apostolic confirmation from Jerusalem. As Peter and John laid hands on the new believers, they, too, received the Holy Spirit, and the gospel continued to advance throughout Samaritan towns and villages (Acts 8:8–25). What had begun in Jerusalem was now unmistakably expanding.

Paul's own conversion and subsequent commissioning marked a decisive turning point in this outward movement. As the gospel took root among gentiles, the Jerusalem church came to recognize that God had indeed "granted repentance unto life" to the nations as well (Acts 11:18). Antioch emerged as a pivotal center of this gentile mission. There, Paul and Barnabas spent a full year teaching and forming a diverse community of believers, Jews and gentiles together, who were first called Christians (Acts 11:25–26). From Antioch, the gospel would continue to

20. Gorman and Gupta, *Cruciformity*, 183–84.

21. Amstutz, *Disciples of All Nations*.

22. Schnabel, *Paul the Missionary*, 256–87.

radiate outward through Paul's apostolic ministry, carried into strategic urban centers whose cultural influence and trade networks facilitated the spread of the faith across the Mediterranean world.[23]

Taken together, Paul's calling, methods, and movements reveal a coherent apostolic vision. He proclaims Christ where he has not been named, forms communities shaped by the Spirit and the teaching of the apostles, and entrusts leadership to local believers so that the gospel might continue to advance long after he moves on. His ministry is both pioneering and pastoral, rooted in divine calling and expressed through adaptable, reproducible patterns that carry the witness of Christ to the nations.

These patterns reveal what may be described as four interrelated stages in the formation of the earliest *national church movements*, movements that penetrated entire regions, crossed cultural boundaries, and ultimately reshaped the Roman Empire. Among peoples who shared common language, culture, and social networks, the gospel consistently took root and expanded through a recognizable process. An initiating stage emerged as the gospel was proclaimed and a church was planted in a strategic center, forming a disciplined community devoted to the apostles' teaching, fellowship, the breaking of bread, and prayer (Acts 2:42–47). This was followed by a nurturing stage, in which the church was strengthened through instruction, pastoral care, and the development of emerging leaders (Acts 6:1–7). As these communities matured, an expanding stage took shape, marked by the multiplication of churches throughout a wider region and the structuring of leadership appropriate to the local context (Acts 8:25; 9:31). Finally, a sending stage emerged, as established churches extended their witness beyond their own regions and commissioned new missionaries for further gospel advance (Acts 11:26–30; 13:1–3).

Throughout this process, the gospel was proclaimed in the power of the Holy Spirit, and its effects were both immediate and enduring. Those who repented and believed were baptized, filled with the Spirit, incorporated into the fellowship of believers, and taught to obey all that Christ had commanded. Discipleship was not static but reproductive. New believers shared the good news within their households and social networks, and churches grew organically as faith spread through relational ties. These emerging communities were nurtured through sustained

23. Major urban centers such as Antioch, Ephesus, Corinth, Philippi, and Thessalonica provided diverse populations, cultural influence, and trade routes that facilitated the spread of ideas. See Meeks, *Urban Christians*, 18.

teaching and embodied models of "sound doctrine," forming believers whose lives reflected the transforming power of the gospel.

As the number of disciples increased, leadership naturally emerged from within the community. Those who demonstrated faithfulness in their households and maturity in character were entrusted with greater responsibility in the life of the church (1 Tim 3:1–13; Titus 1:5–16). The development of such leaders strengthened existing congregations and created the conditions necessary for further multiplication. Churches became increasingly self-supporting, self-governing, and self-propagating, expressing their faith in ways that resonated with their cultural setting while remaining anchored in apostolic teaching.

It is within this missional framework that Paul's sweeping claim in Romans 15 comes into focus. His strategy of proclaiming the gospel in key urban centers and nurturing reproducible communities helps explain how he could say, "From Jerusalem and all the way around to Illyricum I have fulfilled the ministry of the gospel of Christ. . . . I no longer have any room for work in these regions" (Rom 15:19, 23). Paul did not mean that every individual had been reached, but that the gospel had been firmly established through communities capable of carrying the mission forward.[24] With these foundations in place, he was free to look beyond the eastern Mediterranean and set his sights on Spain, trusting that the Spirit-formed churches would continue the work he had begun.

WHY SPAIN?

How did Paul determine where to go? We can find several factors that contribute to how Paul concludes that God is guiding him to a specific people or place. As mentioned above, Paul's mission as an apostle was understood as a divine calling as a chosen instrument to proclaim Christ among the nations (Acts 9:15–16). This calling not only laid the foundation for Paul's self-identity but also guided his mission. The apostle always seemed to be in "go mode," looking for new opportunities.[25]

Throughout his ministry, Paul consistently relies on the guidance of the Holy Spirit, discerning God's direction through both restraint and compulsion. At times, the Spirit closed doors, preventing him from entering regions such as Asia Minor (Acts 16:6–7). At other moments, Paul

24. Amstutz, *Disciples of All Nations*, 17–19.

25. Schnabel, *Paul the Missionary*, 35.

experienced a compelling inner constraint, describing himself as "bound by the Spirit" as he set his course for Jerusalem, fully aware that suffering awaited him there (Acts 20:22–23). Guidance also came through visions and revelations. In Troas, Paul received the vision of a Macedonian calling for help, a moment that redirected the missionary trajectory of the gospel into Europe (Acts 16:9–10). Later, in Jerusalem, the Lord appeared to Paul and assured him that he would bear witness in Rome as well (Acts 23:11), anchoring his mission in divine promise rather than circumstance.

God's guidance, however, was not limited to extraordinary experiences. Paul also recognized the hand of divine providence in ordinary events and open doors for ministry. He interpreted opportunities such as extended seasons of effective work in Ephesus as evidence of God's direction (1 Cor 16:5–9). Frequently, this guidance took relational form through providential encounters with individuals whose lives became entwined with the advance of the gospel. Lydia's hospitality opened a foothold for the church in Philippi (Acts 16:11–15), the conversion of the Philippian jailer transformed a moment of crisis into a new household of faith (Acts 16:25–40), and figures such as Onesimus would later embody the gospel's reconciling power within complex social relationships (Phlm 1). Underlying all of this was Paul's deep commitment to prayer. He sought discernment through prayer, fasting, and communal listening with other believers, trusting that God's direction would emerge through sustained dependence on the Spirit.

Yet in Romans, Paul's guidance takes on a distinctive shape. Rather than recounting visions or dramatic interventions, Paul frames his mission through Scripture, especially the book of Isaiah.[26] As noted earlier, his understanding of apostleship is deeply informed by Isaiah's servant songs (Isa 42:1–4; 49:1–6; 50:4–9; 52:13–53:12). These texts portray the servant as one called to bring light to the nations, to enact God's salvation through faithful obedience, and to fulfill God's purposes through suffering rather than triumphalism. In Romans, Paul implicitly locates his own ministry within this scriptural narrative. His apostolic vocation is shaped not only by the Spirit's immediate leading but also by a sustained, Scripture-formed imagination that understands mission as participation in God's redemptive work for Israel and the nations, even when that path leads through hardship and rejection.

26. See Cole, *Isaiah's Servant in Paul*; and Wagner, *Heralds*.

Paul believed that Jesus fulfilled the role of the suffering servant described in Isaiah. In light of this understanding, Paul saw his own ministry as being modeled after Jesus and the servant described in Isaiah. He saw himself as a servant of Christ, called to proclaim the gospel, suffer for the sake of the gospel, and bring salvation to both Jews and gentiles. Paul saw his ministry as participating in the redemptive work of Christ, following the pattern of the suffering servant.

Paul had completed his ministry in the eastern regions of the Roman Empire and now set his sights on Spain, a major Roman province in the far west. References to Spain in Romans 15:24 and 15:28 have long puzzled interpreters,[27] yet fresh insights suggest clear missional intent.[28]

Spain thus represented a fitting next horizon for the apostle to the nations. Widely regarded as "barbarian" within the Roman imagination, the region lay at the far margins of the empire, with little, if any, Jewish presence and limited integration into Greco-Roman cultural life. It therefore embodied the full scope of Paul's self-understanding as one "indebted both to Greeks and to barbarians" (Rom 1:15). Geographically, Spain completed the northern arc of the Mediterranean world, from Jerusalem through Illyricum and Rome, extending Paul's mission toward what could be envisioned as the symbolic "ends of the earth" (Rom 15:19).

Paul likely also viewed his mission through the lens of Isaiah 66:19, where God sends messengers to Tarshish to proclaim his glory among the nations. In Jewish and early Christian imagination, Tarshish was identified with Tartessos in Spain near the Straits of Gibraltar. It was the edge of the known world. By pressing toward Spain, Paul was not simply expanding territory; he was fulfilling prophecy. His aim was to bring the nations' final "offering" (Rom 15:16), completing the great circle of redemption so that "the full number of the Gentiles" might come in (Rom 11:25). Spain was the culmination of Paul's eschatological vision: the gospel carried to the ends of the earth.

When considering Paul's calling as an apostle to the nations, his sensitivity to the Spirit's guidance in all its forms, and his reading of Isaiah, one can make a case that not only was Spain a reasonable choice for his next season of missionary work, but that it would have been seen by the apostle to be a divine calling and a sacred obligation (Rom 1:14). It was

27. Dunn, *Romans 9–16*, 872.

28. Fitzmyer, *Romans*, 717.

this sacred obligation that compelled Paul to engage with the believers in Rome (Rom 1:15). However, for this partnership to thrive, substantial challenges had to be addressed.

Obstacles to the Spanish Mission

If the congregations in Rome were participating in the Empire's culture of honor and shame, they would have little or no interest in a mission project to the despised people of Spain, for everyone outside the Greco-Roman world were considered barbarians, outside the bounds of recognized humanity.[29] Though Rome initially arrived in Hispania (modern-day Spain) in 218 BCE, the region was not fully subdued until 19 BCE under Emperor Augustus. The conquest of Hispania was a long and arduous process, beginning with Rome's involvement in the Second Punic War and culminating in the defeat of the Cantabri and Astures. However, military dominance did not immediately translate into cultural assimilation. The process of Romanization, the spread of Roman language, customs, and institutions, varied widely across the peninsula. While urban centers and coastal regions, particularly those along the Mediterranean, adapted more quickly to Roman influence, the interior and mountainous areas remained resistant, preserving indigenous traditions and social structures for generations.[30]

Spain, with its stubborn resistance to Greco-Roman culture, was the land of barbarians "par excellence."[31] These Spanish barbarians were on the edge, or perhaps even outside, of humanity; sub-humans to be conquered, not evangelized. Yet, Paul is compelled by Scripture and the Spirit of God to take the gospel even to them.[32] If Paul is to reach Spain, he will need the help of the Roman churches, but if they are blinded by cultural biases, they will not participate in the mission.

Paul thus faced a double challenge: not only persuading the Roman churches to support a mission to a people they regarded as less than fully human but also confronting the practical reality that Spain itself offered

29. Jensen, *Barbarians in the Greek and Roman World.*

30. See Broughton, "Romanization of Spain," 645–51; Vigeura et al., "Romanization of Spain."

31. Schreiner, *Romans*, 924.

32. Bosch, *Transforming Mission*, 148–49.

none of the social, religious, or economic entry points on which his missionary practice normally depended.

Evidence of substantial Jewish settlement in Spain does not appear until the third and fourth centuries CE.[33] The absence of Jewish settlements in Spain created several significant obstacles to Paul's earlier missionary strategy. This lack of synagogues eliminated the avenues that Paul typically used to establish a base of operations. Without the synagogue as a starting point, it would have been extremely difficult, especially for a tentmaker from Paul's social class, to make important contacts with the right patrons. The absence of synagogues would pose an associated economic problem since Jewish travelers often used such buildings as convenient lodgings and places to socialize or develop business contacts. This network formed the economic framework for Paul's self-supporting missionary strategy. In the case of Spain, bases of operations and the recruitment of suitable patrons would be required due to the lack of resources of local synagogues and Jewish contacts.

WHY APPEAL TO THE ROMAN CHURCHES?

Because there was no established Jewish community in Spain, Paul would have needed to rethink his entire missionary strategy for the region.[34] Unlike his work in the eastern Mediterranean, where synagogues often provided an initial point of contact, Spain offered no such social or religious infrastructure. The absence of a Jewish presence, combined with significant cultural, economic, and linguistic barriers, helps explain part of the purpose behind Paul's Letter to the Romans. Moreover, Spain's economy was largely controlled by the Roman Empire. Its mines, industries, and agricultural lands were under direct imperial oversight, meaning that access to the region required political, economic, and relational connections centered in Rome.[35] For Paul, partnership with influential believers in the imperial capital would have been essential for gaining both access and support for a mission to the western edge of the empire.

This raises a critical question. Why would Paul, who did not found the Roman churches, seek their sponsorship for his Spanish mission? The answer lies in the convergence of his theological vision, strategic

33. Bowers, "Jewish Communities in Spain," 400; Richardson, *Romans in Spain*, 262.

34. Jewett, *Romans*, 74–75.

35. Schreiner, *Romans*, 924–29.

planning, and pastoral intent. Paul's appeal is not opportunistic but integrative. He seeks to draw the Roman churches into the global mission of the gospel as active participants rather than passive observers.

Paul's mission was grounded in his conviction that the gospel is "the power of God for salvation to everyone who believes," embracing both Jews and gentiles (Rom 1:16–17). His stated ambition to preach the gospel "not where Christ has already been named" (Rom 15:20) reflects a deliberate commitment to pioneer unreached regions. Within this framework, Rome's geopolitical significance made it an ideal launching point for a western mission. As the administrative and communicative center of the empire, Rome functioned as a hub for trade, travel, and influence. Establishing a partnership with the Roman churches would provide Paul with the resources, connections, and logistical support necessary to carry the gospel to Spain.

Yet Paul frames this support in explicitly theological terms. Sponsorship from the Roman churches was not merely logistical. Their participation would demonstrate alignment with the gospel's universal scope and with God's redemptive purposes for the nations. Paul understood his mission as an extension of God's covenant faithfulness, now unfolding among the nations. By supporting him, the Roman believers would share in this eschatological vision.

Paul's missionary aim is clear in his repeated references to "passing through" Rome on his way to Spain (Rom 1:11–13; 15:22–29). In Romans 15:24, his use of the verb *propempein*, ("to be sent on by you," NRSVue) underscores the concrete nature of the support he sought. This term evokes the customary practices of early Christian mission, including financial assistance, provisions, protection, and relational endorsement. Paul expected the Roman churches to function as an established sending community for work beyond their immediate context.[36]

This strategy reflects a broader missiological principle: the gospel advances into unreached regions through partnerships with established communities. Still, Paul's request is neither transactional nor utilitarian. It is pastoral and theological. By appealing to the Roman churches for support, Paul integrates them into the ongoing story of God's mission. His theological vision, strategic foresight, and pastoral concern converge to align the Roman congregations with God's redemptive purposes in the world.

36. Balz and Schneider, *Exegetical Dictionary*, 2.160.

While Paul's immediate goal was to enlist the Roman churches' support for his mission to Spain, this appeal also served a larger apostolic purpose. Rome was not simply a waypoint but a partner. Paul seeks to unify and mobilize a divided community so that it might faithfully embody the gospel and participate fully in its global advance. His letter addresses internal tensions within the Roman churches, particularly competing Jewish and Greco-Roman claims to cultural and religious superiority (Rom 14:1–15:7). These divisions threatened both the church's internal health and its missional credibility.

Paul's vision is of a reconciled community that bears witness to the gospel's power to create one new humanity in Christ (see Eph 2:14–16). In this new humanity, distinctions such as "Greek and Jew," "circumcised and uncircumcised," "barbarian, Scythian," "slave and free" no longer function as markers of superiority or exclusion.[37] Instead, Jews and gentiles glorify God together "with one voice" (Rom 15:6). Such unity is essential not only for the church's faithfulness in Rome but also for the credibility and effectiveness of Paul's mission to Spain.

Paul's motives, however, extend beyond securing assistance for travel. He also longs to impart spiritual benefit to the Roman believers themselves. "I long to see you," he writes, "so that I may impart to you some spiritual gift to strengthen you," a gift he immediately defines as mutual encouragement in faith (Rom 1:11–12). Participation in his mission would deepen the Roman churches' own missional identity, strengthening their unity, clarifying their calling, and addressing the seriousness of their situation. In inviting them to sponsor his mission, Paul invites them into transformation, shaping them into a community capable of embodying the gospel they are called to proclaim.

The seriousness of the conflict within the Roman churches is unmistakable. Will Timmins identifies three factors that underscore the gravity of the division between the "weak" and the "strong."[38] First, the dispute reflects an unresolved ethnic divide that the gospel itself is meant to overcome. Evidence from Romans 15:7–13 suggests that the "weak" were predominantly Jewish Christians and the "strong" largely gentile believers. Paul's appeal for mutual acceptance is grounded in Israel's Scriptures and the prophetic promise that gentiles would be incorporated into God's redeemed people. Significantly, Paul avoids ethnic labels,

37. Wright, *Paul and the Faithfulness of God*, 1103–1448.

38. Timmins, "Why Paul Wrote Romans," 395–397.

instead addressing both groups as siblings in Christ (14:10, 13, 15, 21). This rhetorical choice reinforces a shared identity rooted in God's saving action for both Jews and gentiles (1:11) and underscores the interdependence of the community, a theme emphasized through Paul's repeated use of "one another."[39]

Second, Paul frames the conflict as a problem of mutual judgment (14:1–6, 13). Both groups are culpable. Some despise, others condemn, and Paul urges both to abandon these practices (14:13). Such judgmentalism echoes the moral posturing condemned earlier in Romans 2, where individuals usurp God's role as judge. For Paul, justification by faith entails a transformed communal ethic. Those who have been justified are called to embody mutual acceptance rather than condemnation (14:4, 10–12).

Third, the division threatens the foundational virtues of faith, hope, and love. These virtues stand at the heart of Christian life and are central to Paul's vision throughout Romans. The weak struggle to disentangle their faith from cultural and religious practices that are no longer determinative in Christ. The strong, while more theologically confident, are warned that careless exercise of freedom can endanger the faith of others (14:13–23). The pursuit of group honor and the mutual shaming that accompanied this conflict jeopardized not only the presence and witness of the gospel in the capital city but also God's mission to reach the ends of the earth with the good news of Jesus Christ.

Such division undermines the gospel's reconciling power, while judgmental attitudes usurp God's rightful role as judge. The consequences are not only internal. Discord threatens the church's identity and credibility as a community shaped by the gospel. Paul's appeal for reconciliation is therefore both pastoral and missional. A church formed in the "obedience of faith" is essential if Paul's broader aim of bringing the nations to the same obedience is to be realized (1:5; 16:26). The unity he envisions is foundational for future mission, including his planned work in Spain. Pastoral formation and missionary advance are inseparable in Paul's thinking. The church's obedience of faith is crucial for the advancement of the gospel.

Paul's pastoral concern is not secondary or preparatory. It is integral to his mission. He seeks to unify Jewish and gentile believers and to clarify their shared covenantal responsibilities before God. Romans

39. Rom 1:12, 27; 2:15; 12:5, 10, 16; 13:8; 14:13, 19; 15:7, 14; 16:16.

proclaims God's redemptive justice in Christ and calls a diverse community to live in faithful harmony.[40] Paul's theology of God's righteousness, Christ's resurrection, and the message of reconciliation shapes his vision for a church that embodies the gospel it proclaims.[41]

Despite his strong sense of obligation to preach the gospel among the nations, Paul never loses sight of the relational dimension of ministry. He is neither a detached theologian nor a purely strategic missionary. He invests deeply in people and communities. His ministry is marked by personal engagement, pastoral attentiveness, and sustained relationships that nurture faith and unity.

Paul devoted himself to discipling believers, mentoring leaders, and addressing concrete spiritual and communal challenges. His letters, filled with personal greetings and expressions of affection, testify to his conviction that the church is an interconnected body rather than a loose network of congregations. This relational emphasis is especially evident in Romans 14–16, where Paul combines pastoral exhortation with extensive personal greetings. By naming individuals across ethnic, social, and gender lines, including Jews and gentiles, enslaved and free, women and men, leaders and ordinary believers, Paul demonstrates that the gospel creates a community defined not by cultural hierarchies but by mutual love and shared belonging. Doctrine and relationship are inseparable in his vision.

This emphasis on reciprocity is already apparent in Romans 1:11–15, where Paul articulates his desire to impart spiritual benefit, experience mutual encouragement, bear fruit among them, and proclaim the gospel. These aims reflect a collaborative vision of mission, one that depends on shared responsibility between local congregations and apostolic initiative.

Romans offers an unparalleled glimpse into the unity of Paul's missiology and ecclesiology. The letter reveals both his missionary motivation (1:1–17) and his missionary strategy (15:14–33). At the same time, Paul writes amid uncertainty. His impending journey to Jerusalem carried real risks, including threats to his safety and concerns over the reception of the gentile collection. Internal tensions within the Roman churches further complicated his plans, particularly disagreements regarding the

40. Bryan, *Preface to Romans*, 89.

41. Bryan, *Preface to Romans*, 11–41.

role of the law. Romans addresses these challenges by laying a theological and relational foundation for partnership.

From a missiological perspective, the letter highlights the mutual dependence of local churches and translocal mission. As Ralph Winter later articulated through his distinction between modalities and sodalities, both structures are essential for the fulfillment of the Great Commission.[42] This framework will be explored in subsequent chapters.

Paul's commitment to both the mission of God and the people of God provides a vital foundation for understanding his theological vision. His letters are not abstract theological treatises but contextual writings shaped by lived realities, communal tensions, and enduring relationships. As this chapter has shown, Paul's ministry holds together theological depth, pastoral care, and missionary urgency. The next section will examine Romans as contextual theology for the church, attending to how Paul addresses the specific challenges of the Roman churches while remaining faithful to the gospel's universal scope.

We will then propose that Romans offers a missional framework for navigating the liminal space between church and mission, between gathered worship and sent witness. In doing so, the letter illuminates the dynamic interplay between modalities and sodalities within God's redemptive purposes.[43] Romans ultimately reminds us that global mission is the work of the whole body of Christ, as local churches and apostolic missions partner together in obedience to the gospel for the sake of the nations.

42. Modalities, such as local congregations, provide the foundation for Christian community, while sodalities, like missionary movements, extend the gospel beyond these boundaries. See Winter, "Two Structures," 121–39.

43. Thomassen, *Liminality and the Modern*.

PART 3

Romans as Missional Theology for the Church

If Romans provides a missiology for the nations, it also offers a missional theology for the church itself. The language of *missional*, rooted in the Latin *missio* ("sending"), reflects a theological vision in which mission is not an activity the church undertakes but a reality in which it participates. The church is not simply an institution that sends missionaries; it is a community defined by being sent, caught up in the *missio Dei*.[1] This vision integrates worship, communal life, witness, and justice and resonates deeply with Paul's theological imagination in Romans.

Romans aims to re-form a fragmented and diverse community around the mission of God. Paul's concern extends beyond individual salvation to the formation of a reconciled people shaped by the gospel. The church emerges not as a collection of converts but as a community called to embody the gospel's reconciling power in its shared life and public witness.

Paul's contextual articulation of the gospel yields a missional theology shaped by the concrete realities facing the Roman churches and interpreted through the Christ event. The letter is forward-looking and participatory, oriented not only toward doctrinal clarity but toward forming a community ready to participate in God's redemptive movement toward the nations. In this way, Romans advances a subversive vision that reconfigures dominant cultural values and equips the

1. See DuBose, *God Who Sends*; Bosch, *Transforming Mission*; Guder, *Missional Church*; and Gelder and Zscheile, *Missional Church*, 15.

church to resist conformity and embody an alternative kingdom ethic as a sent people in the world participating in God's reconciling work in the world.

11

Romans as a Contextualized Gospel

Contextualization is a foundational principle in Christian missiology, concerned with faithfully bridging the universal message of the gospel with the particular cultural, social, and religious realities of a people.[1] It is the process by which Christian faith is expressed and embodied in forms that are intelligible, credible, and transformative within a specific context. This involves translating not only language but also practices, symbols, and patterns of life so that the gospel may take root in local soil rather than remain a foreign import.

Contextualization goes beyond surface adaptation. It entails discerning which cultural elements can be affirmed, reshaped, or challenged in light of Scripture, allowing the gospel to speak in the heart language of a community while remaining faithful to its core message. When practiced well, contextualization empowers local leaders to shape the church from within their own cultural framework, ensuring that faith is incarnated rather than imposed. At its heart, contextualization reflects obedience to the Great Commission (Matt 28:19–20), embodying God's intent that the good news be proclaimed and lived among all nations in ways that honor both the gospel and the diversity of human cultures.

Several realities make contextualization essential for every missionary movement. First, contemporary cultures are vastly different from the world of the Bible. While the message of Scripture remains unchanged, the church must learn how to embody that message within the languages, values, and social structures of its own time and place. Second,

1. Flemming, *Contextualization*, 14–15.

no missionary or church proclaims the gospel from a neutral position. All expressions of faith are shaped by cultural assumptions, traditions, and worldviews. Recognizing this reality calls for humility, attentiveness, and a posture of learning, as the gospel encounters each culture anew. Every church develops its own culture, and every articulation of faith is, to some degree, culturally mediated.

Finally, contextualization lies at the heart of mission itself, since the gospel is always communicated across cultural boundaries. Christianity emerged in a Middle Eastern context and was later articulated within Greco-Roman and Western frameworks, where much of modern theology was formed. Yet theology shaped in one context must continually be reinterpreted as the gospel encounters new cultures and worldviews. Without this ongoing process, the message of Christ risks sounding distant and abstract rather than being received as the living Word that speaks within each people and generation.

Historians and anthropologists help missiologists recognize the indispensable role of history in this process.[2] History is not merely a record of past events but the foundation upon which cultural identity, values, and collective memory are formed.[3] Narratives preserved through story, song, and ritual shape a community's sense of belonging, while art, architecture, and literature embody a people's worldview across generations. Shared experiences of suffering and triumph forge communal identity and reveal patterns of continuity and change. For the missionary, engaging a culture's history is an act of respect and attentiveness, enabling the gospel to take root within a people's lived story rather than displacing it.

Paul's Letter to the Romans offers a paradigmatic example of contextualization. Paul does not dilute the gospel to fit his audience, nor does he present it in culturally abstract terms.[4] Instead, he translates the gospel faithfully into the social, religious, and political realities of the Roman churches, addressing their specific challenges while remaining anchored in the Christ event.[5] For Paul, contextualization is inseparable from the mission of God, allowing the gospel's transformative power to confront and reshape diverse contexts.[6]

2. Hiebert, *Anthropological Insights*, 15–39.
3. Hiebert, *Anthropological Insights*, 113.
4. Flemming, *Contextualization*, 18–20.
5. Longenecker, *Introducing Romans*, 160.
6. Osborne, "Hermeneutics/Interpreting Paul," 396.

Rooted in the incarnation, contextualization reflects the pattern of Christ himself, who entered human culture without compromising his divinity.[7] Just as Jesus communicated God's purposes within a first-century Jewish setting, gospel proclamation requires deep engagement with a culture's language, values, and worldview. This discernment affirms elements that reflect God's truth while confronting practices that distort it, as illustrated in Paul's engagement with Greco-Roman religion in Acts 17:16–34. Contextualization is therefore an imperfect but necessary task, seeking to preserve the gospel's integrity while addressing real human questions.

Romans displays Paul's dual contextualization as he addresses both Jewish and gentile believers.[8] For Jewish Christians, Paul engages themes of law, covenant, and Israel's story. In Romans 1:16—4:25, he frames justification by faith through Abraham, a shared ancestral figure, while Romans 9:1—11:36 wrestles with Israel's place in God's redemptive purposes. Paul affirms God's faithfulness to Israel while insisting that gentile inclusion is not a betrayal but a fulfillment of God's promises.

At the same time, Paul addresses gentile believers by articulating the gospel in broadly accessible categories. In Romans 5:1—8:39, he emphasizes humanity's shared bondage to sin, freedom in Christ, and life in the Spirit. In Romans 12:1—13:14, he offers practical instruction centered on love, humility, and communal responsibility, virtues that transcend cultural boundaries while remaining rooted in the gospel. These exhortations equip believers to embody their faith within diverse contexts without compromising its core.

Romans is therefore both a theological masterpiece and an inherently missiological text. Its missiological significance extends beyond the explicit missionary passages of Romans 1:1–17 and 15:14–33. The entire letter demonstrates how the gospel can address specific cultural realities while maintaining theological fidelity. Paul's engagement with Jewish and gentile audiences reflects his intent to unify a diverse church under the lordship of Christ, confronting cultural assumptions and theological distortions in the process.

Contextualization is not merely a communication strategy but a vital missiological practice that enables the church to serve as a prophetic and cross-cultural witness.[9] Cultures contain genuine beauty and truth,

7. Nicholls, "Contextualization," 215.

8. Longenecker, *Romans*, 27.

9. Flemming, *Contextualization*, 104–5.

yet they are also marked by idolatry, injustice, and disordered allegiances. Faithful contextualization allows the gospel to affirm what reflects God's purposes while confronting what stands in opposition to God's righteousness revealed in Christ.[10] In this way, the gospel becomes a light in the darkness, subversively challenging the powers and principalities embedded within cultural systems.[11] Paul's proclamation of Jesus as Lord exemplifies this dynamic, standing as a direct challenge to Roman imperial ideology, exposing the false claims of Caesar, and reorienting human allegiance toward the reign of God's kingdom.

Through contextualization, the church becomes both culturally engaged and theologically distinct. Faithful contextualization holds together incarnation and transcendence, relevance and resistance.[12] It requires theological clarity, spiritual discernment, and dependence on the Holy Spirit to engage culture without capitulating to it. This tension is not a weakness but a defining mark of Christian witness.

Ultimately, contextualization is inherently transformative and subversive. It aligns the church with God's mission to renew cultures and confront powers that resist God's reign.[13] Contextualized communities embody an alternative way of life, challenging cultural idols such as materialism, nationalism, and individualism while bearing witness to the gospel as the power of God for salvation.[14] By offering a countercultural vision of human flourishing rooted in the life, death, and resurrection of Jesus, the contextualized gospel invites individuals and societies to reimagine their loyalties in light of God's kingdom.[15] In doing so, God's people shine as a light in the darkness, a city on a hill, and a foretaste of the new creation.

THE SUBVERSIVENESS OF THE GOSPEL

The gospel of Jesus Christ is inherently subversive, acting as a transformative agent that infiltrates and corrodes oppressive systems from within. At its best, the gospel is subtle in its subversiveness, bringing about

10. Goheen and Sheridan, *Becoming a Missionary Church*, 79–81.

11. Brueggemann, *Prophetic Imagination*, xii. See also Goldingay, *Israel's Faith*, 228–30.

12. Newbigin, *Gospel in a Pluralist Society*, 142–44, 148–49, 152–54.

13. Goheen and Sheridan, *Becoming a Missionary Church*, 208.

14. Jewett, *Romans*, 72.

15. Newbigin, *Open Secret*, 127, 131, 135.

transformation, not through direct confrontation or political revolution but through a radical redefinition of human identity, relationships, and value systems. It is subversive because it challenges the foundational assumptions of oppressive systems.[16] It exposes the falsehoods of power structures built on domination, exploitation, and dehumanization, replacing them with a vision of God's kingdom where every individual is valued as an image-bearer of God. The gospel's power lies in its ability to reshape relationships. This transformation does not occur through overt revolution but through the quiet infiltration of gospel truths into the very heart of these systems.

As Paul writes in Galatians 3:28, "There is neither Jew nor Greek, slave nor free, male nor female, for you are all one in Christ Jesus." This declaration is not a denial of social distinctions but a theological affirmation that those distinctions no longer determine a person's value or status. This new identity renders oppressive systems untenable because they are incompatible with the gospel's vision of equality and mutual love. The apostle Paul's Letter to Philemon exemplifies this subtle yet powerful subversion. While Paul does not explicitly condemn the institution of slavery, his treatment of Onesimus, a runaway slave, and his appeal to Philemon redefine the social and moral framework that undergirded slavery, planting seeds that ultimately undermine its legitimacy.[17]

PAUL'S SUBVERSIVE APPROACH IN THE LETTER TO THE ROMANS

The apostle Paul's Letter to the Romans is a masterclass in subtle yet transformative subversion. In this epistle, Paul engages the deeply ingrained cultural, social, and religious practices of both Jewish and Greco-Roman

16. Newbigin, *Open Secret*, 135.

17. Philemon showcases the gospel's subversive power by addressing the relationship between Philemon, a Christian slave owner, and his runaway slave, Onesimus. Instead of appealing to legal duty, Paul emphasizes spiritual accountability and brotherhood in Christ. Calling Onesimus his "son" and "beloved brother," Paul humanizes him, challenging Roman norms that upheld slavery. His plea for Philemon to receive Onesimus "as you would receive me" undermines hierarchical oppression, subtly advancing societal transformation through relational equality and love within the Christian community. See Pao, *Colossians and Philemon*, 343–47; Moo, *Colossians and Philemon*, 369–79; Daube, "Onesimos," 40–43; Harrill, "Use of the New Testament in the American Slave Controversy," 149–86; Wright, *Paul and the Faithfulness of God*, 68–74; Moss, *God's Ghostwriters*.

audiences. However, rather than directly confronting these practices, he shines the light of the gospel on their underlying darkness, exposing the sinful bondage inherent within them. Paul's approach is both theological and pastoral, weaving a disruptive critique of cultural norms with a vision of the transformative power of the gospel, which liberates individuals and communities from their captivity to sin and death.

Subversion of Roman Power and the Pax Romana

Paul critiques the Roman Empire's claims to ultimate authority. While not explicitly denouncing Caesar, his language and theology undermined imperial ideology that exalted Rome as the source of salvation and peace.[18] For instance, in Romans 1:1–4, Paul calls Jesus the "Son of God" and "Lord," titles often associated with Caesar. By applying these terms to Christ, Paul challenges the imperial cult's divine claims. Similarly, his assertion that the gospel is "the power of God for salvation" (Rom 1:16) contradicts Rome's narrative of salvation through military and political dominance. This subversion is further emphasized in Romans 8, where Paul depicts creation groaning under bondage and longing for liberation through the Spirit. This imagery critiques the futility of human systems and offers a vision of a new creation under Christ's reign.

Subversion of Social and Cultural Hierarchies

In Christ, the hierarchies of power and privilege are overturned.[19] Paul's theology confronts the deep social and cultural divisions of his time, offering an alternative vision of community shaped by grace rather than status. In Romans 12:3–8, he celebrates the diversity and equality of believers within the body of Christ, where each member has a vital and God-given role. This stands in stark contrast to the rigid class structures of Roman society, which elevated wealth, influence, and patronage as the measures of worth.[20] In Romans 14–15, Paul addresses conflicts between Jewish and gentile believers over dietary laws and sacred days. Rather than imposing uniformity, he advocates mutual acceptance and love, urging believers to "welcome one another as Christ has welcomed

18. Elliott, *Arrogance of Nations.*

19. Wink, *Unmasking the Powers*, 26–58.

20. deSilva, *Honor*, 105–6.

you" (Rom 15:7). By prioritizing mutual welcome in Christ over cultural distinctives, Paul subverts exclusionary practices, calling the church to embody the gospel's transformative power and fostering reconciliation and equality in a divided world.

The Light of the Gospel Against the Darkness of Sinful Culture

At the heart of Paul's subversion is the transformative power of the gospel, which exposes the darkness of sinful cultural bondage. In Romans 5–8, Paul portrays sin as a tyrannical power enslaving humanity and leading to death, resonating with those trapped in systems of oppression, idolatry, and corruption.[21] Yet Paul's message is one of liberation: through union with Christ in his death and resurrection, believers are set free from sin's dominion and empowered to live in righteousness. Paul's call for the renewing of the mind in Romans 12:2 further illustrates his subversive strategy. He urges believers not to conform to worldly patterns but to be transformed by the gospel, enabling them to discern and embody God's will. This renewal critiques cultural values and practices that perpetuate sin and injustice, offering a radically different way of life rooted in the kingdom of God. By embodying this transformation, believers become living testimonies to the gospel's power to redeem and restore.

CONTEXTUALIZATION, NOT ASSIMILATION

While the gospel must be contextualized in order to be communicated faithfully and effectively, the church must remain vigilant against assimilation to the dominant powers of this age. Contextualization seeks to render the gospel intelligible and compelling within particular cultural settings, but it must never compromise the church's allegiance to Christ. His kingdom stands in radical contrast to the systems, ideologies, and spiritual forces that shape this world's order, these "cosmic powers of this present darkness" (Eph 6:12).

Assimilation occurs when the church absorbs the values and priorities of the surrounding culture and, in doing so, forfeits its prophetic witness.[22] This danger is particularly evident when the church aligns too closely with political ideologies, economic systems, or cultural norms

21. Croasmun, *Emergence of Sin*.

22. Newbigin, *Gospel in a Pluralist Society*, 142–44, 148–49, 152–54.

that conflict with the gospel's call to justice, mercy, humility, and love. Sadly, history provides sobering examples of the complicity of Christianity with slavery, colonialism, nationalism, genocide, and systemic injustice.[23] To guard against assimilation, the church must continually evaluate its practices and priorities in light of Christ and the witness of Scripture. The gospel must challenge cultural practices that perpetuate inequality, oppression, or idolatry, calling believers to embody an alternative way of living rooted in God's kingdom.[24]

In the World but Not of the World

The church is to remain in the world without being of the world; engaging culture without conforming to it. This delicate balance is sustained through faithful discernment, rooted in Scripture and guided by the Holy Spirit. True contextualization allows the gospel to speak meaningfully within each culture while also confronting its idols by proclaiming the liberating power of the cross and the transforming hope of the resurrection.[25] In doing so, the church retains its prophetic integrity and shines as a light to the world. Poorly executed contextualization risks syncretism, blending Christian teachings with incompatible cultural elements, or even apostasy, where the gospel is entirely subverted.[26] A sobering example is Christianity in Germany. During the Reformation, Martin Luther's contextualization brought renewal as Scripture was made accessible in the vernacular. Over time, however, the church became syncretistic as it aligned with nationalism and cultural supremacy, culminating in the apostasy of the German Christian movement's support of Nazi ideology during the Third Reich.[27]

23. Noll, *Civil War as a Theological Crisis*, 31–78; Jennings, *Christian Imagination*, 27–89; Heschel, *Aryan Jesus*, 1–42; Ericksen, *Theologians Under Hitler*, 3–30; Sanneh, *Translating the Message*, 159–201; Volf, *Exclusion and Embrace*, 16–38; Longman, *Christianity and Genocide in Rwanda*, 1–25.

24. Lois Barrett et al., *Missional Church*, 124.

25. Goheen, *Light to the Nations*, 4–17.

26. This was Lesslie Newbigin's primary challenge with contextualization. See Stults, *Grasping Truth and Reality*.

27. See Ericksen, *Complicity in the Holocaust*; Heschel, *Aryan Jesus*.

LAYING ALL THINGS BARE IN THE LIGHT OF THE GOSPEL

For Paul, the gospel is not a set of doctrines or a moral code but the manifestation of God's righteousness, revealed through the life, death, and resurrection of Jesus Christ. This revelation exposes the Roman context, uncovering the failures of pagan rebellion and the distortions of religious pride, calling all, Jew and gentile alike, to repentance and faith. Through the gospel, God unveils his plan to set right what humanity has broken, addressing sin and its consequences in a way that is both personal and transformative. Embodied in Christ and accessible through faith, the gospel reveals the divine righteousness that humanity's efforts, whether pagan striving or religious observance, cannot achieve.

As we have seen, Rome embodied cultural diversity, moral disorder, and imperial power, and its Christian communities wrestled with questions of identity, unity, and faithfulness amid these pressures. Paul addresses this complex by exposing everyone to the righteousness of God, declaring that all are subject to judgment because "all have sinned and fall short of the glory of God" (Rom 3:23). At the same time, Paul proclaims that this righteousness is now made available through faith in Christ, fulfilling God's promises to both Jews and gentiles alike (Rom 3:21–26).

The cross stands as the ultimate revelation of God's justice and mercy, reconciling humanity to God. The gospel does not merely disclose truth; it summons a response. Paul therefore exhorts the Roman believers to live in light of God's righteousness, relinquishing the divisions that fracture their common life (Rom 12–15). This lived obedience gives concrete expression to the gospel, calling both individuals and communities to align their lives with God's redemptive purposes. In the end, the gospel reveals God's righteousness as subversive, redemptive, and transformative, making all things new.

12

Reconciliation and Relationships in Romans

ROMANS REVEALS THE GOSPEL'S power to transform and reconcile both individuals and communities.[1] Paul's vision of righteousness, rooted in God's faithful action to restore broken relationships, reveals the inherently relational character of the gospel. For Paul, life in the church is fundamentally relational, shaped by and reflecting the reconciliation that God initiates in Christ.

Paul presents righteousness as deeply relational, faith as wholehearted trust, and love as the fullest expression of the gospel. For Paul, the gospel is not merely proclaimed, it is embodied in the lives of believers. This becomes evident in the diversity of those he greets (Rom 16), a mosaic of transformed lives that together reflect the countercultural nature of the early Christian community.

The inclusion of enslaved and formerly enslaved persons, low-status individuals and women in leadership reveals the radical inclusivity of the gospel. Within the church, these relationships become living testimony to God's reconciling power, showing that the good news does not only speak of restoration, but creates it, forming a community that embodies God's reconciling work in the world.

1. Baker and Wagner, "Righteousness of God and Hurricane Mitch," 108–11.

THE GOSPEL OF RECONCILIATION

Paul's theology of reconciliation stands as one of the central pillars of the New Testament. Reconciliation means the transformation of hostility into friendship, the restoration of broken relationships through God's redemptive work in Christ. Found uniquely within Paul's writings, this theme offers a comprehensive vision of salvation that embraces three dimensions: reconciliation between God and humanity, reconciliation among people, and reconciliation with creation itself.[2]

The verb reconcile (*katallassō*) appears several times in Paul's letters, describing both human and divine reconciliation. It refers to restored human relationships (1 Cor 7:11) and to the renewed relationship between God and humanity (Rom 5:10; 2 Cor 5:18–20). The noun reconciliation (*katallagē*) likewise captures this idea of restored harmony (Rom 5:11; 11:15; 2 Cor 5:18–19), while the compound verb "to reconcile completely" (*apokatallassō*) expands the vision to include the entire created order (Col 1:20, 22; Eph 2:16).

In the wider Greek-speaking world, reconciliation often meant the exchange of hostility for peace, whether between nations or individuals.[3] Yet Paul transforms this concept entirely. Reconciliation, for him, is not a human achievement but God's initiative.[4] It is God who crosses the divide, who acts first, restoring fellowship through Christ and inviting all creation into the peace and wholeness of divine love.

At the heart of Paul's theology is the reconciliation of humanity to God, addressing the estrangement caused by sin. Paul portrays sin as both relational and existential, alienating humanity from God and disrupting creation's intended harmony. In Romans 5:10, Paul writes, "For if, while we were God's enemies, we were reconciled to him through the death of his Son, how much more, having been reconciled, shall we be saved through his life." This reconciliation is entirely God's work, rooted in his love and faithfulness (Rom 5:8). It is accomplished through the death of Christ, which removes the barrier of sin and inaugurates peace between God and humanity.

The gospel is the ultimate expression of God's pathos, his deep, compassionate longing to restore relationship with a fallen and broken

2. Balz and Schneider, *Exegetical Dictionary*, 2.261–63.

3. Arndt et al., *Greek-English Lexicon of the New Testament*, 521.

4. Balz and Schneider, *Exegetical Dictionary*, 2.261–63.

humanity and creation.[5] It is through this divine pathos that God initiates and accomplishes reconciliation, revealing the depth of his love and commitment to his creation. The reconciling nature of the gospel is woven into every aspect of Paul's argument. Paul's message calls the church to embody this reconciliation in their communal life, bearing witness to the gospel as lights in the world.[6]

RIGHTEOUSNESS IS RELATIONAL

Righteousness is not merely a moral attribute of God, it is his covenantal commitment to make things right with the world he created.[7] Through Jesus Christ, God reconciles the world to himself, not counting humanity's sins against them (2 Cor 5:19). This righteousness is revealed in the gospel, where God addresses the alienation caused by sin and reestablishes a relationship with humanity. This act is not transactional or detached but flows from the very heart of God, a deep, passionate desire to see creation restored to its intended relationship with the God who is love.[8] At the core of the gospel is God's righteousness, which Paul portrays as God's faithful action to restore relationships.

Paul also emphasizes that God's righteousness creates what he called in Ephesians 2:15 "a new humanity in Christ" (see also Rom 6:4). The divisions between Jew and gentile, enslaved and free, male and female are overcome through the cross (Rom 3:30; 8:17; Gal 3:28). The church becomes a living testament to this reconciliation, called to embody the unity of one new humanity. As this reconciled community lives as lights in the world, they bear faithful witness to God's redemptive work. The Great Commission gains its true power, not in a coercive call to conformity but in the invitation to join this transformative work of reconciliation which springs from God's yearning to heal his creation (Matt 28:16–20; 2 Cor 5:17–21).

5. Hart, *Hidden and the Manifest*, 56–68.

6. Barth, *Church Dogmatics*, 4/3.1:3–15, 18, 21–22.

7. Brueggemann, *Theology of the Old Testament*, 130–35.

8. Barth, *Epistle to the Romans*, 501.

FAITH, TRUST, AND RELATIONSHIP

Faith in Paul's theology is also fundamentally relational.[9] It is not intellectual assent but trust in God's faithful character and redemptive work through Christ.[10] Faith serves as the means by which individuals are drawn into a relationship with God, receiving the righteousness he offers as a gift (Rom 3:22). This relational trust dismantles the transactional mindset often associated with religious observance.

This trust also lays the groundwork for relationships within the new community of God's people. Central to the gospel and the righteousness of God is the theme of reconciliation restoring fractured relationships.[11] Trust becomes fundamental to the life of the church, for authentic relationships cannot be built on mere feelings of affection but require a solid foundation of trust.[12]

Faith fosters these new relationships within the church by uniting believers not through shared ethnicity, social status, or personal preferences but through their shared life in Christ. Paul repeatedly urges the church to live out this faith in practical ways by showing mutual care, humility, and love. For example, in Romans 12–15, Paul emphasizes that faith should manifest in service, patience, and self-sacrificial love. These actions, rooted in trust, strengthen the bonds of the church and reveals the reconciling power of the gospel. Trust allows believers to embody God's righteousness in their relationships, allowing the transforming power of faith to shape the life of the community.

Trust serves as the glue that binds the church together, allowing it to rise above cultural, social, and ethnic divisions. Faith draws diverse individuals into a shared life in Christ, forming a vibrant community that matures in faith, hope, and love (Eph 3:14–20). Ultimately, faith/trust form the foundation for both individual and communal flourishing.[13] This trust creates space for reconciliation, belonging, and transformative relationships grounded in Christ.

9. Dunn, *Theology of Paul*, 734.

10. Balz and Schneider, *Exegetical Dictionary*, 3.91–92.

11. Chris Kugler, "Faith."

12. Hiebert, *Anthropological Insights*, 83–84.

13. Niebauer, *Virtuous Persuasion*, 83.

LOVE

From the opening greeting to the closing exhortations, Paul paints a portrait of divine love. He begins by addressing the believers in Rome as "loved by God and called to be saints" (Rom 1:7). This declaration grounds their identity in God's initiating love. The love of God is personal and relational, establishing the believers' standing as recipients of grace and peace. God's love is further demonstrated in its sacrificial nature. Paul proclaims that "while we were still sinners, Christ died for us" (Rom 5:8). This act of love is the cornerstone of the gospel. This love, poured into believers' hearts through the Holy Spirit (Rom 5:5), becomes an indwelling force that creates community, sustains hope, and enables transformation.

In Romans 8, Paul lifts the eyes of anxious believers and invites them to stand on unshakable ground. He speaks into a world marked by suffering and uncertainty and assures the church that the love of God is not fragile or conditional. Hardship, loss, and even violence cannot loosen its grip. Neither "tribulation, nor distress, nor persecution, nor famine, nor nakedness, nor danger, nor sword" has the power to sever believers from the love of Christ (Rom 8:35). Far from being overcome by these forces, Paul declares that through Christ's love they are "more than conquerors" (Rom 8:37). His argument crescendos into one of the most sweeping affirmations in Scripture: nothing in all creation, "neither height nor depth," can separate God's people from the love revealed in Christ Jesus our Lord (Rom 8:39). This love is steadfast and victorious, anchoring hope in every circumstance.

Yet Paul does not allow this assurance to remain abstract or merely consoling. The love that holds believers fast is also the love that reshapes their lives together. Having grounded the church in God's unwavering faithfulness, Paul turns in Romans 12 and 13 to the concrete expression of that love within the community. Love, he insists, must be "genuine" (Rom 12:9), embodied in relationships marked by devotion, humility, and mutual care. Believers are called to "love one another with brotherly affection" (Rom 12:10), reflecting in their shared life the same self-giving love they have received.

This love is neither sentimental nor passive. It is ethical and transformative, defined by a rejection of evil and a wholehearted commitment to what is good. For Paul, love reaches its fullest expression in the everyday practice of neighborly faithfulness. Quoting the law's central command, he reminds the Romans that "you shall love your neighbor as yourself" (Rom 13:9). Such love, he explains, "does no wrong to a neighbor" and therefore fulfills the law's true intent (Rom 13:10). In this way, the love that cannot be broken becomes the love that binds the church together, forming a community whose life bears witness to the righteousness and mercy of God in the world.

Love One Another

Paul addresses the practical implications of love within the church, warning believers against actions that could grieve one another. He reminds them that such behavior is not "walking in love" (Rom 14:15). In this context, love is both considerate and sacrificial, prioritizing the well-being of others even when it involves relinquishing personal rights and liberties. Paul concludes by urging believers to strive together in prayer "by the love of the Spirit" (Rom 15:30). This love, sourced in the Spirit, unites believers in their mission and intercession, reflecting God's own compassion and care. In Romans 12–15, he provides practical guidance on how this reconciled community should live. He exhorts believers to present their bodies as living sacrifices, allowing their minds to be transformed and their lives to align with God's will (Rom 12:1–2). This transformation is not merely individual but communal, expressed in mutual love, honor, and care for one another.

Paul's "one another" commands illustrate the gospel's ability to transform relationships.[14] Believers are called to outdo one another in showing honor (Rom 12:10), live in harmony (Rom 12:16), and bear with the weaknesses of others (Rom 15:1). Such exhortations reflect a community shaped by Christ, where love becomes the fulfillment of the law (Rom 13:10). Reconciliation within the church is not only the fruit of the gospel but also a powerful means by which the church bears witness to God's reconciling work in Christ.[15] The climax of this reconciliation among believers is found in welcoming one another, even in the midst of disagreements. Just as God, in Christ, has welcomed them, so too are they called to embrace one another (Rom 14:1, 3; 15:7; 16:2).[16] In doing

14. Rom 1:27; 2:1; 9:21; 12:5, 10, 16; 13:8; 14:5, 13; 15:5, 7, 14; 16:16.

15. Barth, *Epistle to the Romans*, 492–502.

16. Jewett, *Romans*, 833–36.

so, they embody the love of Christ, demonstrating the transformative and unifying power of the gospel.[17]

ROMANS 16: PAUL'S GOSPEL IN HUMAN FACES

Though Paul was driven by his overwhelming sense of obligation to proclaim the gospel to the nations, he prioritized relationships in his life and ministry. His approach to ministry was personal, focusing on discipling believers, mentoring leaders, and addressing the needs of the churches he served.[18] The letters he wrote are filled with greetings and personal references that reveal his strong relationships that cut across social, economic, and ethnic lines. This reality comes into sharp focus in Romans 14–16, where Paul's relational vision for the gospel reaches its fullest expression. In Romans 16 especially, the depth of his concern for genuine, reconciled community is vividly displayed.

Though Paul had not founded or visited the Roman church, his familiarity with many of its leaders reveals both his wide Mediterranean network and the remarkable mobility of the early Christian movement.[19] Prominent figures like Priscilla and Aquila exemplify this mobility, having worked with Paul in Corinth and Ephesus before returning to Rome after Emperor Claudius's death (Acts 18:1–3, 24–26). Paul commends them as "fellow workers in Christ Jesus" who risked their lives for him and hosted a house church (Rom 16:3–5). Paul's greetings also highlight Epaenetus, "the first convert to Christ in Asia" (Rom 16:5), Mary for her diligent work, and Andronicus and Junia, who were "prominent among the apostles" (Rom 16:7 NRSVue). He further acknowledges Urbanus, Stachys, and Rufus, noting Rufus's mother as a maternal figure to him, emphasizing his personal connections and deep respect for those who labored in the gospel (Rom 16:8–13).

Diverse, Inclusive, and Countercultural

The diversity of the individuals Paul greets in Romans 16 is striking. While it was common for Paul to send greetings to and from believers in his letters, Romans 16 is unparalleled by the vast number of people

17. Jewett, *Romans*, 88.

18. Gaventa, "Mission of God," 69–72.

19. Murphy-O'Connor, *Paul*, 325–26.

mentioned.[20] The list includes men and women, Jews and gentiles, Roman citizens, enslaved, formerly enslaved, and even enslavers. Romans 16 is the gospel in human faces. People of every background standing together as one, embodying the grace that levels every distinction and unites all in Christ.[21]

Women such as Phoebe and Prisca (Priscilla) reflect the active roles women played in leadership and ministry within the early church. Paul commends Phoebe as a *diakonos* (minister) of the church in Cenchreae and as a benefactor to many (Rom 16:1–2). Far from describing a subordinate role, Paul's language portrays Phoebe as a trusted leader and co-laborer in the gospel. The term *diakonos*, used elsewhere by Paul to describe his own ministry and that of other missionaries, often denotes those entrusted with preaching, teaching, and oversight within the early church (cf. Rom 11:13; 1 Cor 3:5; 2 Cor 3:6). Phoebe thus emerges not as a mere helper but as a recognized minister, one who embodied the gospel through both service and spiritual leadership. Her commendation affirms the active participation of women in the mission and governance of the earliest Christian communities, revealing a vision of ministry grounded in mutual partnership and shared calling.[22]

Prisca, frequently listed before her husband Aquila (Acts 18:2, 18, 19, 26; Rom 16:3–5; 1 Cor 16:19; 2 Tim 4:19), stands out as another prominent woman in early Christian ministry. Alongside Phoebe and Prisca, Paul also commends other prominent women such as Mary (16:6), Junia (16:7, noted by Paul as an apostle[23]), Tryphena and Tryphosa (16:12), Persis (16:12), Rufus's mother, who "has been a mother to me, too" (v. 13), Julia (16:15), and Nereus's sister (16:15). Together, these women exemplify the leadership, devotion, and diligent labor "in the Lord" that were well known throughout the churches. Paul's inclusion of women demonstrates the inclusive and countercultural nature of the early Christian movement.

20. Park, "What Does Romans 16 Say about the Ministry of Women?" 357.

21. Barth, *Epistle to the Romans*, 100.

22. Jewett, *Romans*, 943–45.

23. Jewett asserts, "The honorific expression ἐπίσημοι ἐν τοῖς ἀποστόλοις should be translated 'outstanding among the apostles' rather than 'remarkable in the judgment of the apostles,' because the adjective ἐπίσημος lifts up a person or thing as distinguished or marked in comparison with other representatives of the same class, in this instance with the other apostles." Jewett, *Romans*, 963.

Enslaved, formerly enslaved, and low-status individuals occupy a visible and theologically significant place in Paul's ministry and in his vision of a new humanity in Christ. Among the more than thirty individuals and households named in Romans 16, scholars commonly estimate that ten to twelve persons, along with members of the households of Aristobulus and Narcissus, were likely enslaved or formerly enslaved.[24] Their presence is not incidental. It reflects the gospel's power to reorder social hierarchies and redefine belonging within the community shaped by Christ.

One especially striking figure is Tertius, the scribe who physically wrote the letter.[25] His name, meaning "third," strongly suggests enslaved or low-status origins, as numerical names were frequently assigned to enslaved persons in the Roman world.[26] In antiquity, scribes were typically enslaved or formerly enslaved individuals whose labor remained invisible, absorbed into the authority of the sender. Yet in Romans 16:22, Tertius breaks this pattern, identifying himself and offering his own greeting: "I, Tertius, who wrote this letter, greet you in the Lord." Such self-reference is highly unusual in ancient epistolary practice and carries profound theological weight.

By allowing Tertius to speak in his own voice, Paul disrupts the social conventions of Roman letter writing and enacts the gospel he proclaims. The scribe who would ordinarily remain unnamed and socially marginalized is no longer merely an instrument of transmission but a recognized participant in the life of the church.[27] This brief but powerful moment embodies the subversive character of the gospel, which transcends and dismantles entrenched hierarchies of status and honor. In acknowledging Tertius and others who were enslaved or formerly enslaved, Paul humanizes those whom Roman society routinely dehumanized, affirming their dignity and agency within the body of Christ. Within the gospel-shaped community Paul envisions, those once rendered invisible are named, acknowledged, and embraced as full members of the body.

Paul's extensive greetings in Romans 16 thus reveal far more than personal familiarity. They offer a window into the gospel's transformative power to create a new kind of community, one in which cultural, social, and economic distinctions no longer determine worth or belonging.

24. See Jewett, *Romans*, 954–84.

25. Gillman, "Tertius (Person)," 6:389.

26. Dunn, *Romans 9–16*, 909–10.

27. Moss, *God's Ghostwriters*, 19–87.

In Christ, there is no privileged status based on ethnicity, class, or legal standing, "for there is no distinction between Jew and Greek" (Rom 10:12). The church that emerges in Romans is a lived expression of this reality: a reconciled community in which the least visible are named, welcomed, and honored as members of God's family.

13

Paul the Theologian

We have examined the historical and cultural context, as well as the genre and content of the letter to the Romans, laying a foundation for understanding Paul's message and intent. Yet, to fully appreciate the significance of Romans, it is necessary to move beyond descriptive analysis and engage with its theological depth and development. Romans is often regarded as Paul's crowning theological achievement that has shaped Christian faith and thought for centuries. Doctrines such as the righteousness of God and justification by faith, sin and the wrath of God, sanctification and life in the Spirit, the role of the law and the situation of the Jewish people, as well as the sovereignty of God are explored with unparalleled depth in this epistle. However, these doctrines should not be viewed in isolation from the overarching purpose of God's mission to restore a fallen world. Paul's theological arguments in Romans are fundamentally missional, rooted in God's plan to redeem and reconcile creation to himself.

In a sense, all theology is mission theology in that nearly all biblical theology will, or should, in one way or another, relate to God's missional purposes in the world and the missionary character of God. Martin Kähler called mission "the mother of theology." The theology in the New Testament developed in the context of the spread of the Christian faith. The encounter with other religions, idolatry, false teaching, syncretism, cultural strongholds, and ethical challenges faced by the nascent Christian movement served as the anvil on which theology was forged.[1] We see

1. Ott et al., *Encountering Theology of Mission*, xviii–xix.

this on full display in Romans as Paul expounds key missional doctrines and confronts the Romans' cultural compromise.

Theology never emerges in a vacuum. It is forged as people wrestle with God's truth within the particular realities of their time and place. Paul stands as the quintessential theologian, yet he is more than that. He is a missionary theologian.

To understand Paul rightly, we must see him within his historical, cultural, and religious world. He lived at the intersection of first-century Judaism and the Greco-Roman Empire, navigating the tension between Jewish faith and gentile diversity. His theology was not abstract speculation but the lived expression of his encounter with the risen Christ and his calling to proclaim the gospel to both Jews and gentiles. Without this context, we risk misinterpreting Paul's message and the missional focus of his work.

PAUL AS NEW COVENANT JEW AND MISSIONARY THEOLOGIAN

The traditional Protestant understanding of Paul's theology, shaped by the Reformation, centers on individual salvation and the doctrine of justification by faith apart from works. In this view, Paul is often portrayed as confronting legalism and rejecting any notion that human effort can secure God's favor.

Beginning in the 1970s, however, a major shift occurred in Pauline studies with the rise of what became known as the New Perspective on Paul (NPP).[2] This movement reexamined Paul within his first-century Jewish context, challenging long-held assumptions. Rather than depicting Judaism as a religion of works-based righteousness, scholars began to show that Jewish obedience to the law was largely understood as a grateful response to God's covenant grace, not a means of earning salvation.[3]

2. Sanders, *Paul and Palestinian Judaism.*

3. While Sanders's work catalyzed the NPP, earlier scholars laid the groundwork for rethinking Paul's relationship to Judaism (Sprinkle, "Old Perspective on the New Perspective"). George Foot Moore's 1921 critique of Christian scholarship exposed biases that portrayed Judaism as a legalistic religion. Moore argued that Judaism, like Christianity, was deeply rooted in God's covenantal grace (Moore, "Christian Writers on Judaism"). He demonstrated that Jewish law was not a means of salvation but a guide for living faithfully within the covenant. This reappraisal challenged long-standing stereotypes and provided a more accurate depiction of Jewish theology. In his 1963 essay, "The Apostle Paul and the Introspective Conscience of the West," Krister Stendahl

This reorientation reframed Paul's message: His critique was not of Judaism itself, but of any system, religious or otherwise, that sought to define righteousness apart from faith in Christ.[4] Paul's theology emerges not from personal angst over the law, but from his encounter with the risen Messiah and his vision of God's covenant expanding to embrace all nations.

Paul did not regard the law as inherently flawed but as limited and ultimately unable to bring salvation. The law had served its purpose within God's covenant, but it could not accomplish the universal redemption that God intended. Salvation, Paul insists, comes through Christ alone, who fulfills and completes God's covenant promises. From this perspective, Christ is the revelation that exposes humanity's true plight, separation from God, and unveils the only path to restoration.

In Paul's letters, "works of the law" are not portrayed as human efforts to earn divine favor but as boundary markers, such as circumcision, dietary laws, and Sabbath observance that distinguished Jews from gentiles.[5] Paul challenges these as barriers to the inclusive, grace-filled community of the gospel. In Christ, God's covenant expands beyond ethnic or cultural boundaries, forming one family of faith in which all are made righteous through trust in him.[6]

This vision reaches far beyond an individual experience of salvation. Paul presents the gospel as a cosmic and transformative reality, God's decisive action in Christ to defeat sin and death and to renew all creation.[7] Paul is not a detached systematizer of doctrine but a missionary theologian, whose thinking is forged in the pressures and possibilities of cross-cultural ministry. His theology is oriented toward forming and sustaining communities that live under the reconciling lordship of Christ.

---

further shifted the conversation by questioning the traditional view of Paul's theology as centered on personal guilt and salvation. Instead, Stendahl argued that Paul's primary concern was Jew–gentile unity within the Christian community. Justification by faith, according to Stendahl, was not about resolving individual struggles with sin but about dismantling barriers to create one unified body in Christ.

4. James D. G. Dunn coined the term "New Perspective on Paul" in 1983, emphasizing that Paul's critique of the "works of the law" targeted boundary markers like circumcision, dietary laws, and Sabbath observance, which distinguished Jews from gentiles. See Dunn, "New Perspective on Paul."

5. Dunn, *Theology of Paul*, 334–40.

6. Wright, *Paul and the Faithfulness of God*, 406–18.

7. Campbell, *Deliverance of God*; Tyson, "'Works of Law' in Galatians"; Howard, "Romans 3:21–31 and the Inclusion of the Gentiles."

This communal understanding of salvation was echoed by early church fathers such as Irenaeus, Origen, and Chrysostom, who consistently emphasized its relational character.[8] For them, God's righteousness was not limited to juridical judgment but encompassed restoration and healing, the reordering of relationships broken by sin. Salvation was understood as incorporation into a redeemed community, the church, where reconciliation with God necessarily entailed reconciliation with one another and where mutual welcome overcame social and ethnic divisions.

Paul's message moves beyond a narrowly individualistic or legalistic framework. Salvation emerges as relational, communal, and covenantal, deeply embedded in the world of first-century Judaism, where belonging to God's people was inseparable from faithfulness to God. This perspective offers a fuller account of Paul's intent and underscores the gospel's power not only to justify individuals but to form a renewed people who embody God's reconciling purposes in the world.

The New Perspective on Paul and the Unity of Scripture

The NPP helps dismantle the misguided belief that the God of the First Testament is fundamentally different from the God revealed in Jesus Christ and the New Testament. This belief, which bears an uncomfortable resemblance to the ancient heresy of Marcionism, undermines the coherence of Scripture and obscures the continuity of God's redemptive plan. Marcionism rejected the First Testament God as a being of wrath, justice, and judgment, incompatible with the God of love revealed in Jesus Christ.[9] However, the God of the First and New Testaments is one and the same, acting consistently in covenant faithfulness, love, and mercy across the entirety of Scripture.[10] One could argue that, rather than the NPP being a new perspective on Paul, it is a resetting of Paul into his original context as a new covenant Jew.

The covenantal relationship between God and Israel reveals a God deeply engaged with his creation, marked by steadfast love (*ḥesed*) and a commitment to justice and restoration.[11] Far from being a God of wrath

8. Irenaeus, *Against Heresies* 1.101 (*ANF* 1:330–31); Origen, *On First Principles*, 69–70; Chrysostom, *On the Priesthood* 6.9 (*NPNF*[1] 9:79).

9. Padgett, "Marcion," 705–8.

10. Jersak, *More Christlike God*.

11. Goldingay, *Israel's Life*, 108–9.

alone, the First Testament portrays Yahweh as compassionate and patient, repeatedly extending grace and opportunities for repentance to his people. The NPP complements this view by showing how Paul's theology, particularly his understanding of God's righteousness, emerges from this covenantal framework. Paul's gospel of justification through faith is not a departure from God's dealings with Israel but their fulfillment in Jesus Christ.[12] This continuity affirms the character of God as unchanging, overturning the false dichotomy between an "Old Testament God" of judgment and a "New Testament God" of grace.

The First Testament's portrayal of God's actions is fully consistent with his character as revealed in Christ. Its theological narrative unfolds God's enduring commitment to bless all nations through the descendants of Abraham, a promise ultimately fulfilled in the gospel.[13] Reorienting our interpretation in understanding the ancient Near Eastern world helps illuminate how biblical authors expressed God's character and purposes within their own time and culture.[14] This awareness deepens our grasp of the unity and coherence of God's revelation across the whole of Scripture, from Genesis to Revelation.

Together, the First and New Testaments form one divine story, a continuous revelation of a God who is just, loving, and faithful. The diversity of voices and settings within Scripture reflects humanity's encounters with this same God across history.[15] What may seem like tension between the Testaments is, in truth, the unfolding of a single redemptive narrative that culminates in Christ.[16] The mercy, justice, and covenant faithfulness revealed in Jesus are not new attributes but the ultimate expression of the character of God who has been at work from the very beginning.

Paul's theology had deep roots within Judaism.[17] His message was not a rejection of his heritage but a transformation of Israel's covenantal story in light of Christ. His calling as a missionary theologian compelled him to reinterpret covenant and community around the reality of Jesus the Messiah, uniting Jews and gentiles under his lordship.

12. Goldingay, *Israel's Faith*, 251–52.

13. Goldingay, *Israel's Faith*, 87.

14. Walton and Walton, *Lost World of the Torah*, 83–88.

15. Enns, *Inspiration and Incarnation*, 168.

16. Enns, *Inspiration and Incarnation*, 103–56.

17. Pitre et al., *Paul, a New Covenant Jew*.

This understanding challenges the church to move beyond any lingering tendency to separate the God of Israel from the God revealed in Christ. The same God who led Israel out of Egypt, spoke through the prophets, and restored his people from exile is the God who took on flesh in Jesus to reconcile the world to himself.

By affirming the continuity of God's character and redemptive purpose across both Testaments, the church can proclaim a gospel rooted in the whole story of Scripture. Such an integrative approach strengthens the church's theological foundation and renews its sense of mission, reminding us that the First Testament is not merely background to the gospel but an essential part of the unfolding story through which God reveals his purposes for the world.

The Broader Impact of the New Perspective on Paul

The renewed understanding of Paul has deeply influenced theology, biblical interpretation, and interfaith dialogue. It has fostered greater appreciation for Paul's identity as a faithful Jew, emphasizing his continuity with Israel's covenant story rather than opposition to it. This perspective challenges long-held interpretations that portray Christianity as replacing Judaism, instead revealing Paul as proclaiming the fulfillment of God's promises through Christ.[18]

At the same time, some have cautioned that emphasizing historical and cultural context must not diminish the universal reality of sin or the personal dimension of salvation.[19] Paul's message holds both together: the cosmic scope of God's redemptive work and the individual's call to faith. A balanced reading recognizes that Paul's theology is neither abstract nor merely historical. It is a living witness to God's reconciling grace that unites people and nations in Christ.

This renewed approach to Paul's theology has redefined how his message is understood, highlighting its communal, covenantal, and missional dimensions. Justification by faith is no longer viewed solely as an individual experience but as God's act of forming a single, unified people in Christ. This understanding emphasizes the inclusiveness of the gospel and the far-reaching, eschatological vision of Paul's message.

18. Nanos and Zetterholm, *Paul Within Judaism*; Eisenbaum, *Paul Was Not a Christian*.

19. Schreiner, "Justification"; Bird, *Anomalous Jew*.

Paul's theology reaches beyond personal salvation to proclaim God's decisive action in history: the triumph of Christ over the powers of sin and death and the restoration of all creation under his lordship.[20] He is, in the fullest sense, a missionary theologian, one whose theology is shaped not only by reflection on Christ and Scripture but by the lived reality of proclaiming that message across cultural, ethnic, and religious boundaries. Paul's theology restores a vision of faith inseparable from mission, concerned not merely with describing who God is but with discerning how God's people are called to live and bear witness to God's redemptive work among the nations.

20. Gaventa: *Our Mother Saint Paul*; *Apocalyptic Paul*.

14

Paul's Theology and the Mission of God in Romans

HAVING ESTABLISHED PAUL AS a missionary theologian, we now turn to key dimensions of his theology viewed through the lens of the mission of God. While earlier discussions have addressed foundational themes such as the righteousness of God, this section explores specific theological developments that reveal the missional thrust of Paul's thought. These include the wrath of God; the tension between Jews and gentiles; the nature of sin; self-exaltation and idolatry; the function of the Torah; the realities of empire and power; and cultural compromise. This is not an exhaustive study, but a focused examination of how these themes together illuminate the dynamic relationship between Paul's theology and the redemptive mission of God in the world.

THE WRATH OF GOD

In Romans 1:16–17, Paul proclaims the heart of his message: "I am not ashamed of the gospel, for it is the power of God for salvation to everyone who believes, to the Jew first and also to the Greek. For in it the righteousness of God is revealed from faith for faith, as it is written, 'The righteous shall live by faith.'" This triumphant declaration highlights the power and universal reach of the gospel. Yet Paul immediately transitions to a sobering subject: the wrath of God. "For the wrath of God is revealed from heaven against all ungodliness and unrighteousness of men" (Rom 1:18). This sharp transition is deliberate. For Paul, the good news cannot be separated from the reality of divine judgment. The same God who reveals righteousness also reveals wrath. Both flowing from God's holiness and covenant faithfulness. Understanding this connection sheds light on the nature of divine judgment and the overarching mission of God.[1]

The wrath of God remains one of the most difficult and often misunderstood themes in theology. It is sometimes imagined as uncontrolled anger or vengeful punishment, a picture that has too often dominated popular portrayals of divine judgment. Jonathan Edwards's famous sermon, "Sinners in the Hands of an Angry God," exemplifies this portrayal, emphasizing divine wrath as a fearful, consuming force poised over sinners.[2] Yet Scripture presents a far different reality. God's wrath is not arbitrary or impulsive, it flows from his love, holiness, and justice.

Divine wrath arises from God's covenantal faithfulness and his refusal to ignore evil or abandon creation to corruption. It is not the opposite of love but its necessary expression against all that destroys life and distorts goodness. Far from being merely punitive, God's wrath confronts sin, exposes injustice, and opens the way for repentance and renewal. It is the fierce compassion of a God who loves the world too much to leave it as it is.

Abraham Joshua Heschel offers a corrective vision of the wrath of God by framing it not as an impersonal force or cold decree, but as *divine pathos*, the deep feeling of a God who is personally involved with his creation. God's wrath cannot be separated from God's love; both arise from the same divine pathos, the same passionate concern for justice, righteousness, and human dignity.

In *The Prophets*, Heschel insists that the wrath of God is not a mood or an outburst, but "the expression of God's sorrow over the ruin of his creation."[3] It is not divine temper, it is divine grief. God's anger is the other side of divine compassion: the protest of a loving God against human cruelty, idolatry, and indifference. To speak of God's wrath, then, is to speak of a God who cares, who refuses to be indifferent to evil, oppression, or moral decay.

1. Tarazi, *Romans*, 51.
2. Edwards, *Works*, 2:7–12.
3. Heschel, *Prophets*, 64.

This insight transforms our understanding of judgment. The wrath of God is not a denial of grace but its precondition; it is the outcry of divine love wounded by injustice, longing to heal what has been broken. In this way, divine wrath is not the end of the story but part of God's redemptive pathos, a movement toward repentance, restoration, and renewal.

Wrath and God's Covenant Relationship

The covenant relationship between God and humanity is central to understanding divine wrath.[4] In the Hebrew Bible, God's covenant with Israel called for justice, mercy, and righteousness. Wrath arises when these covenantal expectations are abandoned. Abraham Heschel described God's wrath as divine pathos, a relational response of love and moral seriousness.[5] Wrath is not opposed to God's love but flows from it. A holy God cannot remain silent or indifferent to the suffering, destruction, and alienation caused by sin. The prophet Ezekiel captures this tension when God declares, "I have no pleasure in the death of the wicked, but that the wicked turn from his way and live" (Ezek 33:11). Here, wrath is not an end in itself but a call to repentance. It is an expression of God's longing to restore shalom, the peace, harmony, and order of creation.[6]

Wrath and God's Justice

The wrath of God is integrally tied to his justice. It is the necessary response of a righteous God to human rebellion. Humanity is called to reflect God's character in their relationships, institutions, and societies.[7] When this moral order is disrupted through idolatry, oppression, injustice, or exploitation, divine wrath becomes a necessary response to the breach of just relationships. God's wrath in the prophets disrupts complacency and injustice, confronting systemic evils that harm the vulnerable.[8] For instance, Amos condemns Israel for trampling the poor and corrupting worship, warning of impending judgment (Amos

4. Goldingay, *Israel's Faith*, 135–36.

5. Heschel, *Prophets*, 358–82.

6. Brueggemann, *Theology of the Old Testament*, 22.

7. Wright, *Paul and the Faithfulness of God*, 163–75.

8. Brueggemann, *Prophetic Imagination*, xii. See also Goldingay, *Israel's Faith*, 228–30.

5:11–12). Yet judgment is paired with a call to repentance: "Seek good, and not evil, that you may live" (Amos 5:14). Divine wrath arises from God's unwavering character.[9] Wrath is not the negation of God's love but its expression against sin and evil. It holds humanity accountable to its covenantal responsibilities and reminds us of the seriousness of sin and its consequences.

Wrath and Repentance

A key aspect of divine wrath is its depiction as the inherent result of human sin rather than an imposed or arbitrary punishment. When individuals and societies reject God's ways, they experience the breakdown of relationships, community, and the created order. Paul captures this dynamic in Romans 1, where he describes divine wrath as God "giving them over" to their sinful desires and actions (Rom 1:24–28). This handing over is not vindictive but a sobering demonstration of sin's futility and destructiveness. Yet, even in its severity, divine wrath is not devoid of grace. It functions as a wake-up call, summoning humanity to recognize its deep need for God and to turn back toward him. Divine judgment is not merely punitive but pedagogical. It exposes ethical failure in order to awaken conscience, disrupt complacency, and redirect life toward righteousness. This understanding stands squarely within the prophetic tradition, where announcements of judgment are never ends in themselves but urgent invitations to repentance, restoration, and renewed covenant faithfulness.[10]

Additional insights emerge when we broaden our focus to include the apocalyptic imagery of Revelation, where God's judgment unfolds through the dramatic scenes of the seven seals, trumpets, and bowls of wrath.[11] These terrifying judgments emphasize the gravity of sin and the urgency of repentance. At least ten times in Revelation, repentance is highlighted as the desired response to divine judgment.[12] For example, despite devastating plagues, humanity's refusal to repent is noted repeatedly: "The rest of humankind, who were not killed by these plagues, did

9. Goldingay, *Israel's Gospel*, 32–33.

10. Brueggemann, *Jeremiah*, 224–26.

11. Seven seals, Rev 6:1–8:1; seven trumpets, Rev 8:2–11:19; and bowls of wrath, Rev 15–16.

12. Rev 2:5, 16, 21, 22; 3:3, 19; 9:20, 21; 16:9, 11.

not repent of the works of their hands" (Rev 9:20–21). God's judgments are not intended to annihilate but to awaken. They are divine appeals to turn away from sin and turn to God.

Wrath and the Mission of God

The wrath of God must be understood within the wider horizon of God's redemptive mission. The *missio Dei* necessarily confronts sin and evil, not to condemn humanity but to heal what has been corrupted. Divine wrath serves this mission by exposing the destructive power of sin and interrupting its dehumanizing effects, creating space for repentance, transformation, and renewal. Paul frames the gospel in precisely these terms. In Romans 1:16–18, the revelation of God's righteousness is inseparably linked to the revelation of God's wrath. The gospel announces God's saving power, yet it does so against the stark reality of humanity's need for deliverance from sin and judgment. Without the backdrop of divine wrath, the gospel's promise of salvation loses its urgency and significance.

At the cross, God's righteousness and wrath converge. At Calvary, the consequences of sin are borne by Christ, and the way is opened for humanity to be reconciled to God. As Paul declares, "Since, therefore, we have now been justified by his blood, much more shall we be saved by him from the wrath of God" (Rom 5:9). The cross makes clear that divine wrath is not God's final word. Rather, it clears the way for the fulfillment of God's mission: the restoration of humanity and creation made new.

Even in its severity, divine wrath is never an expression of despair or abandonment. It is ordered toward restoration, clearing the path for God's kingdom to flourish. The prophetic witness makes this unmistakably clear. Through Ezekiel, God twice reveals his heart, insisting that he takes no pleasure in the death of the wicked but desires their repentance and life (Ezek 18:23; 33:11). His repeated plea—"turn back, turn back"—reveals his patience and desire to see his people abandon their destructive paths and choose the way of life. Judgment is not an end in itself, it is a summons to transformation and renewal.

Divine wrath, then, is redemptive in purpose. It purges what destroys, confronts injustice, and unmasks false securities, and invites humanity to reconciliation with God. Far from negating hope, it reveals the depth of God's commitment to set the world right, inviting humanity to abandon death-dealing ways and to step into the life God offers through Christ.

JEW-GENTILE CONFLICTS

Romans unfolds as a sustained exploration of the relationship between Jews and gentiles in light of the gospel. At the center of Paul's argument stands the revelation of God's righteousness, a righteousness that fulfills God's covenant promises to Israel while simultaneously opening the way of salvation to the nations. God's faithfulness is revealed not by exclusion but by its expansive reach, embracing all peoples within the scope of redemption.[13] This gospel-driven vision presses two fundamental questions to the surface: What role does Israel continue to play in God's redemptive purposes? And how are the nations incorporated into the promises first spoken to Abraham?

Jews and Gentiles and the Universal Scope of Sin and the Need for Salvation, Romans 1–3

One of Paul's most radical and subversive claims in Romans is that all humanity, Jews and gentiles alike, stands bound under the power of sin.[14] He begins by addressing the gentile world, exposing the destructive consequences of idolatry and moral disorder (Rom 1:18–32). Humanity's refusal to honor God leads to a distortion of worship, desire, and social life. Yet just as the reader might expect Paul to conclude with a sharp ethnic contrast, he turns the argument inward. In a deliberate and unsettling reversal, Paul exposes Jewish failure to live in covenant faithfulness, insisting that possession of the law does not guarantee obedience to it (Rom 2:17–29). In doing so, Paul dismantles any illusion of moral or spiritual superiority.

This argument reaches its climax in Paul's sweeping verdict: "All have sinned and fall short of the glory of God" (Rom 3:23). With this declaration, ethnic privilege and cultural hierarchy collapse. Jew and gentile are placed on equal footing before God, not to erase distinction, but to level the ground upon which salvation is received. Justification, Paul insists, comes not through ethnic identity or covenantal badges but through faith in Christ, who is Lord of both Jews and gentiles (Rom 3:28–30). In redefining identity around faith rather than ancestry, Paul challenges Jewish exclusivism, Greek cultural pride, and Roman imperial

13. Barth, *Epistle to the Romans*, 99–100.

14. Barth, *Epistle to the Romans*, 259–60.

claims alike. Allegiance is no longer determined by law, philosophy, or empire, but by participation in Christ.

Paul's critique, however, is not a rejection of the Torah itself but of a distorted understanding of its function.[15] The law was never given as a means of earning righteousness but as a gift within the covenant, intended to guide God's people in faithful relationship with him. What Paul confronts is the temptation to turn the Torah into a marker of superiority or a mechanism of justification. Both Jews and gentiles, he argues, stand equally in need of God's grace, for obedience alone cannot heal the deeper problem of sin that fractures human life.

From Paul's perspective, God's covenant faithfulness has not failed. Rather, its true fulfillment has been unveiled in Christ.[16] In Romans 3:21–31, Paul announces that God's righteousness is now revealed apart from the law yet in continuity with it, through the faithfulness of Jesus Christ. This righteousness gathers Jews and gentiles into a single redeemed community, united under grace and invited to share in the restored covenant life of God. What emerges is not the abandonment of Israel's story but its climactic renewal, as God's long-promised purpose to bless the nations finds its fulfillment in Christ.

Abraham and the Inclusion of the Gentiles, Romans 4

Paul uses Abraham as a model to demonstrate that righteousness comes through faith, not works of the law. In Romans 4, Paul argues that Abraham was justified before circumcision, making him the father of both circumcised (Jews) and uncircumcised (gentiles) believers: "It was not through the law that Abraham and his offspring received the promise . . . but through the righteousness that comes by faith" (Rom 4:13). Paul's use of Abraham shows that the gospel fulfills God's covenant promises to Israel while simultaneously breaking down ethnic boundaries. Abraham becomes the prototype for the multinational family promised by God.[17] The inclusion of the gentiles does not nullify God's promises to Israel, it fulfills them in a way that extends God's saving purpose to all humanity.

15. Sanders, *Paul and Palestinian Judaism*, 236–38, 420–22.

16. Moore, *Judaism in the First Centuries of the Christian Era*, 536.

17. Wright, *Paul and the Faithfulness of God*, 366–67.

Israel's Role and the Problem of Rejection, Romans 9–11

One of the most intricate and emotionally charged sections of Romans is Paul's reflection on Israel's response to the gospel in chapters 9–11. Here Paul writes not as a detached theologian but as a grieving apostle, bearing deep anguish over the fact that many of his fellow Jews have not embraced Christ. Yet his lament is anchored in unshakable confidence. God's promises to Israel, he insists, have not failed (Rom 9:6). Paul's sorrow is not the grief of abandonment but of covenant love, shaped by his conviction that Israel continues to occupy a central place in God's redemptive purposes.[18]

Paul interprets Israel's unbelief not as the collapse of God's covenant but as part of a larger and unfolding mystery of divine mercy. God's faithfulness endures even when his people falter.[19] Even in Israel's stumbling, God's saving purposes move forward. Through Israel's rejection, the gospel has come to the gentiles, not as a replacement but as an expansion of grace meant to provoke longing and, ultimately, restoration. Gentile inclusion, therefore, is not Israel's exclusion, but a stage within God's redemptive economy.

Paul's vision stretches toward hope rather than finality. He anticipates a future in which God's mercy gathers Jew and gentile together, fulfilling the promise that "all Israel will be saved" (Rom 11:26). This hope does not resolve every tension, but it rests in the character of God whose gifts and calling are irrevocable (Rom 11:29). In the end, Romans 9–11 affirms that God's redemptive story remains faithful to its beginnings even as it opens outward to embrace the nations, revealing a mercy vast enough to hold both Israel and the world.

The New Unified Community, Romans 12–15

Paul concludes his letter by turning from theology to its practical outworking. In Romans 12–15, he calls the church to live out the reconciling power of the gospel through mutual acceptance and love: "Accept one another, then, just as Christ accepted you, in order to bring praise to God" (Rom 15:7). This call to welcome one another flows from Paul's

18. Stendahl, *Paul Among Jews*, 2–22.

19. Dahl, *Studies in Paul*, 137–58.

conviction that the gospel creates a new kind of humanity, one defined not by ethnicity or status but by grace.

For Paul, the church is the embodiment of God's righteousness in the world, a new humanity formed through faith in Christ and empowered by the Spirit. The gospel does not reject Israel's story but brings it to fulfillment, extending God's covenant promises to all nations. In this unified community, continuity and transformation meet: God remains faithful to Israel even as he gathers the nations into the same promise. The church thus becomes a living expression of the gospel itself, an agent of reconciliation and a witness to God's redemptive mission in the world.

SIN

Paul's treatment of sin in Romans stands at the center of his gospel and cannot be separated from the mission of God. For Paul, sin is not only a catalogue of moral failures or isolated acts of disobedience. It is a pervasive and enslaving power, a cosmic power that has penetrated the depths of human existence and has corrupted the fabric of creation itself. Sin ruptures humanity's relationship with God, distorts relationships with one another, and disrupts the harmony of creation. It is not simply behavioral but ontological, a condition of existence estranged from God, a disorder that manifests in idolatry, injustice, and self-exaltation.

Throughout Romans 1–8, Paul gives this diagnosis vivid expression. Sin "reigns" like a tyrant, enslaving humanity (Rom 6:6, 12–14). It exploits the law, deceiving and bringing death rather than life (Rom 7:11). Its corrosive effects extend beyond human life to creation itself, which is subjected to frustration and decay as it groans for liberation (Rom 8:20–22). By framing sin in this way, Paul situates the problem within a cosmic horizon. Sin is not merely personal failure but a power that resists God's purposes and corrupts humanity's vocation as God's image-bearers.

Yet Paul never lingers in diagnosis without proclamation. Into this darkened reality breaks the righteousness of God, revealed in Jesus Christ. God's covenant faithfulness and redemptive power confront sin at its deepest level, liberating humanity from its dominion and opening the way for the reconciliation of all things. In Christ's death and resurrection, the reign of sin is decisively challenged and its power broken.

For this reason, Paul's theology of sin is never abstract, moralistic, or detached from mission. Sin is the crisis that summons the mission of God, and the gospel is the announcement that this crisis has been met. The good news Paul proclaims is that the powers of sin and death no longer have the final word. Through Christ, God is restoring broken relationships, reclaiming human vocation, and setting creation itself on the path toward renewal.

Sin as a Universal Human Condition

Paul demonstrates the universality of sin in Romans 1:18—3:20. He indicts gentiles for suppressing the truth of God revealed in creation (Rom 1:18–32) and confronts Jews for failing to uphold the law despite being entrusted with it (Rom 2:17–24). This leads to his climactic summary in Romans 3:23—"For all have sinned and fall short of the glory of God." Paul's diagnosis levels the playing field: All humanity is under sin's power and in need of salvation. The solution to sin is presented in Romans 3:21–26, where Paul proclaims the atoning death of Jesus Christ as the definitive answer. The cross reveals God's justice and serves as the means by which sinners are justified by faith. This act of divine grace upholds God's faithfulness to his covenant promises and extends salvation to all nations (Rom 3:29–30; 15:8–12).

Sin as a Cosmic Tyrant

Paul portrays sin as a pervasive, systemic, and cosmic power that distorts every sphere of life. In Romans 5:12–21, Paul traces the entrance of sin into the world through Adam and describes how death comes to reign over all humanity. Sin is personified as a tyrant: It enslaves humanity (Rom 6:6), exploits and deceives through the law (Rom 7:11), and extends its corrosive reach to creation itself (Rom 8:20–22).[20] This portrayal expands the meaning of sin beyond moral failure to a ruling force that shapes bodies, communities, systems, and even the natural order. A crisis of this magnitude demands a redemption of equal scope.

Romans 7:24 gives voice to that crisis in one of Paul's most anguished and revealing cries: "Wretched person that I am! Who will rescue me from this body of death?" The question is not merely psychological

20. Croasmun, *Emergence of Sin*.

or introspective. Paul is naming a regime, a ruling power under which humanity lives. The "body of death" is not simply a mortal body destined to die, nor is it reducible to personal guilt. It is the corporate reality of life under sin's dominion, a body politic ruled by a tyrant.

Throughout Romans, sin is not treated as a series of bad choices but as an enslaving power. Sin reigns, commands, pays wages, and exercises authority. To be "in sin" is to live under its rule. The "body of death" in Romans 7 therefore names the shared condition of those subject to this power. All who live under sin's lordship belong to this body. It is a collective existence marked by corruption, compulsion, and inevitability. Death is not only the consequence of sin; it is the atmosphere in which this body lives and moves and has its being.

Paul's lament exposes the futility of resistance from within this regime. The law can name the good, but it cannot dethrone the ruler. The self may desire obedience, but desire alone cannot break tyranny. The cry "Who will rescue me?" is the recognition that liberation must come from outside the body of death, through an act of deliverance rather than self-improvement.

The gospel answers that cry immediately: "Thanks be to God through Jesus Christ our Lord!" Rescue does not come through the repair of the old body but through the overthrow of its ruler. In the resurrection and exaltation of Jesus, God decisively breaks the dominion of sin and death. Sin's authority is not reformed; it is displaced. Death is not negotiated with; it is defeated. Jesus is raised as Lord, and with his exaltation comes a transfer of allegiance and belonging.

This is why Paul's language shifts so dramatically from Romans 7 to Romans 8. There is now "no condemnation" because there is now a new realm of life, governed not by sin and death but by the Spirit. Those who belong to Christ are no longer members of the body of death. They have been transferred into a new corporate reality, the body of Christ. This is not merely a metaphor for community; it is a declaration of political and theological allegiance. To be in Christ is to live under a new Lord, to be animated by a new power, and to participate in a new kind of life.

The contrast could not be sharper. The body of death is unified by compulsion, ruled by sin, and destined for decay. The body of Christ is unified by the Spirit, ruled by the risen Lord, and oriented toward resurrection. Membership in the former is universal apart from Christ. Membership in the latter is sheer gift. The church, therefore, is not simply a gathering of forgiven individuals but a liberated people, a community whose very existence testifies that sin no longer reigns.

Romans 7:24 does not end in despair because it was never meant to. It is the final acknowledgment that the old ruler must be overthrown. The gospel proclaims that this has already happened. Jesus Christ has been raised and exalted, and with his exaltation comes a new body, a new belonging, and a new Lord. We are no longer defined by the body of death. We now live as members of the body of Christ, under the reign of grace, awaiting the full redemption of our bodies when death itself is finally undone.

Paul gives voice to this hope in Romans 8:18–25, where creation itself is pictured as groaning under the weight of corruption, longing for the revealing of the children of God. Salvation, in Paul's vision, is not confined to human souls. It is the renewal of all creation.[21]

God's mission encompasses the liberation of both humanity and the created order from bondage to decay, fulfilling the promise of cosmic freedom and reconciliation (Rom 8:21).

This expansive understanding of sin and redemption reshapes the church's sense of vocation. If sin operates not only at the personal level but also within structures and systems, then the mission of God must be equally comprehensive. The defeat of sin through Christ involves more than individual salvation; it entails the confrontation and dismantling of injustice, oppression, exploitation, and alienation in all their forms.[22] As a redeemed community, the church is called to embody this liberation, living as a sign of reconciliation and a foretaste of God's coming kingdom.

Paul's message in Romans thus reveals the full breadth of divine redemption. God's saving work heals the human heart, restores fractured relationships, challenges unjust powers, and sets creation itself on the path toward renewal. The mission of God is nothing less than the restoration of all things to their intended harmony in communion with the Creator.

Sin as a Deadly Wound

Western theology, shaped by figures such as Tertullian, Augustine, and later Anselm, has often interpreted Adam's sin primarily through legal

21. 2 Cor 5:17; Eph 1:9–10; Phil 3:20–21; Col 1:19–20; see also Acts 3:21.

22. Miranda, *Marx and the Bible*, 77–108.

and judicial categories. Humanity's fall is understood as a transgression of divine law that incurred the penalty of death. Through Adam's representative headship, guilt and corruption spread to the entire human race, a condition later described as original sin. Augustine's stark portrayal of humanity as a *massa damnata* ("a horde doomed to hellfire") reflects this emphasis on inherited guilt and condemnation.[23] As a result, much of Western theology has framed salvation in juridical terms, speaking the language of law, guilt, punishment, and justification, and imagining redemption largely within the courtroom of divine justice.

Eastern Orthodox theology, by contrast, approaches sin and redemption through an ontological and relational lens. The fall is not primarily a crime demanding punishment but a rupture in humanity's participation in the life of God. Death, in this view, is less a judicial sentence than the inevitable result of separation from the Source of life.[24] Sin introduces disorder and decay into creation, initiating a movement toward corruption and non-being that distorts God's intended harmony.[25] Redemption is not only acquittal but restoration. It is the healing of human nature, the renewal of life, and the reestablishment of communion between humanity and God.

This emphasis reflects the outlook of much early Christian theology, which did not initially frame sin as the settlement of a legal debt.[26] Sin was more often described as a wound requiring healing rather than a crime demanding punishment.[27] It was understood as a deadly condition that barred humanity from the fullness of life God intended.[28] This corruption called forth divine mercy, culminating in the incarnation, where God moves toward humanity in Christ. Salvation, then, was not simply about clearing a legal record but about restoring communion with God and reclaiming humanity's original vocation. In this framework, salvation is an act of divine healing and restoration. It is God's remedy for sin's corruption.[29] Through Christ's life, death, and resurrection, God overcomes death and restores humanity to the fullness of life.

23. Greenman and Larsen, *Reading Romans Through the Centuries*, 31–32.
24. Athanasius, *On the Incarnation*, 22.
25. Romanides, *Ancestral Sin*.
26. Rybarczyk, *Beyond Salvation*, 48–49.
27. Bray, *Romans*, 141.
28. Dunn, *Theology of Paul*, 212–13.
29. Athanasius, *On the Incarnation*, 52–53.

This restorative vision is inseparable from the mission of God, which centers on renewing creation from the effects of sin and death. The primary consequence of the fall, in this account, is death, introduced when humanity misused its freedom by choosing autonomy over communion with God.[30] This choice resulted in an ontological disconnection that led to corruption and mortality. God's original intent was for humanity to be transformed into beings united with his divine nature. The serpent's temptation twisted this calling into a pursuit of self-sufficient deification, severing humanity from its destiny.[31] Redemption is God's work of restoring humanity to communion, healing what was corrupted, and leading creation back toward its intended fulfillment in union with him.

Sin and the Mission of God

God's purpose is nothing less than the restoration of humanity and creation to their intended design. Sin, as the distortion of that purpose, must therefore be confronted if God's mission is to move forward. In confronting sin, God is not merely rescuing isolated individuals but advancing his cosmic plan to reconcile all things to himself. For Paul, the defeat of sin is both the means by which God's mission unfolds and the evidence of God's unwavering faithfulness, a mission that embraces every nation, every people, and the whole of creation.

This missional horizon comes into sharp focus in Paul's teaching on baptism and new life in Romans 6. Those who are united with Christ in his death are also united with him in his resurrection, drawn into a transformed way of living marked by "newness of life" (Rom 6:4). This union breaks sin's dominion and reorients believers toward a new allegiance. No longer enslaved to destructive powers, they are empowered to offer themselves as instruments of God's righteousness in the world (Rom 6:13). In this way, the defeat of sin is not only foundational for personal salvation but also crucial for advancing God's mission to renew creation.

SELF-EXALTATION AND IDOLATRY

Paul's treatment of idolatry in Romans exposes it as a fundamental betrayal of humanity's relationship with God. In Romans 1:21–25, Paul

30. Bray, *Romans*, 135–36.

31. Oden, *Life in the Spirit*, 382–83.

describes how humanity, though able to know God through creation, chose to suppress that truth. Rather than honoring the Creator, people exchanged God's glory for images and redirected their worship toward created things. Idolatry, in Paul's account, is a cosmic distortion of humanity's vocation, severing the bond between Creator and creation and unleashing a cascade of alienation, moral decay, and relational fracture. The refusal to acknowledge God as Creator becomes the root of humanity's descent into sin, culminating in self-worship and the corruption of God's intended order.

At the heart of idolatry lies the impulse toward self-exaltation. The human tendency to glorify one's own group while excluding or shaming others reflects a deeper spiritual disorder.[32] Throughout Scripture, the elevation of self, tribe, or nation stands as humanity's recurring failure. Idolatry may take many forms, but its core is always the same: the self turned inward, seeking autonomy rather than communion.[33] When humanity places itself at the center, it does not achieve freedom but bondage. Relationships fracture, justice erodes, and the divine economy of love gives way to rivalry and exclusion.[34]

Paul's analysis in Romans 1 makes this dynamic unmistakable. Idolatry begins when humanity refuses its dependence on the Creator and attempts to assume God's place. In suppressing the truth and exchanging God's glory for substitutes, humanity ultimately comes to worship itself.[35] This turn toward self-worship distorts human identity and vocation, giving rise to injustice and hostility while severing the bond between Creator and creation. What begins as theological rebellion inevitably unfolds as social and moral disorder.

This idolatrous pattern also shapes the story of Israel and its relationship with the nations. God's covenant with Abraham was never narrow or exclusive. From the beginning, it envisioned a global horizon: a chosen people through whom all nations would be blessed (Gen 12:1–3; 17:4–5). Israel was called to serve as a priestly nation (Exod 19:6), mediating God's presence, justice, and mercy to the world. Yet, like all humanity, Israel repeatedly struggled with the temptation toward self-exaltation, defining its identity through boundary-making rather than vocation.

32. Sacks, *Morality*, 209.

33. Miranda, *Marx and the Bible*, 35–74.

34. Olson, *Mosaic of Christian Belief*, 201–24.

35. Barth, *Epistle to the Romans*, 48–54.

Instead of embodying election as a call to bless the nations, Israel often transformed it into a marker of superiority. The result was alienation rather than reconciliation, exclusion rather than embrace.[36] Paul confronts this distortion directly in Romans. He warns Jewish believers against boasting in the law while failing to embody its intent (Rom 2:17–24), and he cautions gentile believers against arrogance in their inclusion, reminding them that they stand only by grace (Rom 11:18–21). In both cases, Paul exposes how idolatry reemerges whenever identity is grounded in privilege rather than gift.

The gospel dismantles every boundary erected by pride. Where idolatry produces exclusion, the way of Christ calls forth humble embrace. To embrace another is to recognize the image of God in them and to participate in the reconciling love that defines God's own character. Reconciliation is not merely the absence of hostility but the active pursuit of restored relationship, a way of life that mirrors God's welcome of humanity in Christ.

In Jesus, the promise given to Abraham reaches its fulfillment. Jew and gentile, male and female, educated and barbarian, enslaved and free, are brought together into one new humanity (Eph 2:14–16). This unity is not only a theological reality but a missional calling. As the people of God, the church is entrusted with the vocation once given to Israel: to mediate God's blessing to the nations, resist the idols of nationalism and superiority, and bear witness to a kingdom in which every wall of division is torn down.

God's intention for Israel, and now for the church, is the same: to serve as a kingdom of priests, reflecting divine justice, mercy, and grace to the nations. This calling is undermined whenever self-exaltation replaces service or identity is built on exclusion rather than grace. The promise to Abraham remains the guiding vision for the people of God. Through faith, the global family of believers becomes a channel of blessing to the nations. By rejecting idolatry, practicing humility, and embracing others as God has embraced us in Christ, the church lives into its true identity as a reconciled and reconciling people, a light to the nations, and a witness to the God who is restoring all things.

36. Volf, *Exclusion and Embrace*, 1–23.

TORAH AND SALVATION

Abraham Joshua Heschel famously argued that translating Torah as "Law" is not merely imprecise but theologically distorting. The Hebrew term *torah* derives from a root meaning "to teach" or "to instruct," and thus refers primarily to divine guidance rather than a codified legal system. Rendering Torah as "Law" imports Greco-Roman and modern juridical categories that emphasize regulation, compliance, and impersonal authority, obscuring Torah's covenantal, relational, and pedagogical character. For Heschel, Torah is God's living address to Israel, an expression of divine concern and involvement, before it is a set of commands to be obeyed. While Torah certainly includes *mitzvot*, these commandments are embedded within a broader narrative of promise, redemption, and ongoing relationship. Reducing Torah to "Law" not only flattens its meaning but has also fueled enduring misunderstandings, particularly Christian caricatures of Judaism as legalistic and opposed to grace. In Heschel's vision, Torah is itself a gift of grace: God drawing near to instruct, form, and sustain a people in faithful covenantal life.[37]

The Torah was never intended to function as a means of personal salvation or individual justification. Rather, it was given to shape and sustain Israel's covenant relationship with God and to form their communal identity as his chosen people.[38] Its purpose was fundamentally relational and covenantal. The Torah was not a legalistic system for earning righteousness but a framework for faithful living within God's redemptive purposes, ordering life in response to a living God who seeks relationship rather than mere compliance.

Within the ancient Near Eastern context, law codes, including the Torah, did not operate like modern juridical systems that reduce morality to abstract rules or impersonal enforcement. Instead, they articulated a moral vision, expressing the values, priorities, and commitments of a people in relationship with their God.[39] The Torah gave shape to Israel's vocation as a holy nation, calling them to embody God's justice, mercy, and holiness in the midst of the nations. Obedience was not meant to be mechanical but responsive, an act of attentiveness to God's will and a participation in God's concern for the world.

37. Heschel, *God in Search of Man*, 210–29; Heschel, *Sabbath*, 12–18.

38. Walton and Walton, *Lost World of the Torah*, 154–60.

39. Walton and Walton, *Lost World of the Torah*, 35–36.

For this reason, the Torah was never intended to be a universal or salvific system. It functioned as a covenant charter, ordering Israel's worship, ethics, and communal life in light of their unique relationship with God.[40] Obedience was not a strategy for securing divine favor but a grateful response to the God who had already redeemed Israel and called them to serve as a light among the nations. The law was meant to cultivate sensitivity to God's presence and responsibility toward neighbor, especially the vulnerable, rather than to serve as a boundary of exclusion or self-justification.

This perspective challenges the assumption that Second Temple Judaism generally understood the Torah as a pathway to salvation. Even in that period, the Torah was primarily a marker of covenant membership and communal identity.[41] Yet under the pressures of foreign domination and cultural threat, especially under Hellenistic and Roman domination, certain practices, such as circumcision, dietary laws, and Sabbath observance, increasingly functioned as defensive boundary markers.[42] In these circumstances, attentiveness to God's will could be reduced to rigid observance, and covenantal faithfulness could devolve into legalism.

It is this distortion, rather than the Torah itself, that Paul confronts in Romans and Galatians. His insistence that justification comes by faith rather than "works of the law" addresses the misuse of the Torah as a means of establishing superiority or securing righteousness. Paul does not reject the Torah's covenantal purpose but calls Israel back to its deeper intention: a life oriented toward God's righteousness, mercy, and faithfulness rather than toward self-protection or moral self-exaltation.[43]

Ultimately, the Torah's purpose was covenantal rather than salvific.[44] It was given to form a people attentive to God's call, responsive to God's compassion, and engaged in God's redemptive concern for the world. At the same time, the Torah pointed beyond itself to the necessity of divine intervention through the Messiah, a work the law alone could not accomplish. As Paul affirms, what the law was unable to do because of human weakness, God has accomplished in Christ through the Spirit

40. Walton and Walton, *Lost World of the Torah*, 132.

41. Sanders, *Paul and Palestinian Judaism*, 147–82; and Wright, *Paul and the Faithfulness of God*, 387–89.

42. Wright, *Paul and the Faithfulness of God*, 367–68.

43. Wright, *Paul and the Faithfulness of God*, 1173.

44. Walton and Walton, *Lost World of the Torah*, 159.

(Rom 8:3–4).[45] The Torah coheres fully with the broader biblical narrative of grace and redemption, revealing both God's longing for relationship and humanity's need for renewal within the mission of God.

HONOR AND SHAME

Contrary to the common interpretation of Romans as a treatise on individual justification and forgiveness, the letter is deeply concerned with the cultural realities of honor and shame. These themes run through Paul's argument, reflected in words such as honor, dishonor, glory, praise, boast, and shame. The Roman congregations had been shaped by a society steeped in honor–shame dynamics, where social worth was measured by public recognition and status.[46] Both Jewish and gentile believers had absorbed these values, competing for superiority and thereby undermining the unity Paul sought to establish.

Paul's awareness of these tensions is evident when he refers to categories like "Greeks and barbarians, educated and uneducated" (Rom 1:14). Such distinctions reflected a social mindset that perpetuated exclusion and hindered the church's participation in God's mission, especially to those deemed "barbarians" in regions like Spain. In the broader Roman world, honor and shame governed every sphere of life, politics, religion, family, and economics, reinforcing hierarchies of power and worth.[47]

Paul's letter dismantles this system at its roots. He reframes honor not as a social achievement but as a divine gift grounded in God's grace. In Romans 2:28–29, he confronts Jewish pride by asserting that true circumcision is inward, a matter of the heart and the Spirit. Later, in Romans 14–15, he urges gentile believers to honor Jewish traditions and to "make every effort to do what leads to peace and mutual edification" (Rom 14:19). In this way, Paul redefines honor as humility and service for the sake of unity.

He also challenges the imperial ideology that identified Caesar as the guarantor of peace and honor. By proclaiming Jesus as Lord (Rom 10:9–13), Paul subverts Rome's honor code, presenting Christ's self-giving love as the true measure of glory. In Romans 5:17, he contrasts Adam's reign of death with Christ's reign of life, showing that honor is

45. Walton and Walton, *Lost World of the Torah*, 211.

46. deSilva, *Honor*, 209–10.

47. Beker, *Paul*, 19.

not attained through dominance but received through participation in God's redemptive kingdom.

Finally, Paul extends this redefinition of honor to include those on society's margins. His declaration of indebtedness "to Greeks and barbarians, to the wise and the foolish" (Rom 1:14) affirms the gospel's universality and rejects the hierarchies that devalue people based on ethnicity, education, or social class. For Paul, salvation is not a privilege of the elite but a gift for all who believe. In this radical reframing, the gospel exposes and overturns the honor–shame system of the empire, creating a new community where worth is measured by God's grace alone.

Dismantling and Reshaping the Culture of Honor and Shame

Paul wields the gospel as both mirror and critique, exposing and dismantling the Roman culture of honor and shame. He reveals that such distinctions are rendered meaningless in light of God's righteousness. By interpreting Roman social behavior through the lens of the gospel, Paul challenges every claim to cultural superiority, whether between Jew and gentile, Greek and barbarian, enslaved and free, or between the empire and its margins. In doing so, he redefines honor as a reality rooted not in status or achievement but in faith, grace, and God's redemptive work in Christ. The result is a new kind of community, one in which all stand equal before God and are united in him.

The church's mission has always unfolded amid cultural collisions. In every generation, the gospel confronts societies built on systems of honor, exclusion, self-exaltation, and power.[48] The early church faced fierce resistance from both Jewish and gentile worlds that perceived the gospel as a threat to their established values. Likewise, the modern church often finds itself navigating cultures that prize dominance, power, and tribalism.

When the church embraces the gospel's redefinition of honor grounded in humility and grace, it becomes a prophetic sign of God's kingdom. Rather than conforming to an "us versus them" mentality, the church is called to embody the reconciling power of Christ, standing as a living alternative to cultures of exclusion. To live this way is to challenge every system that marginalizes or dehumanizes and to bear witness to the greater reality of the kingdom of God, where every tribe, tongue, and nation is gathered into one new humanity in Christ.

48. Volf, *Exclusion and Embrace*, 180–85, 193, 196, 213–18.

EMPIRE, IMPERIALISM, AND COLONIALISM

The culture of empire, imperialism, and domination that defined the Roman world forms an essential backdrop for understanding Paul's letter to the Romans and its enduring influence on Christian thought. Rome stood at the center of a vast imperial system sustained by military conquest, political control, and rigid hierarchies of power. Loyalty to the emperor was not only civic but religious. Imperial ideology portrayed the emperor as divinely sanctioned, even as a "son of god," and celebrated Roman rule as the guarantor of peace through force, the *Pax Romana*.[49] This vision of order permeated public life, shaping notions of authority, citizenship, and belonging.

Against this imperial imagination, Paul's proclamation of the gospel emerges as deeply subversive. His insistence that Jesus is Lord (Rom 10:9) directly confronts the imperial cult's confession of Caesar as lord. When Paul speaks of "my gospel" (Rom 2:16; 16:25; 2 Tim 2:8), he proclaims not merely a private message of personal salvation but a public announcement that challenges Rome's claims to ultimate authority. The gospel declares a different ruler, a different peace, and a different vision of justice, grounded not in domination but in self-giving love.

Throughout Romans, Paul reshapes imperial language by presenting God's righteousness as the true foundation of peace and order. Rome claimed to establish justice through law, violence, and hierarchy. Paul counters this claim by revealing a righteousness made known through the faithfulness of Jesus Christ, a righteousness that restores rather than subjugates and that embraces all nations rather than exalting one people over others. God's faithfulness to Jew and gentile alike exposes the fragility of imperial power built on exclusion and coercion, undermining Rome's narrative of superiority over so-called "barbarian" peoples.

Paul also redefines the nature of power and authority. In Romans 13:1–7, he calls believers to respect governing authorities, yet he does so within a framework that clearly subordinates all earthly power to the sovereignty of God.[50] Authority, in Paul's vision, is neither absolute nor self-legitimating. It is accountable to God and measured by its service to the common good. This understanding stands in tension with imperial notions of power rooted in domination and control.

49. Wright, *Paul and the Faithfulness of God*, 294.

50. Elliott, *Arrogance of Nations*, 15.

The contrast becomes even clearer in Paul's exhortations to the Christian community. His call to humility, mutual service, and enemy-love (Rom 12:9–21) offers a radically different social imagination from the competitive and honor-driven values of Roman society.[51] Where empire thrived on rivalry, hierarchy, and exclusion, Paul envisions a community shaped by love, generosity, and reconciliation. In this way, Romans presents not only a theological argument but an alternative way of life, a counter-imperial witness that proclaims the reign of God over against the powers of this age.

Empire Beyond Romans: Christianity and Imperialism

The relationship between Christianity and empire became increasingly complex in the centuries following Paul, particularly with the conversion of Constantine and the establishment of Christianity as the official religion of the Roman Empire. This development marked a decisive turning point in the church's history. Whereas the early Christian movement had largely existed on the margins of imperial power and often stood in tension with its coercive structures, the Constantinian and post-Constantinian eras witnessed a gradual alignment between church and state. Christianity was no longer merely a counter-imperial witness but increasingly became entangled with imperial authority, benefiting from state patronage while absorbing imperial assumptions about power, hierarchy, and control.[52]

As this alliance deepened, Christian leaders and institutions began to adopt imperial language, symbols, and strategies in the promotion of the faith. The church's mission, once rooted in suffering witness and marginality, was increasingly framed in terms of expansion, uniformity, and social order. This fusion of Christianity and empire shaped European Christendom for centuries, embedding the gospel within political structures and cultural dominance. By the time of European colonial expansion, this legacy was firmly entrenched. Colonial powers frequently interpreted their military and economic conquests through a Christian lens, portraying imperial domination as a divine mandate to civilize, convert, and rule non-European peoples.[53]

51. Jewett, *Romans*, 756–79.

52. Bruce, *Spreading Flame*, 293–95.

53. Barrett et al., *Missional Church*, 79–82.

This ideology closely mirrored earlier Roman imperial propaganda, in which cultural superiority and military power were understood as signs of divine favor and instruments of cosmic order. In many colonial contexts, the church functioned alongside the state as both a spiritual and political agent, proclaiming the gospel while simultaneously reinforcing systems of exploitation, racial hierarchy, and economic injustice.[54] Missionary activity was often entangled with colonial administration, blurring the line between evangelization and cultural domination.

Importantly, this fusion of Christianity and empire was not confined to Europe. Similar patterns emerged beyond the European continent, including in the United States, where Christian identity has at times been closely aligned with national expansion, manifest destiny, and political power. Christian language and symbols have been used to sacralize national interests, justify the attempted genocide of Indigenous peoples, legitimize slavery and segregation, and sustain systems of economic and racial inequality. The result has often been a domesticated gospel, reshaped to support national myths and political agendas rather than to challenge them.

Across these diverse settings, the enduring temptation has been the same: to baptize power rather than to submit power to the lordship of Christ. When Christianity becomes intertwined with imperial ambition, it risks abandoning its prophetic vocation and silencing its witness to the crucified and risen Lord. The legacy of Constantinianism and its modern descendants continues to confront the church with a critical question: Will it align itself with the powers of this age or recover its calling to embody a counter-imperial kingdom shaped by the gospel?

Theological Responses to Imperialism

In light of this history, many theologians have recognized the need to confront how empire and colonialism have distorted the message of the gospel.[55] The gospel of Jesus Christ is fundamentally anti-imperial, calling for the liberation of the oppressed and the dismantling of unjust systems.[56] It proclaims the liberation of the marginalized, the restoration of justice, and the peace of God's kingdom breaking into the world. Paul's

54. Ott et al., *Encountering Theology of Mission*, 167–69.

55. Escarfuller, "Repudiating Assimilation in Reading Romans 9–11," 140.

56. Pachuau, *God at Work in the World*, 57.

vision of God's reign, rooted in righteousness, peace, and joy in the Holy Spirit, serves as a direct challenge to every attempt to harness Christianity for imperial or nationalistic ends.[57]

Postcolonial theology has helped recover this liberating dimension of the gospel, exposing how power and privilege have often masked themselves in the language of mission.[58] It insists that the church's mission must reject domination in all its forms and instead embody equity, reconciliation, and the flourishing of all peoples.

Paul's message in Romans becomes subversive—the gospel he proclaims undermines the self-exalting claims of empire and invites the church to bear witness to a different kind of power, which is the self-giving love of God revealed in Christ. This vision continues to offer a prophetic framework for critiquing modern systems of imperialism and for reclaiming the gospel as a message of freedom, justice, and peace for the whole world.

Implications for the Church

The church's historical entanglement with empire serves as both a cautionary tale and a call to return to the radical message of the gospel. Paul's vision of the kingdom of God, as articulated in Romans, offers an alternative to imperial ideologies.[59] It calls the church to embody humility, mutual love, and justice, rejecting the allure of power and privilege. The church's mission, rather than replicating systems of conquest, must reflect the reconciling work of Christ that transcends cultural, ethnic, and political divisions. By reclaiming Paul's counter-imperial gospel, the church can address its historical complicity in imperialism and recommit to the mission of God, one that prioritizes human dignity, justice, and the transformative power of the kingdom of God over the competing claims of earthly empires.[60]

Paul sets the gospel against the Roman cultural mindset, much like a master craftsman wielding a plumbline to reveal the distortions in their values and assumptions.[61] The Roman world was steeped in a hierarchi-

57. Ciampa, "Paul's Theology of the Gospel," 182.

58. Elliott, *Paul Against the Nations*, 48–70.

59. Shohe, "Hermeneutic of Love, Honor, and Hospitality," 231–50.

60. Pannenberg, *Systematic Theology*, 1:148–49.

61. Gregory of Nyssa, *Against Eunomius* 4.8 (*NPNF*[2] 5:168–69).

cal culture of honor and shame, where power, status, and social distinctions, between Jew and gentile, educated and uneducated, enslaved and free, defined a person's worth. Paul's gospel, however, stands as a divine standard that cuts through these constructs, revealing their inconsistency with God's righteousness. Paul dismantles the Roman claims to superiority, whether grounded in imperial propaganda or ethnic pride.[62] Paul's gospel confronts and corrects the misalignments of Roman culture and calls the church to be built on God's justice, mercy, and truth in a way that is worthy of the gospel.

CULTURALLY COMPROMISED

While Paul's Letters to the Corinthians, Galatians, and Colossians confront moral and doctrinal compromises, Romans uniquely addresses cultural compromise. The Roman congregations reflected the cultural complexities of Rome itself, an epicenter of imperial power, societal stratification, and competing honor–shame systems. These dynamics had seeped into the church, creating divisions along ethnic, cultural, and social lines. Far from being abstract cultural phenomena, these tensions directly affected the church's unity, identity, and mission. Jewish believers often viewed their covenantal heritage as giving them a privileged position, while gentile believers, newly liberated from paganism, could disdain Jewish traditions as outdated or irrelevant. Such divisions threatened the church's cohesion and undermined the gospel.

Because Paul lacked a formal relationship with the Roman congregations, he likely adopted a more nuanced and diplomatic approach compared to the direct tone seen in his Letters to the Corinthians, Galatians, and Colossians.[63] This measured tone allowed him to address the cultural compromises within the Roman church while fostering reflection rather than provoking resistance. This strategy enables him to challenge the congregation's compromises effectively while inviting them to embody a transformed identity as the people of God, no longer conforming to the patterns of Roman culture (Rom 12:2).

By reading Romans as Paul's proclamation of the Christ event within the turmoil of cultural and social conflict, the letter emerges as a missiological *tour de force*. Paul proclaims Christ as the redeemer of all

62. Jewett, *Romans*, 745–46.

63. Jewett, *Romans*, 43–44.

nations and calls the church to embody covenant faithfulness in tangible, communal ways. He exhorts believers to rise above ethnic, social, and cultural divisions, forming a unified community that demonstrates the reconciling and transformative power of the gospel amid the pressures of empire.

The Subtextual Becomes the Textual

Beneath Paul's theological argument in Romans lies a network of subtextual concerns addressing the cultural tensions, identity struggles, and potential compromises confronting the Roman church. Though not always stated directly, these issues form the backdrop of his letter and give shape to his theology. The Roman believers wrestled with questions of cultural superiority, the continuing role of the Torah, and the meaning of faith in Christ for their shared identity as God's people. Paul's response reflects both pastoral sensitivity and theological depth, presenting the gospel as the power of God that unites all who believe (Rom 1:16).

Through his argument, Paul brings these underlying tensions to the surface and reinterprets them in light of the Christ event. He transforms cultural and theological conflicts into a framework for understanding how the gospel redefines community, righteousness, and belonging. In this sense, the subtextual becomes the textual: Roman society and church life becomes the very text of his theological reflection. Paul's method of contextualizing the gospel reveals how theology can interpret and ultimately transform the world in which it is proclaimed.

Paul's critique of cultural and religious compromise is incisive. He dismantles Jewish reliance on the law as a source of righteousness, exposing its limits and underscoring the universal need for grace (Rom 3:9–20). Yet he also warns gentile believers against arrogance, reminding them that their inclusion in God's covenant is an act of mercy, not merit (Rom 11:17–24). In holding both groups accountable, Paul dismantles every claim to superiority, religious, cultural, or moral, and calls the church to a shared identity grounded solely in the grace of God revealed in Christ.

Subtle Diplomacy

Although his message is rigorous, Paul delivers his critique with exceptional tact. He opens the letter with a tone of affirmation and humility, expressing gratitude for the faith of the Roman believers and his longing to visit them (Rom 1:8–15). This establishes a relational foundation, making his subsequent critique more palatable. Paul also frames his argument in theological rather than personal terms, grounding his critique in the universal truths of the gospel rather than singling out individuals or groups. Paul's use of inclusive language is another hallmark of his diplomatic approach. Instead of pitting Jews against gentiles or addressing one group in isolation, he consistently emphasizes the shared condition of all humanity: "There is no one righteous, not even one" (Rom 3:10) and "All have sinned and fall short of the glory of God" (Rom 3:23). By leveling the playing field, Paul avoids alienating either group and directs their attention to the sufficiency of Christ's redemptive work.

The brilliance of Paul's approach lies in his ability to confront significant cultural compromises without provoking defensiveness. His critique is woven into a larger theological narrative that highlights God's righteousness, the inclusivity of the gospel, and the church's calling to be a reconciled body. This allows him to address sensitive issues without exacerbating divisions. For example, in Romans 14–15, Paul addresses disputes over dietary laws and the observance of holy days, which were flashpoints for cultural tension. Rather than taking sides, he exhorts both groups to act in love and to prioritize the unity of the body over their cultural preferences: "Let us therefore make every effort to do what leads to peace and to mutual edification" (Rom 14:19). This call to mutual respect and deference cloaks Paul's sharp critique of their divisive behavior, presenting it as an opportunity to embody the gospel rather than a rebuke.

Paul's diplomatic yet incisive approach stands as a masterclass in confronting cultural compromise within the church, compromise that endangered both the integrity of the gospel and the church's capacity for mission. By embedding his critique within a theologically rich narrative and framing it through the gospel's universal scope, Paul ensures that his message rises above the immediate situation of the Roman congregations to speak across generations.

He engages directly with the honor–shame dynamics, Jewish–gentile tensions, and competing claims of cultural superiority that fractured the Roman church. In doing so, Paul demonstrates an awareness that internal division undermines not only the church's witness but its very identity as the covenant people of God, called to embody and proclaim the reconciling power of the gospel. His argument is deeply missional, aimed at forming a reconciled, gospel-centered community capable of carrying the message of Christ into new and challenging frontiers.

Romans thus continues to speak prophetically to the church today, calling believers to confront every form of cultural compromise and division. It summons the people of God to embrace a gospel-shaped identity that transcends ethnicity, culture, and status, an identity that alone sustains authentic partnership and credible witness in a world still fractured by power, pride, and exclusion.

LIGHTS IN THE WORLD: BEARING FAITHFUL WITNESS

Paul's engagement with the Roman congregations reveals not only his concern for their cultural compromises but also his skill as a discerning cultural interpreter. He does not merely address the visible symptoms of division, pride, or moral confusion. Instead, he exposes the underlying cultural narratives that shape their thinking and reorients their entire worldview through the lens of the gospel.

Grounded in the covenant faithfulness of the God of Israel, this gospel redefines what it means to belong, to honor, and to serve. It offers a radically new vision of community and mission shaped by humility, reconciliation, and grace. In this way, Paul presents the gospel as the ultimate criterion by which every culture, value, and pattern of behavior is evaluated. He calls the Roman believers to allow their identities and practices to be reshaped around God's redemptive purpose, aligning their communal life with God's reconciling mission in the world. Through this reorientation, Paul demonstrates the transformative power of the gospel, a power that transcends cultural boundaries, dismantles systems of superiority, and forms a new humanity in Christ.

Romans presents the gospel as God's reconciling power at work in the world, calling the church to embody God's love and righteousness amid fracture and division. Paul rarely, if ever, frames evangelism in terms of programs or techniques. Instead, he emphasizes the witness of a reconciled community whose shared life displays the gospel's credibility and power. As believers live out the gospel together, they offer a faithful witness that resists transactional or coercive evangelism while inviting others into God's reconciling work through presence, faithfulness, and love.

The gospel Paul proclaims addresses every fractured relationship. It restores humanity's communion with God, forms Jews and gentiles into one new people, and shapes the church as a reconciled and reconciling community. At its core, this gospel expresses God's compassionate longing to heal what sin has broken and to reconcile all things in Christ. As the church lives into this reality, it shines as a light in the world, embodying the gospel's transformative power and bearing witness through its shared life to the righteousness and faithfulness of God.[64]

Paul's reorientation of the Roman churches toward the mission of God provided a framework for addressing their internal divisions. Rather than treating their conflicts as isolated pastoral problems, Paul situated them within a broader missional horizon. As the Roman believers embraced their shared participation in God's redemptive mission, they were invited to become a reconciled community whose unity itself bore witness to the gospel. In this way, mission was not an added task layered onto congregational life but the very context within which healing, formation, and renewal could occur.

By addressing both theological fractures and pastoral needs, Paul was equipping the Roman churches to function as a missionary people within the heart of the empire. Their reconciliation across ethnic, cultural, and social boundaries was essential to their credibility as a gospel-shaped community capable of partnering in God's mission to the nations. This dual focus ensured that the churches were not only spiritually renewed but also missionally mobilized. Participation in God's mission became the means by which they rediscovered their purpose, unity, and vitality as the missionary people of God.

RECONTEXTUALIZING ROMANS

Romans has exercised a transformative influence throughout church history, repeatedly igniting renewal at moments of theological, ecclesial, and moral crisis. Its impact is evident in Martin Luther, whose struggle with Paul's teaching on justification by faith reshaped both his conscience and the course of Western Christianity. The same epistle later shaped John Wesley, whose heart was "strangely warmed" while hearing Luther's preface to Romans read aloud, sparking a renewal movement that would spread across continents. In the nineteenth century, Romans

64. Wright, *Paul and the Faithfulness of God*, 1484.

emboldened John William Colenso to challenge the moral assumptions of the British Empire and to advocate for justice on behalf of the Zulu people, grounding his resistance in Paul's vision of God's righteousness as faithful and impartial.[65]

In the twentieth century, during the dark days that led to the Nazi nightmare, Karl Barth again turned to Romans as a theological and prophetic resource.[66] His commentary confronted the church's accommodation to political power and reasserted the radical freedom of God's grace, calling believers back to faithful witness in the face of idolatrous nationalism. In each of these contexts, Romans functioned as a living word that disrupted complacency, exposed false loyalties, and summoned the church to renewed obedience.

Across generations, Romans continues to challenge the church to embody the righteousness of God within complex and contested cultural landscapes. Its enduring relevance lies in its capacity for faithful recontextualization without loss of theological integrity. Each generation encounters Paul's vision anew, discovering how the gospel addresses its particular anxieties, injustices, and missional questions while remaining anchored in God's eternal purposes. The gospel, as Romans presents it, is living and active, continually calling the church to reimagine its identity and vocation in light of God's redemptive mission.

CONCLUSION

Paul's Letter to the Romans stands as a missional masterpiece. Read within its first-century sociopolitical context, Romans reveals how a deeply contextualized gospel speaks both pastorally and prophetically, forming the church while confronting idolatry, cultural accommodation, and religious pride. By addressing internal divisions and simultaneously inviting partnership in his mission to Spain, Paul demonstrates that the health of the local church and the advance of God's mission are inseparable. Unity forged by the gospel is not an end in itself but a means through which the church fulfills its calling to be a light to the nations.

Romans remains a compelling resource for the contemporary church as it navigates pollical polarization, cultural assimilation, and missional uncertainty. It calls the church to remain grounded in the unchanging

65. Colenso, *Romans.* Also, Chapman, *Anglican Theology*, 180–81.

66. Barth, *Epistle to the Romans.*

power of the gospel while faithfully participating in the mission of God. At its heart lies the creative tension between stability and movement, between the gathered life of the church and the outward momentum of apostolic mission. This interplay is not a problem to be solved but a gift to be stewarded. By inhabiting the liminal space between participation in God's mission to the nations and living as one new humanity, the church learns again what it means to live as the missionary people of God.

PART 4

Living Between Church and Mission

The mission of God has always unfolded through partnership, within the creative tension between stability and sending, between the gathered life of the church and the outward movement of mission. From the earliest Christian communities onward, God has worked through both local congregations and boundary-crossing witnesses who carried the gospel into new frontiers. When these expressions remain connected, the church flourishes; when they drift apart, both lose vitality and clarity of purpose.

This section brings together insights from missiology, sociology, anthropology, and organizational theory to reimagine faithful partnership in the contemporary church. Rather than simply describing church and mission structures, it explores how they can collaborate as co-laborers in God's redemptive work. We begin by tracing the historical interplay between church and mission, from the apostolic communities of the first century through monastic movements, missionary societies, and today's global networks. Across these periods, partnership has often emerged through disruption and renewal, revealing that mission structures are not fixed but adaptive expressions shaped by context and calling.

At the heart of this section lies a central question: How can the people of God live as both gathered and sent, rooted in local community while reaching toward the world? Romans, and the gospel itself, call the church to inhabit this creative tension faithfully. It is in this space between stability and movement that the Spirit continues to form a people shaped for the mission of God.

15

Modalities and Sodalities

More than twenty centuries have passed since Paul wrote his letter to the Romans. In that time, the Christian movement has grown from a small network of house churches and itinerant apostolic teams into a global church. What began as a Spirit-led movement in the Mediterranean world has become a complex ecclesial landscape, one that includes both local congregations and specialized mission initiatives. This growth has shaped not only the theological and cultural expressions of Christianity but also how the church understands and organizes its participation in God's mission.

Standing at the intersection of ecclesiology and mission, a persistent question emerges: How can the church's gathered life and its outward-reaching witness function together in harmony rather than in competition?

Among modern efforts to address this question, Ralph D. Winter's framework of modalities and sodalities remains one of the most influential. First presented at the 1973 Lausanne Congress on World Evangelization, Winter argued that the mission of the church has always operated through two complementary structures. The modality refers to the gathered community of believers, the local church with its pastoral, sacramental, and formative life. The sodality refers to specialized ministry and mission communities dedicated to advancing the gospel beyond the congregation's immediate context and ability. Winter's proposal has generated decades of discussion, refinement, and critique, a sign of its enduring importance for both theology and practice.

At the heart of Winter's argument is the conviction that both forms are essential for fulfilling the Great Commission. The local church nurtures, disciples, and sends. Mission and ministry structures pioneer, extend, equip, and establish new expressions of the gospel. Both are biblically grounded and historically necessary. This claim, however, has not gone uncontested. Some argue that mission agencies represent post-biblical developments that risk fragmenting the unity of the church. Others see them as natural continuations of the apostolic missionary bands that carried the gospel across the ancient world.[1]

In the pages that follow, we examine Winter's thesis alongside these competing perspectives, attending to both theological tensions and practical consequences. The goal is to pursue a constructive synthesis that honors the distinct callings of church and mission while cultivating a cooperative partnership shaped by shared faith, mutual dependence, and common participation in the mission of God.

SUMMARY OF RALPH D. WINTER'S "THE TWO STRUCTURES OF GOD'S REDEMPTIVE MISSION"

In "The Two Structures of God's Redemptive Mission," Winter argues that throughout church history Christian mission has been carried out through two distinct but complementary structures: modalities (churches) and sodalities (mission and ministry organizations). He contends that recognizing and maintaining both structures is crucial for the effective fulfillment of the Great Commission.[2]

Redemptive Structures in the New Testament

Winter begins by identifying the New Testament church as essentially a Christian synagogue. Paul's missionary work was primarily centered around synagogues, where he preached the gospel to both Jews and gentiles. Over time, new synagogues emerged that were exclusively Christian, functioning as the early expression of the modality, a structure that included men and women, young and old, as a community of faith.

1. Schnabel, *Paul the Missionary*, 393. Peters, *Biblical Theology of Missions*, 199–243. Tennent, *Invitation to World Missions*, 454.

2. Winter, "Two Structures."

Alongside the local church, Winter identifies a second missional structure: the missionary band, exemplified by the teams led by Paul (see Acts 13–14). These apostolic groups operated beyond the oversight of any single congregation. They depended on the support of multiple churches while retaining freedom to move, adapt, and respond to emerging opportunities for gospel advance. For Winter, Paul's missionary teams provide the prototype for what he later calls sodalities. Sodalities are organized communities of trained and committed individuals set apart to extend the gospel beyond the boundaries of established churches.

Continuity in Church History: Borrowed Patterns

Winter emphasizes that neither of these structures was divinely mandated in a fixed form. Instead, both the synagogue and the missionary band were adaptations of pre-existing Jewish structures.[3] This, he argues, sets a precedent for future generations of Christians to adopt functionally equivalent structures that suit their cultural contexts. The key takeaway is dynamic equivalence, that mission structures should be flexible in form while remaining faithful in function.

Development of the Two Structures in the Roman and Medieval Periods

As Christianity expanded beyond the Jewish world, its organizational structures also evolved. The diocesan system became the dominant expression of the modality, replacing the independent synagogue model. Meanwhile, monastic communities emerged as the functional equivalents of sodalities. These monastic movements played a crucial role in preserving and transmitting Christian teaching, evangelization, and advancing social development.[4]

Winter also challenges the common Protestant tendency to dismiss monastic movements as largely corrupt or missionally irrelevant. While acknowledging periods of decline and abuse, he argues that many monastic orders served as engines of mission, learning, and social renewal. He points especially to the Celtic monastic movements, including the Irish *peregrini*, monks who left their homelands voluntarily and traveled

3. Winter, "Two Structures," 121–23.

4. Winter, "Two Structures," 121–30.

across Europe as "exiles for Christ." From their island monasteries and mobile communities, they crossed borders, preached among pagan peoples, cultivated land, preserved learning, and established new centers of Christian life in regions long beyond the reach of existing churches. These sodalities carried the gospel with an apostolic and spiritual intensity that reinvigorated the wider church.

The Medieval Synthesis and the Role of Monastic Orders

One of the key achievements of the medieval church was the integration of sodalities and modalities. Monastic orders like the Benedictines and later the Franciscans and Jesuits operated alongside diocesan structures, contributing significantly to the spread of Christianity. Bishops (representing the modality) and abbots (leading sodalities) often worked together, though conflicts arose over authority and resources. This symbiotic relationship was a major factor in the survival and expansion of Christianity throughout the medieval period.

The Protestant Reformation and the Loss of Sodality

Winter critiques the Protestant Reformation for initially rejecting sodalities. Martin Luther, dissatisfied with both monastic life and the corruption in the Catholic Church, sought to reform Christianity primarily at the level of local churches. As a result, Protestantism largely eliminated monastic sodalities, leaving only the modality. Winter argues that this was one of the greatest strategic errors of the Reformation. Without sodalities, Protestant churches lacked structured mechanisms for renewal and global mission. It was not until the rise of Pietism and the Anabaptist communities that new expressions of sodality began to emerge. The Moravians and later John Wesley's Methodist societies provided a model for organized spiritual renewal that functioned alongside traditional churches.

The Protestant Rediscovery of Sodality: The Missionary Movement

The most significant recovery of the sodality structure within Protestantism emerged through the modern missionary movement. A decisive turning point came with William Carey's call for the formation of voluntary mission societies dedicated to reaching unreached peoples. This vision ushered in a new era of organized mission, giving rise to societies such as the Baptist Missionary Society, the London Missionary Society, and the Church Missionary Society, which assumed responsibility for coordinated global evangelization beyond the capacity of local congregations alone.

These mission agencies functioned as sodalities by recruiting committed individuals who made a second-level decision to engage in full-time, cross-cultural mission. The rapid proliferation of such organizations in the nineteenth century produced what has often been described as the "Great Century" of missions, a period marked by an unprecedented expansion of Protestant global missions.[5]

Contemporary Misunderstandings and the Need for Balance

Winter identifies a persistent misunderstanding of sodalities within Protestantism. Mission agencies are often treated as secondary or optional, a perception that has frequently produced tension between church leaders and mission organizations. He warns that when ecclesiastical authorities attempt to absorb or tightly control sodalities, mission efforts suffer.

A related problem emerges on the mission field itself. Many missionaries benefit from sodality structures at home but fail to reproduce comparable mission forms in the contexts they serve. Instead, their efforts often focus exclusively on church planting, without cultivating parallel mission structures within the emerging indigenous church. According to Winter, this omission weakens long-term mission capacity, since local congregations alone rarely possess the specialized focus, mobility, and apostolic flexibility required for sustained cross-cultural mission.[6]

The Necessity of Both Structures

Winter concludes by reaffirming the necessity of both modalities and sodalities. The local church sustains worship, pastoral care, and discipleship, while mission sodalities concentrate on pioneering work, cross-cultural evangelism, and renewal. Rather than treating these structures as competitors, he calls church leaders to recognize their complementary roles and

5. Winter, "Two Structures," 131–33.

6. Winter, "Two Structures," 133–36.

to cultivate collaboration and mutual trust. By fostering healthy relationships between modalities and sodalities, the church can more effectively fulfill its mission in the world, avoiding the historical mistakes that have hindered its expansion. Despite ongoing tensions between churches and mission agencies today, both structures remain essential, with each fulfilling distinct yet complementary roles in the mission of God.[7]

DEBATES AND CRITIQUES

Winter's framework of modalities and sodalities has been highly influential but not without challenge. Critics from theological, ecclesiological, and historical perspectives question whether his model unnecessarily separates the church and its mission.

Some theologians argue that Winter's two-structure model risks creating an artificial divide between church and mission. The New Testament portrays the church as both the sender and the sent, mission is not an external function but the church's very identity.[8] To separate the two, they warn, may diminish the church's central role in God's redemptive work.[9]

Some historians also note that many of the movements Winter classified as sodalities were closely connected to established church structures.[10] The Jesuits, for example, remained accountable to the Catholic Church, and early Protestant mission societies often operated under denominational oversight. This historical overlap challenges the notion that sodalities have ever functioned entirely apart from modalities.

Bruce K. Camp argues that mission agencies lack explicit biblical grounding as independent expressions of the church.[11] He sees their value as pragmatic rather than theological: agencies are tools that assist the church's mission, not equal ecclesial structures. Camp emphasizes that local congregations, like the church in Antioch (Acts 13:1–3), bear primary responsibility for both local and global mission.

While Camp rightly emphasizes the importance of the church, Winter helps recover the insight that the church's mission unfolds through two complementary structures. These are not competing institutions but

7. Winter, "Two Structures," 136–37.
8. Bosch, *Transforming Mission*, 468–69; Wright, *Mission of God*, 257.
9. Newbigin, *Gospel in a Pluralist Society*, 146.
10. Walls, *Missionary Movement*, 119–20.
11. Camp, "Theological Examination of the Two-Structure Theory," 197–209.

two interdependent and complementary structures within the *one universal church*, the gathered and the sent, working together to fulfill God's redemptive mission in the world.

THE TENSION BETWEEN MODALITY AND SODALITY IN THE PRACTICE OF MISSION PRACTICE

In theory, the modality–sodality framework envisions churches and mission organizations as complementary partners in the mission of God, each fulfilling distinct yet interdependent roles in the Great Commission. While the theoretical model suggests an equal and mutually beneficial relationship, the lived experience often tells a different story. When institutional, financial, or cultural pressures emerge, churches tend to prioritize internal stability and congregational needs, frequently marginalizing sodalities in the process. The result is a functional hierarchy that reduces mission organizations to auxiliary roles and constrains their capacity for innovation and pioneering engagement.

This persistent imbalance exposes a gap between theological vision and lived practice. Without intentional theological reflection, strategic adaptation, and structural recalibration, the distinct contributions of both modalities and sodalities are diminished. Preserving their interdependence is essential if the church is to remain oriented toward God's mission, especially in seasons of uncertainty and crisis.

The Reality of Ecclesial Consumption

A significant factor driving this imbalance is the power differential between modalities and sodalities. Churches typically control access to people, finances, and institutional legitimacy, which makes mission organizations dependent on them for funding, personnel, and endorsement. This dependence, in turn, allows churches to exercise both formal and informal influence over mission agencies, often shaping their priorities and limiting their freedom to act.

In practice, this control can take many forms. Churches may prioritize internal stability over global engagement, or impose practical, ideological, theological, and bureaucratic constraints that unintentionally blunt missionary effectiveness. Over time, such pressures generate frustration, leading some mission organizations to distance themselves from churches in order to preserve autonomy and pursue their calling with greater flexibility.

At the same time, mission agencies are not without fault. When mission agencies focus solely on mission efforts eclipse concern for the health and sustainability of local churches, trust erodes further. The relationship then becomes increasingly transactional, focused on short-term goals rather than shared vocation. Instead of deep partnership, fragmentation takes hold, weakening the body of Christ's collective capacity to participate faithfully in the mission of God.

The Consequences of a Modality-Only Focus

When the church prioritizes institutional maintenance over cross-cultural and missionary engagement, it risks losing both its vitality and its vocation. History repeatedly shows that when the church subsumes or marginalizes missions the result is stagnation rather than renewal. In seasons of financial or organizational strain, churches often turn inward, prioritizing internal programs, facilities, and congregational needs while relegating global mission to the margins. Over time, this inward posture diminishes the church's capacity to participate fully in God's redemptive work, reducing mission to an optional activity rather than a defining expression of ecclesial life. As Winter observed, the church can become a system of "ecclesial consumption," expending its resources on self-preservation rather than multiplication.

The history of modern missiology offers a telling illustration of this dynamic in the work of Donald McGavran. Serving as a missionary in India, McGavran observed that people most readily come to faith within their own social, linguistic, and cultural networks, an insight that later became known as the Homogeneous Unit Principle. This breakthrough did not arise from abstract theory or congregational strategy but from sustained cross-cultural engagement and close attention to how the gospel took root in indigenous contexts. It was, at its core, a *sodalitic* breakthrough, rooted in the realities of missionary engagement and the contextual dynamics of indigenous church growth.

Ironically, as McGavran's insights were received into Western church settings, they were increasingly reframed through a church-centered lens. What began as a tool for understanding how the gospel spreads among unreached peoples was transformed into a strategy for congregational growth among culturally similar populations. The Church Growth Movement, though rooted in missiological observation, was gradually domesticated into a managerial paradigm aimed at increasing attendance and institutional scale rather than extending the gospel across cultural boundaries. In the process, a missionary insight intended to empower contextual, Spirit-led movements was repurposed to serve institutional expansion.

This inversion reveals a recurring missiological danger. When the church treats mission as secondary to its own success rather than as intrinsic to its identity, it forfeits a primary source of renewal. Theologically, such a posture narrows the church's imagination, shifting its focus from participation in the *missio Dei* to strategies of survival. Structurally, it encourages centralization around measurable outputs such as attendance, budgets, and programs, while neglecting sending capacity and transformative impact. Spiritually, it dulls the church's apostolic and prophetic sensitivity, leaving it less able to discern or join the movement of the Spirit beyond its own walls.

The corrective, however, is not to elevate one structure at the expense of the other, but to recover their mutual interdependence. Paul's Letter to the Romans offers a compelling example. While addressing established congregations, Paul simultaneously invites their partnership in his westward mission to Spain, without collapsing apostolic mission into congregational life or subordinating one to the other (Rom 15:23–24). Both the gathered church and the sending mission are necessary expressions of the one people of God. When this dual calling is embraced, mission is no longer a program the church supports, but the pulse that animates its life, gathered and sent, rooted and reaching, participating together in God's redemptive purpose.

WAYS MODALITIES CONTRIBUTE TO THE IMBALANCE

One of the most common ways this imbalance emerges is through financial prioritization. When economic pressure arises, churches tend to protect what is closest and most visible: staff salaries, facilities, and internal programs. Mission commitments are often perceived as supportive rather than essential. Over time, this pattern reinforces the assumption that mission is optional rather than integral to the church's life.

A second factor is the exercise of church control over missional expression. Although mission sodalities are designed to operate with a degree of autonomy, they remain dependent on churches for funding, personnel, and legitimacy. This dependence can quietly shift into control, as congregations redirect mission efforts toward short-term projects or local initiatives that align with congregational priorities rather than sustaining long-term, frontier engagement.

Often beneath this dynamic lies an unexamined assumption that the church can "do mission better." Because pastors and congregations regularly see their own activities, while the work of missionaries unfolds at a distance and largely out of view, local efforts can appear more effective, immediate, and manageable. This visibility gap easily produces an illusion of competence. The nature of the pastorate can unintentionally reinforce it. Pastors are formed to speak with authority across a wide range of issues, sometimes beyond their specific training, and this posture of leadership can quietly extend into missiology.[12] The result is not overt resistance to mission but a subtle re-centering of control. Whether motivated by sincerity or a concern for faithful stewardship, pastors and church leaders can unintentionally domesticate mission, reshaping it to fit familiar patterns of church life and leadership and, in the process, constraining the adaptive, contextual freedom that frontier and cross-cultural mission requires.

Underlying all of this is a powerful psychological and cultural pull toward the local. This tendency is not born merely of apathy but of proximity. Churches naturally invest in what is near and tangible: weekly gatherings, pastoral crises, and visible outcomes. Global mission, by contrast, is distant, slow, and often marked by ambiguity and setback. In cultures that prize measurable success and immediate results, cross-cultural mission struggles to compete for attention and resources. Over time, this inward gravity reshapes the church's imagination. Mission becomes one ministry among many rather than the outward expression of the church's identity.

12. The global COVID-19 pandemic exposed this dynamic with particular clarity. In numerous instances, pastors and church leaders issued authoritative medical and public health declarations despite having no training in medicine, epidemiology, or the sciences informing such guidance. What was often framed as pastoral leadership or theological conviction functioned, in practice, as the assertion of expertise outside one's competence. This episode revealed how the habitual authority of the pastoral role can overflow its proper limits, with consequences that are not merely theoretical but tragically concrete.

Doctrinal, political, and institutional pressures further complicate the relationship. When secondary theological or political disputes arise, mission agencies are frequently vulnerable to decisions made far from the field. Projects may be halted, missionaries recalled, or partnerships dissolved, not because of ethical failure, but because of misalignment with shifting institutional or ideological commitments. In such moments, the protection of institutional identity eclipses the demands of mission itself.

This dynamic becomes especially visible in contested contexts such as Gaza. Efforts to offer humanitarian aid, pastoral care, or gospel witness among Palestinians often encounter resistance, not from those being served but from sending churches shaped by polarized political narratives. When allegiance to institutional identity or political ideology eclipses fidelity to the gospel's reconciling work, the church becomes more concerned with defending its boundaries than crossing them, and mission becomes distorted, constrained, selective, and conditional.

Recovering that vision requires intentional formation. Churches must learn to see beyond the local horizon, to cultivate empathy for the global body of Christ, and to remember that the church exists not only in the world but for the world.

WAYS SODALITIES CONTRIBUTE TO THE IMBALANCE

Mission sodalities can also contribute to imbalance when the pursuit of focus and effectiveness leads to increasing distance from the church. In seeking flexibility, speed, and innovation, some mission agencies operate with minimal accountability to congregational life. While this independence can enhance agility, it carries relational costs. Over time, separation from the worship, discernment, and shared life of the church can foster the perception that mission agencies function as self-contained enterprises rather than as integral expressions of the body of Christ.

As this disconnect widens, trust erodes on both sides. Churches may hesitate to support organizations they perceive as distant or unaccountable, while missionaries may view churches as inward-looking or detached from the realities of mission. The result is mutual misrecognition, with each interpreting the other through frustration rather than shared calling. Restoring partnership requires a renewed commitment to shared responsibility for both church health and mission vitality.

A related tension arises from frustration with church bureaucracy. Missionaries often encounter slow decision-making processes, layered hierarchies, and internal politics that can delay or derail timely responses to emerging opportunities. Financial approvals, doctrinal gatekeeping, and administrative complexity can blunt missionary responsiveness in fast-moving or fragile contexts. In response, some agencies seek alternative funding streams or organizational arrangements outside traditional church structures. While this can increase operational freedom, it also risks reinforcing an us-versus-them mentality, in which missionaries perceive churches as obstacles and churches view agencies as unaccountable or rogue. The result is further fragmentation within the body of Christ and a weakened collective witness.

Mission sodalities may also contribute to imbalance when mission urgency eclipses concern for church health. Agencies driven by specialized goals or project-based outcomes can unintentionally neglect the long-term vitality of the churches they partner with. When attention centers on deliverables rather than discipleship, the deeper work of leadership development, spiritual formation, and congregational resilience may be sidelined. In such cases, missionaries risk being perceived, not as partners in the gospel but as outsiders pursuing narrow agendas. Sustainable mission, however, depends on strengthening local churches as enduring witnesses of God's kingdom, not working around them in the name of efficiency. By strengthening the church rather than working around it, missionaries build trust, deepen collaboration, and help ensure that the fruit of their labor remains, enduring beyond their immediate presence and carried forward by the body of Christ.

Finally, an overemphasis on measurable success can strain relationships with churches. Under pressure to demonstrate impact, mission agencies may privilege quantifiable outcomes such as church plants, conversions, or completed projects. While metrics can serve accountability, they can also distort the imagination of mission when numbers replace formation as the primary measure of faithfulness. Churches that value depth, patience, and relational investment may feel alienated by approaches that prioritize speed and scale. Faithful mission requires holding these tensions together. Fruitfulness matters, but so does formation. Expansion is essential but so is depth. When sodalities align their practices with the long work of nurturing churches rooted in love, integrity, and faithfulness, partnership deepens and mission bears fruit that endures.

ADDRESSING THE IMBALANCE

For modalities and sodalities to function in healthy partnership, both must recognize their interdependence rather than operate as competing forces. Churches are called to embrace the mission of God, not as an optional program but as a core expression of their identity. Mission sodalities, in turn, must remain meaningfully connected to the life, worship, and discernment of the church. When the relationship moves beyond transactional exchange toward long-term collaboration, both structures are strengthened and the church's participation in God's mission becomes more faithful and resilient.

The consequences of failing to sustain this balance are significant. When churches absorb or subordinate mission efforts, apostolic initiative is diminished and long-term missionary vitality suffers. When mission organizations pursue their calling without sustained attention to the spiritual health of local churches, the church itself is weakened. The future of global mission depends on partnerships capable of holding together stability and sending, rootedness and risk, pastoral care and apostolic innovation.[13]

Paul's Letter to the Romans offers a compelling biblical vision for such a relationship. Writing to an established congregation, Paul invites their partnership in his westward mission to Spain (Rom 15:23–24). He does not ask the church to manage or control his apostolic work, nor does he operate independently of them. Instead, he envisions a cooperative relationship in which the church supports, sends, and participates in the mission while allowing it to retain its distinct apostolic character.

At the same time, Paul affirms the vital role of the local church. He longs to visit Rome in order to strengthen the believers and to experience mutual encouragement through shared faith (Rom 1:11–12). Mission, for Paul, does not bypass the church, nor does the church replace the apostolic calling. Together, these two structures form one body, distinct yet inseparable, interdependent rather than autonomous. By cultivating healthy, collaborative relationships, both modalities and sodalities can thrive in their unique callings while enriching one another spiritually and missionally. This dynamic approach helps ensure that the church remains both rooted and expansive, faithfully responding to the evolving needs of the world while staying anchored in its calling. This pattern offers a corrective to institutional dominance on either side and points

13. Ott et al., *Encountering Theology of Mission*, 198.

toward a model of mission shaped by shared authority, reciprocal trust, mutual dependence, and common purpose in the mission of God.

For this kind of partnership to flourish, both modalities and sodalities must move beyond rigid structural identities and enter what may be described as a liminal space. This is the dynamic and often ambiguous terrain where pastoral ministry and apostolic mission overlap, where established forms loosen and new expressions emerge. In this space, the church is freed from fixed institutional boundaries and becomes more responsive, adaptive, and attentive to the Spirit's leading. It is to this liminal dimension of mission and partnership that we now turn.

16

Liminality: Understanding the In-Between Space

Every season of meaningful change begins in an in-between space. Old patterns loosen before new ones fully take shape. What once felt stable becomes uncertain, familiar assumptions are questioned, and identities that once seemed settled begin to shift. These moments are often uncomfortable, even disorienting, yet they are also the places where creativity, renewal, and transformation most often emerge. This threshold experience is what scholars describe as *liminality*.

Liminality names a transitional space or time in which the usual boundaries of structure, identity, and behavior become fluid. In such moments, the rules that once governed life lose some of their authority, opening room for imagination, risk, and reconfiguration. While these seasons can feel destabilizing, they are also deeply generative. It is precisely when the old no longer sustains life and the new has not yet arrived that genuine transformation becomes possible.

The concept of liminality emerged from the work of the French anthropologist Arnold van Gennep, who observed that societies across cultures mark significant transitions through shared rituals. In *The Rites of Passage*, Van Gennep described transformation as unfolding through three movements: separation from a previous state, a liminal phase marked by ambiguity and suspension, and reincorporation into a renewed identity shaped by the passage through uncertainty.[1] Liminality,

1. Van Gennep, *Rites of Passage*.

in this account, is not a detour from formation but the space in which formation actually occurs.

Building on this insight, the British anthropologist Victor Turner extended the concept to describe how communities and societies experience liminal moments together.[2] Turner observed that when established structures are temporarily set aside, new forms of social life can emerge. He called this phenomenon *communitas*, a way of being together marked by shared vulnerability, mutual dependence, and a loosening of hierarchy. In *communitas*, people encounter one another not through status or institutional role, but as companions navigating uncertainty side by side.[3]

For the church, liminality is not merely a sociological category but a missional reality. Mission consistently draws the people of God into liminal spaces, across cultural boundaries, into unfamiliar contexts, and amid shifting social and political realities. The missionary encounter itself places the church at the threshold, between what it has been and what it is becoming. In these spaces, inherited structures and assumptions are tested, and the church is forced to discern anew how the gospel takes flesh in changing contexts.

It is within such liminal settings that *communitas* often takes shape, as believers learn to depend on the Spirit and on one another rather than on established forms of authority or control. Mission strips away illusions of self-sufficiency and invites the church into deeper relational solidarity, humility, and attentiveness to God's leading. Again and again, renewal emerges not from the preservation of familiar systems, but from faithful presence in these in-between spaces.

Liminality is the primary context of the church's mission. At the threshold, the church is stripped of settled assumptions and rediscovers itself as a pilgrim people, sent rather than secure, responsive rather than rigid. It is in these unsettled spaces, between cultures, structures, and certainties, that the Spirit most often forms the church for faithful participation in God's still-unfolding mission.

2. Turner, *Ritual Process*.

3. Turner, *Ritual Process*, 101–10.

COMMUNITAS

The interplay between liminality and structure is not an abstract theory but a lived reality at the heart of the church's mission. Mission consistently carries the people of God into seasons of transition, uncertainty, and dislocation, moments when established roles, traditions, and hierarchies are loosened or set aside. In these spaces, familiar patterns no longer function as they once did, creating room for the Holy Spirit to form new expressions of community, identity, and witness.

Victor Turner's concept of *communitas* helps clarify what often takes shape in liminal contexts. He described *communitas* as a form of unmediated relational connection, a mode of belonging that transcends status, role, and institutional position.[4] Turner understood it as an essential human bond, inseparable from the experience of liminality itself.[5] *Communitas* is not engineered through organizational design; it emerges organically when people meet one another in shared vulnerability, dependence, and purpose.

Where institutions rely on defined roles, authority, and norms, *communitas* arises when those boundaries are temporarily set aside. Pilgrimage, rites of passage, exile, and crisis all create such conditions. These are also the very settings in which mission most often unfolds. Crossing cultures, navigating uncertainty, and living as guests rather than hosts repeatedly draw the church into liminal spaces where *communitas* can take root and reshape how God's people relate, discern, and bear witness together.

The early church offers an example of this dynamic. In Acts 2:42–47, the first believers lived under conditions of instability and threat, navigating persecution, social dislocation, and economic uncertainty. In this liminal setting, deep communal bonds formed that transcended social, ethnic, and economic divisions. Their unity was not imposed by institutional authority but forged through shared faith, shared suffering, and shared life. This Spirit-formed koinonia became the soil from which mission naturally flowed.

In such moments, hierarchy gives way to mutual submission. People meet one another not as holders of status or authority but as companions on the way. The church recovers something close to its original shape—a fellowship animated by the Spirit, where unity is experienced rather than

4. Turner, *Ritual Process*, 94–130.

5. Turner and Turner, *Image and Pilgrimage*, 250.

enforced, and mission emerges naturally from shared life in Christ rather than a managed program. The same dynamic appears whenever believers prioritize relationship over hierarchy and collaboration over control. When mission is approached as shared participation in God's work rather than as an institutional project, *communitas* becomes a source of renewal and shared imagination.

Yet *communitas*, by its very nature, is fluid. Turner was careful to note that it cannot sustain itself indefinitely. Over time, it either dissipates or becomes embodied in structures that seek to preserve the bonds formed in liminality. The challenge is not to eliminate structure but to ensure that structure remains porous and responsive, capable of carrying forward the vitality born in liminal moments without stifling it through rigidity or control.

This rhythm between *communitas* and structure is essential for the life of the church and its mission. Structure without *communitas* hardens into bureaucracy. *Communitas* without structure fades into sentiment. Held together in creative tension, they allow the church to remain both rooted and adaptive, stable and sent. It is within this ongoing movement between liminality and form that the Spirit continues to renew God's people for faithful participation in the mission that is still unfolding.

CLARIFYING LIMINALITY'S SCOPE

It is important to recognize that liminality itself does not produce transformation. It is not a force that drives change, but a condition, a threshold between what has been and what is still emerging. Liminality names the space between structures, a transitional state that unsettles established patterns of thought, behavior, and identity.[6] It describes a temporary and potentially transformative in-between state, a place of possibility where ambiguity opens the way for discovery and change. While liminality does not create change, it creates the conditions in which change can occur. Its significance lies in how individuals and communities respond within it.[7]

Liminality challenges rigid distinctions between structure and agency. Periods of disruption loosen the grip of inherited forms and open space for new meaning, new relationships, and new configurations of communal life. Transformation rarely emerges from stability alone. It is

6. Carson et al., *Crossing Thresholds*, 28–45.

7. Thomassen, *Liminality and the Modern*, 7.

born in tension, when old forms no longer suffice and new ones have not yet taken shape. This insight is especially important for mission theology, where the liminal space between modalities and sodalities is embraced not as a problem to be resolved, but as a transformative in-between threshold where the Spirit breathes new life into the mission of God.

At its core, liminality names those sacred thresholds where old certainties fade and new realities are still being formed. It is a time of disorientation and openness, when identities, roles, and boundaries blur. Yet it is precisely within this blurring that the Spirit invites trust, creativity, and deeper dependence. Liminality is not confined to anthropology or theory. It is the lived experience of the church as it moves between stability and sending, between settled patterns and missional risk.

The church inhabits this liminal space whenever it is stretched between the familiar and the frontier. In such moments, mission becomes more than a strategy or institutional task. As Paul's appeal for partnership in Romans 15 suggests, it becomes a shared pilgrimage of faith. Stability and innovation meet, established congregations and apostolic movements depend on one another, and the Spirit forms *communitas*, a deep bond of shared purpose and mutual care that resists hierarchy and control.

The challenge for the church is not to avoid these moments, nor to rush past them through premature institutionalization. It is to honor their vitality, to remain supple in the hands of God, open to reformation, and willing to be reshaped for new seasons of mission. Liminality reminds us that the people of God are always on the way, pilgrims living between promise and fulfillment, learning to trust that even in the uncertainty of transition, God is already at work, forming a renewed community to bear witness to his unfolding redemptive story.[8]

Liminality helps us see more clearly where modalities and sodalities actually meet. These two expressions of God's redemptive purpose most often encounter one another in transitional spaces, where stability and sending overlap and familiar patterns no longer suffice. It is within these thresholds that collaboration is either resisted or rediscovered, and where the Spirit invites the church to hold structure and movement together as distinct yet interdependent expressions of the one body of Christ.

8. Carson et al., *Crossing Thresholds*, 219.

LIMINALITY AS AN ARENA FOR TRANSFORMATIONAL PARTNERSHIPS

In Romans 15:23–24, Paul extends a bold and deeply personal invitation to the believers in Rome: to join him in advancing the gospel westward to Spain. This appeal marks a decisive threshold in Paul's ministry, a moment when his pioneering apostolic work intersects with the stability of an established congregation. What unfolds here is not simply a logistical arrangement but a liminal encounter, a meeting point between what has already been accomplished and what has not yet been imagined.

Paul stands at the edge of one season and the beginning of another, inviting the Roman church to step with him into unfamiliar territory. He is not asking merely for funding or hospitality, but for participation. His vision presses beyond the familiar boundaries of the Mediterranean world toward what many would have understood as the farthest reaches of the known world. In doing so, Paul draws a settled church into a shared act of trust, calling them to move from being recipients of the gospel to partners in its ongoing advance.

This moment reveals something essential about the nature of mission. The church in Rome, though organized and established, is not asked to control or absorb Paul's apostolic work. Nor does Paul pursue his mission independently of the church's discernment and support. Instead, he imagines a relationship of mutual dependence, one in which the church strengthens mission and mission, in turn, strengthens the church.[9] This reciprocal partnership resists institutional dominance on either side and reframes mission as a shared vocation rather than a delegated task.

Such partnership takes shape most fully in liminal space. It is here, between stability and sending, that modalities and sodalities encounter one another, not as rivals but as co-laborers. Liminality becomes the arena where established structures are tested, apostolic imagination is renewed, and collaboration is forged through trust rather than control. In this in-between space, mission ceases to function as a program managed by institutions and becomes a shared pilgrimage of faith.

Within these liminal moments, *communitas* often emerges as the relational texture of mission. When pastors, missionaries, and local believers meet one another, not through hierarchy or role but through shared vulnerability and dependence, a deeper form of unity takes root. Mission flourishes, not as a project to be executed but as a shared life shaped

9. Carson et al., *Crossing Thresholds*, 101–15.

by grace, sacrifice, and mutual responsibility. Hierarchy recedes, and the Spirit forms a fellowship bound together by shared purpose rather than institutional authority. The mission depends on cooperation, not control, on Spirit-led surrender, not institutional strength.

Such partnerships require a posture of adaptability. Liminality demands openness to change, a willingness to release rigid plans in order to remain responsive to the Spirit's leading. Paul's repeated acknowledgment that his travel plans had been hindered and reshaped (Rom 15:22–25) reflects a missional agility grounded not in control but in discernment. Healthy mission partnerships breathe.[10] They adjust, listen, and learn as contexts shift and new possibilities emerge.

At the same time, liminal partnerships require humility and shared strength.[11] Neither churches nor mission agencies can embody God's mission alone. When churches relinquish the impulse to dominate and mission organizations resist the temptation toward independence, both rediscover the gift of co-laboring in God's redemptive work. Power and provision are no longer wielded as tools of leverage, but shared as expressions of trust and mutual care. Mission is sustained not by institutional dominance, but by an economy of grace in which resources circulate for the sake of the whole body.

These partnerships are nurtured most deeply in spaces of shared discernment. When churches and mission networks create room for joint theological reflection, shared ministry, and collaborative experimentation, they cultivate the kind of liminal environments where new missional expressions can emerge organically. Such spaces are not engineered for efficiency, but opened for attentiveness, where listening precedes action and faithfulness matters more than predictability.

Liminality also resists the temptation of quick resolution. It calls the church to embrace a slower, deeper transformation that unfolds over time. Mission is not a task to be completed but a journey to be undertaken together. In these in-between places, new missional expressions often emerge, not by design but by discovery. The future of mission depends not on institutional strength or strategic mastery, but on patient participation in what God is already doing in the world.[12]

This reorientation invites the church to move beyond programmatic approaches to mission and into active participation in God's ongoing

10. Carson et al., *Crossing Thresholds*, 103.

11. Carson et al., *Crossing Thresholds*, 111.

12. Heifetz and Linsky, *Leadership on the Line*, 31–50.

work. Rather than centering mission on measurable success or organizational achievement, the church is called to attend to God's agency, trusting that the Spirit is already at work beyond its structures and plans.[13] To center mission on ourselves is to risk a subtle form of practical atheism.[14] To center mission on God is to recover humility, freedom, and hope.

In these liminal spaces, the church learns again to live between decision and discernment, action and listening.[15] Like the sons of Issachar, who understood the times and knew what Israel should do, God's people are called to attend carefully to the Spirit's movement amid uncertainty. Such discernment gives rise to communities defined, not by rigid boundaries but by shared direction, centered, not on institutional identity but on faithful movement toward Christ.[16]

In this way, liminality becomes not a threat to the church's mission, but one of its primary gifts. It is in these thresholds that the church is freed from self-preservation and drawn into deeper dependence on God and one another. Here, as stability and innovation meet, the Spirit continues to form a people capable of bearing faithful witness to God's unfolding redemptive story in the world.

LIVING IN THE LIMINAL SPACE

Liminality is not a threat to the church's mission; it is its proving ground. It is the space where stability meets movement, where structure remains open to the Spirit's leading, and where new forms of faithfulness take shape. When churches and mission agencies learn to inhabit this space together, partnership is no longer driven by control or efficiency but by shared discernment, mutual dependence, and attentiveness to God's work in the in-between.

The relationship between modalities and sodalities, then, is not a problem to be solved but a tension to be lived. This creative tension unfolds in liminal space, where uncertainty is not an obstacle to mission but the context in which transformation often begins. Rather than rushing toward fixed solutions, the church is invited to remain present at the threshold, cultivating mutual dependence, deep relational trust,

13. Newbigin, *Gospel in a Pluralist Society*, 84.

14. Keifert and Rooms, *Forming the Missional Churchmatic*, 5.

15. Carson et al., *Crossing Thresholds*, 109–10.

16. Hiebert, *Anthropological Insights*, 253.

and adaptive forms of life that allow mission to emerge rather than be imposed.

The future of God's mission does not rest in static institutions or isolated pioneers, but in interdependent communities willing to navigate liminality together. In these spaces, the church learns again to discern where the Spirit is already at work and to participate faithfully in what God is bringing into being. Here, competition gives way to cooperation, fragmentation to communion, and institutional survival to Spirit-led renewal.

This raises a crucial question: If mission takes shape most faithfully in these in-between spaces, how does transformation actually occur without centralized control? How do new patterns of mission and church life emerge through shared discernment, relational trust, and Spirit-led responsiveness? To explore these questions, we now turn to emergence theory, a framework that helps illuminate how God's people are formed and sent through dynamic, decentralized, and deeply relational processes.

17

Emergence Theory

EMERGENCE THEORY, DRAWN FROM complexity science, offers a way of understanding how new structures, behaviors, and patterns arise through the interaction of simpler elements.[1] Rather than being imposed from above, order in emergent systems develops through decentralized processes, as individual components relate to one another in ways that generate outcomes that are adaptive, dynamic, and often unpredictable.[2] This phenomenon is observable across a wide range of disciplines, from biology and physics to sociology, artificial intelligence, and organizational studies, and it provides a valuable lens for rethinking the dynamics of mission and ecclesial life.[3]

At its heart, emergence helps us pay attention to what happens when people, ideas, and contexts interact in ways no one could have scripted in advance. New realities do not come into being simply because someone designed them in a boardroom. They take shape through relationships, pressures, opportunities, and through the quiet and persistent work of the Spirit. When the church is viewed through this lens, familiar either-or categories begin to lose their hold. Church and mission, modality and sodality, stability and sending are no longer seen as opposites, but as interwoven realities that continually shape one another.

This is often how mission actually unfolds. A local congregation grows and unexpectedly discovers a passion for global engagement.

1. Jensen, *Complexity Science*, 5–9.

2. Clayton, *Mind and Emergence*, 3–7.

3. Clayton and Davies, *Re-Emergence of Emergence*.

Elsewhere, a mission initiative takes root and, over time, gives rise to a new worshiping community. Neither outcome was carefully engineered from the start. Both emerged through shared life, faithful response, and openness to God's leading. Mission is less a program we design and more a reality that unfolds as God's people step into the world, attend to need, and trust the Spirit to do what only the Spirit can do.

Unlike reductionist approaches, which attempt to explain systems by breaking them down into their smallest parts, emergence theory recognizes that the whole often displays qualities that cannot be found in the components alone.[4] Simple interactions at the local level can give rise to complex and unforeseen patterns at the macro level. The coordinated movement of bird flocks, the self-regulation of ecosystems, the growth of cities, and the spontaneous expansion of church-planting movements all exhibit this dynamic.[5] In each case, no single agent directs the system from above; order arises from within through relational interaction.[6]

A helpful way to grasp this is through the idea of emergent properties, characteristics that belong to a system as a whole but are absent from its individual parts. Water, for example, is wet, yet wetness is not a property of hydrogen or oxygen. It emerges only when these elements interact. Similar dynamics appear in biological systems, where the blue coloration of birds such as blue jays and eastern bluebirds arises not from pigment but from microscopic feather structures that scatter light, producing an optical effect that emerges only at the level of the whole.[7]

At higher levels of complexity, memory offers another example. A single neuron does not remember, yet memory emerges through the interaction of neural networks.[8] Similarly, in economic systems, money functions as an emergent social property. A twenty-dollar bill has no intrinsic value in its physical form, yet within a complex socioeconomic system of trust, law, and exchange, it acquires significance as a medium of exchange.[9] In each case, new realities arise that cannot be reduced to their constituent parts, even though they depend upon them.

4. Jensen, *Complexity Science*, 21–45.
5. Jensen, *Complexity Science*, 325–49.
6. Clayton and Davies, *Re-Emergence of Emergence*, 1–28.
7. Croasmun, *Emergence of Sin*, 23–24.
8. Clayton and Davies, *Re-Emergence of Emergence*, 149–60.
9. Croasmun, *Emergence of Sin*, 24.

Taken together, these examples reveal the interpretive challenge at the heart of emergence.[10] Emergent realities are not illusions; they possess real and formative power, yet they cannot be fully understood by reducing them to individual components.[11] Through patterns of local interaction at the micro level, new realities arise at the macro level, realities that in turn shape, guide, and constrain the behavior of the parts themselves.[12] This reciprocal relationship between parts and whole resists simple, linear explanation and calls for a more integrative account of how complex systems and living communities function.[13]

Scripture reflects this same dynamic in its vision of communal life, where God's work is not confined to isolated individuals but unfolds through the shared, Spirit-formed life of the body. In this sense, emergence offers a language for naming how God brings order, meaning, and transformation within creation and the church, not by bypassing human interaction, but by working through it.

For mission and ecclesiology, this insight is especially important. It suggests that vibrant movements of faith do not depend primarily on centralized control or institutional design. Instead, they emerge through decentralized, relational, and Spirit-led interactions that exceed managerial predictability. Recognizing emergence helps churches and mission organizations embrace organic growth, relational networks, and adaptive forms of leadership. More importantly, it invites renewed trust that God's mission advances, not only through what we plan but through what the Spirit brings into being as we live, respond, and follow faithfully in a complex and changing world.

KEY CHARACTERISTICS OF EMERGENCE SYSTEMS

Emergent systems operate in ways that resist traditional top-down control. Rather, they develop through dynamic interaction among their components. This pattern is evident in biological ecosystems, social systems, and human organizations, and it offers important insight for understanding how mission and ecclesial life take shape in complex and changing environments. Attending to these characteristics helps

10. Clayton, *Mind and Emergence*, 3–33.

11. Clayton, *Mind and Emergence*, 143–44.

12. Corradini and O'Connor, *Emergence in Science and Philosophy*, 25–43.

13. Clayton, *Mind and Emergence*, 9–10.

churches and mission agencies cultivate movements that are resilient, responsive, and Spirit-led rather than rigid or overly centralized.[14]

Self-Organization: Order Arises Through Local Interaction

A defining feature of emergence is self-organization, the capacity of a system to generate order without external control.[15] In such systems, coherent patterns naturally arise through local interactions rather than centralized command.[16] Biological examples abound. Ant colonies, for instance, function without a single directing agent. Instead, ants coordinate their behavior through pheromone trails and feedback loops, enabling them to forage efficiently, build complex nests, and defend their colonies.

Mission often unfolds in similar ways. Church-planting movements frequently grow, not through micromanaged strategies but through local discipleship, relational networks, and contextual responsiveness. As communities of faith respond to local needs and cultural contexts, they develop contextualized expressions of church life. Mission flourishes, not when it is tightly controlled, but when space is given for faithful, localized response guided by the Spirit.

Nonlinearity: Small Actions Can Produce Disproportionate Effects

Emergent systems are nonlinear, meaning that cause and effect are not proportionate or predictable.[17] Small inputs can generate significant and unexpected outcomes. In meteorology, minor atmospheric disturbances can contribute to large-scale weather events, a dynamic often described as the butterfly effect, where a seemingly insignificant event can trigger a chain reaction of massive systemic shifts.[18]

In mission, this nonlinearity helps explain how seemingly modest initiatives can catalyze widespread transformation. A small Bible study in a restricted context, a single act of hospitality, or a faithful witness in obscurity may ignite movements far beyond their original scope. This

14. Clayton and Davies, *Re-Emergence of Emergence*, 1–28.

15. Corradini and O'Connor, *Emergence in Science and Philosophy*, 253–254.

16. Kauffman, *At Home in the Universe*, 71–92.

17. Clayton, *Mind and Emergence*, 122.

18. Clayton and Davies, *The Re-Emergence of Emergence*, 79–80.

challenges linear models of planning and evaluation, reminding the church that faithfulness, not scale, is often the seedbed of transformative mission.

Interdependence: Relationships Shape Outcomes More Than Isolated Components

Emergent systems are defined less by their individual parts than by the relationships between them. No element functions in isolation; each one both influences and is shaped by the wider network.[19] In an ecological system, for example, the health of a rainforest is dependent not just on its individual species but on the interactions between trees, animals, fungi, and microorganisms. The loss of one species can set off a domino effect that destabilizes the entire ecosystem.

This dynamic is equally visible in mission. Churches and mission organizations are most effective when they operate in collaborative interdependence rather than competition or control. When churches dominate mission agencies, or when missions detach themselves from ecclesial life, the broader mission suffers. Emergence underscores the need for relational models of mission grounded in mutual trust, shared discernment, and ongoing dialogue.

Adaptability: Systems Evolve in Response to Changing Conditions

Emergent systems are adaptive. They respond dynamically to shifting environments through feedback, learning, and adjustment.[20] Rather than remaining static, they evolve over time. Technological systems such as search algorithms provide a familiar example, continually refining themselves in response to new data.

The spread of the gospel has always depended on such adaptability. The early church responded creatively to persecution and displacement. When believers were scattered from Jerusalem, they did not retreat but carried the gospel into new regions and cultures (Acts 8:1–4). In every era, faithful mission has required discernment, flexibility, and attentiveness to how the Spirit is moving within changing contexts.

19. Jensen, *Complexity Science*, 6–15.

20. Kauffman, *At Home in the Universe*, 196–98.

Irreducibility: The Whole Is More Than the Sum of Its Parts

Perhaps the most striking feature of emergence is irreducibility. The behavior and character of the whole cannot be fully explained by analyzing its components in isolation. To return to the example of water, for example, wetness is not present in individual hydrogen or oxygen molecules; it emerges only through their collective interaction. In the same way, a community's culture, identity, and shared practices arise from relationships and shared history, not from individuals considered on their own.

Paul's vision of the church as the body of Christ reflects this same reality (1 Cor 12:12–27). The church is not an aggregate of autonomous individuals but a Spirit-formed body, knit together through diverse members into a living whole. Each part belongs to the others, and together they bear witness to God's reign in ways no individual could accomplish alone. For this reason, mission cannot be generated through institutional strategy alone. It emerges as the Spirit gathers, gifts, and sends a people whose shared life, obedience, and mutual dependence form a collective witness that surpasses intentional design and gives visible expression to the work of God among them.

MANAGING EMERGENT PHENOMENA IN MODALITIES AND SODALITIES

In organizational settings, emergence theory challenges traditional hierarchical models by drawing attention to the spontaneous and often unpredictable ways systems develop. Innovation, adaptability, and resilience do not arise primarily through rigid control but through the collective actions of people responding to their environment. This insight is especially relevant in a world marked by complexity, rapid change, and cultural flux, where effective leadership increasingly depends on attentiveness, flexibility, and responsiveness rather than command and control.

Stephen J. Guastello's work on nonlinear dynamics in organizations provides a helpful framework for understanding these processes.[21] His analysis highlights how organizations function as complex systems shaped by feedback loops, thresholds, and decentralized interactions. Applied to ecclesial life, this perspective challenges assumptions that

21. Guastello, *Managing Emergent Phenomena.*

relationships between churches and mission organizations can be managed through linear or hierarchical models alone. Instead, emergence theory helps us see how modalities and sodalities evolve, adapt, and influence one another in fluid and relational ways, often producing outcomes no single actor could have planned in advance.

Nonlinear Dynamics and the Modality–Sodality Relationship

A central insight of nonlinear dynamics is the rejection of static organizational models in favor of adaptive systems in which patterns emerge through interaction. Traditional approaches to mission have often framed the relationship between modalities and sodalities competitively, with churches seeking to control mission agencies or mission agencies operating independently of ecclesial structures. Emergence theory reframes this relationship as a dynamic system in which new forms of partnership arise through ongoing interaction rather than institutional dominance.[22]

As in biological and social systems, church–mission relationships are shaped by context, trust, and shared practice. A congregation may initially hesitate to partner with a mission organization, yet over time, repeated interactions, shared discernment, and mutual dependence can give rise to collaborative models neither side anticipated at the outset. These partnerships are not imposed; they emerge through faithful engagement.

Catastrophe Theory and the Tensions Between Stability and Change

Guastello's use of catastrophe theory offers an additional lens for understanding moments of rapid change.[23] In complex systems, gradual pressures can accumulate until a threshold is reached, resulting in sudden and dramatic transformation. Church history reflects this pattern. The Protestant Reformation's rejection of monastic sodalities represents one such threshold, where accumulated theological and institutional tensions led to the near disappearance of missionary orders, only for sodalities to re-emerge later in the modern missionary movement.

Tensions between modalities and sodalities are not necessarily signs of failure but indicators that a system may be approaching a point of transformation. Rather than resisting such moments, leaders can learn

22. Guastello, *Managing Emergent Phenomena*, 15–54.

23. Guastello, *Managing Emergent Phenomena*, 46–51.

to recognize them as invitations to adaptive change. By cultivating flexibility and openness, churches and mission organizations can navigate transitions more faithfully, allowing new forms of partnership to emerge without unnecessary rupture.

Self-Organization and Adaptive Leadership in Mission Partnerships

Emergence theory also underscores the importance of self-organization, the capacity of systems to generate order through decentralized interaction.[24] In contrast to top-down leadership models, emergent systems thrive when space is given for initiative, experimentation, and relational learning. This has direct implications for mission partnerships.

For churches, this means approaching mission, not as an external activity to be managed, but as an integral expression of ecclesial identity that develops through shared vision and practice. For mission organizations, it calls for resisting rigid structures that inhibit contextual responsiveness. Adaptive leadership focuses less on directing outcomes and more on cultivating environments in which collaboration, trust, and innovation can take root.

When modalities and sodalities embrace these principles, mission partnerships become sites of emergence rather than arenas of control. Leadership shifts from enforcing alignment to nurturing attentiveness, from managing compliance to facilitating discernment. In such contexts, the Spirit is given space to form new patterns of faithfulness, enabling churches and mission organizations to respond creatively and courageously to the demands of God's mission in a complex and changing world.

EMERGENCE THEORY AND THE MISSIONAL CHURCH: TRUSTING GOD'S UNFOLDING WORK

Emergence theory offers a refreshing and humbling way of seeing how God often works, not through rigid, top-down control but through the Spirit's quiet, dynamic, and frequently surprising activity in and through relationships, decisions, and moments no single person or institution could have planned. At its core, emergence describes how complex patterns, structures, and movements arise from simple, local interactions

24. Guastello, *Managing Emergent Phenomena*, 45–46.

without a central authority dictating outcomes. This pattern is woven throughout Scripture, particularly in the life of the early church.

The scattering of believers following Stephen's death (Acts 8:1–4) was not the result of a carefully crafted mission strategy, yet it propelled the gospel far beyond Jerusalem. Paul's apostolic ministry unfolded in a similar way. His partnerships with local churches and missionary companions were not governed by formal institutional frameworks, but by relational bonds, shared discernment, and responsiveness to the Spirit's leading. Out of these interactions emerged new communities of faith and new horizons for mission that no single plan could have anticipated. Mission advanced not by design alone, but by participation in God's unfolding work.

What makes emergence so compelling for the missional church is the posture of trust it requires. Trust that the Spirit is already at work beyond our ability to manage or predict. Trust in one another as co-laborers rather than competitors. Small acts of faithfulness, planting a house church, extending hospitality, supporting a missionary, often generate outcomes far beyond their apparent scale. Emergence reminds us that living movements of mission arise not from institutional mastery, but from Spirit-formed communities where relationships, obedience, and shared life converge in ways that exceed intentional design.

Emergence challenges churches and mission agencies to relate differently. Modalities and sodalities are not rivals competing for control, but companions called into shared discernment. Stability and pioneering vision belong together. Mission is not a program to be managed but a journey to be shared, one in which God's people learn to move together in step with the Spirit, confident that the Spirit is always bringing new life into being.

PRACTICING EMERGENCE IN MISSION

Attending to emergent dynamics equips church and mission leaders to navigate the complexity of modality–sodality relationships with greater wisdom and humility. Traditional hierarchical models often struggle to respond to rapidly changing cultural, political, and spiritual realities. Emergent approaches, by contrast, foster collaboration, adaptability, and long-term resilience by privileging relationship over rigidity and discernment over control.

One of the strengths of an emergent approach is its capacity for self-organization. Rather than imposing predetermined structures, leaders learn to observe how mission is actually taking shape through local interactions, relational networks, and Spirit-led initiatives. This allows mission to develop in culturally resonant ways, attentive to context rather than constrained by uniform models.

Emergent systems also learn through feedback. Healthy mission partnerships depend on open communication, iterative learning, and attentiveness to insight from the field. When churches and mission agencies create space for reflection, shared evaluation, and honest dialogue, mission remains responsive rather than static. In such environments, strategy emerges from lived experience rather than being imposed from a distance.

Flexibility is equally essential. Fixed organizational structures and centralized decision-making often slow responsiveness and inhibit innovation. By contrast, decentralized and networked leadership models allow mission initiatives to adapt to shifting realities. This pattern mirrors the expansion of the early church, where the gospel spread through relational networks rather than institutional directives (Acts 13–16). Leadership in emergent systems focuses less on directing outcomes and more on cultivating conditions in which faithful response can flourish.

Emergence also helps leaders recognize patterns that naturally stabilize over time. Certain missional practices gain traction because they resonate deeply with local realities. Rather than resisting these patterns or forcing alternative models, wise leaders learn to discern why particular approaches flourish and to support their growth. In the same way, partnerships that arise organically through shared calling and trust often prove more resilient than those engineered through formal agreement alone.

Finally, emergence prepares leaders for moments of transition. Complex systems rarely change in smooth, predictable increments; more often, they shift suddenly when accumulated pressures reach a critical threshold. Such moments may take the form of leadership transitions, funding disruptions, theological tensions, or geopolitical upheaval. Rather than responding defensively or attempting to reassert control, leaders are invited to recognize these moments as thresholds of possibility, occasions for adaptive change shaped by humility, flexibility, and prayerful discernment.

Discernment in such seasons begins by asking powerful questions that surface what is already unfolding beneath the surface. Are tensions emerging between churches and mission agencies that signal deeper structural strain? Are funding patterns shifting in ways that threaten long-term sustainability? Is a new generation of leaders rising whose vision and instincts challenge inherited forms of authority? Attending to these signals allows the church to engage transition proactively rather than reactively.

When such shifts are recognized, churches and mission organizations can respond with practices that support faithful transition, such as preparing for leadership succession, diversifying funding streams, or creating space for theological dialogue before disagreement hardens into division. In this way, emergence, self-organization, and adaptive leadership help move the church beyond institutional rigidity toward a more dynamic, Spirit-led, and collaborative future. The goal is not the preservation of familiar forms, but faithful participation in what God is bringing into being, ensuring that mission remains contextually responsive, relationally grounded, and spiritually transformative as the church moves into the future.

At stake in these emergent and liminal dynamics is not merely organizational adaptability or innovative ministry practice, but the formation of a particular kind of ecclesial life. When the partnership between church and mission is faithful, the question is not simply whether the gospel has crossed new boundaries, but whether it has taken root deeply enough to generate local responsibility, sustainability, witness, and discernment. Over time, churches that flourish in such environments begin to exhibit recognizable capacities: They assume authority for their own life, sustain ministry from within their context, bear witness beyond themselves, and engage Scripture with a growing theological voice of their own. These capacities do not arise all at once, nor can they be engineered in advance. They emerge as signs that the gospel has moved from arrival to habitation. It is this form of ecclesial maturity, often described in missiology as "four-self" life, that provides a lens for recognizing when the church has truly become contextualized, a theme to which we will return in greater depth.

LIVING IN THE TENSION OF MISSION

The story of the church has always unfolded between movement and structure, gathering and sending, modality and sodality. These are not competing forces but complementary expressions of God's redemptive purpose. The church gathers to be formed into a faithful community; it is sent to bear witness beyond itself. When these dimensions remain in rhythm, the gospel flourishes. When one dominates or eclipses the other, mission falters and the church drifts into survival and self-consumption.

Liminality offers a way forward. These in-between spaces, where familiar patterns loosen their hold and new forms of faithfulness begin to take shape, are not signs of failure but of formation. Scripture consistently portrays such moments as sites of becoming, where God reshapes his people for the next chapter of his unfolding work. Just as the early church navigated the tension between Jewish inheritance and gentile inclusion, so today's church is called to inhabit uncertainty with trust, attentiveness, and courage, learning to assume responsibility for its life and witness in new contexts.

Emergence theory helps us see that mission often advances not by decree but by discovery. The most vibrant movements arise through networks of prayer, relationship, and shared obedience. These communities learn to sustain their common life, adapt their practices, and respond to their context in ways that cannot be scripted in advance. In such settings, faith takes on local texture and durability, embodied in communities whose life together reflects both rootedness and openness to the Spirit's leading.

Paul's appeal to the Romans offers a final image of this dynamic partnership. Standing between past labor and future hope, Paul invites the Roman believers to participate in God's unfolding mission to Spain. His vision assumes a community capable of discerning its calling, bearing responsibility for its shared life, and extending the gospel beyond its immediate boundaries. The vitality of local congregations and the pioneering impulse of mission belong together, forming a single rhythm of participation in God's redemptive work.

The task before the church, then, is not the preservation of familiar structures but the cultivation of openness to the Spirit who always goes ahead of us. When modalities and sodalities learn to walk together, neither clinging to control nor retreating into independence, they bear witness to the gospel itself: diverse yet united, stable yet dynamic, rooted yet moving.

18

Overcoming Church Challenges by Reengaging the Mission of God

Paul's engagement with the Roman churches offers two enduring insights for the life of the church. First, there are challenges the church cannot resolve apart from renewed participation in the mission of God. When congregations turn inward, consumed by internal disputes, cultural differences, or questions of status and belonging, they lose sight of their vocation. The Roman churches were caught in cycles of judgment, suspicion, and division precisely because they had forgotten that they existed as participants in and witnesses to the gospel. Paul lifts their gaze beyond immediate tensions and locates their identity within God's redemptive movement unfolding in history.

Second, there are mission frontiers that will never be reached without deeper and more intentional partnership between apostolic initiatives and local congregations. Paul's appeal for support in his mission to Spain makes clear that apostolic calling does not stand apart from the church but depends upon it. The local church is not merely a logistical platform or funding base but a primary site of spiritual formation, communal discernment, and sustained faithfulness. Certain spiritual resources necessary for long-term mission are found only within the shared life of the congregation. Missionaries need this life-giving connection, just as churches need the outward pull of apostolic vocation.

Together, these insights frame Paul's response to division in Rome and offer a lens for understanding the church's present challenges. The advance of the gospel requires collaboration between gathered communities and sending movements. Theologically, this reflects the mutual interdependence of modality and sodality within God's redemptive purpose. When these dimensions are held together in creative tension, the church is freed to be both deeply rooted and faithfully sent.

Many churches today find themselves in a similar struggle. Cycles of internal conflict, identity confusion, and institutional fatigue consume energy while producing little fruit. Disputes over leadership, worship, theology, and cultural engagement are often treated as technical or organizational problems requiring better structures or clearer messaging. Yet beneath these symptoms lies a deeper issue. When the church loses sight of its participation in the mission of God, it turns inward, and its shared life begins to fracture.

Paul's letter to the Romans addresses this dynamic directly. The Roman congregations were marked by tension and competing claims of honor and superiority. Paul does not resolve these conflicts by appealing to hierarchy, control, or cultural alignment. Instead, he reframes the church's life around a shared vocation in God's reconciling mission. Jew and gentile are called to glorify God together, not by securing uniformity or dominance, but by participating in the gospel that reconciles and sends. For Paul, inward division is healed not through self-protection but through outward orientation.

This insight is especially pressing in the contemporary Western context. The decline of Christianity's cultural dominance has left many churches anxious and defensive. Long-held assumptions about moral authority, public influence, and social legitimacy no longer hold. In response, some congregations attempt to reclaim influence through political alignment or appeals to national identity. Others retreat into insularity, preoccupied with internal survival. Both responses misunderstand the nature of the gospel and misread the church's vocation.

One of the more subtle responses to cultural displacement is the temptation to narrate the church primarily as a victim. Often sincere and rarely malicious, this posture nonetheless reshapes imagination and discipleship over time. What begins as vigilance hardens into suspicion. What begins as conviction curdles into fear. When perceived opposition becomes the dominant lens through which cultural change is interpreted, the church risks misdiagnosing its moment and quietly deforming its witness.

Within such a narrative, resistance is easily mistaken for righteousness. Opposition becomes proof of faithfulness, and suffering is assumed rather than discerned. Group identity intensifies, nuance fades, and humility erodes. From this posture, antagonism follows naturally. Those who disagree are no longer neighbors to be loved but threats to be resisted. People become issues, complex lives are reduced to symbols and slogans, and compassion gives way to ideology. Dialogue collapses, criticism is dismissed as hostility, and repentance becomes increasingly difficult. The result is not resilience but spiritual insulation.

This posture stands in sharp contrast to the way of Christ and to Paul's vision in Romans. Jesus did not secure faithfulness through grievance or fear but through self-giving love. He refused to define his mission over against enemies and instead absorbed hostility without returning it. Paul likewise did not respond to opposition by retreating into defensiveness. He called the church outward into shared participation in the mission of God. The gospel calls the church to be cruciform, humble, and courageous, shaped by love rather than fear and formed for witness rather than self-protection.

Throughout history, the church has repeatedly struggled with the allure of Christendom. When Christianity aligns itself with empire, nation, or cultural dominance, it forfeits its prophetic voice and becomes captive to the very powers the gospel is meant to transform. Romans stands as a sustained challenge to such arrangements. Ethnic, social, and political hierarchies are relativized in light of God's mercy. Allegiance to Christ displaces every other claim to ultimate loyalty.

The present moment can be understood as a liminal one. Old certainties no longer hold, yet new forms of ecclesial life have not fully emerged. Such seasons are disorienting, but they are also generative. Liminality exposes what has been taken for granted and creates space for deeper discernment. For the church, this in-between time invites renewed engagement with the missio Dei, not as a strategy for institutional survival but as the rediscovery of its true vocation.

Romans offers a way forward by calling the church beyond self-referential concerns into shared participation in God's mission. Paul's vision is relational and decentralized. Local congregations and apostolic movements are not competitors but partners in the gospel. Congregations provide formation, hospitality, and communal life. Apostolic initiatives carry the gospel into new spaces, often at great personal cost. Together they embody the gathered and sent life of the church.

Reengaging the mission of God does not eliminate tension or difficulty. Paul never promises that it will. Faithfulness is forged through radical welcome, shared struggle, mutual dependence, and hope sustained by grace. The church's calling is not to secure its future but to bear witness to the gospel in whatever circumstances it finds itself. This witness is inherently communal, shaped through partnership rather than individual effort or institutional dominance.

What follows in this book turns from theological and missiological groundwork to lived expression. The movement is from the articulation of a gospel-shaped vision for the people of God to its concrete expression within a particular community. The Foursquare Church is taken up here, not as an idealized model but as a living tradition in which the dynamics of modality and sodality, gathering and sending, are worked out in real time. By attending closely to Foursquare's history, structures, and practices, we are able to trace how a missional imagination takes form within a specific church context and how its struggles and innovations may serve, in turn, as a gift for the wider body of Christ.

PART 5

The Foursquare Church as Modality and Sodality

The New Testament portrays the church as a Spirit-formed people who gather in worship and are sent in witness, holding local formation and apostolic movement together as a single participation in the mission of God. Here, in Part 5, we look at The Foursquare Church as a contemporary case study of that enduring vocation. Founded in 1923 by Aimee Semple McPherson, Foursquare emerged through the convergence of congregational life and missionary imagination, shaped from the beginning by revival, mobility, and a global horizon. From its earliest days, the movement sought to hold together what the church has often struggled to sustain: rooted communities and outward-moving mission.

This section traces how Foursquare has embodied that dual calling across its history, and where the tension between stability and sending has become difficult to maintain. Attending to the interplay of theology, organizational structure, and missional practice, it examines how authority, resources, and imagination are negotiated within a single denominational system. Foursquare is not presented here as an exception, but as a revealing example of a challenge the wider church continues to face: how to remain a gathered people without turning inward and a sent people without becoming fragmented.

19

The Origins and Development of The Foursquare Church

THE ORIGINS OF THE Foursquare Church are rooted in the extraordinary life and ministry of Aimee Semple McPherson, a pioneering evangelist whose bold faith, theological instincts, and imaginative leadership gave rise to a global disciple-making movement. From the outset, Foursquare was marked by spiritual vitality, cultural creativity, and missionary urgency. McPherson's ministry consistently held together what others often separated—the local and the global, the spiritual and the social—embodying the twin impulses that would come to define Foursquare's identity as both a gathered church and a sending movement.

From its earliest years, the Foursquare movement carried a missionary horizon that extended far beyond the United States. Evangelists and missionaries carried the gospel across cultural and geographic boundaries with a blend of Pentecostal fervor and practical faith. By the late 1920s, Foursquare workers were planting churches in places such as India, China, the Philippines, Bolivia, and Panama, each shaped by contextual adaptation and emerging local leadership. In the decades that followed, new movements took root across Latin America, Africa, Asia, Europe, and the Middle East. These churches bore the same formative DNA as the founding movement: evangelistic proclamation, Spirit-empowered ministry, and a commitment to the full gospel of Jesus Christ.

Today, that same Spirit-led vision continues to shape The Foursquare Church as a global family of more than ten million believers worshiping in over one hundred thousand churches across more than 150 nations.

What began as a single congregation ignited by missionary passion has matured into a worldwide network of churches and mission partnerships. Its enduring strength lies in the ongoing interaction between local congregations and global initiatives, between stability and movement, structure and Spirit. Foursquare's vitality has always depended on the creative tension between modality and sodality, the gathered and the sent, held together rather than separated.

The theological identity of The Foursquare Church emerges from the convergence of its historical development, cultural ethos, and doctrinal convictions.[1] Together, these forces shape its ecclesiology, missiology, and governance, enabling it to function as both a rooted church movement and an apostolic missionary force. Recognizing this interdependence is essential for discerning Foursquare's present challenges and future direction.

1. James R. Nieman argues that theology remains an essential function of denominations, particularly at the national level, and that its influence is often more significant than it appears. Traditionally, denominational theology might be assessed by comparing denominational events and issues against official doctrines, creeds, and belief statements, looking for alignment or divergence. However, this conventional approach assumes that theology is primarily systematic, a speculative discipline centered on abstract ideas and academic reflection. In such a model, theology primarily functions as a regulatory tool, setting behavioral norms, defining organizational boundaries, and legitimizing institutional actions. This narrow perspective not only exaggerates the role of formal doctrines but also neglects the many other ways theology is genuinely expressed within denominations.

Nieman advocates shifting the focus away from established doctrinal statements toward the full spectrum of denominational practices, including rituals, procedures, habits, and structural elements to uncover "operative theologies." These theologies emerge naturally through lived ecclesial practices, revealing theology as a dynamic discourse deeply embedded in communal actions rather than confined to intellectual or speculative propositions. This holistic approach relocates theology from an exclusively academic sphere into its authentic ecclesial context within the life of the church as a community called into being by God. Rather than functioning as a static system of ideas, theology is a dynamic discourse that orients, explains, and discerns God's activity in the world through a particular expression of the body of Christ.

Nieman's concept of operative theology is evident in apostolic models, especially Paul's ministry in Romans. Paul's missiological strategy provides insight into the dynamic and contextual nature of theology as he effectively navigates linguistic, cultural, and religious challenges to communicate the gospel within diverse Greco-Roman contexts.

This understanding of theology being grounded in practice and embedded in communal identity, challenges The Foursquare Church to reflect on its missional theology, not merely through doctrinal statements but through its lived experience as a Spirit-filled community engaging in the mission of God. See Nieman, "Theological Work of Denominations," 625–53.

To understand this more fully, we turn to the movement's origins, tracing its journey from a single church with a global vision to a global church with a single vision to make disciples of all nations. Throughout this story, the relationship between modality and sodality is theological at its core, revealing how stability and mission together continue to shape Foursquare's character, resilience, and capacity for adaptation.

AIMEE SEMPLE MCPHERSON AND THE FOUNDING OF THE FOURSQUARE CHURCH

Aimee Semple McPherson emerged from the ferment of early twentieth-century Pentecostal revival as a gifted preacher, visionary leader, and pioneering communicator. Blending spiritual fervor with practical compassion and remarkable creativity, she reshaped the contours of modern evangelism. One of the most unconventional and influential religious figures of her era, Aimee defied both social convention and ecclesial expectation, breaking through cultural and institutional barriers that sought to limit women's voices in ministry.[2] Her life and work embodied a rare convergence of revivalist passion and organizational imagination, a combination that would give rise to what became The Foursquare Church.

Born Aimee Elizabeth Kennedy in 1890 in rural Ontario, Canada, she was raised in a Salvation Army household that emphasized both personal conversion and social concern. This integration of evangelism and compassion would remain a defining feature of her ministry. At seventeen, she encountered Pentecostal revival through the preaching of evangelist Robert Semple.[3] The experience marked a decisive turning point, as she embraced a calling to proclaim the gospel empowered by the Holy Spirit.

In 1908, Aimee married Robert Semple, and together they set out as missionaries to China, a decision that reflected their shared commitment to global mission. Their work was brief and marked by tragedy. Robert contracted malaria and died in 1910, leaving Aimee widowed, pregnant, and far from home. Returning to North America, she gave birth to her daughter Roberta and gradually began to share her story publicly, gaining recognition as a dynamic and Spirit-filled communicator.

2. Van Cleave, *Vine and the Branches*, 1–8.

3. McPherson, *This Is That*, 31.

A second marriage to Harold McPherson brought a short season of partnership and relative stability. Together they conducted revival campaigns along the East Coast, marked by fervent preaching, reports of healing, and widespread conversions. During this period, their son Rolf was born. The demands of itinerant ministry soon took their toll. Harold grew weary of the constant travel and the unconventional life of revival work, eventually leaving Aimee to return to his previous life, while Aimee pressed forward, convinced that she remained under a divine mandate to preach.[4]

Accompanied by her mother, Minnie Kennedy, and her two children, Aimee embraced a life of itinerant ministry, preaching in tents, theaters, and auditoriums across the United States.[5] Her preaching combined dramatic storytelling, theological clarity, and an unmistakable emphasis on salvation, healing, and Spirit baptism. By the early 1920s, she had become a national figure, widely known for her ability to communicate the gospel in ways that were both imaginative and accessible.

Aimee's ministry entered a new phase with her relocation to Los Angeles. In 1921, she established the Echo Park Evangelistic Association, an umbrella organization that coordinated evangelism, missions, publishing, and ministerial training. Two years later, this vision took concrete form with the opening of Angelus Temple, a 5,300-seat auditorium that quickly became the largest Pentecostal meeting place in the world.[6] Angelus Temple became a spiritual and cultural landmark, a living symbol of revival, creativity, and compassion and the beating heart of what would soon emerge as a global movement. In 1923, she founded Echo Park Evangelistic and Missionary Training Center (later LIFE Bible College, now Life Pacific University) to train ministers and missionaries, ensuring that the movement would outlast her own leadership. Angelus Temple also became a center of social compassion. During the Great Depression, Aimee mobilized her congregation to provide food, clothing, and assistance to more than 1.5 million people.[7]

Aimee's methods were as innovative as her message. While many evangelists relied on traveling campaigns alone, she embraced emerging technologies to extend the reach of the gospel. Her illustrated sermons and theatrical presentations brought Scripture to life for diverse

4. Blumhofer, *Aimee Semple McPherson*, 99–134.

5. Epstein, *Sister Aimee*, 6–77.

6. Anderson, *Introduction to Pentecostalism*, 268.

7. Van Cleave, *Vine and the Branches*, 18.

audiences. In 1924, she launched radio station KFSG, becoming one of the first religious broadcasters in the United States.[8] Through radio, print media, and an expanding publishing ministry, her message reached millions who would never attend a revival meeting, anticipating the media-driven ministries of later generations.[9]

Aimee's public life was not without controversy. Her highly publicized disappearance in 1926, along with the strain of multiple marriages, drew intense media scrutiny. Yet even amid scandal and criticism, her influence endured.[10] Her capacity to communicate, organize, and mobilize people around a compelling vision of the gospel sustained the movement's momentum.

In 1943, while ministering in Mexico, Aimee contracted a bacillus infection that began eroding the walls of her intestinal tract, leaving her in chronic pain and deteriorating health. Though weakened, she pressed on with her demanding preaching schedule, refusing to slow down. The infection, compounded by exhaustion and the heavy burden of years in public ministry, ultimately contributed to her death on September 27, 1944, at the age of fifty-three.[11] Her life ended much as it had been lived, marked by relentless commitment, public intensity, and unyielding devotion to the calling she believed God had entrusted to her.

Aimee Semple McPherson left an indelible mark on global Christianity. At a time when women were rarely recognized as religious leaders, she founded one of the most influential Pentecostal movements of the twentieth century. More significant for this study, however, is not simply what she built, but how she held together forces that are often pulled apart. McPherson demonstrated that revivalist energy could be organized without being domesticated. Her ministry was driven by evangelistic urgency and missionary imagination, oriented toward expansion rather than consolidation, yet she did not resist structure. By establishing churches, training leaders, and launching missionary networks, she translated a Spirit-driven, sodalitic impulse into institutional forms capable of sustaining and extending the movement.

In doing so, she embedded within The Foursquare Church a defining tension between revival and organization, spontaneity and structure,

8. KFSG: Kall Foursquare Gospel; "K" was the standard US prefix for radio stations west of the Mississippi River.

9. Noll, *Old Religion in a New World*, 158, 297.

10. Epstein, *Sister Aimee*, 229–381.

11. Epstein, *Sister Aimee*, 438.

the gathered church and the sending movement. This tension did not resolve into a settled equilibrium; it became a constitutive feature of the movement's identity. Foursquare's vitality has never depended on choosing between these impulses, but on holding them together. Forged in McPherson's life and ministry, this dynamic between modality and sodality continues to shape the movement's missional imagination and global witness.

FOURSQUARE AFTER AIMEE

By the time of Aimee's death in 1944, the movement she launched had already begun to take on a more durable form. Through the interlocking development of the Echo Park Evangelistic Association, Angelus Temple, the Bible college, and the formal incorporation of The International Church of the Foursquare Gospel,[12] revival had been translated into an integrated ecclesial system. Evangelism, congregational life, ministerial formation, global missions, and denominational identity were no longer parallel efforts but parts of a single missional ecosystem. The apostolic impulse remained, but it increasingly depended on structures capable of preserving coherence beyond the life of its founder.

That work of consolidation accelerated under the leadership of her son, Rolf K. McPherson, who served as president from 1944 to 1988. During his tenure, governance structures were formalized, regional oversight expanded, and systems of pastoral accountability established. These developments provided stability during a period of significant growth and secured Foursquare's place within the broader evangelical landscape, symbolized by its entry into the National Association of Evangelicals in 1952. The movement had gained durability, but its center of gravity had begun to shift. Missionary zeal did not disappear during these years, yet increasing attention was directed toward congregational health, administrative continuity, and denominational maintenance. What had once been driven by expansion increasingly came to be measured by sustainability.

Subsequent denominational leadership of the US Foursquare Church reflects the persistence of this rhythm. Periods of consolidation have repeatedly given way to moments of renewal, each responding to the pressures of scale, culture, and organizational complexity. The

12. Incorporated in 1927.

movement has not advanced along a straight line, but through recurring cycles in which expansion produced structure, and structure eventually demanded reimagining. This pattern reveals both strength and vulnerability: Foursquare has endured by learning to live within the tension between rooted community and apostolic movement, continually renegotiating that relationship rather than attempting to resolve it once and for all. Yet history also shows that such balance is never self-sustaining. Structures that once served mission can, over time, begin to redefine it, quietly redirecting attention, authority, and imagination.

Renewed apostolic energy within Foursquare has often arisen from sodalic-type leaders whose influence extended far beyond the local churches they served. This dynamic was exemplified by Jack Hayford, who demonstrated that Spirit-led renewal need not originate outside established structures in order to reshape them; at The Church on the Way, he transformed a local congregation into a national center of charismatic renewal by integrating theological depth, Spirit-filled worship, and pastoral leadership. Similar patterns appeared elsewhere. At Beaverton Foursquare Church, Ron Mehl modeled grace-centered teaching and relational integrity that fostered deep local formation while extending influence outward, while Roy Hicks Jr., as pastor of Faith Center, strengthened the denomination's leadership pipeline through mentoring systems, conferences, and training initiatives that equipped pastors and church planters for sustained, long-term ministry.

Though firmly embedded within denominational life, these leaders exercised translocal influence. Their ministries assumed apostolic dimensions, reintroducing risk, innovation, and outward momentum from within established structures. That pattern has not ended. Similar forms of influence continue today among pastors, church planters, and movement leaders who work within Foursquare's institutional life while extending its reach beyond local congregations. Together, they demonstrate that institutional stability need not extinguish apostolic vitality; under the right conditions, it can become the soil in which renewal takes root.

STRUCTURAL AND FINANCIAL CHALLENGES TO MODALITY-SODALITY INTEGRATION

Because structure and money carry theological weight, they become decisive arenas in which a movement's deepest commitments are tested.

Every movement must organize and steward resources; the more probing question is whether its structures and budgets are intentionally ordered to serve mission rather than subtly displace it. Without sustained vigilance, even faithful decisions tend to drift toward what is most visible, immediate, and controllable. The present moment therefore invites closer examination of the pressures created by Foursquare's unitary organizational structure and recent financial realignments, and how these dynamics shape, and at times strain, the movement's capacity to live faithfully as both a rooted church and a sending movement.

Two interconnected pressures are especially significant. The first concerns the strain inherent in sustaining congregational life and apostolic mission within a single institutional framework. The second emerges through Foursquare Reimagined, a reform initiative launched in the late 2000s that sought to renew the movement's missional effectiveness by aligning more explicitly with the Great Commission, reshaping national and district offices toward a catalytic leadership culture, and redirecting a substantial portion of the national tithe back to local churches. Together, these structural and financial shifts have materially reshaped how Foursquare understands and practices its mission, both nationally and globally. What is ultimately at stake is not organizational efficiency but theological faithfulness: whether Foursquare's structures and financial practices continue to sustain its apostolic vocation alongside congregational life, or whether local priorities increasingly eclipse the movement's calling to participate in God's mission to the nations.

Foursquare's Unitary Structure

Sociologist Mark Chaves has offered one of the most helpful organizational insights for understanding modern denominations. In his analysis of American religious institutions, Chaves argues that denominations are often mistakenly treated as single, unitary organizations, when in fact they typically operate through two parallel structures: a religious authority structure and an agency structure. These structures function simultaneously but differently, responding to distinct environments, managing different forms of uncertainty, and exercising separate lines of authority. For Chaves, this dual arrangement is not incidental but fundamental, so much so that it should stand at the center of any serious analysis of denominational organization. In missiological terms, denominations ordinarily function as both modality and sodality.

What makes The Foursquare Church distinctive is that it does not neatly fit this dominant pattern. Chaves identifies Foursquare as one of the few American denominations that has retained a largely unitary organizational structure. Such structures often trace their origins to charismatic founders who built movements around personal authority, typically with a president functioning as the movement's senior pastor.[13] Foursquare's historical development under Aimee Semple McPherson reflects precisely this pattern.

Ironically, however, despite its formally unitary design, The Foursquare Church has developed functional parallels to the dual structures Chaves describes. Over time, the movement has differentiated between domestic church life and global mission through two primary entities: the US Church and Foursquare Missions International (FMI). The US Church attends to the life of local congregations through pastoral care, credentialing, governance, and leadership development, while FMI bears responsibility for global mission strategy, missionary deployment, and international partnerships. Though housed within a single denominational framework, these entities embody distinct callings that correspond closely to modality and sodality.

Viewed through the combined lenses of Paul, Winter, and Chaves, Foursquare's structure appears less as an organizational anomaly and more as a crucible. It exposes the persistent difficulty of holding church and mission together without allowing one to eclipse the other. The task before the movement is not to abandon unity or to artificially separate its structures, but to recover a theological imagination robust enough to sustain both modalities and sodalities as indispensable expressions of one body, called together into the mission of God.

The challenge, however, is that within a unitary structure these parallel commitments inevitably compete for attention, authority, and resources. Winter warned that unless deliberately safeguarded, the modality will always tend to absorb the sodality. The local church, by virtue of its visibility, immediacy, and pastoral proximity, naturally commands loyalty, funding, and institutional focus. Global mission, by contrast, requires sustained theological intentionality and deliberate structural

13. Chaves, "Dual Structures," 165–68.

protection if it is to remain central rather than peripheral to the movement's life.

In Foursquare's case, this tension is intensified by the concentration of authority within the office of the president. Because presidential leadership shapes strategic priorities, budgetary allocation, and organizational emphasis across the entire movement, decisions made at this level simultaneously affect both domestic church life and global mission engagement. Over time, and especially as movements mature, institutional gravity tends to pull leaders toward consolidation, risk management, and pastoral stability rather than apostolic expansion.

For this reason, anchoring Foursquare's identity explicitly and continually in its dual calling as both church and mission is not optional but essential. Structures and budgets alone cannot preserve this balance. It must be named, taught, and intentionally stewarded so that future leaders inherit not only authority, but a clear theological mandate to hold modality and sodality together with wisdom and courage. Without such anchoring, the tension is not resolved but quietly collapsed, and the apostolic dimension of the movement risks being diminished by the very structures designed to sustain it.

A Structural Culture

An added challenge lies not only in formal organization but in the movement's cultural imagination. In practice, The Foursquare Church places primary emphasis on the local congregation and its senior pastor, a focus that unintentionally intensifies the tension between modality and sodality. Foursquare rightly understands itself as a Great-Commission movement, yet it often narrates its identity primarily through local churches and pastoral leadership. While this emphasis affirms the indispensable role of congregational life, it can also narrow the biblical vision of the church by equating "church" almost exclusively with the local assembly.

This narrowing obscures the broader scriptural witness to the church as the whole people of God, participating in God's mission through multiple forms and callings. When ministry is collapsed entirely into the activity of local congregations, other expressions of Christian vocation are recast as secondary or auxiliary rather than integral to God's redemptive work. Such assumptions, often framed as pragmatic or empowering, reflect a constricted ecclesiology that overlooks the New

Testament's affirmation of both gathered communities and specialized, sent ministries. Within this imagination, sodalities are rarely rejected outright, but they are easily diminished, treated as optional rather than essential expressions of the church's shared participation in the mission of God.

This constricted vision is reinforced by the way Foursquare narrates its own origins. The movement commonly identifies the opening of Angelus Temple as the beginning of The Foursquare Church, rather than the incorporation of the Echo Park Evangelistic Association or the formal establishment of The International Church of the Foursquare Gospel in 1927. While Angelus Temple rightly carries deep symbolic significance, privileging it as the primary point of origin subtly centers the local congregation and its senior pastor as the normative locus of ministry. Over time, this narrative shapes a ministry imagination in which legitimate Christian work is assumed to flow almost exclusively through the local church, while translocal, apostolic, and mission-focused expressions are treated as derivative or supplementary.

The consequence of this imagination is that translocal and apostolic structures oriented toward specialized ministry and frontier mission can be diminished, marginalized, or even functionally erased. Yet, as Ralph Winter repeatedly observed, the church has never existed without both modalities and sodalities. Whatever form Christianity takes, there have always been organizational expressions centered on congregational life alongside others devoted to specialized mission. History confirms this pattern again and again: bishops and abbots, dioceses and monastic orders, parishes and mission societies, churches and Bible colleges, pastors and missionaries. When either expression is neglected, the church's witness is weakened.

If the church has never existed without both modalities and sodalities, then the erosion of either is never abstract. It takes concrete form in decisions about authority, focus, and funding. Over time, such decisions reveal what a movement truly expects its churches to carry and what it is willing to sustain collectively. For Foursquare, this tension comes sharply into view in a series of financial and structural reforms aimed at renewing mission by strengthening local congregations, even as they placed new strain on the apostolic structures tasked with global witness.

Foursquare Reimagined: Funding, Focus, and the Strain on Mission

For much of its history, The Foursquare Church sought to sustain the relationship between congregational life and global mission through a funding model designed to hold both together. Local congregations retained 90 percent of their tithes and offerings to pursue their own local mission, vision, and ministry while contributing 10 percent to the denomination to support the mission, vision, and ministries of the national church. In addition, churches and individuals supported the Global Missions Fund, through which FMI deployed missionaries to strategic regions of the world. Together, these practices embodied a shared responsibility for mission, allowing local churches to flourish in their particular contexts while participating collectively in apostolic work beyond their immediate reach.

In the early 2000s, FMI initiated a significant shift in its approach to global mission. Moving away from a fully centralized funding model, FMI adopted a self-funded strategy in which those called to international service raised their own support. The stated aims were greater flexibility, broader participation, and long-term sustainability. This change empowered individual missionaries and strengthened relational partnerships with sending churches, while also relocating much of the financial responsibility for global mission from the denominational center to decentralized networks. At the same time, the Global Missions Fund continued to underwrite essential leadership functions, including the work of global associate directors and regional coordinators, preserving a measure of strategic coherence even as frontline funding became more localized.

A second, more far-reaching transition followed with the launch of Foursquare Reimagined in 2009. Unlike earlier seasons of renewal driven primarily through influential leaders and congregations, Foursquare Reimagined represented an intentional, denomination-wide effort to recalibrate structures and resources in service of mission. Framed in explicitly missional language, the initiative pursued three interrelated aims: to align the movement more clearly with the Great Commission; to reshape national and district offices toward a catalytic leadership culture; and to redirect a substantial portion of denominational tithes back to local churches through what became known as the Return on the Tithe (ROT). The stated purpose of this financial realignment was to strengthen congregations for leadership development, church multiplication, and local mission, on the assumption that renewed local capacity would generate broader missional vitality across the movement.

Central to this recalibration was the ROT. Approved in 2014 and implemented in 2015, ROT fundamentally restructured denominational finances by redirecting a portion of national tithe income back to local congregations. The program initially returned 20 percent, approximately $6 million annually. A second phase introduced in 2020 expanded this return to 40 percent, with an additional 10 percent allocated specifically for pastor retirement funding, bringing the annual redistribution to roughly $12 million, alongside the approximately $300 million already retained each year by local churches. Over its first decade (2015–2025), ROT redistributed an estimated $105 million to congregations. This shift represented one of the most significant financial restructurings in Foursquare's history, materially redefining how the national church understands and enacts its mission.

One of the most immediate consequences of this financial reorientation was a reduction in centralized funding for mission-related initiatives. Ministries such as Native American outreach, the Black Pastors' Network, and immigrant-focused programs, which had depended on denominational support, experienced significant budget constraints. At the same time, with greater resources retained locally, many congregations understandably prioritized immediate pastoral and congregational needs over long-term global mission engagement.

The reallocation of funds assumed that strengthening local churches would naturally result in renewed growth and missional expansion. The data following Foursquare Reimagined, however, shows that this assumption has not been borne out. In 2009, Foursquare reported 1,859 churches with a combined attendance of 262,616. By 2024, the number of churches had increased only marginally to 1,890, while total attendance declined to 190,283, a decrease of more than 72,000 people. These trends indicate that the initiative did not produce the kind of sustained growth or multiplication envisioned by its designers.

The challenge before The Foursquare Church is not administrative or financial, but theological. The question is how to recover a missional imagination in which strengthening local churches and sustaining global mission are not competing priorities, but mutually reinforcing expressions of faithfulness. Like the Roman Christians addressed by Paul, Foursquare is invited to rediscover that the church flourishes most fully when it gathers faithfully and sends generously, holding modality and sodality together in service of God's redemptive purpose in the world.

HOLDING CHURCH AND MISSION TOGETHER

The story of The Foursquare Church is a story of creative tension stewarded across generations. From its origins in the revivalist imagination of Aimee Semple McPherson to its maturation as a global denomination, Foursquare has flourished not by choosing between structure and movement, but by holding congregational life and apostolic mission together in dynamic relationship. When evangelistic urgency has been paired with institutional durability, the movement has expanded and adapted. When either impulse has been privileged at the expense of the other, its witness has narrowed.

This history makes clear that neither structure nor funding is neutral. Both carry theological weight, shaping not only what the church does but how it understands itself. Foursquare's unitary structure, formed in charismatic origins and sustained through strong presidential leadership, has provided coherence and continuity across decades of growth. At the same time, it has intensified pressure to define the church primarily through local congregations and pastoral leadership, leaving sodalitic expressions of mission vulnerable to marginalization. Recent financial realignments, particularly through Foursquare Reimagined and the ROT, further reveal how easily budgetary decisions can recalibrate missional imagination, often in ways that extend beyond their original intent.

Seen through a Pauline lens, the question is not whether local churches should be strengthened. Paul never pits congregational health against apostolic mission. Rather, he assumes that the maturity of the church is demonstrated precisely through its participation in God's outward-moving work. The church does not preserve itself by turning inward but discovers its identity by gathering faithfully and sending generously, sharing people, prayer, and resources so that the gospel may take root beyond its own borders.

The challenge facing The Foursquare Church, therefore, is not whether its current structures or financial strategies are prudent in themselves. Every movement must organize, adapt, and steward resources wisely. The deeper question is whether these structures and budgets are being intentionally and theologically guarded so that they serve, rather than quietly redefine, Foursquare's dual vocation as both church and mission. Without such vigilance, institutional gravity will inevitably favor what is most visible, immediate, and controllable, allowing local consolidation to eclipse apostolic imagination.

Yet the present moment is not only one of risk; it is also one of opportunity. The vitality of local congregations, the ongoing work of global mission through FMI, and the movement's deep historical memory provide fertile ground for renewal. If Foursquare can anchor its identity explicitly and consistently in its calling as both modality and sodality, it can model a form of ecclesial life capable of sustaining stability without sacrificing mission.

The future of The Foursquare Church will not be secured by structure alone, nor by funding strategies, nor by charismatic leadership in isolation. It will depend on whether the movement continues to steward the theological imagination that gave it birth: a vision of the church as a gathered people and a sent people, pastoral and apostolic, held together by the Spirit and participating together in God's redemptive mission to the nations. When this rhythm is rediscovered, the church becomes once again what it was always meant to be, not an institution to preserve, but a people formed and sent for the sake of the world.

20

The Global Expansion of The Foursquare Church

From its earliest days, Foursquare carried within its DNA a distinctly missionary impulse shaped by the Pentecostal revivals of the early twentieth century. Its global expansion was not the result of a single strategic plan nor merely an act of unstructured enthusiasm. Rather, it emerged from a foundational missiology that held together local church formation and apostolic mission, modality and sodality, in a dynamic and reproducible pattern.

Ted Vail identifies four formative commitments that shaped the spiritual DNA of The Foursquare Church and help explain its global spread.[1] First, Aimee Semple McPherson's unwavering commitment to exalting Jesus Christ stood at the center of the movement. The person and work of Christ were not abstract theological commitments but the animating force behind both the emerging denominational structure and the outward thrust of mission. This Christ-centered passion generated, at the same time, a strong local church expression at Angelus Temple and an apostolic impulse that propelled trained leaders into the world.

Second, church planting was central from the outset. Angelus Temple functioned not only as a thriving congregation but also as a sending hub. Early Foursquare churches emerged in diverse cultural and linguistic contexts, including Jewish Christian congregations and Native American ministries. Growth was not driven by the replication of a

1. Vail, "Foursquare Missiology," 155–68.

single ecclesial model but by contextual adaptation to the cultural "soil" in which the gospel took root. From the beginning, Foursquare demonstrated an instinctive capacity to translate mission into local expression without sacrificing theological coherence.

Third, a deep concern for holistic care shaped Foursquare's missional imagination. Influenced by McPherson's Salvation Army upbringing, her experience as a widowed missionary in China, and her encounters with poverty during evangelistic travels, ministry was understood as addressing both spiritual and material need. This conviction became especially visible during the Great Depression, when Angelus Temple's Commissary provided food and clothing through unconditional generosity. The same holistic vision accompanied early missionaries, whose churches often functioned as centers of spiritual formation, education, and social care. Here again, modality and sodality worked together, institutional stability serving outward-facing mission.

Fourth, McPherson recognized early that sustained mission required Bible-centered leadership development. Within the first year of Angelus Temple's opening, she established a Bible college to train pastors and missionaries. This commitment ensured that revival would not dissipate but multiply through trained leaders. Significantly, she extended this vision cross-culturally by launching a Spanish-language Angelus Temple and LIFE Bible College under Hispanic leadership, independent of the English-speaking institution. This decision reflected an instinctively contextual, reproducible, and apostolic approach to mission.

These four commitments were not abstract ideals. They generated a missionary impulse that moved quickly beyond Los Angeles and into the nations. Empowered by the Holy Spirit and compelled by the urgency of the gospel, early missionaries crossed cultural, linguistic, and geographic boundaries to plant churches where the name of Jesus was scarcely known. Some were Americans formed in revival who ventured into unfamiliar contexts. Others were immigrants, sailors, and laborers who encountered Christ in Los Angeles, were discipled, and then sent back to their homelands as bearers of the gospel. Mission flowed in multiple directions, carried by relationships rather than centralized control.

From its earliest decades, Foursquare's global expansion followed a discernible rhythm. Missionary pioneers crossed cultural and geographic boundaries with evangelistic urgency, forming congregations that initially depended on translocal initiative but gradually matured into self-governing, self-supporting, and ultimately missionary-sending churches. What began as sodalitic mission did not remain external or permanent. Responsibility was progressively transferred, leadership localized, and ministry contextualized. Over time, churches born through missionary movement became stable ecclesial bodies capable of sustaining their own life and extending their witness beyond themselves. This rhythm of planting, indigenizing, and multiplying became one of the defining characteristics of Foursquare's global development.

Two cases illustrate this pattern with particular clarity. In the Philippines, early missionary work in Iloilo initiated by Vincente DeFante was intentionally released into Filipino leadership, later strengthened by the Ilauans and Tuzons. What began as missionary-driven initiative developed into a robust national church marked by contextualized ministry and sustained church planting. Growth from 279 to 616 churches reflected not the consolidation of external control, but the long-term fruitfulness of leadership entrusted to local hands. The movement matured by relinquishing dependence rather than preserving it.

A similar dynamic unfolded in China, though under far more constrained conditions. The Lawler family and later collaborators established congregations in Shanghai and surrounding regions, but political upheaval eventually forced missionary withdrawal. Rather than extinguishing the movement, this disruption reshaped it. Through Hong Kong, under the leadership of Edwin and Beulah Lee, Foursquare developed a training and sending center that resourced Chinese churches across shifting geopolitical realities. Mission adapted without retreating, sustaining ecclesial life through new forms of partnership and translocal support.

Across every inhabited continent the pattern held. Where mission was practiced as initiation and formation rather than permanent control, churches took root with resilience. When responsibility was transferred rather than retained, local leadership emerged capable of contextual discernment and sustained growth. Foursquare's global expansion was shaped by this repeated willingness to allow sodalitic mission to give way to indigenous ecclesial life, and, in time, to recover its apostolic vocation through churches that sent others in turn.[2]

Remarkably, this global expansion occurred with relatively few Western missionaries. In the 1960s, this phenomenon drew the attention of researcher James Montgomery, whose work in the Philippines

2. This summary is adapted from Van Cleave, *Vine and the Branches*.

documented rapid gospel growth despite a limited missionary presence. His findings demonstrated that Foursquare's expansion was not driven by centralized Western control but by a missiological method that empowered local leaders.[3] Stable structures and apostolic freedom were held together in a way that fostered adaptability without dependency.

Taken together, these stories reveal more than numerical expansion or institutional success. They disclose a deeper form of missional fruit: the emergence of churches capable of assuming responsibility for their own life, witness, and discernment within their cultural context. Across regions and generations, Foursquare flourished not simply where missionaries were present or structures were replicated, but where missionary initiative and local church development were held together in mutual dependence. The movement's vitality has never rested solely on structure or spontaneity, strategy or charisma. It has emerged through the sustained synergy between the sending and the sent, the pioneering and the pastoral, the missionary impulse and the local congregation.

What becomes visible in these accounts is a recurring pattern of ecclesial maturation. As the gospel took root, churches gradually developed the capacity to govern themselves, sustain their common life, bear witness beyond their immediate context, and engage Scripture with a growing theological voice of their own. These capacities did not appear simultaneously, nor were they produced by uniform methods. They emerged unevenly, often through tension, transition, and improvisation, as local communities learned to inhabit the gospel within their own social and cultural worlds.

Over time, this pattern of maturation did not remain merely implicit. As leaders reflected on decades of global mission practice, the movement began to recognize that these recurring capacities could be named, nurtured, and safeguarded without being forced. This recognition gave rise to what would later be articulated as Foursquare's four-stage model of national church development. Importantly, this model did not invent the process it describes. It emerged as a way of attending to life already present, offering language for how churches tend to grow toward maturity when modality and sodality remain in creative partnership.

The four stages function not as a prescriptive sequence but as a descriptive framework. They name rhythms that repeatedly surface when mission is practiced with patience, trust, and restraint. Together with the

3. Montgomery, *New Testament Fire in the Philippines*.

four-self vision of ecclesial maturity, they provide a coherent missiological grammar for understanding how contextualized churches are formed over time—churches that are neither permanently dependent nor prematurely autonomous, but capable of participating fully in God's mission from within their own context.

21

The Foursquare Church as Modality and Sodality

VAIL'S ANALYSIS OF THE Foursquare Church's founding DNA, together with the four-stage model of church-planting movements and the four-self missiology, provides indispensable frameworks for understanding how a single congregation in Los Angeles grew into a global movement. Yet even with these interpretive lenses, one additional dimension warrants closer attention. From its earliest days, Aimee Semple McPherson and the emerging Foursquare movement intentionally leveraged the complementary strengths of local congregations as modalities and ministry agencies as sodalities. They understood that the dynamic interplay between these two structures could both deepen congregational life and propel the gospel beyond local boundaries. This partnership was not incidental; it was a constitutive feature of how Foursquare embodied mission. Long before these patterns were named or systematized in formal models, they were already being practiced as the movement learned to gather and send, stabilize and expand, in faithful participation in the mission of God.

Aimee Semple McPherson's ministry began, not as a local church but as a sodality: the Echo Park Evangelistic Association (EPEA). Its central place in her vision is evident in her own descriptions. When she spoke in 1922 of constructing Angelus Temple, she framed it not primarily as the founding of a congregation but as a strategic development for the EPEA, calling the Temple "the base for the activities of The Echo Park

Evangelistic Association."[1] Financial support for LIFE Bible College likewise flowed through the EPEA rather than through Angelus Temple, and in 1924 McPherson commissioned Alfred Kleinschmidt and Carl Linden as missionaries to India through the EPEA. Even after the incorporation of the International Church of the Foursquare Gospel in 1927, Foursquare publications continued to be produced by the EPEA for nearly fifteen years following McPherson's death, underscoring its enduring role as the movement's primary sending and coordinating body.[2]

Subsequent retellings of Foursquare's origins often treat the EPEA, Angelus Temple, LIFE Bible College, and the International Church of the Foursquare Gospel as successive stages in a single institutional trajectory. While historically understandable, this narrative flattens the distinct missional functions each structure served. In practice, these entities existed in a symbiotic relationship: A sodality (the EPEA) generated and sustained a modality (Angelus Temple), which in turn provided a stable base for the sodality's ongoing apostolic work, including church planting and global mission. Together, church, training, and mission formed an integrated ecosystem rather than a linear progression from one form to another.

Over time, however, the movement came to narrate its origins primarily through the opening of Angelus Temple rather than through the earlier incorporation of the EPEA or the later formation of the International Church of the Foursquare Gospel. While this choice is symbolically powerful, it has also shaped Foursquare's self-understanding in significant ways. Anchoring the movement's identity in the local congregation subtly elevates the church and its senior pastor as the primary, and sometimes exclusive, locus of ministry.

This emphasis reinforces Foursquare's pastoral identity, yet it also intensifies the inherent tension between congregational life and apostolic mission. Foursquare continues to affirm its identity as a Great Commission movement, but it often frames that identity almost entirely through the language of local churches and pastoral leadership.[3] This tension becomes explicit in statements such as one frequently voiced during the Foursquare Reimagined initiative: "Districts and denominations do not do ministry; only local churches do ministry." While intended to affirm congregational vitality, such claims reflect a constricted ecclesiology that

1. Echo Park Evangelistic Association, "About EPEA."

2. Van Cleave, *Vine and the Branches*, 11.

3. Van Cleave, *Vine and the Branches*, 295–305. Foursquare Church, "Our Mission and Approach."

equates "church" exclusively with the local assembly gathered around a senior pastor.

This reduction obscures the broader biblical vision of the church as the whole people of God, participating in God's mission through diverse callings and structures. Apostolic, missionary, and para-congregational ministries are not secondary add-ons to the church's work; they are essential expressions of the church's vocation to bear witness to the gospel beyond its immediate boundaries. When the church is defined solely in congregational terms, these sodalitic expressions are easily marginalized, minimized, or functionally erased.

Yet sodalities remain indispensable for disciple-making and church-planting movements. They provide specialized leadership, training, and translocal coordination that cannot be sustained by local congregations alone. As Ralph Winter famously argued, whatever form Christianity takes, "there will still be two kinds of structures that will make up the movement," and mission will be most effective only when both are fully and properly engaged.[4]

This bears repeating, because history confirms it again and again. In every era of the church, tensions have emerged between these two structures. These structures are not inherently opposed, but unless intentionally guarded, the modality will absorb the sodality, church will consume mission. Local congregations, by virtue of their immediacy and visibility, naturally command attention, loyalty, and financial support. Global mission, by contrast, requires deliberate theological imagination and structural protection if it is to remain central rather than peripheral.

For The Foursquare Church, sustaining this balance is not only an organizational concern but a theological one. Faithfulness to its founding vision requires ongoing vigilance to ensure that both modality and sodality are honored as essential partners in the church's shared participation in the mission of God.

FOUR-STAGE MODEL AND THE SYMBIOTIC RELATIONSHIP BETWEEN MODALITIES AND SODALITIES

The four-stage model of national church development offers a practical way of visualizing the symbiotic relationship between mission and

4. Winter, "Two Structures," 121.

church, between sodality and modality. Taken together, the stages reflect the church's dual vocation as a sent, apostolic movement and a gathered, pastoral community. Neither dimension is sufficient on its own; both are required for the gospel to take root, mature, and multiply.

Stages one and four form what might be described as the apostolic arc of the model. In these stages, the gospel is initiated among unreached peoples, and mature churches are sent outward again in missionary expansion. This work is typically carried by sodalitic structures: missionaries, apostolic teams, translocal networks, mission agencies, training institutions, and relief organizations that cross cultural, linguistic, and geographic boundaries. These structures specialize in pioneering, adaptation, and multiplication.

Stages two and three form the pastoral arc of the model. Here the focus shifts to nurturing disciples, developing leaders, organizing congregational life, engaging local communities, and establishing durable churches. This work is most naturally carried by modalities, local congregations that provide relational depth, spiritual formation, accountability, and long-term presence within a particular context. These stages ensure that gospel witness is not fleeting but embedded in stable communities of faith.

The model therefore resists a false choice between mission and church. Modalities and sodalities are not competing expressions but complementary ones. Modalities offer contextual intimacy and sustained discipleship, while sodalities provide broader vision, strategic coordination, and specialized capacity. When held together, this partnership enables both depth and reach, local rootedness and global expansion.

At the same time, this dynamic is not without tension. Questions of authority, funding, visibility, and decision-making inevitably arise between congregations and mission agencies, pastors and missionaries, local priorities and global commitments. These tensions must be navigated intentionally. Yet when approached collaboratively rather than competitively, they generate a synergistic effect in which grassroots engagement and strategic coordination strengthen one another. The early Foursquare ecosystem offers a clear historical example of this synergy in practice, particularly in the interplay between the EPEA, Angelus Temple, LIFE Bible College, the International Church of the Foursquare Gospel, and later FMI.

Ralph Winter's modality–sodality framework helps clarify why this balance is so essential. Winter insisted that the fulfillment of the

Great Commission depends on the full and proper involvement of both church-focused and mission-focused structures.[5] The four-stage model demonstrates how this theoretical insight functions in lived practice. The two "hemispheres" of the model are not rivals; one cannot exist without the other. Apostolic mission gives birth to the church, and the church, when healthy, becomes apostolic again.

What ultimately distinguished Aimee Semple McPherson's legacy was not her charisma, communication skill, or miracle ministry alone. Many revivalists have possessed similar gifts. What allowed her work to outlast her lifetime was the intentional integration of sodalitic and modalitic structures.[6] Revival energy was institutionalized without being domesticated, and missionary momentum was sustained through churches, training centers, and organizational frameworks.

As the movement expanded, this differentiation became more explicit. Domestic church life and global mission were eventually expressed through distinct yet interconnected structures, most notably the US Church and FMI. In Winter's terms, the US Church functions primarily as a modality, supporting congregational life, while FMI functions as a sodality, advancing translocal and cross-cultural mission.

The Foursquare Reimagined initiative reflects a contemporary attempt to renegotiate this relationship. Proposals such as aligning the US Church and district offices toward a more catalytic culture signal a desire to recover sodalitic energy within domestic structures.[7] If realized, such shifts could foster greater innovation, church planting, and mission mobilization. At the same time, they raise critical questions about funding priorities, resource allocation, and the ongoing role of local congregations within a unitary denominational system.

Winter's warning remains instructive here. Without deliberate theological clarity and structural safeguards, modalities tend over time to prioritize their own maintenance and gradually absorb the missionary sodalities that once renewed them. The four-stage model therefore functions, not only as a descriptive framework but as a diagnostic tool, helping the church discern whether it is sustaining the creative tension necessary for long-term missional vitality.

5. Winter, "Two Structures," 121.

6. Anderson, *Introduction to Pentecostalism*, 159.

7. Foursquare Church, "Up-to-Date Information on the Five Stakes."

CONCLUSION

The story of the church has always been a story of tension and grace, of holding together what so easily comes apart. Across the centuries, the people of God have been called to live in the rhythm of gathering and sending, worship and witness, community and mission. When this balance is sustained, the church becomes a living expression of the gospel, rooted in love and reaching toward the world.

Yet this balance is never automatic. Every generation faces the temptation to turn inward, to preserve what is familiar rather than risk what faithfulness may require. Structures that once served mission can slowly become ends in themselves. Without ongoing discernment and renewal, apostolic passion gives way to maintenance, and the church's outward movement begins to stall. Still, when local faithfulness and global vision are held together in prayerful partnership, something more than strategy emerges. The Spirit breathes life into the whole body once again.

Paul's vision in Romans offers a pattern for this kind of integrated faithfulness. He labored to strengthen local communities even as he pressed toward places where Christ had not yet been named. For Paul, church and mission were never separate pursuits. They flowed together as a single vocation shaped by the gospel. The church today is called to that same integration, to live what it believes, to let its theology take form in its practices, and to allow its structures to serve the life of the Spirit rather than contain it.

The future of Christian mission will belong to communities able to live within this creative tension, anchored in worship, generous in sending, humble in partnership, and attentive to the Spirit's surprising work in a changing world. When the church learns again to hold structure lightly and love deeply, it will rediscover its true calling: to embody the gospel locally and to extend it globally, until the earth is filled with the knowledge of the Lord as the waters cover the sea.

22

The Church Contextualized, Thriving, and Indigenous

The global expansion of the Foursquare movement invites more than historical description; it demands theological interpretation. What unfolded across nations and decades cannot be adequately explained by strategy, organizational design, or charismatic leadership alone. As the gospel took root in diverse cultural, social, and political settings, deeper patterns began to surface. Where mission partnerships were marked by patience, trust, and a willingness to release control, similar forms of church life emerged again and again.

These churches were not replicas of one another. They differed in language, worship, leadership patterns, and social location, and they were not the product of a single model imposed from the outside. Yet across this diversity, recognizable capacities appeared again and again. Churches learned to govern their own life, sustain ministry, bear witness within their own relational networks, and discern faithfulness through Scripture and lived experience. Over time, many followed recurring rhythms as they moved from initial gospel presence toward mature participation in God's mission.

Crucially, Foursquare did not invent these patterns. They were not designed in advance or codified through strategic planning, but recognized over time through sustained engagement with Scripture, attentive listening to missiologists and anthropologists, and decades of lived missionary experience. As leaders reflected on the movement's global story, they began to name what they were already witnessing: the marks of mature, contextualized churches and the pathways through which such maturity takes shape.

This recognition was deeply biblical. Again and again, leaders returned to Acts and to the letters of Paul, where the gospel advances through communities first formed by apostolic initiative, then entrusted to local leadership, sustained through shared responsibility, and propelled outward in mission. Contemporary experience echoed the scriptural witness: the church grows not by remaining dependent, but by receiving the gospel deeply enough to take responsibility for its life and witness.

From this convergence of Scripture, experience, and reflection emerged what have come to be known as four-self missiology, the four stages of church development, and the concept of indigeneity. These frameworks do not function as blueprints to be imposed, but as interpretive lenses that help name what emerges when the gospel is entrusted locally and mission is practiced as partnership. They draw attention to capacity rather than outcomes, to formation rather than efficiency, and to faithfulness over time rather than rapid expansion.

This chapter brings these insights together around a demanding question: What does it look like when the gospel truly takes root and the church becomes at home in its context? By exploring the church as contextualized, thriving, and indigenous, the discussion moves beyond questions of growth to consider the nature of ecclesial maturity itself. What the global Foursquare story ultimately reveals is not a proprietary method but a theological conviction: When mission is practiced with humility and responsibility is entrusted rather than retained, the church learns not only how to grow but also how to live.

CONTEXTUALIZING THE CHURCH: FOUR-SELF MISSIOLOGY

Up to this point, the discussion has focused on structures, movements, and spaces: churches and mission agencies, stability and sending, centers and frontiers, thresholds and transitions. These categories are essential for understanding how the church and mission interact, yet they still leave a more fundamental question unresolved. What does faithfulness actually look like when the gospel has truly taken root in a local community? How do we recognize when a church is no longer merely present in a context but has become capable of living, growing, and bearing witness from within that context? In other words, faithful mission requires more than the contextualization of the gospel: It also requires the contextualization of the church itself, its leadership, practices, patterns of life, and capacities, so that the good news is not only proclaimed in a local language, but embodied through a local people.

The frameworks of modality and sodality help us discern how God carries out his redemptive purposes through his people and why tensions inevitably arise between stability and movement, rootedness and sending. Together, they draw our attention to the liminal relational and structural spaces in which churches and mission are shaped and reshaped through encounter, disruption, transition, and participation in God's work. What these frameworks do not yet name explicitly is the character of the life that is forming through mission itself. To discern that, we must shift our focus from ecclesial structures and missional dynamics to ecclesial maturity: What does it look like when the gospel truly takes root and a church is born? What signs indicate when a community has moved beyond mere presence and has become a living, contextualized expression of the gospel? Four-self missiology provides a way of naming that maturity.

Four-self missiology, then, is an expression of what faithful contextualization looks like when the gospel is allowed to shape the life of a community from within. At its core, contextualization affirms that both the gospel and the church are translatable without being diluted, incarnational without being captive to culture, and universally true while being locally embodied. The four-self framework gives concrete form to this theological conviction by shifting attention away from methods and programs toward the capacities that emerge when the gospel is genuinely received, owned, entrusted to a local community of faith, and embodied in its shared practices, leadership, and witness.

By *capacity*, we do not mean competence in a technical or managerial sense, nor the possession of institutional resources or polished systems. Capacity names the church's ability to sustain faithful life from within its own context over time. It refers to the deep, often invisible formation that enables a community to discern, decide, adapt, and respond responsibly to the demands of discipleship, mission, and change. Capacities are not installed through training alone, nor secured through external oversight. They emerge gradually as practices are lived, authority is exercised, mistakes are made and corrected, and trust is formed within the life of the community. To speak of ecclesial capacity, then, is to speak of resilience, responsibility, and the ability to bear the weight of the gospel in a particular place without constant external intervention.

The four selves do not function as benchmarks to be achieved or outcomes to be measured, but as names for the capacities that signal ecclesial life taking root. They help discern when responsibility is shifting from external agents to local leaders, when sustainability is emerging from within the community, when witness is becoming indigenous rather than imported, and when theological discernment is being exercised locally rather than outsourced. The four selves offer a grammar for recognizing maturity, not by uniform appearance or rapid growth, but by the presence of life capable of enduring faithfully over time.

When the gospel takes root in a new context, it does not arrive as a finished product. It enters particular languages, economies, social hierarchies, political pressures, and religious imaginations. It is heard, interpreted, embodied, and lived within concrete histories and everyday realities. The gospel always comes as good news *to someone, somewhere*, and it is received and lived within the constraints and possibilities of a specific place. Four-self missiology recognizes that a church becomes truly local, not simply when it adopts cultural forms but when it develops the internal capacities necessary to live the gospel responsibly from within its own context.

These capacities include the ability to govern its communal life, sustain its ministry, bear witness beyond itself, and engage Scripture theologically in light of local realities. They are more than organizational milestones or institutional achievements. They are signs that the gospel has been received deeply enough to generate life from within rather than dependency from without, to form a community capable of faithful obedience, resilience, and discernment over time.

Historically, the original three-self formulation—self-governing, self-supporting, and self-propagating—emerged in the nineteenth century as a response to mission practices that unintentionally produced dependency and prolonged external control.[1] Figures such as Henry Venn and Rufus Anderson, and later Roland Allen, observed that churches could grow numerically and yet remain structurally fragile, culturally foreign, and indefinitely supervised by missionary agents. Their concern was not efficiency or speed, but ecclesial faithfulness: the formation of

1. See Shaw and Gitau, *Kingdom of God in Africa*, 171; Allen, *Missionary Methods*.

churches able to assume responsibility for their own life and witness under the lordship of Christ.

Over time, missiologists recognized that these three capacities, while essential, were incomplete without a fourth. Self-theologizing was needed to name the church's capacity to interpret Scripture, discern faithfulness, and articulate the gospel meaningfully within its own cultural horizon.[2] Without this capacity, churches could function administratively and missionally while remaining theologically dependent. Together, these four principles describe not a linear sequence to be completed, but a pattern of life that emerges as the church becomes rooted, responsible, and resilient within its context.

Self-Governing: Contextual Authority and Local Discernment

Self-governing reflects contextual authority exercised within the life of a local church. Leadership is no longer borrowed, translated secondhand, or mediated primarily through external decision-makers. Instead, local leaders discern, decide, and shepherd in ways that are intelligible and credible within their own social world, drawing on shared cultural knowledge, relational networks, and pastoral wisdom shaped by proximity to the community they serve.

This principle does not imply isolation from the wider body of Christ, nor does it deny the importance of accountability, mutual learning, or theological correction. Rather, it affirms that responsibility and agency are rightly located where the Spirit is already at work. Contextualization here is expressed as trust—trust that the same Spirit who called the church into being is capable of guiding it from within, through leaders formed in that context and accountable to one another in community.

When authority remains indefinitely external, churches may function, but they do not mature. Decision-making becomes reactive rather than discerning, leadership development is constrained, and responsibility is continually deferred. Over time, this produces fragility rather than resilience. Self-governance signals a decisive shift from supervision to responsibility, from control to trust. It marks the moment when leadership has become indigenous rather than merely delegated, capable of bearing the weight of discernment and direction for the life of the church.

2. Hiebert, *Anthropological Insights*, 186–90; Bosch, *Transforming Mission*, 447–52; Newbigin, *Gospel in a Pluralist Society*, 222–33; Bevans, *Models of Contextual Theology*, 3–12.

Self-Supporting: Contextual Sustainability and Economic Dignity

Self-support expresses contextual sustainability rooted in economic dignity. Economic life is never neutral. The ways communities give, share, and steward resources are shaped by culture, history, patterns of exchange, and lived realities. Four-self missiology therefore resists the *practice* of long-term financial dependence as a normative feature of mission. Even when dependence is unintended, habitual patterns of external funding can quietly shape expectations, distort power relationships, and delay the transfer of responsibility. By contrast, four-self missiology frames economic maturity as a theological good—one tied to responsibility, freedom, and full participation in the shared life and witness of the church.

Self-supporting does not imply isolation from global generosity or the rejection of mutual aid. Rather, it emphasizes ownership, dignity, generosity, and responsibility. Churches remain interconnected within the wider body of Christ, and moments of shared burden and reciprocal generosity are often expressions of true partnership. What self-support resists is the normalization of dependency. Churches that rely indefinitely on external funding are subtly shaped by outside priorities, timelines, and power dynamics. Over time, this distorts discipleship, undermines local initiative, and weakens the church's capacity to discern its own mission. It also constrains reproducibility, as new church plants may come to assume that viability requires outside financial support rather than local participation. In such settings, multiplication becomes contingent on external resources rather than on the gospel's capacity to take root and generate life within the community itself.

When local churches learn to sustain ministry in ways appropriate to their context, the gospel becomes embedded in the rhythms of everyday life. Giving becomes an expression of belonging rather than obligation. Stewardship becomes a spiritual practice rather than a technical requirement. Self-support functions as a sign of church vitality, indicating that the church is sustaining life from within rather than surviving through continual external intervention.

Self-Propagating: Contextual Mission and Indigenous Witness

Self-propagation reveals contextual mission. The gospel, once internalized, naturally seeks expression beyond its point of arrival. A contextualized church resists copying foreign forms, strategies, or organizational models. Instead, it bears witness and multiplies in ways that are culturally intelligible, relationally grounded, and responsive to local realities.

Mission becomes intrinsic rather than imported. Evangelism and church planting arise through social networks already embedded in the life of the community—family systems, friendships, workplaces, and shared spaces of trust. New communities of faith emerge not as replicas of the sending church, but as fresh embodiments of the same good news, shaped by the cultural soil in which they take root.

This principle resists the monopolization of growth by external agents and affirms that the Spirit's missionary agency is already active among local believers. When churches propagate the gospel in ways that feel natural rather than imposed, they demonstrate that faith has moved from reception to participation, from something received to something shared. Self-propagation signals that the church has become a bearer of the gospel it has received.

Self-Theologizing: Contextual Meaning and Ecclesial Voice

Self-theologizing brings contextual meaning to the surface. Every community encounters Scripture with its own questions shaped by suffering and hope, injustice and resilience, family structures, social pressures, and historical memory. Four-self missiology insists that theology is not complete until it is wrestled with locally, within the concrete realities of a particular people and place.

This does not relativize truth or undermine the apostolic witness. Rather, it honors the way truth is apprehended, confessed, and embodied in specific contexts.[3] Theology that remains permanently imported may preserve correct formulations, but it does not cultivate discernment. Churches may learn what to say without learning how to think theologically, how to interpret Scripture faithfully in light of lived experience, or how to speak the gospel credibly to their own world.

A church that can name the gospel in its own theological voice has moved beyond reception into ownership.[4] It has learned not only to repeat inherited answers, but to engage Scripture deeply, to discern

3. Bevans, *Models of Contextual Theology*.

4. Greenman and Green, *Global Theology in Evangelical Perspective*, 9.

faithfully, and to articulate hope in ways that address local questions while remaining accountable to the wider Christian tradition. Self-theologizing reflects confidence in the Spirit's guidance and trust in the church's capacity to discern truth together as a community formed by word and Spirit.

HOLDING FAITHFULNESS AND CULTURE IN TENSION

Taken together, the four-self vision resists two equal and opposite distortions of mission. On one side lies cultural domination, where the gospel becomes entangled with the habits, leadership models, and institutional assumptions of the sending context. In these settings, faithfulness is quietly redefined as resemblance. Churches are assessed by how closely they mirror the forms and practices of those who brought the gospel, rather than by their capacity to live it responsibly within their own world. The result is often numerical growth without depth and organizational continuity without genuine rootedness.

On the other side lies uncritical accommodation, where contextualization collapses into cultural conformity and the gospel's distinctive claims are muted. When the church simply reflects the surrounding culture without discernment, the good news loses its power to confront, heal, and transform. Instead of calling people into a new way of life, it becomes a religious echo of prevailing values and power structures.

Four-self missiology holds gospel faithfulness and cultural particularity together in a necessary and dynamic tension. It affirms that the gospel is always at home in culture, yet never captive to it. The good news of Jesus Christ takes on local form, speaks every language, and inhabits every social world, even as it calls every culture into judgment and renewal. Contextualization is neither imitation nor accommodation, but faithful translation expressed through embodied obedience.

The measure of ecclesial maturity, therefore, is not resemblance to the sending church, nor mere cultural relevance, but the emergence of a community capable of living the gospel faithfully within its own context. Such a church bears witness, not by looking like Christians elsewhere but by embodying Christ in ways that are recognizable, resilient, and transformative where it has been planted.

Four-Self as a Grammar of Ecclesial Life

Four-Self Missiology provides a grammar for recognizing ecclesial life. Rather than prescribing what churches must do, it helps us discern what living churches look like. The four selves name capacities that emerge when the church is alive rather than merely organized, responsive rather than managed, and formed from within rather than sustained by external control.

These capacities do not appear all at once, nor do they mature evenly. Churches may exhibit strong self-propagation early while remaining fragile in governance or theological discernment. Others may develop deep theological reflection while remaining economically dependent. Such unevenness should not be interpreted as failure or deficiency. It is characteristic of living systems, which grow through complexity, adaptation, and time rather than through uniform progression.

Four-self missiology functions as a way of discerning life rather than producing it. Just as living organisms exhibit recognizable characteristics that signal health without explaining the mystery of life itself, mature churches display observable capacities that indicate whether the gospel has truly taken root. These signs do not exhaust the meaning of faithfulness, but they help distinguish between communities that are sustained by ongoing intervention and those that have developed resilience from within.

The goal of mission, therefore, is not the reproduction of our church models, nor the indefinite extension of external oversight. It is the emergence of mature, faithful communities through whom Christ is made visible in every culture. When the four selves begin to take shape, they signal not the end of mission but its fulfillment: the gospel taking flesh in new places, carried forward by communities who have learned to live it as their own.

Because the four selves have often been reduced to slogans or treated as a checklist, it is important to clarify how this framework is intended to function. Four-self missiology does not describe a linear progression through which churches advance in orderly sequence, nor does it offer a program or exportable model to be replicated elsewhere. The four selves do not prescribe structures, budgets, or leadership forms. They name capacities rather than templates, and they assume that churches mature unevenly and in contextually specific ways. Neither does selfhood imply isolation or the abandonment of partnership. Mature churches remain deeply relational, interconnected, and mutually accountable within the global body of Christ. At its best, four-self missiology also resists cultural domination and missionary overreach by calling sending structures to release control rather than extend it indefinitely. Understood in this way, the four selves orient mission away from efficiency and toward faithfulness, away from reproduction alone and toward formation over time.

If four-self missiology names the capacities that characterize a contextualized and mature church, it does not yet explain how those capacities typically take shape within real communities shaped by history, leadership, culture, conflict, and change. Churches do not awaken fully formed, nor do the four selves emerge evenly or simultaneously. They are cultivated through lived processes, relational patterns, and seasons of growth that unfold within concrete mission contexts.

To attend to these formative dynamics, we turn now to the four stages of church development—not as a formula to be imposed, but as a descriptive framework that traces the recurring rhythms through which contextualized churches are formed, strengthened, and eventually released into generative participation in God's mission. If the four selves name the destination, the stages describe the terrain.

THE CHURCH THRIVING: THE FOUR STAGES OF CHURCH DEVELOPMENT

Foursquare's global expansion has emerged through a sustained commitment to reproducibility, indigenous leadership, and collaborative partnership. Over time, these commitments were clarified and articulated through what has come to be known as the four stages of national church development.[5]

5. Amstutz, *Disciples of All Nations.*

National Church Development - Four-Stages

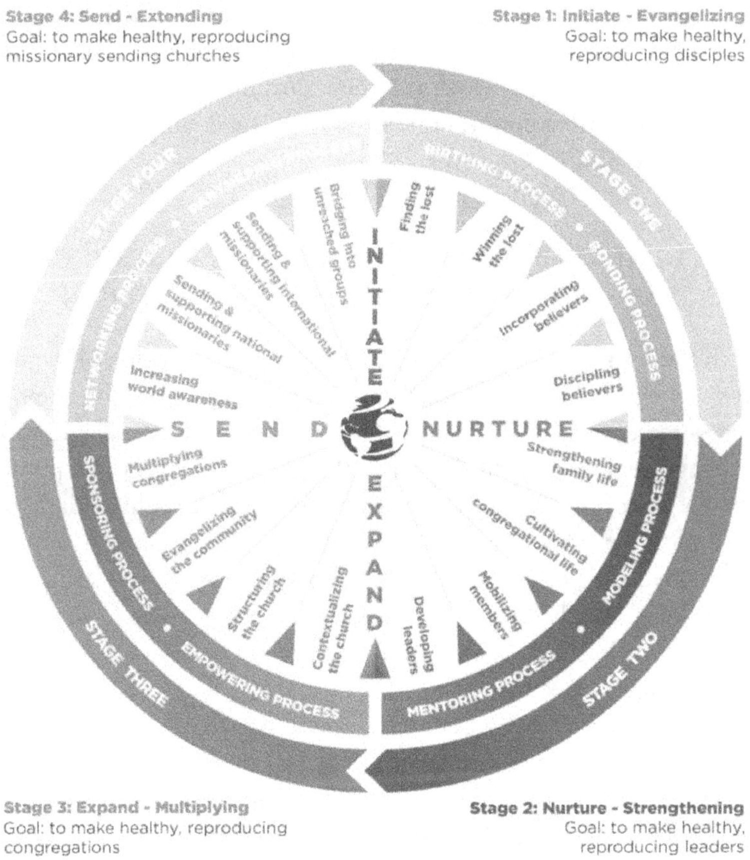

Stage 4: Send - Extending
Goal: to make healthy, reproducing missionary sending churches

Stage 1: Initiate - Evangelizing
Goal: to make healthy, reproducing disciples

INITIATE · NURTURE · EXPAND · SEND

Stage One: Birthing Process • Bonding Process — Finding the lost; Winning the lost; Incorporating believers; Discipling believers

Stage Two: Modeling Process • Mentoring Process — Strengthening family life; Cultivating congregational life; Mobilizing members; Developing leaders

Stage Three: Empowering Process • Sponsoring Process — Contextualizing the church; Structuring the church; Evangelizing the community; Multiplying congregations

Stage Four: Networking Process — Increasing world awareness; Sending & supporting national missionaries; Sending & supporting international missionaries; Bridging into unreached groups

Stage 3: Expand - Multiplying
Goal: to make healthy, reproducing congregations

Stage 2: Nurture - Strengthening
Goal: to make healthy, reproducing leaders

As *Disciples of All Nations* makes clear, the four stages reflect a theological conviction grounded in Scripture: The gospel advances most faithfully when churches are formed in ways that are locally rooted, culturally appropriate, and oriented toward multiplication rather than dependency. This conviction mirrors the apostolic logic of Acts, where gospel proclamation, community formation, leadership development, structural maturation, and missionary sending unfold in a recognizable rhythm across diverse contexts, from Jerusalem to Antioch to Ephesus.

At its core, the four-stage framework assumes that the church exists simultaneously as a gathered community and a sent movement.

Luke's narrative consistently holds these realities together. The church gathers for worship, teaching, fellowship, and prayer (Acts 2:42), yet it is repeatedly scattered by persecution, calling, and the leading of the Spirit (Acts 8:1; 13:2–3). Rather than treating stability and sending as competing impulses, Acts presents them as mutually reinforcing dimensions of the same missional life. The four stages describe how this dynamic unfolds over time as gospel witness moves from initiation to maturation and ultimately to multiplication, so that churches themselves become missionary-sending movements.

STAGE ONE—INITIATE: MAKING DISCIPLES AND LAYING THE GOSPEL FOUNDATION

The initiating stage corresponds to moments in Acts where the gospel enters a new social or cultural space through apostolic proclamation empowered by the Spirit. Pentecost itself functions as the paradigmatic initiating event. The Spirit descends, the gospel is proclaimed publicly, and new believers are gathered into a nascent community marked by repentance, baptism, and shared life (Acts 2:37–47). Similar initiating dynamics recur throughout Acts as the gospel crosses new boundaries: in Samaria through Philip (Acts 8:4–8), among gentiles in the household of Cornelius (Acts 10), and in key urban centers such as Antioch (Acts 11:19–21).

In each case, the gospel is carried forward primarily through translocal, apostolic actors who cross cultural, linguistic, and geographic boundaries. Yet even at this early stage, congregational life begins to take shape. New believers are baptized, incorporated into fellowship, and instructed in the way of the Lord. Luke emphasizes that initiation is never merely individual conversion; it is always oriented toward the formation of a worshiping, learning community. The initiating stage therefore holds together proclamation and incorporation, announcing Christ while planting the seeds of communal life.

STAGE TWO—NURTURE: DEVELOPING LEADERS AND COMMUNITY LIFE

As communities formed through gospel proclamation begin to mature, Acts consistently depicts a second phase focused on nurture, teaching, and leadership development. In Jerusalem, this stage becomes visible as the apostles devote themselves to prayer and the ministry of the word while delegating practical responsibilities to emerging leaders (Acts 6:1–7). The result is both organizational stability and continued numerical growth, suggesting that leadership development is integral to spiritual vitality rather than a distraction from mission.

The church in Antioch provides another clear example. Barnabas and Saul spend a full year teaching and forming the community (Acts 11:25–26), grounding believers in the faith while allowing local leadership to emerge. This nurturing work is not only instructional; it is relational and formative, shaping a community capable of discerning the Spirit's leading together. Importantly, apostolic figures remain present during this stage, not as permanent authorities but as mentors and equippers who strengthen the community for greater responsibility.

STAGE THREE—EXPAND: CULTIVATING NEW COMMUNITIES OF FAITH

As churches grow in confidence and capacity, Acts depicts a stage of expansion marked by contextualization, structural clarity, and regional multiplication. Luke highlights how churches take responsibility for their own life and witness, developing patterns of worship, leadership, and governance appropriate to their context. Paul's extended ministry in Ephesus illustrates this stage vividly. Through sustained teaching and public engagement, a strong local church emerges that becomes a catalyst for gospel spread throughout the province of Asia (Acts 19:8–10).

This stage is characterized, not simply by numerical growth but by reproductive capacity. Churches plant churches, leaders reproduce leaders, and the gospel takes root across entire regions (Acts 9:31). Apostolic figures remain involved, but their role shifts from direct leadership to catalytic encouragement, theological guidance, and translocal connection. The Jerusalem Council (Acts 15) exemplifies this dynamic, providing theological clarity without imposing cultural uniformity, thereby enabling gentile churches to mature on their own terms while remaining connected to the wider body of Christ.

STAGE FOUR—EXTEND: MULTIPLICATION AND MISSION SENDING

The final stage becomes visible when mature churches recover an explicitly missionary posture, extending the gospel beyond their own cultural and geographic boundaries. Antioch again serves as the clearest example. In a context of worship, prayer, and fasting, the Spirit sets apart Barnabas and Saul for translocal mission (Acts 13:1–3). Significantly, this sending initiative arises from within a healthy local church rather than being imposed externally.

At this stage, church/modality does not disappear; it provides the spiritual, relational, and material support that makes sending possible, while sodalic/apostolic teams carry the gospel into new regions. Paul's missionary journeys, supported by local churches and networks of partners, embody this rhythm repeatedly (Acts 16–20). The extending stage thus completes a missional cycle, initiating new gospel movements that will, in turn, pass through the same stages of development.

Crucially, the extending stage is not an endpoint. Missionary sending initiates the cycle anew as gospel witness takes root in contexts where no established church yet exists. What began as a gathered community becomes a catalytic force for new movements, embodying the reproducible rhythm at the heart of the four-stage model: The church gathers in order to be sent, and is sent so that new churches might be formed.

These stages are not a rigid sequence to be completed in orderly succession, nor a mechanistic process resembling an assembly line. In lived reality, they are overlapping, recursive, and often messy, reflecting the organic life of the body of Christ rather than an engineered system. Churches may inhabit multiple stages at once, revisit earlier stages in new contexts, or experience seasons of regression and renewal. The four-stage model is therefore best understood as a set of missional health markers, describing how the gathered and sent expressions of the church develop over time. When modality and sodality remain in dynamic partnership, the church retains both stability and apostolic vitality, continually renewed for participation in God's mission.

WHAT LIVING MOVEMENTS LOOK LIKE

The church is often evaluated by what it produces: programs, attendance, initiatives, or expansion. Yet activity can persist long after vitality has begun to fade. The more fundamental question is not whether something is happening but whether life is present. Living communities possess internal capacities that allow them to grow, adapt, reproduce, and endure over time. Where those capacities are absent, motion may continue, but life slowly drains away.

This way of seeing finds a helpful parallel in the biological sciences. Biologists do not identify living organisms by a single defining trait. Life is recognized instead through a pattern of integrated capacities—organization, regulation, responsiveness to the environment, growth, reproduction, adaptation, and continuity. No single capacity proves life on its own. A system may exhibit movement or complexity and still be inert. Life becomes visible when these capacities function together as a coherent, self-sustaining whole.

This insight provides a clarifying lens for church vitality. Churches, like all organisms, can display impressive activity while lacking the internal capacities required for long-term health. Conversely, communities that appear small or unimpressive may nonetheless be deeply alive if these capacities are present and integrated. The four-self principles and the four-stages framework do not function as strategies or metrics. They name the essential capacities through which ecclesial life takes shape and matures, enabling communities to participate freely and faithfully in God's mission.

The four-self principles correspond closely to the core capacities of living systems. Self-governing life parallels regulation: a community capable of ordering its own life and exercising authority internally without constant external control. Self-supporting life reflects metabolism: the ability to receive resources, transform them, and sustain common life over time. Self-propagating life corresponds to reproduction: bearing witness, making disciples, and forming new communities. Self-theologizing life parallels adaptation and responsiveness: the capacity to interpret Scripture faithfully, discern God's will amid change, and respond wisely to new challenges without losing identity.

None of these capacities stands alone. A church may reproduce rapidly while lacking regulation, leading to instability. Another may be well ordered yet unable to adapt, slowly ossifying. Vitality is not proven by strength in one area, but by the integration of all four capacities working together.

The four-stages framework describes how these capacities typically emerge and mature over time. As the gospel takes root, communities respond and grow. Over time, patterns of regulation and support develop. With maturity comes the capacity for reproduction and outward participation in mission. Continuity is established as leadership is entrusted locally and the community becomes resilient amid change. These stages are not rigid steps but recurring rhythms that reflect how life normally unfolds.

Seen together, the four selves and four stages function as a diagnostic framework. They do not prescribe uniform forms or timelines, nor do they guarantee success. Instead, they help leaders ask better questions: Where is life strong? Where is it constrained? Which capacities are emerging, and which require patient cultivation? The goal is not acceleration but health.

This perspective reframes leadership. Leaders are not engineers tasked with producing outcomes but stewards of life. Their role is to notice where vitality is present, protect it from distortion, and create conditions in which it can mature. Like physicians attending a living body, they work with the grain of life rather than imposing control from outside.

It also reframes success. Numerical growth, institutional complexity, or geographic spread may accompany vitality, but they do not define it. Life reveals itself over time through coherence, resilience, and fruitfulness. A living church can endure disruption, adapt to new contexts, and release leadership without collapse. These are not signs of efficiency but of health.

For this reason, living movements do not remain inward-facing. Life naturally seeks expression beyond itself. Communities that possess integrated capacities will, over time, bear fruit beyond their own boundaries. They engage new contexts, form new leaders, and participate in wider mission not because they are pressured to expand, but because life overflows.

At the same time, vitality requires continuity. Life reproduces according to its nature. As churches take root in new settings, Scripture, shared practices, and communal memory function like a genetic code, ensuring that what emerges remains recognizably shaped by Christ even as it takes on local form. In this way, movements remain both adaptive and faithful, contextual and connected.

The relationship between biological life and ecclesial life is therefore more than metaphor. It is a way of seeing. Where the four-self capacities emerge and mature through the rhythms named by the four stages, life is present. Where they are fragmented or suppressed, activity may continue, but vitality diminishes. Living movements are recognized not by speed or scale but by the quiet coherence of life taking shape over time.

Stages Are About Direction and Integration, Not Rank and Graduation

All of this brings us to an essential clarification about how the four stages function. One of the most common misunderstandings is the assumption that the stages operate like rungs on a ladder, as though a church graduates from stage one to stage two, or from stage three to stage four, leaving earlier stages behind as it advances. That instinct is understandable, but it misunderstands how life actually works.

Maturity does not mean abandoning earlier capacities. A grown body does not outgrow the need for breathing, nourishment, or coordination. Rather, maturity is marked by the integration of these functions into a coherent whole. The stages are best understood not as steps in a sequence, but as dimensions of life that must be held together.

At their deepest level, the four stages function as quality markers of church vitality. They name essential dimensions of life: making disciples, developing leaders, multiplying churches, and reaching new frontiers. A healthy church does not simply pass through these dimensions. It continues to embody all four. Stage language does not answer the question "How far along are we?" but rather "Which dimensions of life are flourishing, and which remain underdeveloped?"

Why We Still Use Stage Language for Churches and Movements

This is why stage language remains useful when describing national churches and emerging networks. It serves as missional shorthand, not as a spiritual scorecard. When a movement is described as stage one or stage two, we are naming which capacities are structurally present and reproducible at that moment. For example, a national church may send a missionary and yet lack robust leadership development or sustainable multiplication at home. Such sending is faithful and worthy of celebration, but sending alone does not constitute stage-four life. True stage-four vitality is not defined by isolated acts of mission but by the integration of all four dimensions working together. Sending flows from strength, not from substitution.

Stage four, then, is not something that comes after stages one through three. It emerges from within them. A church or movement is stage four to the extent that it is making disciples, developing leaders, multiplying churches, and engaging new frontiers at the same time, in ways appropriate to its context. The difference is not presence versus absence but degree of integration.

In the end, the goal is not to become a "stage-four church." The goal is to become a living church, animated by the Spirit, sufficiently integrated that it can be trusted to reproduce itself, adapt to new contexts, and participate faithfully in God's mission to the ends of the earth (Rom 8:14; 15:18–21).

Taken together, four-self missiology and the four stages offer a way of describing the church as both *contextualized* and *thriving*. The four selves name the capacities required for faithful life to take root within a particular context, while the four stages trace how that life grows, integrates, and bears fruit over time. Yet a further question remains: What do we call the kind of church that emerges when these capacities are both present and enduring? What language helps us describe a church whose life is no longer dependent on constant external input, but has learned how to belong, adapt, and sustain itself within its own social and cultural environment? It is here that the language of indigeneity becomes essential.

THE CHURCH BECOMES INDIGENOUS

The term *indigenous* is often misunderstood as a claim about origin. In biology and agriculture, however, indigeneity refers, not to where something began but to how fully it has become embedded, adapted, and capable of sustaining life within a particular environment. Indigeneity is not about historical purity; it is about ecological maturity.[6] Two familiar examples—the kiwi fruit and the camel—illustrate this distinction with particular clarity.

The kiwi fruit, closely associated with New Zealand and even named after the nation's iconic bird, did not originate there. Its botanical

6. Odum and Barrett, *Fundamentals of Ecology*, 5–7.

origins lie in China, where it was cultivated for centuries.[7] When introduced to New Zealand in the early twentieth century, however, it entered a long process of adaptation. Farmers selected varieties suited to local soil and climate, developed cultivation practices responsive to regional conditions, and integrated the fruit into local agricultural systems. Over time, the kiwi became self-sustaining, reproducible, and economically viable without constant external dependence. It is now rightly regarded as indigenous to New Zealand—not because it began there, but because it belongs there through adaptation and participation.[8]

A similar pattern appears in the history of the camel. Although camels are almost universally associated with the Middle East, North Africa, and Central Asia, paleontological evidence indicates that their earliest ancestors evolved in North America.[9] After migrating out of their place of origin, camels became locally extinct there but survived and continued to evolve elsewhere. Environmental pressures in Asia and Africa gradually shaped their adaptation to arid and semi-arid environments. Their physiology—water retention, temperature regulation, and endurance—reflects generations of selection within desert ecosystems. Today, camels are integral to the ecology, economy, and culture of regions where they did not originate yet where they have become fully indigenous.[10]

These examples clarify an essential point: indigeneity is not defined by where something comes from, but by whether it has learned how to live. Indigenous life sustains itself, reproduces itself, and responds to change from within a particular environment without constant external intervention.[11] It is shaped by its context even as it contributes to that context's stability and resilience.[12]

This distinction matters for how the church understands itself in mission. The gospel did not originate in most of the places where it now flourishes. Christianity crossed borders from its earliest days.[13] Churches therefore become indigenous not by denying their missionary history, nor by preserving the cultural forms of their origin, but by allowing the

7. Ferguson, "Origin and Development of the Kiwifruit Industry," 15–29.

8. Zespri Kiwifruit, "What Is the Origin of Kiwifruit?"

9. Honey et al., "Camelidae."

10. Croft, *Horned Armadillos and Rafting Monkeys*, 112–14.

11. Davis, *Invasion Biology*, 12–15.

12. Odum, *Ecology and Our Endangered Life-Support Systems*, 31–33.

13. Schnabel, *Early Christian Mission*, 1:448–456.

gospel to be so fully received that it can be lived, sustained, interpreted, and transmitted from within a particular people and place.

Just as the kiwi became indigenous to New Zealand not by preserving its Chinese form, and just as the camel became indigenous to desert regions not by remaining North American, so the church becomes indigenous, not by replicating the forms of its missionary origin but by adapting faithfully to the soil in which it is planted. Indigeneity marks the transition from dependence to belonging, from importation to habitation.[14] It is one of the clearest signs of the gospel's universality: the gospel demonstrates its power not when it looks the same everywhere but when it becomes capable of sustaining faithful life anywhere.

Indigeneity and Church Life

Building on this ecological understanding of indigeneity, the language of indigenous church life names not origin, appearance, or cultural purity, but the capacity for sustained, self-renewing ecclesial life within a particular social, cultural, and theological environment. To speak of an indigenous church is therefore not to invoke nostalgia or romantic authenticity but to make a claim about belonging and maturity—the ability of a community of faith to live, reproduce, and discern faithfulness from within its own context.

In this sense, indigeneity does not describe whether a church exists in a place but whether it has learned how to live there. An indigenous church participates deeply in the rhythms, limits, and relationships of its environment, responding to change, not through continual external correction but through internal capacity shaped over time. Its life is locally accountable, contextually intelligible, and resilient in the face of social, cultural, and political change.

The contrast with invasive species clarifies the missional stakes. In ecology, invasive species often spread rapidly and appear successful, yet they do so by overwhelming local systems rather than belonging to them. Their expansion depends on disruption, displacement, and the absence of natural constraints. In missional terms, churches can function similarly when growth, replication, or institutional expansion outpaces contextual integration. Such movements may multiply quickly, draw resources efficiently, and achieve visible influence, yet they remain dependent on

14. National Research Council, *Ecological Indicators for the Nation*, 21–24.

external leadership, funding, or cultural templates. Their apparent success often masks fragility, as vitality must be continually imported rather than generated from within.

Indigenous life follows a different logic. Rather than maximizing speed or scale, it prioritizes integration, adaptability, and long-term sustainability. Applied to church life, this means cultivating leadership, theology, and practice that emerge from within the local context and are capable of enduring beyond the presence of external catalysts. Indigenous churches strengthen their social and spiritual environment even as they are shaped by it. They contribute to the resilience of the wider ecclesial ecosystem rather than exhausting it.

This distinction offers a clarifying lens for ecclesiology. A church is not indigenous simply because it is locally led, culturally expressive, or numerically established. Nor is indigeneity guaranteed by organizational autonomy alone. A church becomes indigenous when it has developed the capacity to govern its life, sustain its ministry, bear witness beyond itself, and interpret Scripture faithfully from within its own cultural horizon—without remaining structurally dependent on outside systems for its vitality.

Missional discussions of indigeneity often focus on visible markers such as language, worship style, leadership demographics, or institutional independence. While these matter, they are secondary indicators. In ecological terms, appearance does not determine indigeneity; function does. What matters is whether life can be sustained, renewed, and reproduced under changing conditions, and whether that life contributes to the health of the environment in which it exists.[15]

An indigenous church, then, is not one that merely looks local, but one that can bear the weight of its own life over time. It is capable of faithful continuity and creative response, rooted deeply enough to endure disruption and flexible enough to adapt without losing coherence. Indigeneity names the ecological condition in which a contextualized and thriving church can endure, integrate, and participate fully in the ongoing mission of God.

15. Allen, *Missionary Methods*, 85–92.

When the Church Learns How to Live

At its heart, mission is about life—whether the gospel has been received deeply enough to generate communities capable of living, discerning, adapting, and bearing witness from within their own context. Four-self missiology, the four stages of church development, and the language of indigeneity each attend to this same question from a different angle. Together, they offer a coherent way of recognizing when the church is not merely present, not merely active, but truly alive.

This vision of life has been present within the Foursquare movement from its earliest days. When Aimee Semple McPherson called believers to take the "Foursquare Gospel" to the ends of the earth, she did not offer a detailed plan for global expansion, nor did she imagine a tightly controlled international system. What she offered instead was a summons, an apostolic imagination shaped by urgency, faith, and trust in the Spirit's capacity to work through ordinary people in unfamiliar places. Early Foursquare missionaries did not go out as technicians carrying a finished ecclesial product. They went as witnesses, convinced that the same gospel that had transformed them could take root elsewhere and give rise to new communities of life.

Many of those early missionaries responded directly to this call with little more than conviction, prayer, and a willingness to cross boundaries. They entered contexts vastly different from their own, linguistically, culturally, politically, and economically, and discovered, often through trial and failure, that the gospel could not simply be transplanted whole. It had to be received, interpreted, embodied, and sustained locally. Over time, patterns began to emerge. Where missionaries exercised patience, released control, and entrusted responsibility to local believers, churches did more than survive. They learned how to live.

Four-self missiology names the capacities that appeared again and again in those settings. Churches learned to govern their own life, sustain their ministry with dignity, bear witness beyond themselves, and engage Scripture with theological responsibility. The four stages, in turn, describe the recurring rhythms through which those capacities were formed, strengthened, and eventually released into wider mission. Indigeneity names the condition that resulted when this life endured—when churches were no longer dependent on constant external input but had become capable of sustaining faithful life from within their own cultural soil.

Importantly, these frameworks emerged in reflection after the fact, as leaders looked back on decades of global engagement and recognized patterns that were already present. Language followed life. Experience was interpreted in light of Scripture. What Foursquare eventually named was not a proprietary method, but a reality discerned through the convergence of biblical imagination, missionary practice, and historical memory.[16]

These frameworks function best as a grammar for discernment. They help distinguish between activity and vitality, between growth and maturity, between churches sustained by ongoing intervention and churches capable of bearing the weight of their own life. They caution against confusing rapid expansion or visible influence with ecclesial health, and they call leaders to attend more carefully to integration, resilience, and responsibility over time.

This vision resonates with the apostolic witness of Scripture. Paul's concern in Romans is never merely whether communities are functioning, but whether they are walking in newness of life, led by the Spirit, and bearing fruit that endures. Acts likewise portrays churches formed through proclamation, strengthened through shared life and leadership development, entrusted to local authority, and eventually drawn into God's wider mission. The story Foursquare discovered in its own global experience echoes the story Scripture has been telling all along.

The implications are both liberating and demanding. They call sending churches and mission agencies to resist the temptation to retain control, to extend oversight indefinitely, or to equate faithfulness with resemblance. They also call receiving churches to embrace responsibility, discernment, and participation as gifts rather than burdens. Partnership, in this light, is not a mechanism for managing outcomes, but a shared commitment to steward life until it can stand on its own.

Ultimately, the goal of mission is the emergence of communities in every culture that can live the gospel as their own, interpret Scripture with integrity, sustain their common life with dignity, and bear witness beyond themselves in freedom and faith. When this happens, the church becomes truly indigenous because it has learned how to live where it has been planted.

Indigeneity is not the end of mission but its completion. It marks the moment when the call to go into all the world has been answered

16. Amstutz, *Disciples of All Nations*, 9–10.

not only by crossing borders, but by trusting the Spirit to give life that endures. The goal toward which mission moves is not uniformity but communion: a people drawn from "every nation, from all tribes and peoples and languages" (Rev 7:9), standing before the throne and before the Lamb, distinct yet united in worship. In that vision, the gospel has not erased differences but redeemed them. Mission reaches its culmination when the church no longer depends on being sent from elsewhere, because faithful life has taken root everywhere.

PART 6

Partnerships Between the Western District and FMI in MENACA and Europe

The global landscape is shifting in ways that demand new forms of missionary partnership. As the gospel advances amid religious plurality, political instability, migration, and cultural fragmentation, mission can no longer depend primarily on inherited models of sending and support. What is required are partnerships that are relationally grounded, theologically attentive, and capable of shared discernment and adaptive leadership within complex settings.

In 2021, the US Foursquare Church responded to these realities by aligning its districts with the global associate directors of FMI. This structural shift reflected a broader recognition shared across the global church: Effective mission today depends on deeper integration between local ecclesial bodies and transnational mission networks. Partnership, in this vision, is not transactional or hierarchical but relational and reciprocal, shaped by shared vocation and mutual responsibility in the mission of God.

Here, we examine one expression of such partnerships through the collaboration between the Western District of Foursquare Churches and FMI in MENACA (Middle East, North Africa, Central Asia) and Europe. While grounded in a specific denominational context, this case offers transferable insights for the wider body of Christ. Informed by the theological vision of Romans and interpreted through the frameworks of modality and sodality, liminality, and emergence theory, these chapters explore how relational partnership can foster faithful presence, contextual responsiveness, and sustained witness in rapidly changing mission fields.

23

The Context of the Western District

The Western District of Foursquare Churches spans California, Arizona, Nevada, and Utah, a region marked by extraordinary demographic diversity and cultural volatility. These states are a formative environment that actively shapes leadership, ecclesial imagination, and missional practice. Migration, religious pluralism, economic inequality, and political polarization press the church beyond inherited models of Christendom toward adaptive, relational, and theologically grounded forms of witness. Understanding this terrain is essential for grasping the district's strategic posture and why it has emerged as a critical partner in global mission.

This context does not simply present challenges to be managed. It exerts formative pressure on the kind of church that can faithfully exist here. The Western District's environment requires leadership that is adaptive rather than dominant, partnerships that are relational rather than transactional, and a missional imagination rooted in Scripture yet attentive to cultural reality. In such a setting, replication of inherited ecclesial forms proves insufficient. What is required instead is discernment, humility, and creative faithfulness.

Theologically, this moment resonates with the world addressed by Paul in Romans. Writing to a divided community at the heart of the empire, Paul envisioned churches shaped not by cultural dominance but by reconciliation, mutuality, and shared participation in the mission of God. His concern was not only what the church believed but how it lived together and bore witness amid political complexity and social fragmentation. In many respects, the Western District inhabits a similarly liminal space, called to embody the gospel within a context marked by instability, diversity, and contested identities.

Here, we examine the Western District as a missional context formed by geography, demography, culture, and leadership. By attending to these realities, we gain insight into how the district has been shaped for its present vocation and why it functions as a bridge between local faithfulness and global mission.

DEMOGRAPHICS OF THE FOUR STATES SERVED BY THE WESTERN DISTRICT

California

Home to nearly thirty-nine million people, California is the most populous and among the most diverse states in the United States. Its population reflects deep ethnic plurality, with large Hispanic or Latino, non-Hispanic white, Asian, and Black communities shaped by sustained immigration and global mobility. As a cultural and economic hub, California exerts outsized influence in technology, entertainment, and international trade, even as persistent poverty and stark income inequality expose deep social fractures. With more than a quarter of its residents foreign-born and over a third holding a bachelor's degree or higher, the state embodies globalization and cultural hybridity. Increasingly post-Christian and religiously plural, California reveals the limits of inherited Christendom models and calls the church toward Spirit-led mission marked, not by cultural dominance but by humble, creative, and incarnational witness.[1]

Arizona

Arizona's 7.1 million residents live within a state shaped by deep Indigenous roots and accelerated urban growth. Its population reflects significant cultural plurality, with substantial non-Hispanic white, Hispanic or Latino, and Native American communities. Metropolitan Phoenix, among the fastest-growing urban areas in the country, continues to attract residents from higher-cost neighboring states, intensifying both opportunity and strain. Economic expansion in aerospace, technology, and healthcare coexists with persistent poverty and uneven access to

1. US Census Bureau, "California."

education. Culturally and spiritually, Arizona occupies a liminal space where inherited social and religious structures are increasingly unsettled, creating fertile ground for relational, contextual, and locally rooted expressions of Christian witness.[2]

Utah

Utah, with a population of 3.3 million, remains relatively homogeneous, shaped by a strong non-Hispanic white majority alongside a growing Hispanic or Latino population. The LDS Church continues to exert significant cultural, political, and religious influence, forming a highly structured religious environment. At the same time, the expansion of the "Silicon Slopes" corridor near Salt Lake City is attracting a younger, more globally connected workforce, introducing new social and cultural dynamics. Supported by a strong economy, low poverty, and high educational attainment, Utah is well positioned for innovation. Yet Christian witness in this context must navigate a landscape shaped by religious consolidation and theological divergence, calling for patient, deeply relational, and incarnational forms of engagement rather than confrontational or programmatic approaches.[3]

Nevada

Nevada's 3.1 million residents are concentrated largely in urban centers such as Las Vegas and Reno, producing a context shaped by mobility, transience, and cultural plurality. Its population reflects significant ethnic diversity, with substantial non-Hispanic white, Hispanic or Latino, and Black communities. While long associated with entertainment and gaming, Nevada's economy is increasingly diversifying into logistics, technology, and renewable energy, even as educational attainment and economic security lag behind national averages. In a social environment often shaped more by consumerism than by inherited religious tradition, Nevada presents a distinctive missional landscape. Here, postmodern disillusionment can become an opening for spiritual exploration, inviting

2. US Census Bureau, "Arizona."
3. US Census Bureau, "Utah."

churches to practice imaginative, relational, and contextually grounded forms of discipleship.[4]

A MOSAIC OF DIVERSITY AND GROWTH

Taken together, these four states embody many of the paradoxes shaping the early twenty-first century: rapid growth alongside deep inequality, spiritual curiosity amid widespread religious disaffiliation, and cultural fragmentation accompanied by a longing for meaningful community. The Western District's demographic complexity therefore calls for a ministry posture that is contextual, adaptive, and prophetic.

In this setting, the decline of American Christendom is not primarily a loss to be lamented but a kairos moment to be embraced. Stripped of cultural privilege and political alignment, the church is invited to recover a more faithful missional identity. No longer sustained by social dominance, it must bear witness through embodied allegiance to Jesus as Lord. The church is sent into the world as a Spirit-led, boundary-crossing community, participating in God's reconciling mission as Christ was sent by the Father (John 20:21).

These states are more than sociological territories, they are theological fields in which the gospel confronts and reconfigures lives, relationships, and systems. The Western District is thus positioned to respond, not through nostalgia or institutional preservation but through faithful presence shaped by humility, courage, and love across lines of race, culture, and class.

LEADERSHIP AND MISSIONAL FOCUS

The Western District is guided by a seasoned and diverse leadership team whose collective wisdom and cultural breadth mirror the complexity of the district itself. District supervisor Mark Slomka serves alongside associate supervisors Grace Kladnik, Tim Russell, and Joe Hernandez, forming a supervisory team shaped by varied cultural, ethnic, and spiritual backgrounds. Together, their leadership embodies the district's lived diversity and reflects the broader Foursquare commitment to multiethnic and collaborative governance.

4. US Census Bureau, "Nevada."

The supervisors are supported by a gifted team of leaders who advance the district's mission across multiple domains, forming an integrated leadership ecosystem well suited to navigating a rapidly changing and pluralistic context. Brittany Johnstone oversees communications and events, strengthening connection and shared identity across the district. Johanna Oddo serves as district mission mobilizer, cultivating both global and local missional engagement. Jennifer Thigpenn leads initiatives that empower immigrant and cross-cultural leaders while fostering multicultural and multigenerational communities. Dan Britton directs NextGen ministries, investing in the spiritual formation and leadership development of emerging generations. Together, this team reflects a collaborative and integrative approach to ministry in a complex and evolving environment.

The district's missional priorities center on multiplication, expansion, leadership resourcing, encouragement, celebration, and mutual service. These commitments echo Paul's vision in Romans of a reconciled community formed for participation in God's mission. From urban centers to rural communities, the district's nearly four hundred congregations engage an extraordinary range of social and cultural environments. More than 1,700 credentialed ministers serve within its borders, reflecting a wide spectrum of callings and embodying Paul's vision of one body with many members (Rom 12:4–8).

A CONTEXT FORMED FOR PARTNERSHIP

The Western District's context reveals more than a set of challenges; it discloses a vocation. Shaped by pluralism, migration, and cultural flux, the district has been formed in a crucible where inherited authority yields to relational credibility and discernment. What may appear as instability instead emerges as missional preparation, a setting uniquely suited for partnership, experimentation, and shared leadership in service of the gospel.

This context clarifies why partnership is not optional but essential. No single congregation, district, or agency can adequately respond to the scope of opportunity and challenge present here. Faithful participation in God's mission requires collaboration across cultures, structures, and geographies, relationships marked by trust, mutual learning, and shared discernment.

The Western District is not only adapting to a changing world; it is being shaped for participation in God's mission beyond its own boundaries. Its story prepares us to understand the partnerships that follow, particularly its collaboration with FMI in MENACA and Europe. Here mission is not treated as a program to be managed but as a shared journey requiring humility, courage, and attentiveness to the Spirit.

Context matters because formation matters. The Western District has been formed into a community ready for relational mission, poised to engage both local and global frontiers. It is within this crucible that the partnerships explored in the following chapters take shape, offering a living example of how the church can remain faithful and fruitful in a complex and changing world.

24

FMI MENACA and Europe in Context

FMI's ENGAGEMENT IN EUROPE and MENACA represents one of the most demanding frontiers in the church's global mission. Though geographically expansive and culturally diverse, these regions share a defining reality: They are among the most spiritually complex and least-reached contexts in the contemporary world. MENACA, once the cradle of the early Christian movement, has undergone such profound religious transformation that it must now be approached missiologically as pre-Christian.[1] Europe, by contrast, is broadly post-Christian, marked by the erosion of traditional belief, declining institutional affiliation, and widespread skepticism toward organized religion.

Across Europe, secularization and religious pluralism have reshaped the public landscape. Many now identify as non-religious or "spiritual but not religious," and the church's historic influence on public life, moral formation, and social imagination has significantly diminished.[2] In both regions, inherited Christendom assumptions no longer provide a viable framework for mission. These contrasting yet complementary contexts help explain why partnership, rather than programmatic expansion or hierarchical control, has become the primary missional logic shaping FMI's work in MENACA and Europe.

Within these post-Christian and pre-Christian settings, FMI's work is necessarily pioneering and deeply incarnational. Mission advances not through visibility or institutional strength, but through

1. Jenkins, *Lost History*, 240.

2. Krastev, *After Europe*.

cross-cultural humility, apostolic imagination, and theological depth. Situated within the global vision of The Foursquare Church, FMI operates through collaborative, polycentric partnerships that prioritize indigenous leadership and contextual discernment. By cultivating gospel-shaped communities and navigating complex social, political, and religious realities, FMI participates in a Spirit-led movement that is both locally rooted and globally connected.

MENACA

The MENACA region, encompassing the Middle East, North Africa, and Central Asia, forms one of the most diverse and strategically significant mission contexts in the world. Stretching from Morocco across North Africa and the Levant and Arabian Peninsula into Central Asia, the region comprises a vast mosaic of peoples, languages, religions, and political systems shaped by centuries of empire, migration, and trade. Its importance is not only demographic or geopolitical but deeply theological, as the birthplace of monotheism and the early Christian movement.

With a population exceeding six hundred million, MENACA is marked by pronounced youthfulness, rapid urbanization, and persistent economic inequality. Many countries in the region have among the youngest median populations globally, creating both opportunity and volatility. High youth unemployment, uneven governance, and social fragmentation have driven significant migration, both within the region and beyond it. Major cities such as Cairo, Istanbul, Tehran, Riyadh, Dubai, and Casablanca function as cultural and economic hubs, reshaping social, political, and religious life across national boundaries.

Islam provides the dominant religious framework across MENACA, encompassing diverse Sunnī and Shīʿa traditions alongside smaller sects such as ʿAlawī and Druze. Together, these expressions shape legal systems, social norms, and public life in varied and context-specific ways. Christian communities persist throughout the region, ranging from ancient historic churches—such as the Coptic Church in Egypt and Assyrian communities in Iraq and Syria—to newer evangelical and Pentecostal movements. In many settings, Christians face legal restriction, social marginalization, or persecution. Yet these communities often demonstrate remarkable resilience, sustaining faith through relational networks, adaptive forms of discipleship, and quiet, faithful witness.

Economic conditions vary widely across MENACA, from resource-rich Gulf states to nations marked by chronic instability and poverty. Dependence on oil and gas, combined with political unrest and corruption, has fueled both opportunity and vulnerability. Armed conflict and regional tensions—particularly in the Middle East and North Africa—have generated large-scale displacement and humanitarian crises.[3] Central Asia, meanwhile, navigates post-Soviet transition amid competing Russian, Chinese, and Western influences, alongside internal challenges related to political authoritarianism and religious regulation.

Despite these challenges, MENACA presents significant missional opportunity. Its youthful populations, accelerating urbanization, and growing spiritual openness—especially among marginalized and disillusioned communities—create space for contextualized witness. FMI's engagement in the region emphasizes relational evangelism, indigenous leadership development, business as mission, and humanitarian service. Ministry advances here not through scale or publicity, but through trust, presence, and long-term faithfulness.

Middle East

The Middle East stands at the intersection of history, faith, and geopolitics. It is the region of Abraham's call, Israel's covenantal story, and the emergence of Christianity, and it has long functioned as a bridge between Africa, Europe, and Asia. For centuries, empire, trade, and religious tradition have converged here, shaping a complex and often contested social landscape.

Today the region is predominantly Arab, alongside significant Iranian and Turkic populations and enduring minorities such as Jews, Assyrians, Copts, and Druze. Islam provides the dominant religious framework, shaping legal systems, social norms, and public life, while Christianity and Judaism persist as living but frequently marginalized traditions.[4] Mission in this context unfolds within highly regulated political and religious environments, requiring patient, relational, and

3. Ventura, "Poorest Countries in the World 2025."

4. Britannica Editors, "Middle East."

deeply incarnational forms of witness shaped by theological sensitivity and long-term presence.

North Africa

North Africa extends from the Atlantic coast to Egypt and from the Mediterranean into the Sahel, encompassing societies shaped by centuries of migration, conquest, and trade. While Arabic language and Islamic identity provide a shared civilizational framework, this unity overlays deep ethnolinguistic and cultural diversity.

Indigenous Amāzīgh (Berber) peoples retain distinct languages and regional identities across Morocco, Algeria, Libya, and the Sahara, while Egypt adds further complexity through its Coptic Christian, Nubian, and Bedouin communities. Colonial legacies continue to shape education and public life, particularly through the influence of French in the Maghreb. Although Islam predominates, historic Christian communities—most notably the Coptic Orthodox Church in Egypt—endure alongside growing evangelical fellowships and small Jewish populations. Mission in North Africa requires attentiveness to layered identities and social constraints, engaging urbanizing societies through contextual, relational, and discreet forms of discipleship.[5]

Central Asia

Central Asia stretches from the Caspian Sea to western China, encompassing vast steppes, deserts, and mountain ranges that historically linked East and West. Once central to the Silk Road, the region has long served as a corridor of commerce, empire, and religious exchange and today occupies a strategic geopolitical position shaped by Russian, Chinese, and Islamic influences.

Historically influenced by Iranian-speaking cultures and later transformed through Turkic migrations, Central Asia remains linguistically and ethnically diverse. Persian (Tajik) continues to shape cultural life in Tajikistan, while Afghanistan reflects particularly complex ethnic and linguistic patterns. Islam predominates across the region, largely Sunnī with notable Shīʿa minorities, while traces of pre-Islamic traditions remain embedded in cultural memory. Christianity persists as a minority

5. Worldometer, "Northern Africa Population."

presence, most visibly through Orthodox and smaller Protestant communities. Mission here unfolds amid political restriction and religious regulation, requiring wisdom, restraint, and relational credibility.[6]

MISSIONAL IMPLICATIONS AND OPPORTUNITIES IN MENACA

Taken together, the Middle East, North Africa, and Central Asia form a vast and interwoven mission field shaped by deep historical memory, cultural plurality, and constrained public space for Christian witness. From the Sahara to Central Asia, this region has long stood at the crossroads of civilizations, faiths, and empires—the setting of Abraham's call, Israel's exile, and the early church's expansion, the soil in which monotheism took root and from which the gospel first went forth. Though internally diverse, these societies share common dynamics: dominant religious frameworks, complex political environments, and youthful, mobile populations shaped by both continuity and disruption.

In such contexts, mission advances less through visibility or institutional expansion than through faithful presence, relational trust, and contextual discernment. These realities clarify why partnership in MENACA cannot be driven by uniform strategy or centralized control but must be adaptive, locally rooted, and sustained through long-term relational commitment. The Foursquare family in MENACA now includes more than one hundred churches across fourteen nations. At the same time, security concerns affecting both FMI personnel and local believers complicate traditional approaches to partnership, funding, and visibility. These conditions necessitate heightened discretion, strengthened security practices, and innovative partnership models that differ significantly from those employed in less restricted environments.

EUROPE AS A MISSIONAL LANDSCAPE

Where MENACA requires adaptive mission under constraint, Europe demands reimagined witness amid institutional decline. Once the heartland of Christendom, Europe is now largely post-Christian, shaped by secularization, religious pluralism, and widespread disengagement from

6. Britannica Editors, "Central Asia."

institutional religion. Yet beneath this surface of decline, meaningful opportunities for gospel witness and renewal persist.

Europe is not monolithic. Its nations reflect diverse histories and ecclesial trajectories, from historically Catholic, Protestant, and Orthodox contexts to societies that are increasingly secular or religiously indifferent.[7] Effective mission therefore requires nuanced, contextual approaches capable of engaging both Europe's residual Christian memory and its present spiritual dislocation.

Within this landscape, both Foursquare Europe and FMI Europe seek to embody a posture that holds together stability and movement, pastoral care and pioneering vision. Foursquare Europe refers to the network of local congregations and national churches established across the continent, while FMI Europe names the missionaries and apostolic workers serving alongside these churches in cross-cultural and frontier contexts. Having developed over a longer period than its counterpart in MENACA, the European Foursquare movement reflects a greater degree of institutional maturity in both church life and mission structures. Together, these two expressions demonstrate a collaborative partnership that honors national church identity while participating in the wider mission of God across Europe.

FOURSQUARE EUROPE (MODALITIES)

The Foursquare Church maintains a substantial presence across Europe, encompassing more than four hundred congregations and ministries in approximately thirty nations, with over nineteen thousand adherents. Thirteen fully nationalized Foursquare churches now operate across the continent, cooperating through the Fellowship of European Foursquare Churches. These national bodies provide stable ecclesial structures rooted in local language, culture, and leadership, forming the primary modalities of Foursquare's witness in Europe.[8]

7. The number of nations in Europe varies slightly depending on classification criteria, particularly regarding transcontinental states such as Russia and Turkey. Most standard sources identify forty-four sovereign countries as part of Europe. See United Nations Statistics Division, *Composition*; Windley et al., "Europe."

8. For more information, visit www.foursquare-europe.com.

FMI EUROPE (SODALITIES)

Alongside these national churches, FMI Europe supports workers serving in more than fourteen nations. These workers operate in diverse contexts, from urban centers shaped by secularism and migration to rural regions experiencing depopulation and economic transition. Their ministries reflect a missional flexibility suited to Europe's uneven spiritual and social terrain.

FMI Europe's work includes leadership development, church planting, humanitarian response, youth mobilization, refugee care, theological training, and interdenominational collaboration. Together, these initiatives embody a holistic vision of mission grounded in the conviction that Europe's renewal depends on credible, relational, and embodied witness.

FMI LEADERSHIP FOR MENACA AND EUROPE

In my role as FMI global associate director for MENACA and Europe, I serve alongside a team of trusted co-laborers committed to advancing the gospel across two of the world's most diverse and strategically significant regions. Brandon and Marcie Brazee, based in Cologne, Germany, serve as FMI Europe regional administrators, providing essential relational and operational support to a growing network of churches and missionaries across the continent. Paul and Marie serve as regional coordinators for FMI MENACA, guiding ministry throughout the region with wisdom, courage, and deep contextual awareness.[9]

With the contextual realities of both the Western District and FMI MENACA and Europe now in view, it becomes clear that effective partnership requires far more than structural alignment. It calls for a model that is theologically grounded and missionally agile—capable of bridging cultures, systems, and callings. For leaders in both regions, the task is the cultivation of relationships that are mutually beneficial, contextually responsive, and spiritually transformative.

The following chapter turns to the lived experience of this partnership, drawing on the voices of leaders from the Western District and FMI MENACA and Europe. Their reflections illuminate the essential elements of collaborative mission: relational trust, theological clarity, and a

9. Identities withheld for security purposes.

shared commitment to the church's global calling—tested not in theory but in lived partnership.

25

Stakeholder Perspectives and Relational Insights

The unfolding partnership between the Western District and FMI comes into focus most clearly through the voices of those who inhabit it. Over the course of several days, I conducted in-depth interviews with district leaders and pastors, as well as FMI leaders serving in Europe and MENACA. These conversations reveal a partnership shaped not only by strategy and structure but also by relationships forged through shared prayer, proximity, and trust. Again and again, interviewees described a missional ecosystem sustained as much by friendship and mutual learning as by formal agreements or organizational alignment.

These leaders do not speak of partnership as a finished system, but as a living, evolving reality, one continually negotiated at the intersection of calling and context. Their testimonies illuminate both the promise and the strain of cross-cultural mission in a season marked by the decline of inherited Christendom models and the emergence of new expressions of church life. Taken together, these voices reveal a church in motion, learning to navigate complexity with humility, faith, and hope.

RELATIONAL INFRASTRUCTURE AS MISSIONAL FOUNDATION

Across every interview, one theme surfaced with unmistakable clarity: Relationships are the essential infrastructure of mission partnership.

Whether discussing strategy, finances, theology, or leadership development, participants consistently emphasized that without relational proximity and trust, collaboration becomes abstract, transactional, or brittle. Relational infrastructure is not a supplement to mission; it is its sustaining core.

Several leaders warned that when mission is disconnected from lived relationships, it is easily marginalized. Brittany Johnstone observed that without personal connection, global mission risks becoming "another budget line item," detached from the shared imagination of local congregations.[1] Communication alone, she noted, cannot generate lasting engagement unless it is anchored in relationships that allow people to know names, stories, and fruit. Mission becomes compelling when it is personal and embodied.

Paul and Marie echoed this conviction from the field, stressing that healthy partnerships require shared implementation, as well as shared vision. Strategies developed without deep consultation often feel imposed rather than empowering. "Shared implementation leads to shared ownership," Paul noted, underscoring the importance of trust and local agency.[2] Their insight aligns closely with emergence theory, which suggests that adaptive systems flourish when authority is decentralized and local actors are empowered to shape outcomes from within their own contexts.

Johanna Oddo highlighted how relational exposure can catalyze long-term engagement. She described the impact of pastors traveling to Bosnia-Herzegovina and Croatia, praying and ministering alongside field leaders. These encounters transformed abstract concern into concrete commitment. "It's about people, not projects," she explained.[3] Such experiences generate what Victor Turner described as *communitas*, a bond formed in liminal spaces where institutional roles loosen and mutual transformation becomes possible.

Grace Kladnik reinforced this point succinctly: "Relationships are more powerful than programs." Missional activation, she argued, occurs when people are personally invited into something larger than themselves.[4] This reflects a shift away from functionalism toward a relational ecclesiology that prioritizes presence over performance and participation

1. Johnstone, interview by author, March 19, 2025.
2. Paul and Marie, interview by author, March 21, 2025.
3. Oddo, interview by author, March 24, 2025.
4. Kladnik, interview by author, March 24, 2025.

over persuasion. District pastor Jimmy Darter articulated the impact of this model from a rural perspective.[5] Mission can feel episodic and reactive, surfacing primarily through funding appeals rather than sustained relational engagement.

Timothy Russell brought theological depth to the conversation by grounding mission in the *imago Dei*. Mission, he insisted, begins with proximity rooted in love.[6] "If you value someone, you don't want them to be hungry or without shelter," he explained. For Russell, generosity is not performative but reflexive, a spiritual discipline shaped by Christ's incarnational love. "We can't export what we haven't learned to embody," he concluded, naming the danger of a mission theology disconnected from lived discipleship.

Other leaders named the relational fractures that weaken mission. Jennifer Thigpenn spoke of "invisible walls" separating missionaries from pastors, creating silos that undermine the church's witness.[7] District pastor Jon McIntosh noted that while many people are willing to engage, they are not always meaningfully connected.[8] Joe Hernandez framed the issue biblically, reminding leaders that sending is not only institutional deployment but relational commissioning (Rom 10:15).[9] Without belonging and trust, mission becomes transactional and loses its spiritual vitality.

STRUCTURAL TENSIONS AND SYSTEMIC TENSIONS

While relational infrastructure forms the heart of the partnership, interviews also surfaced significant structural tensions that constrain its full potential. These challenges, financial, organizational, and theological, do not signal failure so much as transition. They reflect a system living in what Turner described as *liminality*: an in-between space where inherited forms are unsettled and new configurations are still emerging. Emergence theory reminds us that in such environments, coherence must be cultivated rather than assumed.

5. Darter, interview by author, March 20, 2025.
6. Russell, interview by author, March 21, 2025.
7. Thigpenn, interview by author, March 21, 2025.
8. McIntosh, interview by author, March 21, 2025.
9. Hernandez, interview by author, March 20, 2025.

Financial Disparities and Theological Dissonance

One of the most persistent critiques concerned the denomination's financial architecture and the theological signals it sends. Multiple leaders pointed to a symbolic and practical asymmetry between the expectations placed on missionaries and those placed on churches. Missionaries are required to raise their own support and contribute an administrative fee of 10 percent of all funds raised, while, under Foursquare Reimagined, churches effectively contribute approximately 5 percent to the denomination overall and may remain compliant with global mission expectations by giving as little as one dollar annually to missions.[10] Hernandez described this arrangement as "symbolically weak and practically ineffective," warning that it communicates an ecclesiology in which mission appears optional rather than constitutive of the church's identity.

McIntosh pressed the issue further, insisting that financial structures do more than allocate resources; they form theological imagination. When churches are asked for little and missionaries are asked for much, the imbalance sends a clear signal, eroding mutuality at its roots. Small policies, he observed, generate outsized cultural effects, quietly reinforcing the assumption that mission belongs at the margins rather than at the center of ecclesial life. Without accessible and equitable pathways for participation, congregations remain spectators instead of stakeholders.

Russell named the concern with theological precision: "Our budget is our theology in numbers." If the church truly confesses the centrality of mission, that conviction must be visible not only in its statements but in its financial priorities. Stewardship is not administrative; it is doxological.

Fragmented Initiatives and Narrative Drift

A second tension emerged around the proliferation of initiatives. Leaders described a crowded landscape of programs—church planting, global partnerships, disaster response, leadership development—often pursued without an integrating narrative. Even worthy efforts, when disconnected from a shared story, can compete for attention, producing initiative fatigue and eroding clarity about what truly matters.

Kladnik and Thigpenn both warned that participation weakens when a coherent narrative is absent. "When everything feels urgent,

10. As mentioned earlier, the compliance standard was revised during the final stages of this study.

nothing feels essential," Thigpenn observed. From the perspective of emergence theory, this fragmentation is not only a management problem but a systemic one: adaptive systems require shared narratives that link diverse activities to a common purpose. Without such coherence, momentum dissipates and mission becomes episodic rather than formative.

POST-CONSOLIDATION COMPLEXITY

Structural factors have further intensified this sense of dissonance. Oddo pointed to the challenges created by the 2021 consolidation that merged the Central Pacific, Southwest, and SoCal districts into the Western District. While administratively necessary, the merger disrupted longstanding relationships and introduced new layers of complexity. "Each area had its own history with FMI," she noted, "some with deep trust, others with confusion or indifference." The result is a district still negotiating its identity, not only structurally, but missionally, seeking a shared sense of direction amid inherited differences.

MODALITY, SODALITY, AND LEADERSHIP IMBALANCE

One of the most sustained concerns across interviews involved a perceived structural bias toward modality, local church systems and senior pastoral leadership, at the expense of sodality expressions such as missionaries, cross-cultural leaders, and apostolic workers. While often unintentional, this imbalance reflects deeper assumptions that prioritize maintenance over movement and stability over sending.

Hernandez extended the critique by naming the cost of a modality-dominated imagination: "When churches act like they own the mission, rather than being part of it, they end up protecting turf instead of expanding the kingdom." When modality becomes the primary lens through which the church understands itself, it risks losing sight of its sent-ness, its identity as an apostolic people called not to inward consolidation but to outward movement in the mission of God.

Thigpenn was particularly direct. She described a system where pastoral-centered metrics, attendance, finances, buildings, often determine influence and funding, while missionaries and mission mobilizers are sidelined despite operating at the frontier of the church's witness. She called for a more holistic model of leadership that recognizes apostolic, prophetic, and cross-cultural gifts as central to the church's identity and health.

Several leaders framed this imbalance as a discipleship issue. Mark Slomka insisted that pastors must be formed into a missional ecclesiology that sees congregations not as destinations but as launchpads.[11] Britton echoed this concern, particularly regarding younger leaders.[12] Exposure trips, camps, and cross-cultural experiences function as liminal spaces where vocation awakens and calling is discerned. These relational environments often form leaders more durably than formal instruction.

McIntosh and Kladnik both pointed to leadership pipelines that naturally center pastoral roles while overlooking apostolic and cross-cultural callings. Encouragingly, they noted growing awareness of this gap and early efforts to broaden leadership formation.

Brandon and Marcie Brazee added perspective from Europe, noting that modality bias can also shape international partnerships. "Sometimes it feels like the church in the US is only interested when they can be the lead story," Marcie said. Brandon cautioned against performance-based engagement centered on visibility rather than mutuality: "When partnerships are filtered through who gets platformed, we lose the essence of mutual mission." Their comments highlight how modality bias can unintentionally shape even cross-cultural relationships in ways that mirror domestic church hierarchies, privileging visibility over presence and control over collaboration.[13] Paul and others noted that missionaries often feel structurally invisible despite carrying significant burdens. Oddo suggested that the discomfort surrounding these tensions is itself a sign of liminality, a necessary stage in discerning new models.

The parallel to Paul's appeal in Romans is instructive. In Romans 15, Paul seeks partnership not through hierarchy but through mutual encouragement and shared mission. Hierarchical efficiency, while useful, often constrains the adaptive capacity required for missional emergence. Faithful leadership structures must therefore embody collaborative discernment reflective of the gospel's reconciling power.

11. Slomka, interview by author, March 20, 2025.

12. Britton, interview by author, March 19, 2025.

13. Brazee and Brazee, interview by author, March 22, 2025.

THE SACREDNESS OF BEING SENT

Beneath structural debates lies a deeper theological conviction voiced repeatedly in the interviews: Mission is not a program of the church; it is the church's identity. Leaders spoke of sending not as deployment, but as sacred vocation.

Joe Hernandez described mission as "sacred sending," emphasizing that apostolic identity is relational and Spirit-driven rather than managerial. Oddo highlighted the necessity of attentiveness to the Spirit and context, resisting prepackaged strategies. Kladnik emphasized the relational dynamics of calling and sending. "People are activated not by obligation, but by invitation," she noted. For Kladnik, sending is not a managerial function but a spiritual practice: discerning what the Spirit is already doing in a person's life and blessing that work into fuller expression.

Paul spoke candidly of the cost of being sent. "The calling to be sent isn't glamorous," he said. "It's rooted in sacrifice, patience, and learning to see people the way Jesus does." Slomka explicitly connected this missional identity to the theological vision of Romans. "The church is not just a gathered body; it is a scattered one," he reflected. Thigpenn pressed the implications further, insisting that professed theology must be matched by aligned resources and priorities.

Brandon and Marcie Brazee highlighted the relational cost of neglecting mutuality in mission: "When we don't hear from anyone for a year, we start to wonder if people still care," Marcie shared. When communication wanes, trust erodes. In emergent systems, relational touchpoints function as the bloodstream of coherence.

NAVIGATING LIMINAL SPACE TOWARD MISSIONAL RENEWAL

The partnership between the district and FMI reveals a church in motion, complex, relational, and charged with promise. Across conversations with pastors, missionaries, and district leaders, one conviction emerged with clarity: mission cannot be sustained by strategy alone. It requires relationship, trust, theological depth, generosity, and the courage to remain in the liminal space where inherited forms are released and new patterns of faithfulness begin to emerge.

Taken together, these voices articulate a shared theological vision: Mission is not a department or initiative but the church's very identity.

The sacredness of being sent is measured not by effectiveness but by faithfulness, formation, and Spirit-led discernment. From Hernandez's articulation of sacred sending to Russell's insistence on missional discipleship, from Oddo's attentiveness to context to Thigpenn's prophetic demand for alignment, the church is being summoned back to its apostolic imagination, to become a people shaped by the gospel and sent for the sake of the world.

In a moment marked by fragmentation, institutional anxiety, and cultural fatigue, the way forward for the church is not preservation but participation. To be sent is to enter the ongoing mission of God, to be formed by cruciform love rather than control, and to follow Christ beyond the center toward the margins. This is the vocation unfolding before the people of God in every place: to inhabit the tension between modality and sodality faithfully, trusting that in this liminal space the Spirit is already at work, forming a church renewed for the life of the world.

26

The Partnership in Practice

THE PRECEDING CHAPTER TRACED the voices, tensions, and theological convictions shaping the partnership between the district and FMI. Those conversations revealed both deep relational strength and significant liminal pressure, a system being stretched by cultural change, organizational complexity, and renewed missional calling. This chapter turns from listening to embodiment. If mission is not a program of the church but its very identity, then it must take visible shape in lived practice. What follows examines some of the ways partnership is enacted on the ground, how relationships function as missional infrastructure, and how theological conviction is translated into shared patterns of life.

This chapter argues that partnership becomes transformative not through structure or scale, but through relational presence that re-forms imagination, practice, and identity. The question is not simply whether churches and mission agencies cooperate, but how such cooperation reshapes what the church understands itself to be.

A PARTNERSHIP ROOTED IN PRESENCE

What began as a small number of intentional connections between the district and FMI has matured into a multidirectional collaboration marked by mutual encouragement and shared labor in the gospel. This partnership is defined by sustained presence and theological alignment. In this sense, it reflects Paul's vision in Romans of a church that is both gathered and sent, rooted in local communities while oriented toward God's reconciling purposes in the world.

On the ground, this partnership takes shape through joint gatherings, shared leadership, co-creation of initiatives, pastoral vision trips, and ongoing engagement with local churches across Europe and the MENACA region. Leaders prioritize listening before acting and collaboration before direction, investing in long-term relationship rather than short-term outcomes. Mission is not managed through control but cultivated through communion and co-creation. Across cultures and geographies, relationships emerge that no single institution or region could generate alone. In shared prayer, friendship, and faithful presence, partnership becomes not a program to administer but a way of inhabiting the church's calling together.

BUILDING RELATIONSHIPS AS MISSIONAL INFRASTRUCTURE

Over time, this partnership has matured beyond programmatic cooperation into a shared theological and missional commitment. What began as intentional relationship-building has developed into a way of working together marked by mutuality, trust, and co-laboring in the gospel. Through sustained relational presence and contextual attentiveness, the district has increasingly walked alongside FMI, not as a patron or sponsor but as a genuine partner in mission.

This shift became especially visible during pastoral visits to Croatia and Bosnia-Herzegovina led by Johanna Oddo. Her presence is more than logistical or symbolic, it is relational and catalytic. For Mario Dučić, senior pastor of The Foursquare Church in Zagreb, serving alongside district leaders embodied a crucial reality: The district was neither distant nor abstract but tangibly present. The encounter reinforced that mission is not something one group does for another but a shared and incarnational participation in the life of the gospel. Here, witness emerged through proximity and mutual engagement rather than one-sided action.

The district's regular participation in FMI's annual workers' gatherings further reflects this movement from episodic involvement to sustained partnership. What might once have functioned as symbolic attendance has become consistent relational presence. Expressions of care from local churches through personal notes, thoughtful gifts, and tangible support communicate more than generosity; they express belonging. In this way, missionaries are received not as functionaries but as members of a shared household, a community bound together through hospitality and shared life.

This commitment also extends beyond centralized events. District pastors and leaders regularly attend regional conferences across Europe and MENACA, not to teach, supervise, or direct but to listen, learn, and build trust with field leaders. Time spent in homes and local communities invites leaders into the lived realities of mission, fostering relationships that are participatory rather than performative. Such practices quietly disrupt hierarchical assumptions and reinforce the conviction that mission is not a departmental activity, but the shared life of the church in motion.

Taken together, these patterns mark a transition from institutional patronage toward spiritual kinship. Ministry emerges not through centralized control, but through relational trust, shared discernment, and the empowerment of local agency, conditions under which partnership becomes not only effective, but formational.

VISION TRIPS AS LIMINAL ENCOUNTERS

Johanna Oddo's pastoral vision trips have become a defining practice of relational mission within the partnership. These journeys are not logistical site visits or evaluative tours but intentionally liminal encounters, spaces of humility, discovery, and shared transformation in which district pastors step beyond familiar contexts to encounter the church in diverse cultural settings.

Each trip is structured to cultivate genuine relationship between district pastors and local leaders across Europe and MENACA. Connection is formed through shared meals, worship, prayer, and the ordinary rhythms of daily life. Participants do not arrive as experts or assessors but as learners and companions. This posture fosters trust and mutual encouragement and reflects a missional approach that listens attentively, adapts patiently, and remains open to the Spirit's leading as understanding and vocation take shape together.

Functioning as sacred disruptions, these trips place leaders in in-between spaces where assumptions are unsettled and imagination is reformed. They are not curated experiences designed to showcase success but encounters with the front lines of global mission, often messy and marked by instability, scarcity, and human suffering. In these settings, district leaders find themselves drawn into ministry rather than observation, offering prayer, presence, and pastoral discernment amid situations that resist easy resolution.

What pastors carry home is a widened sense of belonging to a larger body. They return with relationships rather than techniques and with community rather than control. In this way, the vision trips embody Paul's vision in Romans 15, where partnership in the gospel is shaped not by hierarchy or efficiency but by shared calling, mutual encouragement, and participation in both the suffering and hope of God's mission.

LOCAL CHURCHES LIVING A GLOBAL IDENTITY

Across the district, a growing number of local congregations are rediscovering what it means to be both gathered and sent, deeply rooted in their local communities while actively participating in God's mission among the nations. In these churches, global mission is no longer an external obligation but an expression of ecclesial identity.

Antioch Church in Simi Valley, California, exemplifies this posture. Rather than engaging global mission at a distance, Antioch has become a relational partner alongside FMI's regional coordinators for MENACA. Their partnership is pastoral and formative rather than merely financial, marked by prayer, shared vision, and sustained encouragement. Through practices such as a MENACA-focused Vacation Bible School and a congregation-wide prayer campaign using the *MENACA Field Guide*, the church is being shaped as a priestly community that intercedes for the nations and participates in God's reconciling work.[1]

The Rock Church in Anaheim offers a different yet complementary expression of global engagement. Its discipleship framework, Jesus Disciple, emerged as a local initiative but has taken on translocal significance.[2] Through simple, reproducible practices rooted in Spirit-led obedience, believers are equipped for everyday discipleship and witness. In the United Kingdom, this framework has contributed to the formation of house churches and new believers receiving baptisms; in Spain, it is multiplying through generational discipleship; and in MENACA, it is

1. Dupont, *2025 MENACA Field Guide.*

2. See www.jesusdisciple.com.

being introduced discreetly as a tool for underground church planting. Here, the boundary between local congregation and apostolic mission dissolves, as a locally rooted practice becomes a catalyst for renewal across diverse contexts.

A third district congregation, choosing to remain anonymous, made a substantial financial commitment to support the establishment of Foursquare in Egypt. Their desire for anonymity underscores a key mark of authentic partnership: mission pursued, not for visibility or control but as an act of obedience and solidarity with the global body of Christ.

Together, these examples reveal a movement taking shape within the district. Local churches are embracing global mission not as a program or budget line, but as a lived expression of who they are. Through prayer, generosity, and relationship, ordinary congregations are rediscovering their place within God's global story.

INVESTING IN THE NEXT GENERATION

The decision to send teams of young people to the annual Foursquare Europe Youth Conference represents more than a logistical commitment; it reflects a theological investment in the church's future. The district's presence signals solidarity with the global body of Christ and a deliberate focus on forming the next generation within a shared missional imagination.

For young people navigating questions of identity and faith amid cultural skepticism and social instability, the relationships cultivated through this partnership embody the gospel as belonging rather than consumption. The conference functions as a formative space where emerging leaders encounter the Spirit through cross-cultural relationships, shared worship, and mutual encouragement. In these liminal settings, faith is learned, not primarily as information or performance but as participation in the life of God's people.

By investing in Europe's youth, the district affirms a vision of the church that privileges formation over programming and presence over performance. Showing up not to lead but to listen and serve, the district enacts Paul's vision of a Spirit-formed family extended across generations and cultures, bearing witness to Christ's reconciling work in the world.

"ONE MILLION DOLLARS IS TOO SMALL"

A defining moment in the partnership emerged during a conversation about future collaboration. When the possibility of setting a goal to raise one million dollars annually for advancing the gospel in unreached and under-reached contexts was raised, District Supervisor Mark Slomka paused and responded, "I think that amount is too small."

The significance of the moment lay not in the figure itself, but in a shared conviction that imagination must be shaped by the scope of the gospel rather than constrained by existing systems. The response signaled a shift from transactional support to prophetic imagination—from reacting to immediate needs toward discerning what becomes possible when trust, relationship, and shared vision converge. In that exchange, vision was allowed to lead strategy, reflecting confidence that faithfulness begins not with limits, but with the expansive horizon of God's mission.

Missiologically, this was not a budgetary statement but an emergent moment, one arising in the space between faith and uncertainty, where relational trust had created room for theological imagination. Structure followed Spirit rather than the reverse. When local congregations and apostolic movements operate within this posture, the church is freed to imagine participation in God's mission at a scale commensurate with the gospel itself, echoing Paul's vision in Romans 15 of a Spirit-led movement extending toward new horizons.

FMI AS A FORMATIVE PRESENCE WITHIN THE DISTRICT

While much attention is rightly given to the district's support of global mission, the relationship is reciprocal. FMI has become a formative presence within the district itself, contributing not only resources and relationships abroad but theological imagination and missional competence at home. This reciprocity reflects a maturing partnership in which formation, encouragement, and equipping flow in both directions.

FMI's influence within the district is both theological and practical. Formed in cross-cultural and often resistant contexts, FMI leaders bring insights shaped by ministry in settings marked by religious pluralism, social constraint, and post-Christian dynamics. Through leadership training, mission intensives, seminars, workshops, and sustained relationships, FMI has helped pastors and congregations recognize their own neighborhoods as mission fields and to lead with Spirit-led adaptability rather than inherited assumptions.

This formative role is especially visible in FMI's participation in the district's Fall Leaders' Conferences and ongoing training events. These engagements are not symbolic appearances, but substantive contributions to the district's theological and missional formation. FMI leaders speak into the district's identity, offer practical equipping, and model the church's dual calling as both sent and sending. Their presence extends beyond platforms into workshops, preaching, shared ministry contexts, and long-term pastoral relationships, generating what might be described as operative theology, faith lived and practiced rather than merely articulated.

These dynamics have, in turn, sharpened the district's engagement with its own context. Serving one of the most culturally diverse regions of the United States, district churches increasingly recognize that mission is not confined to distant places but embedded in everyday life. The missional imagination cultivated through global partnership reshapes how congregations engage neighbors formed by diverse religious and secular worldviews. Mission thus becomes both near and far, woven into the ordinary rhythms of congregational life.

TOWARD COHERENCE AND MISSIONAL IMAGINATION

What is emerging in the partnership between the district and FMI is not simply an effective strategy but the lived embodiment of the ecclesial vision Paul articulates in Romans. Romans offers a vision of the church as both gathered and sent, rooted and mobile, local and global. This dual identity is not a problem to be solved but a vocation to be embraced. To read Romans as a missional framework is to accept the gospel's formative power, to become a people reshaped by God's reconciling work and capable of bearing faithful witness across boundaries of culture, ethnicity, and geography.

Ralph Winter's articulation of modality and sodality gives conceptual language to what Paul embodies in Romans. Congregational life and apostolic mission are not competing structures but complementary expressions of a single calling. Paul strengthens local churches while simultaneously inviting them into shared participation in God's mission to the nations. Romans itself emerges from a moment of transition: Paul writes between completed work in the East and an anticipated mission to the West. The Roman churches, likewise, occupy a liminal space, negotiating identity amid ethnic diversity, theological difference, and cultural complexity. The letter functions not only as theological proclamation but as missiological intervention, calling the church into a coherent identity shaped by shared vocation.

From these foundations, new initiatives emerge organically rather than by imposition. They are adaptive, relational, and Spirit-empowered, arising where theological depth, relational trust, and apostolic imagination converge. What takes shape is an ecclesiology formed in liminality, where renewal through mission and expansion through partnership belong together. Having traced how these dynamics are embodied in practice, we now turn to examine how they unfold more intentionally within specific contexts.

CONCLUSION

Viewed through the lens of Romans and embodied in the collaboration between local congregations and apostolic movements, this study has shown that the future of global mission depends less on structural alignment than on relationship, trust, shared discernment, and co-creation. The church was never intended to function as a collection of disconnected institutions but as a living body, formed by the Spirit, sustained by the Scriptures, governed by love, and sent into the world for the sake of God's reconciling purposes.

Paul's vision invites the church to imagine mission, not as a one-directional enterprise but as a mutual and transformative partnership. Congregational life and apostolic movement exist in creative tension, each calling the other toward greater faithfulness, humility, and obedience. When grounded in theological depth and sustained through relational proximity, such partnerships become more than pragmatic strategies; they become embodied signs of the *missio Dei* at work in and through the church.

In a time marked by instability, fragmentation, and the unraveling of inherited ecclesial forms, these partnerships offer a different horizon of hope. They reveal how God's mission is continually renewed in liminal spaces, where uncertainty becomes the soil for emergence and new life. As the people of God learn to inhabit this tension with courage and grace, mission is recovered not as a specialized activity, but as the shared identity of the whole church. In that rediscovery lies the promise of renewal, that through humble partnership and faithful presence, the church may once again bear credible witness to the reconciling love of God among the nations.

This pattern now invites closer examination. While the partnership between the district and FMI has served as a primary lens, it represents a broader assortment of partnerships unfolding across MENACA and Europe rather than an isolated or exclusive model. Having traced how partnership takes shape relationally and theologically, the chapters that follow turn to the concrete realities of national church development in these regions. Through a series of contextual case studies, I will explore how these dynamics unfold across differing stages of maturity, cultural constraint, and historical complexity, and how shared participation in God's mission gives rise to durable, indigenous expressions of the church.

PART 7

National Church Development in MENACA and Europe

Spirit-led mission depends on relationships marked by mutuality, cultural attentiveness, and shared commitment to the gospel's transforming witness. Mission advances through communities discerning together how the gospel takes root in particular places. These commitments are especially vital in regions shaped by religious plurality, political volatility, migration, and historical trauma—realities that mark much of MENACA and Europe. Such contexts are deeply liminal, defined by tension and transition.

The following chapters examine how these convictions take concrete shape through case studies drawn from the Foursquare movement, with relevance beyond its denominational context. What appears local and culturally specific is precisely where the universals of the gospel become visible. In settings of real constraint, recurring patterns emerge—calling and resistance, sending and staying, innovation alongside inherited forms. The particular does not obscure the universal; it discloses it.

Focusing on Romania, Egypt, Kazakhstan, and Turkey, these studies explore how contextualized partnership supports national church development across diverse settings. Together they show that when theological vision, contextual sensitivity, and missional partnership converge, the church is positioned to flourish even in challenging environments, bearing witness to God's mercy among the nations.

27

National Church Development in Egypt

Egypt is a nation marked by layered history, cultural complexity, and deep spiritual memory. In the biblical narrative, it appears as both a place of oppression and refuge, judgment and deliverance, a threshold space where divine purpose unfolds amid political power and human vulnerability (Exod 1; Matt 2:13–15). This ambivalence is not incidental. It signals Egypt's enduring role as a liminal setting in which faith must be lived under constraint.

In the early centuries of Christianity, Egypt proved remarkably receptive to the gospel. According to tradition, the apostle Mark brought the Christian message to Alexandria, from which emerged some of the church's most influential theologians and spiritual leaders, including Clement, Origen, and Anthony the Great. The deserts of Egypt became the cradle of Christian monasticism, shaping global Christian spirituality through the witness of the desert fathers.[1] This legacy endures in the Coptic Orthodox Church, one of the world's oldest Christian communities and a living testimony to theological depth, spiritual resilience, and sustained faithfulness.

Yet this extraordinary heritage exists alongside long-standing fragility. Centuries of political upheaval, religious marginalization, and social pressure have constrained the public life of Christianity in Egypt. What was once a vibrant center of Christian thought has, in many places, become cautious and inward-facing, not from theological weakness but from the realities of survival under restriction. Contemporary mission

1. Jenkins, *Lost History*, 65–72.

in Egypt therefore encounters, not a blank slate but a complex ecclesial landscape shaped by ancient faithfulness and enduring limitation.

This chapter examines the development of The Foursquare Church in Egypt as a case study in patient, partnership-based mission. Still in its embryonic stages of development, the Foursquare presence in Egypt offers a window into how ecclesial life begins to take shape under conditions that demand restraint, trust, and long-term commitment. The chapter explores how contextual sensitivity, relational credibility, and the careful, gradual entrusting of responsibility contribute to the emergence of sustainable church life. Egypt thus illustrates both the challenge and the promise of national church development in constrained contexts, where vitality depends less on visibility or scale than on faithfulness, relationship, and time.

MODERN EGYPT AS A MISSIONAL CONTEXT

Meaningful engagement in Egypt requires attentiveness to the realities that shape everyday life. As the most populous nation in the Arab world, Egypt occupies a position of cultural, political, and religious gravity within the Middle East and North Africa. Political centralization, economic strain, demographic pressure, and religious regulation converge to form a context marked by volatility and constraint, yet also by relational openness and deep spiritual longing. For Christian mission, Egypt presents neither a closed society nor an open marketplace but a setting where faith must be lived carefully, relationally, and over time.

Political Dynamics

Modern Egyptian politics has been shaped by strong centralized authority punctuated by brief moments of upheaval. Since independence from British rule, successive regimes have consolidated power through nationalism, security frameworks, and tight regulation of public life.[2] Political participation remains limited, civil society is closely monitored, and religious expression operates within narrowly defined legal boundaries.

The 2011 uprising momentarily expanded space for reform, but the return to authoritarian governance following 2013 reasserted restrictions in the name of stability and national security. For Christian communities,

2. Smith, "Egypt."

particularly those outside state-recognized structures or those involving converts from Islam, this environment creates ongoing vulnerability. While official rhetoric promotes interfaith coexistence, legal ambiguity and social pressure persist.[3]

For mission leaders, this political reality demands restraint rather than visibility and discernment rather than haste. Faithful ministry in Egypt requires cultural literacy, legal awareness, and long-term trust-building. Strengthening the church within Egypt carries regional implications as well, given Egypt's historical and cultural influence across the Arab world.[4]

Economic and Demographic Pressures

Egypt's economy remains under sustained strain from rapid population growth, underemployment, inflation, and inequality. With more than 110 million people, nearly 60 percent under the age of thirty, demographic pressure shapes nearly every dimension of social life. Many young adults enter adulthood with limited access to stable employment, contributing to widespread underemployment and frustration.[5]

Labor migration and remittances play a critical role in household survival, even as rapid urbanization overwhelms infrastructure in cities such as Cairo and Alexandria.[6] Inequality remains stark, with wealth concentrated among a small elite while millions live near or below the poverty line.

From a missional perspective, economic precarity both constrains and opens space for the gospel. While instability increases vulnerability, it also heightens receptivity to holistic forms of Christian witness. Ministries that integrate discipleship with education, vocational training, trauma care, and economic empowerment align closely with lived realities and embody a gospel attentive to human flourishing.

Migration further intensifies Egypt's complexity. Internal migration reshapes urban life, while Egypt has also become a major destination and transit corridor for refugees from Sudan, Syria, Eritrea, Ethiopia, and

3. Dunne, "Limits of Authoritarian Resilience," 34–48.

4. Volf, *Public Faith*, 93–108.

5. Little, "Egypt."

6. Little, "Egypt."

beyond.[7] Many refugees live in legal and economic limbo, carrying deep trauma and spiritual need.[8] For the church, this reality calls for a theology of hospitality expressed through trauma-informed, cross-cultural ministry rooted in hope and presence.[9]

Gender inequality remains a persistent feature of Egypt's social landscape, shaping access to education, economic participation, public leadership, and personal security. Cultural expectations, legal gaps, and social pressures often limit women's visibility and authority, particularly in conservative or economically vulnerable settings.[10] For the church, this reality directly shapes who is heard, who is trusted, and who bears responsibility. National church development therefore cannot be understood apart from the slow, relational work of forming communities in which women's dignity, agency, and spiritual authority are recognized and responsibly entrusted.

RELIGIOUS LANDSCAPE

Religion in Egypt is both constitutionally significant and culturally foundational. Islam is the state religion,[11] and while freedom of belief is affirmed, it is generally recognized within the framework of the three "divine religions" (Islam, Christianity, and Judaism). Roughly 90 percent of Egyptians identify as Sunnī Muslims, while approximately 10 percent are Christians, the vast majority belonging to the Coptic Orthodox Church.[12]

Sunnī Islam in Egypt is woven deeply into daily life, shaping moral imagination, social expectation, and communal rhythm.[13] Religious language permeates ordinary speech, and popular piety—festivals, local

7. Human Rights Watch, *World Report 2025*, 141.

8. UNHCR, "Refugee Context in Egypt."

9. Carroll, *Christians at the Border*, 115–30.

10. Omran and Bilan, "Female Labour Force Participation," 1–12.

11. Saleh and Kraetzschmar, "Politicized Identities, Securitized Politics," 545–62.

12. Majumdar, *Government Restrictions on Religion*, 42.

13. Ḥanafī Islam reflects a historically moderate and adaptable form of Sunnī jurisprudence shaped by the teachings of Imām Abū Ḥanīfa (699–767 CE). As the oldest and most widespread Sunnī school of law, the Ḥanafī tradition emphasizes reasoned interpretation (*qiyās*), practical legal judgment, and the integration of Islamic principles within diverse cultural settings. Under the influence of the Abbasid and later the Ottoman and Mughal empires, Ḥanafī Islam became deeply rooted in Egyptian Muslim religious life, where it blended with local customs (*'ādāt*) and Ṣūfī devotional practices. See Khalid, *Islam after Communism*.

customs, and devotional practices—adds texture beyond formal doctrine. Institutions such as Al-Azhar University play a significant role in shaping religious discourse, even as the state tightly regulates religious expression to guard against instability.[14]

Christianity in Egypt is ancient and resilient, yet socially constrained. Today, "Egyptian Christians think of themselves as the descendants of the ancient Egyptians and see the Arab Muslims who conquered them in the seventh century as foreign invaders."[15] Alongside the Coptic Orthodox Church exist smaller Catholic, Orthodox, Anglican, and Protestant communities, many operating within recognized structures such as the Protestant Churches of Egypt. Despite constitutional protections, Christians may face discrimination in employment, education, and bureaucratic processes.[16] Church construction, conversion, and public evangelism remain sensitive and sometimes dangerous issues.[17] Periodic violence and social hostility have left deep communal memory, reinforcing caution and inward-facing survival strategies.[18]

This environment does not render the church powerless, but it shapes how mission must be carried out.[19] Evangelism, discipleship, and church planting require legal literacy, cultural discernment, and what might be called a *prophetically gentle* posture, courageous in witness, cautious in method, and committed to the long obedience of faithful presence.[20]

MISSIONAL IMPLICATIONS

Taken together, Egypt's political, economic, demographic, and religious realities place the nation in a liminal space between tradition and transformation. Long-standing assumptions about faith, nation, gender, and generation are increasingly contested, producing both disorientation and unexpected openings. Egypt thus occupies a strategic place in the missional imagination of the twenty-first century, at once a crossroads

14. Ruthven, *Islam in the World*, 290–92.
15. Chapman, "Christians in the Middle East," 92.
16. Marlin, *Christian Persecution*, 81–95.
17. Little, "Egypt."
18. International Christian Concern, "Middle East."
19. Brownlee, *Violence Against Copts in Egypt*.
20. Kateregga and Shenk, *Muslim and a Christian in Dialogue*, 25–27.

shaped by deep religious memory and a threshold where new forms of social and spiritual life are emerging.

Within this shifting environment, culturally resonant expressions of Christian community can take root, forms of ecclesial life that honor Egypt's ancient Christian heritage while engaging contemporary realities. In such contexts, discipleship and leadership development are not primarily programs but pathways toward identity, healing, and purpose. Especially among youth, women, migrants, and displaced populations, the church's witness becomes credible not through visibility or scale, but through relational depth, contextual wisdom, and patient trust cultivated over time.

Egypt's missional landscape therefore calls for neither triumphalism nor retreat, but for a discerning, hope-filled presence attentive to the slow and often hidden work of God. The task before the church is not merely to establish institutional presence but to nurture indigenous expressions of discipleship capable of embodying the gospel within Egypt's dense urban networks and rural communities alike. In this complex and contested soil, marked by a rich Christian past and an uncertain present, national church development must take root quietly, carefully, and with enduring faith, trusting that God continues to work persistently, even when growth remains largely unseen.

FOURSQUARE IN EGYPT

In March 2023, the FMI regional coordinator for MENACA and I traveled to Egypt with a posture of prayerful discernment, seeking to identify relational pathways through which new expressions of ministry might emerge. During that visit, we formed relationships with a range of Christian ministries, including a hospital in the Nile Delta, refugee-serving organizations, and local Christian leaders. These connections provided relational entry points into an already active and complex ecclesial landscape.

A significant development followed a few weeks later when an Egyptian-American couple, trained through Foursquare Multiply,[21] expressed a desire to return to Egypt to serve among their family and relational networks. Subsequent visits focused on deepening trust, clarifying calling, and discerning sustainable forms of engagement. This couple

21. The US Foursquare Church's church-planter training program.

has since been commissioned as FMI workers, marking a transition from exploratory presence toward sustained partnership rooted in local relationship and responsibility.

At present, Foursquare engagement in Egypt remains intentionally relational rather than institutionally defined. FMI workers and regional leaders are cultivating networks with pastors, educators, medical professionals, and refugee-serving ministries. These relationships have opened pathways for mentoring, theological formation, humanitarian engagement, and collaborative ministry. In a highly relational society marked by curiosity and hospitality, such networks function as access points into everyday life rather than as platforms for formal expansion. What is emerging is a growing web of trust.

Several leaders within these networks have expressed interest in mentoring and connection with a wider community of practice, particularly in leadership development and theological education. At the same time, demand for accredited and globally recognized training has created avenues for influence that do not require public institutional growth. Partnerships with organizations such as Healthbridge Global have further expanded opportunities for medical and community-based ministry, particularly among vulnerable populations and refugees. Together, these developments point toward the gradual formation of ecclesial life grounded in local responsibility and shared mission.

PARTNERSHIP, FORMATION, AND CONTEXTUAL WITNESS

Ministry in Egypt unfolds within a Muslim-majority, politically regulated, and highly urbanized environment. In such settings, faithful witness depends less on visibility than on credibility. Relationships must be patient, respectful, and sustained over time.[22] The gospel advances, not through confrontation but through presence shaped by humility, compassion, and integrity. Love, rather than technique, becomes the primary medium of witness.

Contextualization requires attentiveness to cultural norms, religious sensibilities, and urban realities.[23] Cities such as Cairo are marked

22. Smartley, *Encountering the World of Islam*, 151–69.

23. Conn and Ortiz, *Urban Ministry*, 340–57; Hiebert and Meneses, *Incarnational Ministry*, 363–375; Keller, *Center Church*, 154–63; Kim, *Mission Strategy*, 81.

by density, inequality, and rapid change, demanding adaptive and incarnational approaches to ministry. Holistic witness, expressed through hospitality, education, healthcare, and pastoral care, creates space for the gospel to be heard as good news rather than foreign intrusion. Effective urban ministry must be incarnational, modeled on Jesus Christ, who entered into the human experience to redeem it.[24] At the same time, ministry must honor deep communal traditions and local wisdom, learning from leaders who navigate these realities from within.[25]

Across these contexts, prayer and spiritual discernment remain central.[26] As Paul reminds the church in Romans, the advance of the gospel is not human achievement but Spirit-led work sustained through intercession and mutual encouragement (Rom 1:9–12; 15:30–32).[27] In Egypt, such dependence on the Spirit shapes both the pace and posture of mission. Formation, rather than acceleration, becomes the guiding priority.

LEADERSHIP DEVELOPMENT AND HUMANITARIAN ENGAGEMENT

Leadership development in Egypt is taking place through both formal and informal means. FMI workers engage emerging leaders through mentoring, coaching, and training gatherings, while exploring connections with broader theological networks. The aim is not credential accumulation, but the formation of leaders who are biblically grounded, culturally fluent, and capable of shepherding communities under constraint. In many of these contexts, women emerge as primary carriers of pastoral care, relational trust, and spiritual resilience, even when formal leadership roles remain socially or institutionally constrained.

Humanitarian engagement functions as an integral expression of ecclesial life rather than a parallel activity. Medical outreach, refugee care, and community development respond to tangible needs while strengthening trust and credibility. Partnerships such as those with Healthbridge Global[28] demonstrate how compassion and proclamation

24. Conn and Ortiz, *Urban Ministry*, 27; Hiebert and Meneses, *Incarnational Ministry*, 363–375; Keller, *Center Church*, 149; Kim, *Mission Strategy*, 36–37.

25. Kim, *Mission Strategy*, 75.

26. Smartley, *Encountering the World of Islam*, 433–65.

27. See Rom 15:30; Phil 1:19; Col 4:3; 1 Thess 5:25; 2 Thess 3:1–2; Phlm 22; 2 Cor 1:11.

28. See www.healthbridgeglobal.org.

can be held together without instrumentalizing either. In Egypt's context, acts of mercy are not peripheral to the gospel; they are among its most intelligible forms.[29]

A CONCRETE EXPRESSION OF PARTNERSHIP IN PRACTICE

A women's leadership initiative in March 2025 offers a concrete illustration of how partnership and formation converge. An all-women team served alongside Egyptian leaders among Sudanese refugees, engaging in teaching, prayer, and pastoral care. Preparation emphasized spiritual formation, shared leadership, and cultural humility, allowing ministry to emerge collaboratively rather than being tightly directed.

The response exceeded expectations. Although the team prepared for five hundred participants, nearly seven hundred women arrived. Local leaders stepped into visible authority with confidence, and the Spirit's work became evident through moments of healing, encouragement, and communal solidarity. In a context where women's leadership is often constrained or rendered invisible, the initiative did not contest cultural realities directly, but quietly reconfigured them by entrusting responsibility, voice, and spiritual authority to local women within a shared ecclesial space. Workshops, children's activities, prayer ministry, and simple acts of generosity fostered an atmosphere marked by dignity and care. Despite limited resources, every need was met—a quiet testimony not to organizational capacity, but to what becomes possible when responsibility is shared and the Spirit is trusted.

The significance of this gathering lay not in its scale, but in its pattern. Leadership was entrusted rather than retained. Ministry emerged organically rather than being scripted. In these dynamics, one can glimpse the contours of an indigenous church learning to bear the weight of its own life.

MATURING THROUGH THE STAGES

The long-term vision for Foursquare in Egypt is to cultivate forms of church life capable of sustaining faithfulness within Egypt's social, cultural, and spiritual realities. Such maturity includes the emergence of

29. Greenlee et al., "Exploring the Intersection of Community Development," 105–18.

locally exercised leadership, trustworthy and contextually appropriate governance, theological discernment rooted in lived experience, sustainable patterns of ministry, and outward-facing witness. This kind of life cannot be rushed or engineered. It must be cultivated through patience, trust, and the willingness to release control.

What is taking shape in Egypt is therefore not a finished structure but a discernible trajectory of growth. Early exploratory relationships and apostolic initiative are giving way to sustained partnership with an expanding network of local leaders and communities connected to the Foursquare family. This movement signals, not completion but increasing responsibility. Egypt is no longer merely a site of initial engagement; it is becoming a context in which the foundations of a rooted and enduring expression of church life are being laid.

At the center of this process is leadership formation. FMI workers invest intentionally in Egyptian leaders through mentoring, discipleship, coaching, and shared ministry, not to replicate external models, but to cultivate the internal capacities needed to shepherd communities and discern faithfulness from within their own context. This formation necessarily includes the patient recognition and development of women leaders, whose participation and entrusted responsibility serve as quiet but decisive indicators of whether ecclesial maturity is genuinely taking root. Together, these practices reflect a deliberate shift from external initiation toward local ownership, from oversight toward trust. Leadership is no longer provisional or borrowed but gradually and responsibly entrusted.

As ecclesial life matures, the need for structure emerges organically. Rather than imposing institutional templates, Foursquare leaders walk alongside local partners as they discern governance practices grounded in shared values, relational accountability, and cultural credibility. These emerging structures exist to anchor communal life, protect relationships, and support discernment as responsibility increasingly rests with local leaders.

Alongside leadership development, ministries of compassion are becoming visible and integral expressions of the church's presence in society. Health initiatives, educational support, humanitarian care, and community-based ministries are natural extensions of the gospel embodied in daily life. In this way, witness is not confined to proclamation alone, but woven into patterns of service that build trust and respond to real human need.

The horizon toward which this work moves is the gradual emergence of an indigenous church capable of bearing the weight of its own life, leadership, and mission. Such a church is self-governing without isolation, sustainable without dependency, and missionally engaged without external pressure. It remains relationally connected to the MENACA region and the global Foursquare movement, not as a dependent outpost, but as a contributing member of the wider body of Christ.

What is unfolding in Egypt illustrates a central conviction of this book: Ecclesial maturity cannot be accelerated or imported. It emerges through patient partnership, faithful presence, and the courage to entrust responsibility to local leaders. Read through the lens of the four-self vision and the four stages of national church development, Egypt's present moment reflects the fragile but necessary early phases in which self-governance, self-support, self-propagation, and self-theologizing are only beginning to take shape. The foundations being laid are therefore measured less by visible expansion than by the quiet growth of resilience, responsibility, and life from within. With continued prayer and discernment, these early signs point toward a church that is not only present in Egypt but increasingly at home there.

28

National Church Development in Romania

ROMANIA STANDS AT A geographic and cultural crossroads in Europe, shaped by centuries of movement between empires, traditions, and identities. Situated between Central and Eastern Europe and bordered by Ukraine, Moldova, Hungary, Serbia, Bulgaria, and the Black Sea, the country has long functioned as both bridge and boundary between East and West, Orthodoxy and pluralism, continuity and disruption. Its physical landscape, marked by the Carpathian Mountains and the Danube River, mirrors a national story defined by endurance amid repeated external pressures. With a population of approximately nineteen million people, Romania today ranks as the sixth most populous member of the European Union.[1]

National church development in Romania is taking shape through patient, incarnational partnership slowly cultivated in the soil of history, marginalization, migration, and trust. Romania resists missionary speed. It exposes the limits of managerial approaches to mission and instead demands long obedience in place. As such, Romania serves as a revealing test case for how the gospel takes flesh when mission is practiced as presence rather than performance.

Romania's historical development reflects a persistent tension between indigenous identity and foreign domination. From ancient Dacian roots and Roman colonization to centuries of Ottoman influence in the

1. Hitchins, *Concise History of Romania*, 13; European Commission, *Eurostat Regional Yearbook*, 25–27.

south and east and Habsburg rule in Transylvania, Romanian identity was forged under overlapping imperial regimes.[2] The unification of Moldavia and Wallachia in 1859 marked the emergence of the modern Romanian state, later expanded after World War I through the incorporation of surrounding regions into what became known as Greater Romania.[3] Yet this consolidation unfolded within an unstable geopolitical environment, repeatedly disrupted by war, shifting borders, and competing ideologies.

The twentieth century proved especially formative. Fascist movements, Soviet occupation, and the imposition of Communist rule reshaped political, social, and religious life, culminating in the forced abdication of King Michael I and the establishment of a socialist republic.[4] The Communist period left deep scars through the suppression of civil society, the surveillance of religious institutions, and the erosion of public trust. The revolution of 1989 marked a dramatic rupture, opening Romania to democratic governance, economic reform, and eventual integration into the European Union.[5]

Today, Romania occupies a paradoxical position. It is firmly embedded in Euro-Atlantic structures such as NATO and the EU, increasingly connected to global economic and cultural networks, yet still shaped by historical memory, social inequality, and unresolved religious tensions.[6] The Romanian Orthodox Church remains a dominant cultural force, shaped by both national identity and its accommodation to past political regimes. At the same time, minority and evangelical communities have become more visible, navigating a religious landscape marked by freedom, suspicion, and renewed spiritual searching. Mission in Romania therefore unfolds within a complex field of inherited loyalties and cautious openness, requiring historical awareness, cultural humility, and attentiveness to the slow formation of trust.

2. Hitchins, *Concise History of Romania*, 6–10; Kalkandjieva, "Comparative Analysis," 591–93.

3. Hitchins, *Concise History of Romania*, 113–44; Clark, *Why Angels Fall*, 204–5.

4. Stan and Turcescu, *Religion and Politics*, 89–91.

5. Stan and Turcescu, *Religion and Politics*, 92–94.

6. Kalkandjieva, "Comparative Analysis," 592–93; World Tourism Organization, *Tourism Highlights*, 46–47.

ORTHODOXY, EMPIRE, AND BELONGING

Eastern Orthodoxy has been the dominant religious tradition in Romania since the early medieval period, functioning not only as a spiritual authority but as a primary bearer of national identity. Across centuries of foreign domination, the Romanian Orthodox Church provided cultural continuity, shaping language, art, architecture, and communal rhythms that remain deeply embedded in everyday life.[7] Orthodoxy in Romania is more than a confessional identity; it is a marker of belonging, memory, and continuity.[8]

During centuries of Ottoman suzerainty, the Orthodox Church functioned as a stabilizing force within Romanian society. Although the Ottomans exercised political and economic control, they largely permitted Orthodox institutions to operate, recognizing their role in maintaining social order.[9] In this context, Orthodoxy became both a symbol of cultural continuity and a quiet form of resistance, preserving communal identity in the face of external domination and Islamic rule.[10] In the absence of political sovereignty, faith served as a vessel of cultural survival, binding religious practice and national identity into a shared memory that endured without statehood.

In Transylvania, under Habsburg and later Austro-Hungarian rule, Orthodoxy functioned differently but no less powerfully. Imperial governance introduced Catholic and Protestant institutions that reshaped the region's religious landscape and aligned closely with political authority and ethnic elites.[11] Within this context, Orthodoxy became the spiritual home of Romanian peasants and townspeople, offering continuity amid foreign rule.[12] Through liturgical life, ecclesial structures, and the rhythms of the church calendar, Orthodoxy reinforced linguistic and cultural distinctiveness. Over time, these patterns further fused Orthodox faith with Romanian ethnic identity, particularly in contrast to Hungarian and German communities.[13]

7. Clark, *Why Angels Fall*, 204.
8. Clark, *Why Angels Fall*, 201–4.
9. Hitchins, *Concise History of Romania*, 30-36.
10. Hitchins, *Concise History of Romania*, 30–31.
11. Clark, *Why Angels Fall*, 204; Hitchins, *Concise History of Romania*, 130–32.
12. Hitchins, *Concise History of Romania*, 30–31.
13. Clark, *Why Angels Fall*, 205; Stan and Turcescu, *Religion and Politics*, 44–46.

This fusion persists in contemporary Romania. The Orthodox Church enjoys significant public trust, constitutional recognition, and cultural authority. While this legacy has provided social cohesion, it also complicates religious pluralism. Minority and evangelical movements are often perceived not simply as theological alternatives but as cultural intrusions.[14] Conversion can be interpreted as cultural betrayal. Any account of church development in Romania must therefore reckon seriously with the depth of this historical association between faith, nation, and belonging.

COMMUNISM AND THE FRACTURE OF TRUST

The twentieth century introduced a devastating rupture in Romania's religious life. From 1947 to 1989, Communist rule subjected religious institutions to strict state control and repression. Churches were surveilled, clergy were coerced, and religious expression was tightly regulated.[15] The Orthodox Church occupied an ambiguous position. While clergy and faithful endured harassment and fear, the institutional church was often compelled to collaborate with the regime, becoming entangled with state power in ways that compromised its moral authority.

Minority communities suffered even more directly. Roman Catholics, Greek Catholics, Protestants, and evangelical movements faced confiscation of property, imprisonment of clergy, suppression of education, and the closure or forced merger of institutions.[16] Religious life for these communities was driven underground or reshaped into rigid forms acceptable to totalitarian ideology.

The legacy of this period persists long after the fall of the regime. Decades of enforced conformity and compromise produced deep mistrust toward institutions and authority. For many Romanians, religious identity remains culturally significant yet institutionally suspect. Mission in Romania unfolds amid unresolved wounds where memory, fear, and faith remain tightly intertwined.

14. Stan and Turcescu, *Religion and Politics*, 89–92.
15. Stan and Turcescu, *Religion and Politics*, 44–46.
16. Stan and Turcescu, *Religion and Politics*, 89–92.

POST-1989 PLURALISM AND EUROPEAN INTEGRATION

The revolution of 1989 marked a decisive turning point. The collapse of the Communist regime ended state-imposed atheism and opened space for religious freedom.[17] New constitutional protections allowed long-suppressed traditions to reemerge, including the Greek Catholic Church, while Protestant and evangelical communities experienced renewed growth.[18] International mission agencies entered Romania with enthusiasm and hope, often assuming that openness would naturally yield rapid church expansion.[19] However, decades of religious control and compromise under totalitarian rule weakened the moral authority of many religious institutions and left a residue of mistrust toward organized religion.[20]

Yet pluralism arrived unevenly. The Orthodox Church retained a privileged position in public life, while minority groups often encountered bureaucratic obstacles and social suspicion, particularly in rural areas.[21] Formal guarantees of equality coexist with informal hierarchies of belonging. Freedom on paper did not immediately translate into trust on the ground.

Romania's accession to the European Union in 2007 strengthened legal protections for religious liberty and minority rights.[22] EU frameworks provided mechanisms for accountability and advocacy, even as local practice lagged behind formal commitments.[23] For mission practitioners, this context offers both protection and complexity. The law may permit pluralism, but culture and memory still regulate belonging. The gap between legal inclusion and lived acceptance remains a defining feature of Romania's religious landscape.

17. Stan and Turcescu, *Religion and Politics*, 89–92.

18. Stan and Turcescu, *Religion and Politics*, 90; Hitchins, *Rumania*, 130–32.

19. Romocea, "Church–State Relations in Post-1989 Romania," 243–77.

20. Stan and Turcescu, *Religion and Politics*, 44–46.

21. Stan and Turcescu, *Religion and Politics*, 160; Clark, *Why Angels Fall*, 210–12.

22. Stan and Turcescu, *Religion and Politics*, 157–60.

23. Romocea, "Church–State Relations in Post-1989 Romania," 243–77; Stan and Turcescu, *Religion and Politics*, 158.

MIGRATION, URBANIZATION, AND SOCIAL DISLOCATION

Post-Communist transition and EU integration generated dramatic migration patterns.[24] Millions of Romanians left rural communities to seek employment across Western Europe. Families were fractured, villages depopulated, and children left in the care of grandparents or state institutions. These dynamics reshaped the social fabric and created new forms of vulnerability, particularly among the young and elderly.[25]

At the same time, urban centers such as Bucharest, Cluj-Napoca, and Timişoara became sites of economic opportunity and cultural experimentation.[26] Cities displayed greater openness to new forms of Christian community and leadership, making them strategic spaces for mission.[27] Urban mission emerged as a liminal space where inherited identities loosened and new forms of belonging could be imagined.

These dynamics have produced a Romania marked by mobility, dislocation, and reconfiguration of identity. For the church, they present both challenge and invitation. Mission must respond to fragmentation with community, to institutional mistrust with credibility, and to historical memory with patient, incarnational presence.

HUNGARIAN COMMUNITIES: FAITH AS MEMORY

Romania's ethnic mosaic adds significant depth to its religious, cultural, and political life. Among its most prominent minorities is the Hungarian community, comprising approximately 6.5 percent of the population and concentrated primarily in Transylvania, a region long shaped by shifting borders and contested sovereignties. This presence reflects Transylvania's incorporation into the medieval Kingdom of Hungary and later the Austro-Hungarian Empire, before its transfer to Romania following the Treaty of Trianon in 1920. As a result, many Hungarian communities continue to maintain strong linguistic, cultural, and religious ties to Hungary, shaping both internal cohesion and relations with the Romanian state.[28]

24. Ciobanu, "Diverging or Converging Communities?," 65–84.
25. Ciobanu, "Diverging or Converging Communities?," 70–73.
26. Ciobanu, "Diverging or Converging Communities?," 76.
27. Clark, *Why Angels Fall*, 210–12.
28. Hitchins, *Concise History of Romania*, 54, 192–95.

For ethnic Hungarians, religious affiliation functions as a central expression of communal identity. Most belong to Roman Catholic, Reformed, or Unitarian traditions, churches that have long served as guardians of language, memory, and social cohesion within a predominantly Romanian Orthodox context.[29] Through congregational life, education, and cultural programs, these communities have preserved Hungarian identity across generations, particularly in rural or mono-ethnic regions where faith and ethnicity remain closely intertwined.

At the same time, Hungarian communities have faced sustained pressures related to twentieth-century nation-building and centralization. Tensions around language rights, religious autonomy, education, and political representation persist, despite formal commitments to pluralism and minority protections.[30] Ongoing disputes over church property restitution and Hungarian-language schooling reveal how religious institutions in minority contexts function not only as spiritual centers, but also as sites of cultural preservation and communal resilience.[31]

For mission engagement, these dynamics underscore the need for historical awareness and cultural humility. Ministry among Hungarian communities must recognize the weight churches carry as bearers of collective memory and identity. Faithful engagement requires approaches that honor inherited traditions, attend to long-standing wounds, and resist collapsing religious difference into ethnic or political categories.

THE ROMA: HISTORY, STRUCTURAL SIN, AND GOSPEL EMERGENCE

If the Hungarian experience reveals how faith and ethnicity intertwine through contested memory, the Roma expose something even more unsettling: the persistence of structural sin embedded in European history.[32] Roma communities have been present in Romania since at least

29. Hitchins, *Concise History of Romania*, 57.

30. Verdery, *National Ideology Under Socialism*, 110–14.

31. Crowe, *History of the Gypsies*, 84–85.

32. In the context of European policy, including definitions employed by the Council of Europe, the term *Roma* functions as an umbrella designation encompassing a wide array of related groups sharing common Indian origins, cultural elements, and a history of marginalization in Europe. This category includes populations often identified by subgroup names such as Roma (in Central and Eastern Europe), Sinti (in German-speaking countries and parts of Italy), and Kalé (in Spain and Wales). The term *Roma* generally refers to communities descended from migratory populations who

the thirteenth century, yet few peoples have endured such sustained exclusion, violence, and erasure, or have been so persistently spoken *about* rather than listened *to*.[33]

Although outsiders often speak of "the Roma" as a single ethnic group, Roma communities are remarkably diverse. More than forty distinct subgroups exist, each with its own dialects, customs, histories, and social structures. For many Roma, identity is shaped less by pan-ethnic labels than by family networks, local affiliations, and lived experience. External attempts to define "the Roma" frequently flatten this complexity, reducing living communities to administrative categories or policy targets.[34] Historically, Roma have been identified by names imposed from outside, including *Gypsy* in English, *Țigan* in Romanian, and *Zigeuner* in German. These terms are now widely recognized as pejorative because of their association with centuries of stereotyping, criminalization, enslavement, and exclusion. While many Roma activists and institutions have reclaimed *Roma* as a self-designation, some individuals and communities continue to use older terms in familiar or localized ways.[35] Such usage reflects the ongoing negotiation of identity under conditions of long-standing marginalization rather than endorsement of their historical meanings.[36] As a result, efforts at inclusion often fail when they treat Roma communities as objects of reform rather than as subjects of their own history.[37] Meaningful engagement must therefore attend to the contested and evolving ways Roma identity is lived, interpreted, and expressed within particular local contexts.

---

arrived in Europe from the Indian subcontinent between the tenth and fourteenth centuries. By contrast, *Travelers* refers to groups in Western Europe with distinct cultural and historical origins separate from the Roma migration. Irish Travelers and Scottish Travelers, for example, are indigenous to the British Isles. While these groups share certain socioeconomic experiences with Roma, including itinerant traditions and histories of marginalization and discrimination, they do not descend from the South Asian migratory movements characteristic of Roma origins. Travelers maintain their own languages (such as Shelta among Irish Travelers) and cultural traditions that developed independently of Roma groups. The Council of Europe and related bodies often use the compound term *Roma and Travelers* to acknowledge these distinct communities while addressing their shared experiences of exclusion, human rights concerns, and the need for policy interventions. See Council of Europe, "Roma History Factsheets"; Crowe, *History of the Gypsies*, 17–19; Clark and Greenfields, *Here to Stay*, 10–12.

33. Crowe, *History of the Gypsies*, 110–14.

34. Mirescu, "Exclusion, Inclusion, Illusion," 57.

35. Giordano and Boscoboinik, *Roma "Problem,"* 11–18.

36. Laederich, *Roma Cultural Identity*, 19–26.

37. Achim, *Roma in Romanian History*, 74–86.

The Roma people, Europe's largest and most marginalized ethnic minority, occupy a paradoxical place in contemporary European life. Present on the continent for centuries and rich in cultural resilience, they remain among its most persistently excluded peoples. Despite growing political recognition, many Roma continue to live within entrenched cycles of poverty and discrimination that are both historic and structural. Numbering an estimated ten to twelve million across Europe and more than fifteen million worldwide, the Roma are everywhere present yet often unheard, their identities flattened, their histories obscured, and their contributions ignored.[38] Their marginalization is not accidental or recent but the result of layered injustice carried across generations.

In Wallachia and Moldavia, Roma were subjected to legalized slavery for nearly five centuries. This system was upheld, not only by political authorities but also by social and religious institutions, normalizing the ownership of human beings within Christian societies.[39] Roma families were bought, sold, inherited, and punished under the sanction of law and custom.[40] Emancipation in the nineteenth century arrived without land, compensation, or meaningful legal protection.[41] Liberation without repair hardened into inherited vulnerability, leaving Roma communities exposed to poverty, exploitation, and criminalization. Only in recent years has the Orthodox Church begun to name this history and reckon, however tentatively, with its own complicity.[42]

The twentieth century brought further catastrophe. Under the Nazi regime, tens of thousands of Roma from Romania were deported to Transnistria, where many died from starvation, disease, and exposure. This genocide, known among Roma as the *Porajmos*, "the Devouring," remains inadequately acknowledged in European public memory.[43] Communist rule did little to dismantle these patterns.[44] While Roma were formally included as citizens, inclusion often took the form of surveillance, forced settlement, coerced labor, and educational segregation. Marginalization was reorganized rather than undone.

38. *Roma at a Glance*, 1.

39. Mirescu, "Exclusion, Inclusion, Illusion," 59–60.

40. Mirescu, "Exclusion, Inclusion, Illusion," 61.

41. Mirescu, "Exclusion, Inclusion, Illusion," 57–63.

42. Mirescu, "Exclusion, Inclusion, Illusion," 60.

43. Hancock, *We Are the Romani*, 53–59; Mirescu, "Exclusion, Inclusion, Illusion," 57–58.

44. Mirescu, "Exclusion, Inclusion, Illusion," 57; *Roma at a Glance*, 2.

These histories continue to shape contemporary realities. Many Roma communities face limited access to education, healthcare, employment, and legal documentation. Children are disproportionately placed in state care. Settlements remain segregated. Official statistics frequently undercount Roma populations, reflecting both stigma and fear of self-identification. Inclusion often remains symbolic: rights without belonging, policies without trust. The persistence of Roma marginalization cannot be understood apart from this long accumulation of injustice.

Here Paul's insistence in Romans that sin operates not only in individual acts but in powers and structures becomes illuminating. What was once sanctioned by law continues to exert force long after formal abolition. Sin embeds itself in social arrangements, shaping habits, expectations, and exclusions that appear normal rather than violent. In such contexts, repentance cannot be reduced to individual morality alone; it must also involve the naming and undoing of distorted social orders.

Yet the Roma story is not only one of suffering. Across Romania, evangelical and Pentecostal movements have taken root among Roma communities through sustained relational presence rather than institutional power. These movements did not spread through mass campaigns or external control but through kinship networks, shared hardship, and trusted leadership. Churches emerged in villages long dismissed as hopeless, often meeting in homes or simple structures and led by Roma pastors shaped by lived experience rather than formal credentials.

For many Roma believers, conversion represents more than a change of belief. It is experienced as the recovery of dignity, agency, and moral vocation long denied.[45] Churches become places where families are known by name, where leadership is possible, and where identity is not defined solely by exclusion. Discipleship unfolds through example and proximity rather than abstraction. Trust precedes structure. In these communities, the gospel takes flesh not as foreign intrusion but as lived hope. Life emerges from within rather than being imposed from above. Authority is earned relationally. Formation is slow, embodied, and communal.

The Roma are not peripheral to the mission of God; they stand near its center.[46] Their long history of suffering and perseverance echoes the biblical witness that God chooses what the world overlooks. Here,

45. Laederich, *Roma Cultural Identity*, 19.

46. González, *Out of Every Tribe and Nation*, 58–63.

reconciliation takes lived form, practiced in communities where wounds are named, dignity is restored, and hope is relearned.[47]

In Roma churches, the gospel confronts Europe's unfinished repentance and offers a vision of a new humanity formed not by power or respectability, but by grace. What we encounter is not a problem to be solved, but a people through whom God is at work, embodying hope in places long marked by exclusion.[48]

FOURSQUARE IN ROMANIA: FROM ATTEMPTS TO INCARNATION

Given Romania's complex historical and cultural landscape, meaningful missional engagement requires historical awareness, relational sensitivity, and spiritual patience. This is especially evident in ministry among marginalized Roma communities, among Hungarian populations where faith has long functioned as a vessel of memory and identity, and within contexts shaped by Orthodox dominance and Communist repression. Contextualization here is not simply a matter of translation or cultural adaptation; it demands a restorative, incarnational approach that takes seriously lived experiences of exclusion, mistrust, and longing. Any ministry that hopes to endure must be shaped *with*, rather than *for*, local communities, allowing the gospel to take root within Romania's particular social and spiritual soil.

Over the past two decades, several attempts to establish Foursquare ministries in Romania, including outreach among Roma communities, were marked by sincere vision but struggled to sustain long-term presence. In retrospect, these limitations reflect, not a lack of zeal but the need for slower formation, deeper partnership, and greater space for local leadership to emerge.

A new season began in 2018 with the deployment of FMI missionaries Tim and Dhana Wimberly. From the outset, their posture emphasized humility, long-term presence, and relational investment. Rather than importing predetermined structures, they committed to listening, learning, and walking alongside Romanian believers and Roma leaders. Over time, this approach has begun to bear fruit, with signs of life emerging among both ethnic Romanian and Roma communities.

47. Giordano and Boscoboinik, *Roma "Problem,"* 24–25.

48. *Roma at a Glance*, 3–4.

Rooted in relational leadership, the Wimberlys have focused on family ministry, leadership development, and community formation through shared practices rather than centralized programs. Building homes for refugees, mentoring young leaders, and strengthening families have become means through which trust is cultivated and ministry is lived.

A pivotal development emerged through partnership with Ad van der Heiden and Foursquare Netherlands, which connected the Wimberlys with Nelu and Anca Cocos, respected Roma leaders with broad regional influence. This relationship has opened new pathways for gospel witness among Roma communities and strengthened the relational foundations of the emerging movement. What is taking shape in Romania is a living process, one marked by patient discipleship, shared leadership, and contextual faithfulness. Foursquare's future here will be measured not by the speed of expansion, but by the depth of belonging it learns to embody. The work develops at the speed of trust.

LIVES THAT BECAME ECCLESIOLOGY

The emerging Foursquare movement in Romania is best understood through lives rather than plans. The ministry of Tim and Dhana Wimberly embodies an incarnational theology shaped by relationship, cultural humility, and patient presence. Rather than arriving with a prepackaged ecclesial model or strategic blueprint, they entered Romania with a long-horizon vision marked by listening, vulnerability, and embedded discipleship. Their posture has been to learn before leading and to dwell before building.

Central to their approach is a willingness to inhabit liminal space—social, cultural, and spiritual thresholds where identity and belonging remain uncertain. Romania, shaped by post-Communist ambivalence, Orthodox dominance, and suspicion of outsiders, is precisely such terrain. From the outset, the Wimberlys recognized that fruitfulness would require time. Rather than resisting this reality, they embraced it, remaining present amid uncertainty as others held inherited religious traditions alongside the possibility of new life in Christ.

Through relationships with leaders such as Nelu and Anca Cocos, Sergiu and Adriana Szabo, Istvan and Alina Muntean, and Kwame and Jessica Obeng, the Wimberlys cultivated a relational network bridging ethnic, cultural, and social divides. These partnerships are mutual and Spirit-led, marked by shared vulnerability rather than hierarchy, and they resist reproducing Western church models in favor of indigenous leadership and authentic expressions of Christian community.[49]

What is taking shape in Romania is a contextualized Foursquare movement, Romanian and Roma, rooted in Scripture and open to the Spirit. It arises from cruciform presence rather than managerial control. As one leader observed, the Wimberlys "build people" by seeing them as God sees them, restoring dignity and calling where suspicion and marginalization have long prevailed. Their ministry reflects not only the message of the gospel, but its form: incarnational, patient, and transformative.

A Church Is Born

The story of Sergiu and Adriana Szabo illustrates how ecclesial life can emerge organically when discipleship precedes structure. Their journey began, not with denominational strategy but with hospitality. Friends and neighbors gathered around their table for prayer, worship, and Scripture, and over time a shared rhythm of spiritual life took shape.

"We didn't start out thinking we were planting a church," Sergiu recalled. "We just wanted to follow Jesus and invite others to do the same."

As the community grew, a question emerged through conversation with Tim and Dhana Wimberly: *Are we a church?* The question prompted deeper theological reflection. If people are gathering in Jesus' name, growing in faith, serving one another, and living on mission, what else could it be called?

Rather than rushing toward formal recognition, Sergiu and Adriana allowed the community's identity to emerge from shared life. Eventually, with affirmation from the Foursquare family and a shared sense of calling, their house fellowship formally affiliated with Foursquare, becoming an indigenous expressions of the movement in Romania.

49. Timothy and Dhana Wimberly, interview by author, July 9, 2024; Nelu Cocos, interview by author, July 10, 2024. Sergiu and Adriana Szabo, interview by author, July 9, 2024. Istvan and Alina Muntean, interview by author, July 10, 2024. Kwame and Jessica Obeng, interview by author, July 11, 2024. Ad van der Heiden, interview by author, July 9, 2024.

From Orphan to Advocate: Embodied Gospel Witness

Istvan and Alina Muntean's ministry offers a compelling example of the gospel's restorative power among Romania's marginalized. Istvan grew up in a state-run orphanage during the Communist era, while Alina came to faith as a teenager through evangelical outreach. Together they founded Rise Together, a ministry serving orphans and vulnerable youth in Târgu Mureş through therapy, evangelism, and long-term relational care. "Because I was an orphan," Istvan explained, "I have to be there for them."

Central to their approach is sustained relational presence. Alina describes this as getting one's "boots in the mud," a metaphor for ministry that resists abstraction and embraces proximity. Rather than quick fixes or distant programs, they choose the slow work of shared life. "Just be with people that are different from you," she urged. "This will also make a huge difference."

Today, through mentoring, summer camps, and partnership with Foursquare teams in Romania and abroad, the Munteans serve predominantly Roma children, many abandoned by parents who migrated for work within the EU. In these relationships, the gospel takes root not as abstraction but as embodied hope.

From Refugees to Bridge-Builders

Kwame and Jessica Obeng's journey reveals how displacement can become vocation. Originally from Ghana and Nigeria, they sensed God's call to Eastern Europe and eventually settled in Ukraine, serving students and forming relational communities of faith. When Russia's full-scale invasion in 2022 forced them to flee, they arrived in Cluj-Napoca carrying trauma, uncertainty, and an undiminished calling.

Rather than retreat, they opened their home. Prayer gatherings formed, followed by discipleship and community. Today, their fellowship includes people from more than fifty nations—students, refugees, professionals, and migrants drawn together by shared faith rather than shared nationality. "When people come," Kwame explained, "they find home."

The Obengs now pastor one of the most ethnically diverse Christian communities in the region. As part of the emerging Foursquare movement in Romania, their ministry models a diaspora-led, relationally rooted, and missionally vibrant expression of the church. From refugees to shepherds of the nations, Kwame and Jessica embody the power of faithful witness lived out in liminal spaces. Their story reminds us that God often works through displacement, forming communities of hope in the very spaces marked by upheaval.

A Movement of Discipleship Among the Roma

For more than two decades, Nelu and Anca Cocos have served as pastors and church planters among Roma communities in central Romania. What began as a single congregation in the village of Bahnea has grown into a network of seven churches. Central to this expansion is the New Life Bible School, a mobile, two-year training program for Roma leaders founded by Nelu's brother, Moise, and now operating in multiple regions. As Nelu explains, nearly all current leaders have passed through the school, a process that has deepened both theological formation and practical ministry capacity.[50]

Nelu describes a quiet but steady renewal unfolding among the Roma. New churches continue to emerge, shaped, not only by the expressive worship characteristic of Roma culture but by a discipleship model grounded in trust and example rather than abstraction. "You build trust together," he explains, "and when you show a good example, then the Roma people are willing to learn, to be discipled."[51] Formation happens through shared life before it takes shape through instruction.

Yet this movement unfolds amid persistent challenges rooted in long histories of exclusion. Deep mistrust remains, shaped by generations of discrimination. "It's very hard for Roma people to believe that someone wants to help them simply out of love," Nelu admits. Structural barriers also persist within parts of the wider church. Even where congregations are entirely Roma, leadership is often withheld at the highest levels. "You can be an elder," Nelu notes, "but there will still be a Romanian pastor above you."[52] These realities reveal how easily mission can replicate patterns of control rather than restore dignity.

In response, Foursquare leadership is exploring with Nelu the formation of a recognized Foursquare Roma Church, a distinct yet non-segregated expression within the global Foursquare movement, equal

50. Nelu Cocos, interview by author, July 10, 2024.

51. Nelu Cocos, interview by author, July 10, 2024.

52. Nelu Cocos, interview by author, July 10, 2024.

in standing with other national churches. "For where we are right now," Nelu explains, "having our own organization works best." The aim is not separation but entrusted responsibility: a church able to order its own common life, bear the weight of its calling, and participate fully in the sending work of God beyond itself. Ultimately, Nelu dreams of a sustainable, self-governed, and missionary Roma church. "We always need help, but our desire as Roma is to support each other to continue the mission that God has entrusted to us," he said. His vision includes Roma leaders bringing revival "not just in Romania, but also for the nations."

At the heart of Nelu's vision is a theology of family shaped by mutual respect rather than power. Reflecting on his relationship with Foursquare, he observes, "Being a family means respecting each other. It's not about power. Only God is the boss, and we are all his servants." This conviction is echoed by Ad van der Heiden, who has worked closely with Roma communities for nearly a decade and insists that Roma ministry must be led by Roma leaders themselves.

Looking ahead, the hope is for a contextualized, thriving, and indigenous Foursquare Roma movement built on the foundations already laid. What is needed now is not control or acceleration, but deeper relational investment, sustained presence, and global partnership. The invitation to the wider church remains simple and urgent: "Come over and help us."[53]

DISCIPLESHIP AMONG THOSE ALREADY ON THE WAY

A defining feature of the emerging Foursquare movement in Romania is that many of those being discipled are not new converts in a narrow sense, but believers already formed in different Christian traditions. Some come from Orthodox backgrounds shaped by deep liturgical memory but limited participatory discipleship. Others arrive from evangelical or Pentecostal contexts marked by vibrant worship yet longing for deeper formation, stability, and mission. This pattern is not a departure from apostolic mission; it is distinctly Pauline.

When Paul entered new territories, he rarely encountered religious blank slates. His practice was to engage those already oriented toward the God of Israel, Jews and God-fearing gentiles gathered in synagogues, and invite them into a deeper, Christ-centered way of life (Acts 13:5;

53. Ad van der Heiden, interview by author, July 9, 2024.

14:1; 17:1–4). These communities possessed Scripture, prayer, and moral frameworks, yet still required formation into the full life of the gospel. Paul's work was therefore not limited to initial conversion, but was fundamentally formative, drawing believers into a reconfigured identity in Christ and shared participation in God's mission.

Timothy provides a clear example. Nurtured in the Scriptures from childhood through the faith of his mother and grandmother (2 Tim 1:5; 3:15), he was not converted from paganism but formed through mentoring, shared ministry, correction, and commissioning. Paul did not dismiss Timothy's prior faith but refined and redirected it toward apostolic service.

This pattern recurs throughout Paul's letters. He writes to communities already "in Christ" yet still in need of instruction, encouragement, and growth. The believers in Rome were known for their faith (Rom 1:8), yet Paul longed to visit them in order to strengthen and be strengthened through mutual encouragement (Rom 1:11–12). Discipleship is not a linear movement from unbelief to belief, but an ongoing formation into maturity, unity, and mission. The task is not to replace existing faith, but to reorder it around shared discipleship and missional participation. The gospel takes root not by erasing spiritual histories, but by redeeming them, forming communities capable of faithful witness within their own cultural and historical soil, and of joining in God's sending work beyond themselves.

THE EMERGING FOURSQUARE MOVEMENT IN ROMANIA

Through the patient ministry of Tim and Dhana Wimberly, together with a growing circle of Romanian, Roma, and international leaders, a contextualized Foursquare movement is quietly taking root in Romania. What is emerging is a way of being church shaped by presence, partnership, and trust in the Spirit's work over time.

This movement was not planned in advance. It has grown slowly from relationships, shared life, and attentiveness to what God was already doing in Romanian soil. Its shape becomes visible, not through organizational charts but through lived patterns—missionaries who dwell rather than direct, communities that form before they formalize, and leaders who emerge from within their own contexts. What is unfolding can be named, but not controlled.

Tim and Dhana function as catalytic partners rather than institutional architects. Sent by FMI, they operate beyond established congregational structures, investing in people, nurturing leaders, and creating space for new ecclesial expressions to emerge. Their role has been to make disciples, and through that churches come into being. This dynamic is evident in the story of Sergiu and Adriana Szabo. Their community in Târgu Mureş began around a table with hospitality, prayer, Scripture, and shared discipleship. Only later did they ask the question, *Are we a church?* The question did not signal a rush toward structure, but a recognition that shared life in Christ had already become ecclesial.

Romania itself is a liminal space, shaped by post-Communist mistrust of institutions, a deep Orthodox heritage, and rapid social change. Rather than resisting this in-between reality, the Wimberlys embraced it as part of their calling. From the beginning, they understood that fruit would take time. Their ministry has been marked by patience rather than urgency, accompaniment rather than control.

That same liminality appears in the story of Kwame and Jessica Obeng. Displaced by war in Ukraine, they arrived in Romania as refugees, beginning again from loss rather than strength. What emerged was a community shaped by hospitality and shared vulnerability, students, migrants, professionals, and refugees from more than fifty nations gathering around prayer and mutual care. In their story, displacement became vocation, and liminality fertile ground for mission.

Across Romania, similar patterns of emergence are visible. Roma churches connected to Nelu Cocos, the Rise Together ministry of Istvan and Alina Muntean, and house-based fellowships among Romanians and internationals have grown from local initiative and relational trust rather than centralized planning. These communities are not replicas of imported models. They are culturally credible, locally led, and increasingly self-sustaining. Leadership is shared, discernment is communal, and growth is measured less by speed than by depth.

Underlying this movement is a distinctly Pauline imagination. Like Paul, the Wimberlys have often begun not with religious blank slates, but with believers already shaped by other traditions, inviting them into deeper discipleship. Authority is exercised through relationship rather than command, and unity is forged through mutual welcome rather than uniformity. Romanian, Roma, and diaspora leaders are not absorbed into a single pattern, but invited to contribute their gifts to a shared mission.

This emphasis on belonging came into sharp focus at the 2025 Foursquare Europe Conference in Croatia. For many Romanian leaders, the gathering felt less like a conference and more like a homecoming. They were received, not as projects or guests but as family. Shared worship softened cultural boundaries, affirmed callings, and reshaped identity through relationship rather than strategy.

Sergiu and Adriana Szabo experienced the gathering as confirmation of their pastoral vocation and a widening vision of church as relational and inclusive. Adriana was struck by the visibility of women in ministry. "This is not just about rules," she reflected. "It's about the Spirit." Istvan and Alina Muntean described the conference as renewal and reassurance. For Kwame and Jessica Obeng, the experience was restorative. "We arrived as refugees," Kwame said, "but we left as leaders again." Nelu Cocos spoke of being received as a brother, strengthening his confidence among Roma congregations. As Tim Wimberly observed, "They saw they weren't alone. And that changed everything."

At the heart of this emerging movement is a shared commitment to dwelling before building. Ministry unfolds through slow obedience: learning rhythms, earning trust, and walking with people over time. Istvan and Alina speak of keeping their "boots in the mud," remaining present among those shaped by trauma and abandonment. Nelu describes pastoral authority born from shared suffering and faithfulness. Kwame and Jessica speak of beginning again with nothing but a table and the Spirit. In each case, the church emerges from shared life before structure.

This posture mirrors Paul's own approach to the Roman church. He sought partnership rather than control, mutual encouragement rather than hierarchy. "Welcome one another," he urged, "just as Christ has welcomed you" (Rom 15:7). That same gospel logic now shapes the Romanian context. Incarnational, relational ministry is not optional; it reflects the very form of the gospel—God with us, God among us, God through us.

Within Romania's complex social landscape, three complementary expressions of contextualization have taken shape. In urban centers, church has emerged as relational and intercultural community, formed around tables rather than programs. Among orphans, Roma families, and marginalized youth, trauma-informed presence has given rise to healing-centered ministry rooted in proximity and patience. And among

Roma communities, a transnational ecclesial vision is emerging, one that seeks entrusted responsibility rather than dependency, affirms Roma leadership, and remains fully connected to the wider body of Christ.

Across these expressions, a coherent pattern becomes clear. Proximity precedes proclamation. Healing accompanies witness. Structure serves life rather than defining it. What is emerging in Romania is not yet complete, nor is it uniform. But it is unmistakably alive. Rooted in Scripture, attentive to history, and open to the Spirit, this movement offers a picture of ecclesial life formed from within. In a land marked by memory and transition, the gospel is learning once again how to dwell—and, in doing so, is giving birth to a church that truly belongs.

LEARNING TO BEAR THE WEIGHT OF LIFE

What has emerged in Romania is a church learning to live faithfully in the in-between spaces that define the nation itself—between empire and identity, Orthodoxy and pluralism, inherited faith and renewed discipleship, memory and hope. This movement has not rushed to resolve these tensions. Instead, it has learned to dwell within them, trusting that faithfulness, not control, is the proper posture of the gospel in such soil.

The foundations of this work are unmistakably incarnational. Churches have not been born from strategy documents or institutional momentum, but from tables and homes, from shared suffering and patient presence, from long obedience practiced in particular places. Trust has preceded structure. Formation has mattered more than speed. Life has been allowed to emerge before it was named or organized.

Viewed through the four-stages and four-self framework, what is unfolding in Romania is not linear advancement but growing capacity. Discipleship, leadership development, communal life, and outward witness are taking shape together rather than sequentially. Likewise, self-governance, self-support, self-propagation, and self-theologizing are not imposed as benchmarks but cultivated as signs of maturing responsibility. The central question has never been whether churches can move forward through stages, but whether they can bear the weight of their own life with faithfulness and integrity.

Theologically, this pattern resonates deeply with Paul's vision in Romans. Authority is exercised through relationship rather than command. Unity is forged, not through uniformity but through mutual welcome.

The church is revealed, not as a finished product but as a Spirit-formed body learning how to live reconciled life together. In Romania, that vision has moved from abstraction to practice. Roma leaders are stepping into responsibility long denied to them. Romanian pastors are discovering renewed confidence and shared vocation. Missionary families are planting roots, not as experts but as co-laborers. Even proposals such as the recognition of a Roma Foursquare Church signal that this vision is beginning to reshape not only practice, but structure.

The future of Foursquare in Romania will not be measured primarily by numerical growth or institutional expansion. It will be measured by faithfulness, by whether the gospel continues to take flesh in Romanian soil, among Roma villages and urban centers, among the displaced and the rooted, among those long excluded and those newly gathered. Across these contexts, the church's calling remains the same: not simply to grow or expand but to learn how to bear the weight of life together in Christ, so that the gospel may be faithfully given away.

29

National Church Development in Kazakhstan

THE GROWTH AND CONTEXTUALIZATION of Christianity in Kazakhstan cannot be understood apart from the region's complex historical, cultural, and religious landscape. From early Christian presence along the Silk Road, through the expansion of Russian Orthodoxy, to the systematic suppression of all religion under Soviet atheism, Kazakhstan has long functioned as a contested spiritual frontier. These overlapping layers of trauma, resilience, and shifting religious authority continue to shape the country's spiritual imagination in the post-Soviet era.

In this context, Christian mission encounters both challenges and opportunities. Drawing on historical memory, sociopolitical realities, and theological reflection, it becomes clear that contextualization in Kazakhstan is not simply cultural courtesy, it is a theological necessity. As the gospel takes root in a pluralistic and post-Soviet society, it must do so with sensitivity to Kazakhstan's ancient Christian heritage, its contemporary regulatory environment, and the enduring search for meaning among its people.

This chapter traces the emergence of the national church in Kazakhstan as a slow, contextual, and Spirit-led process shaped by historical rupture, cultural plurality, and indigenous leadership. In such a setting, contextualization is not only a pragmatic strategy or a gesture of cultural sensitivity; it is a theological necessity. Faithful mission must attend carefully to Kazakhstan's ancient Christian memory, its contemporary regulatory realities, and the enduring search for meaning among a people formed by coercion, loss, and resilience. The church does not arrive here on neutral ground. It must learn how to dwell.

KAZAKHSTAN'S HISTORICAL AND CULTURAL LEGACY

Kazakhstan occupies a pivotal place in Central Asia, historically situated within the broader region of Transoxiana, north of the Oxus River (modern Amu Darya), and intersecting the trade networks of the Silk Road. For centuries, this territory functioned less as a fixed political entity than as a corridor of movement, shaped by migration, exchange, and encounter. Nomadic peoples decisively formed its cultural and social patterns, and Kazakh identity traces its roots to Turkic nomads who emerged within a khanate in the sixth century CE. Mobility, kinship, and adaptability were defining features of life on the steppe.[1]

This nomadic world came under increasing pressure with the expansion of Russian imperial power and, later, Soviet rule. Both regimes pursued aggressive policies of sedentarization that disrupted patterns of life refined over centuries. Under Soviet control, Kazakhstan became a laboratory for economic experimentation, agricultural collectivization, and large-scale resource extraction. These initiatives radically altered land and society. Over roughly 130 years, the population became highly diverse, shaped in significant part by forced deportations during the Stalinist era. By independence in 1991, more than one hundred ethnic groups resided within Kazakhstan's borders.[2]

Independence brought both promise and profound challenge. Political leaders, particularly President Nursultan Nazarbayev, invoked continuity with ancient Turkic heritage to anchor national identity, yet the realities of post-Soviet transition proved far more complex.[3] Early optimism gave way to authoritarian consolidation, systemic corruption, and increasing restrictions on religious expression.[4] The tension between symbolic nationhood and lived insecurity remains a defining feature of Kazakhstan's social and spiritual landscape.

1. Sawatsky, "Kazakhstan," 106–10.
2. Allworth et al., "Kazakhstan."
3. Cummings, *Kazakhstan*, 14–37.
4. Cummings, *Kazakhstan*, 108.

Several twentieth-century developments continue to shape collective memory. Khrushchev's Virgin Lands Campaign (1953–59) temporarily increased grain production but devastated nomadic economies and caused lasting environmental damage.[5] Soviet irrigation projects contributed directly to the catastrophic shrinking of the Aral Sea, one of the most severe ecological disasters of the modern era.[6] In each case, progress was pursued through coercion, with little regard for local knowledge or long-term consequence.

Kazakhstan was also deeply marked by the Soviet military-industrial complex. The Baikonur Cosmodrome and the Semey nuclear testing site were both located on Kazakh territory, the latter hosting 479 nuclear tests between 1949 and 1989. The environmental and public health effects persist today. In addition, more than seventy gulag-style forced labor camps operated across the country, embedding trauma and mistrust into the social fabric.[7]

Geographically vast yet sparsely populated, Kazakhstan stretches nearly three thousand kilometers east to west and two thousand kilometers north to south, while maintaining one of the lowest population densities in Asia. Demographically, independence arrived amid unusual conditions: ethnic Kazakhs comprised only 46 percent of the population, while Russians accounted for roughly 35 percent, alongside nearly one million ethnic Germans.[8] At the same time, Soviet investment in education produced a highly literate society, with literacy rates rising from approximately 2 percent in the 1930s to near universality by the early 1990s.[9]

These gains came at immense human cost. Forced collectivization during the 1930s led to the deaths of an estimated 1.75 million Kazakhs, nearly half of the ethnic population. World War II claimed an additional 350,000 lives. After independence, roughly three million non-Kazakhs emigrated, draining skilled labor and hollowing out entire regions. In places such as Qostanay, unemployment soared as factories closed and communities collapsed.[10]

5. Cummings, *Kazakhstan*, 89.
6. Britannica Editors, "Aral Sea."
7. Sawatsky, "Kazakhstan," 108–9.
8. Allworth et al., "Kazakhstan."
9. Allworth et al., "Kazakhstan."
10. Allworth et al., "Kazakhstan."

Culturally and linguistically, Kazakhstan remains suspended between multiple spheres of influence. The Kazakh people, identified in medieval sources as "White Huns," are a Turkic people whose language has been repeatedly reshaped by political transition. During the Soviet period, Kazakh was written in Cyrillic, while Russian functioned as the language of governance and intellectual life. Following independence, Kazakh was declared the official language, but debates over script reform, ranging from Arabic to Latin, continue. These debates function as markers of deeper questions of belonging and future orientation: toward the Turkic world, the post-Soviet sphere, or the broader Islamic *ummah*.

This layered historical and cultural legacy forms the soil into which the gospel is received and the church takes shape. Mission in Kazakhstan cannot be approached as a blank slate. It requires attentiveness to trauma, disrupted trust, and the long memory of imposed change. Faithful witness depends not only on linguistic or cultural competence, but on patience, humility, and the recognition that resilience here has often been forged through suffering. Kazakhstan offers a sobering lesson: The past is not behind the people; it is carried with them, shaping how authority, belief, and hope are understood today.

NESTORIAN CHRISTIANITY IN CENTRAL ASIA AND EARLY CHRISTIAN PRESENCE IN KAZAKHSTAN

Christianity in Central Asia extends deep into the first millennium through the eastward expansion of the Church of the East,[11] a tradition often labeled "Nestorian" in Western polemics, though the term obscures the church's own theological self-understanding.[12] For centuries, this tradition was misunderstood because of its association with early Christological controversies and its rejection of the Council of Chalcedon (451 CE). Contemporary scholarship has corrected many of these caricatures, demonstrating that the Church of the East articulated a biblically grounded Christology marked by theological depth, intellectual vitality, and extraordinary missionary energy.[13]

What most clearly distinguished this tradition was its orientation beyond the Roman world. While Western Christianity largely expanded

11. Not to be confused with Eastern Orthodox Christianity.

12. Sawatsky, "Kazakhstan," 107–8.

13. Jenkins, *Lost History*, 45–69.

within imperial boundaries, the Church of the East moved eastward across Persia and along the Silk Road, establishing Christian communities from Mesopotamia to India and China. Syriac functioned as its primary liturgical and literary language, yet missionaries demonstrated striking cultural adaptability. Scripture was translated, local leaders were trained, and Christian life was embedded within diverse social and ethnic settings. Mission advanced not through imperial replication, but through adaptive presence.[14]

By the early fifth century, Christianity had gained legal recognition within the Persian Empire. In 409 CE, Shah Yazdegerd I issued an edict of toleration that allowed the East Syrian Church to organize openly. Synod records from this period list bishops from regions as far east as Samarqand, north of the Oxus River, and possibly extending into areas corresponding to modern Kazakhstan. These sources confirm that Christianity had already taken root well beyond its Mediterranean origins and was firmly established in Central Asia.

Mission among Turkic and nomadic peoples is especially well attested. During the exile of Shah Kavadh I (497–501 CE), Church of the East clergy accompanied him northward, ministering to Christian captives and preaching among nomadic tribes. Their approach combined evangelism, baptism, education, and economic development. They cooperated across theological boundaries, even partnering with Armenian Miaphysite leaders, and introduced written language and agricultural practices alongside Christian teaching. As Samuel Moffett observed, this work represented a "full-rounded blend of spiritual and practical missionary methods," offering a holistic vision of mission centuries before the term existed.[15]

Missionary expansion reached a high point under Patriarch Timothy I (780–823 CE). His correspondence describes renewed outreach beyond the Persian frontier, including a notable request from the "king of the Turks" for bishops and priests to be sent to his people, likely referring to Turkic populations inhabiting regions that now comprise much of Kazakhstan. By this period, Samarqand had become a metropolitan see overseeing a wide network of bishops across Central Asia. Churches, monasteries, and centers of learning existed throughout present-day Kazakhstan, Uzbekistan, and Tajikistan.[16]

14. Sawatsky, "Kazakhstan," 107–8.

15. Moffett, *History of Christianity in Asia*, 1:209.

16. Sawatsky, "Kazakhstan," 107–8.

Traces of this Christian presence persisted for centuries. In southern Kazakhstan, Baptist communities in Zhambyl (ancient Taraz), a major Silk Road city, maintain that Christian activity continued there into the tenth century. These claims align with archaeological and historical evidence of monasteries across Central Asia that functioned as centers of worship, education, hospitality, and healthcare. Monastic networks supported both spiritual life and economic exchange, providing infrastructure for merchants traveling between Persia and China. In this way, Christian faith became woven into the region's social and commercial life.[17]

By around 1000 CE, the Church of the East may have numbered as many as twelve million adherents across Asia, alongside roughly thirty-two million Christians in Byzantine and Western territories. Yet this expansive presence proved fragile. From the eighth century onward, Christians experienced increasing marginalization under Islamic rule, though Islam did not become dominant across much of Central Asia until the fourteenth century. In the southern regions of Central Asia, such as Bukhara in modern-day Uzbekistan, Islamic institutions grew rapidly, and Bukhara became a significant center of Islamic learning, third in stature only to Mecca and Medina. A major blow to the Church of the East came in the early fifteenth century through the brutal campaigns of Timur, which devastated remaining Christian communities, destroying churches, monasteries, and clergy.[18]

Why This History Matters for Mission Today

This history reframes contemporary mission in Kazakhstan. Christianity here is not a foreign intrusion but a recovery of deep roots. The Church of the East modeled mobility, contextual translation, indigenous leadership, and partnership across cultures, precisely the capacities required for faithful witness in Kazakhstan today. Its disappearance was the result of political violence and structural marginalization.

This legacy also explains why imported ecclesial models often struggle to take root. Kazakhstan's spiritual soil has been shaped by movement rather than settlement, emergence rather than institution, and survival rather than dominance. Mission that seeks control, replication, or rapid

17. Sawatsky, "Kazakhstan," 107–8.

18. Allworth et al., "Kazakhstan."

institutionalization risks repeating the coercive patterns of empire that scar the nation's memory. By contrast, mission that embraces emergence, patient, relational, and locally led, resonates with the deepest currents of Kazakhstan's Christian past.

Recovering this story does more than correct historical amnesia. It invites the church to imagine its future, not as novelty but as renewal—the gospel returning to soil where it once bore fruit, and where, by the Spirit's work, it may yet do so again.

RUSSIAN AND SOVIET ERAS: THE RESHAPING OF RELIGION IN KAZAKHSTAN

Orthodox Expansion and Imperial Settlement

When Roman Catholic missions resumed long-distance evangelization in the sixteenth century, they largely bypassed Central Asia in favor of maritime routes to India and China. Christianity's reentry into the Kazakh steppe therefore did not occur through Catholic renewal but through the gradual eastward expansion of Russian Orthodoxy, closely intertwined with imperial conquest and settlement.

Although earlier Russian principalities had intermittent contact with Turkic and Mongol peoples through the Golden Horde, sustained engagement with Kazakh territories began with the rise of Muscovy and intensified under Peter the Great (r. 1682–1725). Full political incorporation into the Russian Empire unfolded over the nineteenth century, culminating in formal annexation by 1860. What followed was large-scale Slavic settlement that permanently reshaped Kazakhstan's religious and demographic landscape.[19]

By 1890, more than 500,000 settlers, primarily Russians and Ukrainians, had relocated to Kazakh lands. Prime Minister Pyotr Stolypin's agrarian reforms (1906–11) accelerated this process, resettling nearly 438,000 peasants in northern and eastern regions. Ethnic Germans also arrived in significant numbers, many from earlier colonies in European Russia. Though they represented a small proportion of the population, German settlers constituted a disproportionately large share of Kazakhstan's educated elite.[20]

19. Allworth et al., "Kazakhstan."

20. Cummings, *Kazakhstan*, 87.

This demographic transformation brought a wide array of Christian traditions. Alongside Russian Orthodoxy came Lutherans, Roman Catholics, Mennonites, and Baptists, many of whom established congregations, schools, and mutual aid networks. By the early twentieth century, Orthodox, Mennonite, and Baptist communities had initiated limited missionary engagement among Kazakhs, including early efforts at Scripture translation. Christianity never became dominant among the indigenous population, yet it became embedded within Kazakhstan's emerging multiethnic fabric.

Soviet Atheism and Religious Repression

The Bolshevik Revolution introduced a decisive rupture. From 1929 to 1991, the Soviet state pursued systematic religious repression, targeting all faith traditions. Churches, mosques, and religious schools were closed; clergy were imprisoned or executed; and atheism was institutionalized as state ideology. In Central Asia, the number of mosques fell from approximately twenty-six thousand in 1917 to just over thirteen hundred by 1942.

Although restrictions eased briefly during World War II, repression soon resumed. In 1943, the state established the Spiritual Administration of Muslims of Central Asia and Kazakhstan (SADUM), ostensibly to organize Islamic life but in practice to monitor clergy and suppress independent religious expression. By the mid-1980s, only two officially sanctioned madrasahs operated across Central Asia, and fewer than one hundred registered mosques remained throughout the USSR. At the same time, unregistered mosques proliferated underground, often led by informal or self-taught leaders. These communities preserved religious continuity but also became sites where alternative and sometimes radical interpretations of Islam could develop.

Orthodox Christianity retained a limited, highly regulated presence. A bishopric was established in Alma-Ata, and by 1958 the Russian Orthodox Church operated approximately sixty registered congregations in Kazakhstan. These numbers declined under Khrushchev's renewed anti-religious campaigns but rebounded modestly during *perestroika*. By independence in 1991, Orthodoxy remained institutionally visible yet ethnically bounded, serving primarily Russian and Ukrainian populations and remaining firmly under Moscow's ecclesiastical authority.

Protestant Witness Under Pressure

Protestant and evangelical communities endured especially severe conditions, yet they demonstrated remarkable resilience. Many Baptists, Mennonites, and Lutherans were deported to Kazakhstan during Stalin's purges and assigned to labor camps or industrial regions such as Qaraghandy. Under these conditions, churches formed not through institutional support but through shared suffering, underground worship, and mutual care.

By the 1930s, Baptists in Kazakhstan had organized into regional unions, often led by ethnic German believers whose educational background provided theological stability. By 1988, more than 150 Baptist congregations and groups existed across the country, though leadership shortages were acute. Periods of intensified repression produced internal divisions, particularly over whether churches should register with the state. The formation of the Council of Churches of Evangelical Christians-Baptists (1962) marked a decisive refusal to submit to state control. Despite arrests, surveillance, and imprisonment, the movement sustained robust underground networks, including clandestine publishing and support for imprisoned believers.[21]

Other Protestant traditions persisted as well. Pentecostals, Adventists, Lutherans, and Mennonites maintained small congregations, many of them unregistered. By the 1980s, Soviet reports acknowledged growth among these groups, even as officials portrayed unregistered leaders as threats to social order. Ironically, these documents testify to the vitality of religious life that survived decades of systematic repression, sustained not by power or privilege, but by conviction, community, and hope.[22]

MISSIONAL IMPLICATIONS

Imperial expansion, forced migration, and ideological control have left deep and lasting scars on Kazakhstan's religious landscape. Christianity, though never a majority faith, became closely associated with migration, marginalization, and endurance. It survived, not because it was protected but because it adapted—decentralized, relational, and often hidden from

21. Sawatsky, "Kazakhstan,"107–8.

22. Sawatsky, "Kazakhstan," 107–8.

view. Faith endured through networks of trust rather than institutional stability.

For contemporary mission, this history matters deeply. It helps explain widespread suspicion of organized religion, the resilience of informal and underground communities, and the persistent hunger for spiritual meaning in a post-atheist society. It also cautions against approaches that rely on visibility, scale, or formal recognition. In Kazakhstan, faith has often flourished most fully at the margins. Any new movement, including the Foursquare Church, must therefore engage this landscape with humility, historical awareness, and respect for communities that learned to believe under pressure.

CONTEMPORARY TENSIONS FOR CHRISTIANITY AND ISLAM IN KAZAKHSTAN

Since independence in 1991, Kazakhstan has presented itself as a secular, multiethnic, and multireligious nation. Enshrined in the constitution, secularism was intended to safeguard religious tolerance in a society shaped by both Islam and Russian Orthodoxy. In practice, this commitment has been uneven. The country's religious environment has moved through alternating periods of openness and restriction, shaped by anxieties over national identity, fears of extremism, and the state's desire to manage religious expression.[23]

Religious Liberalization and Early Openness

The collapse of the Soviet Union created an unprecedented opening for religious life. The 1992 Law on Religious Activity marked a decisive break from decades of repression, allowing religious organizations to register, worship publicly, and engage in social ministry. Historic communities—Orthodox Christians, Muslims, Baptists, Lutherans, and Catholics—re-emerged, while evangelical and Pentecostal churches experienced rapid growth.

This period coincided with severe economic crisis. Faith-based organizations stepped into the vacuum left by the retreating state, providing humanitarian aid, education, and social services. Between 1994 and 1996, thousands of NGOs, many with religious affiliations, were

23. Yemelianova, "Islam, National Identity and Politics," 286–301.

established to meet urgent needs, a phenomenon described by one analyst as "the great donor tsunami."[24] During this same period, Christianity began to take root among traditionally Muslim ethnic groups, including Kazakhs, Uzbeks, and Uighurs. By the late 1990s, indigenous Christian expression was visible through worship in Turkic languages and the emergence of local leadership.[25]

Rising Restrictions and Policy Shifts

Despite early openness, concerns over national security and religious extremism soon began to reshape policy. From the late 1990s onward, legislation increasingly restricted religious activity. Laws introduced between 2002 and 2005 imposed mandatory registration, limited unregistered gatherings, and required missionaries to operate under state-recognized religious bodies.[26]

Although framed as safeguards against extremism, these measures disproportionately affected groups labeled "non-traditional," including independent evangelical churches, Pentecostals, and Islamic movements outside official structures. Ḥanafī Sunnī Islam and Russian Orthodoxy retained privileged status, while others faced heightened scrutiny.[27] High registration costs, vague definitions of extremism, and inconsistent enforcement created an atmosphere of uncertainty.[28] Incidents such as the demolition of Hare Krishna homes near Almaty and the detention of members of Tablighi Jamaat illustrate how quickly religious activity could be reclassified as a threat to public order.[29]

International Critique and Civil Liberties

Kazakhstan's religious policies have drawn sustained criticism from international human rights organizations. Reports document arrests for peaceful religious activity, censorship of religious literature, and pressure

24. Ruffin and Waugh, *Civil Society in Central Asia*, 35.
25. Sawatsky, "Kazakhstan,"107–8.
26. Khalid, *Islam After Communism*, 185–86.
27. Ruffin and Waugh, *Civil Society in Central Asia*, 47–48.
28. Yemelianova, "Islam, National Identity and Politics," 286–301.
29. Majumdar, *Government Restrictions on Religion*, 12, 20.

on unregistered communities.[30] At times, Kazakhstan has been recommended for international watch lists. While government responses have included selective reforms and dialogue with global institutions, structural issues persist. National security narratives continue to justify restrictions, particularly in regions where religious minorities are perceived as socially or politically suspect.[31]

Secularism and the Problem of Partiality

Although secularism aspires to neutrality, in practice it has produced selective recognition. The state consistently favors "traditional" religions, Ḥanafī Islam and Russian Orthodoxy, as partners in national identity formation, while other expressions are treated as foreign or destabilizing.[32] Many unregistered communities such as house churches, informal mosques, and underground fellowships, operate outside the legal framework not out of defiance, but because of mistrust, fear, or bureaucratic exhaustion.[33]

This dynamic exposes a deeper tension. The state seeks stability through regulation, while religious life resists total control. As a result, spiritual vitality often flourishes in informal, relational, and liminal spaces rather than within official institutions.

30. US Commission on International Religious Freedom, *2025 Annual Report*; Human Rights Watch, *World Report 2025*.

31. US Commission on International Religious Freedom, *2025 Annual Report*, 56.

32. Ḥanafī Islam, the predominant legal tradition in Kazakhstan and across Central Asia, reflects a historically moderate and adaptable form of Sunnī jurisprudence shaped by the teachings of Imām Abū Ḥanīfa (699–767 CE). As the oldest and most widespread Sunnī school of law, the Ḥanafī tradition emphasizes reasoned interpretation (*qiyās*), practical legal judgment, and the integration of Islamic principles within diverse cultural settings. Under the influence of the Abbasid and later the Ottoman and Mughal empires, Ḥanafī Islam became deeply rooted in Central Asian religious life, where it blended with local customs (*ʿādāt*) and Ṣūfī devotional practices. In Kazakhstan, this produced a form of Islam that is generally flexible, pragmatic, and oriented toward social harmony, a dynamic that continues to shape the country's religious landscape and its approach to faith, identity, and public life. See Khalid, *Islam after Communism*.

33. Majumdar, *Government Restrictions on Religion*, 33.

Religious Freedom in a Complex Landscape

Kazakhstan continues to promote itself internationally as a model of interfaith harmony, hosting global forums and emphasizing tolerance, the lived experience for many religious communities tells a more complicated story.[34] For registered communities, this image often reflects reality. For others, especially converts from Islam or members of unregistered churches, life remains precarious. Social pressure from family and community frequently compounds legal vulnerability.[35]

From independence to the present, Kazakhstan's religious environment has been shaped by ongoing tension: openness and control, indigenization and regulation, hospitality and suspicion. This is the soil into which the gospel must be planted today. Faithful mission in Kazakhstan requires more than legal awareness. It calls for spiritual discernment, cultural humility, and the formation of disciples resilient enough to grow amid ambiguity, constraint, and quiet resistance.

THE FOURSQUARE CHURCH OF KAZAKHSTAN

In the years following Kazakhstan's independence in 1991, amid renewed religious openness and tightening state regulation, a new chapter began in the global story of the Foursquare Church. Rooted in indigenous leadership and strengthened through apostolic partnerships from Germany and the United States, the Foursquare movement in Kazakhstan emerged as a Spirit-led initiative and has matured into a vibrant national church. Today it functions, not only as a local church community but as a sending movement across Central Asia and beyond.

The story of Foursquare's emergence in Kazakhstan comes into focus through the lives of three key leaders: Thomas Thomasov, national leader of Foursquare Kazakhstan; Ewald Zelmer, director of missions for Foursquare Germany; and A. Sadik, who serves alongside both men while directing the Bible Institute. Their intertwined journeys, marked by trauma and healing, vision and discernment, partnership and perseverance, trace the organic formation of a church learning to govern itself, sustain its life, articulate its theology, and extend its witness. In their lived experience, the four-self principles and the four stages of national church

34. Congress of Leaders of World and Traditional Religions, "About the Congress."

35. Cummings, *Kazakhstan*, 14–37.

development are not abstract frameworks but embodied realities, revealing how a Spirit-formed ecclesial life has taken root within the particular cultural, political, and spiritual soil of Kazakhstan.

Theological and Missiological Liminality

Foursquare Kazakhstan emerged within the unsettled terrain left by Soviet secularism, postcolonial identity formation, and competing ideological pressures. As A. Sadik observed, Kazakhstan's spiritual landscape is shaped by three dominant trajectories: the rise of radical Islam among youth, a materialist orientation drawn toward Europe and the United States, and the residual influence of historic Christianity. Within this contested space, the Foursquare movement came to occupy a liminal position, neither aligned with radicalism nor consumerism, and distinct from inherited institutional Christianity.

This in-between identity was not accidental. As Sadik later explained, the movement learned to operate "outside the social norm," offering a Spirit-formed alternative capable of affirming indigenous identity while resisting cultural conformity. These tensions were not theoretical; they were embodied in the lives of Foursquare leaders themselves.

Thomas Thomasov's conversion during an unjust imprisonment in the early post-Soviet period exemplifies this theological liminality. "After three days in jail," he recalled, "I understood that nobody could help me. . . . Someone had to be above this terrible world. . . . Someone who could love me."[36] His encounter with divine goodness, experienced not through institution but through desperation, became the seed of a faith shaped by existential hunger and direct encounter.

Thomasov's journey from a religiously mixed family through Soviet atheism into charismatic Christian leadership mirrors the threshold dynamics explored throughout this book. Foursquare Kazakhstan reflects Paul's vision in Romans: a gospel that dismantles inherited boundaries and forms a Spirit-empowered community across ethnic, social, and religious lines.

36. Thomas Thomasov, Ewald Zelmer, and Alisher Sadik, interview with author, April 17, 2025.

Contextual Theology and Symbolic Reorientation

As the movement matured, contextualization emerged as a theological necessity. Leaders recognized that the gospel could not take deep root if it remained clothed in imported aesthetics or Western ecclesial forms. It needed to speak through the symbols, stories, and structures of Kazakh life.

One emblematic expression of this commitment was the adaptation of the Foursquare logo to incorporate the *shanyrak*, the circular crown of the traditional Kazakh yurt. This was not cosmetic branding. As Sadik explained, "It's not just a cultural picture; it's a message. The *shanyrak* points to the sky, to God. It means family, blessing, openness to heaven. That is also who we are in Christ."[37]

Traditionally associated with continuity, hospitality, and the connection between earth and heaven, the *shanyrak* became an indigenous theological metaphor, a Christ-centered cosmology expressed in Kazakh form. This act of symbolic reorientation embodied incarnation in context: the gospel spoken from within a culture rather than imposed upon it.

Emblems of The Foursquare Church | *Emblems of Foursquare Kazakhstan*

By embedding a national symbol within its identity, Foursquare Kazakhstan enacted a theological act of redemption rather than cultural accommodation. The message was clear: Following Jesus did not require cultural erasure. As Sadik put it, "You don't need to become something else to follow Jesus. You can meet him right here in your land, your

37. Thomas Thomasov, Ewald Zelmer, and Alisher Sadik, interview with author, April 17, 2025.

language, your story."[38] This theological move also carried missional consequence, fostering legitimacy among local authorities and enabling believers from Muslim and Orthodox backgrounds to perceive Foursquare, not as foreign but as faithfully local.

APOSTOLIC CONVERGENCE AND DIASPORIC MISSION

At the heart of Foursquare Kazakhstan's emergence lies the intentional convergence of two missionary streams—German and American—whose intersection in the early 2000s catalyzed the formation of a unified national movement. This convergence was neither accidental nor merely strategic; it was a prayerful resistance to the fragmentation that often marks transnational church-planting efforts.

The German stream, led by Ewald Zelmer, carried deep historical resonance. A descendant of ethnic Germans deported to Kazakhstan under Stalin, Zelmer understood his return as an act of spiritual reconciliation. "I was born and raised in Kazakhstan," he explained. "We felt called to come back, not as exiles, but with the gospel."[39] His cultural fluency and relational credibility enabled him to function as a bridge, planting churches long before formal denominational alignment emerged.

Running parallel was the American stream, shaped through John Weed's ministry. Already serving in Kazakhstan, Weed was introduced to the Foursquare movement through relationships with Mike McIntosh and others. A pivotal meeting in 2003 brought Weed, Thomasov, and Foursquare leaders together for extended theological dialogue and discernment. "By the end of the day," Thomasov recalled, "we said, 'This is us. These are our values.'"

Rather than competing or operating in parallel, the leaders chose unity. Weed was affirmed as national leader, not because of origin but because of trust and calling. "We didn't care where he came from," Thomasov explained. "He loved Jesus. We trusted him." This trust became the foundation for a movement shaped not by nationality or hierarchy but by theological resonance, relational fidelity, and Spirit-led discernment.

38. Thomas Thomasov, Ewald Zelmer, and Alisher Sadik, interview with author, April 17, 2025.

39. Thomas Thomasov, Ewald Zelmer, and Alisher Sadik, interview with author, April 17, 2025.

"We decided from the beginning," Thomasov reflected, "we will not be German Foursquare or American Foursquare. We will be Jesus Foursquare."[40] This centering allowed a contextual church to emerge, globally connected yet locally owned, apostolic without being colonial.

Formation, Sending, and a Contextual Ecclesiology

Education became central to this process of maturation. Rather than importing rigid curricula, leaders adapted Discipleship and Leadership Training (DLT)[41] into a dialogical, relational model responsive to legal constraints and cultural plurality. "We're building leaders," Sadik explained, "not ticking boxes."[42] Formation unfolded slowly, allowing space for bivocational leaders, rural pastors, and first-generation believers to engage Scripture as lived theology rather than abstract system.

This approach proved both formative and apologetic. In a society shaped by Soviet secularism, Orthodox memory, Islamic pressure, and Western materialism, theological education functioned as cultural translation forming leaders capable of articulating a gospel that made sense in their context and could withstand scrutiny.

As the movement matured, it moved through the overlapping stages of initiating, nurturing, expanding, and sending. What began as scattered fellowships has become a self-governing, self-propagating, self-supporting, and self-theologizing church. Today, Foursquare Kazakhstan releases leaders across Central Asia and the Caucasus, embodying the logic of Antioch rather than dependency on outside control.

This ecclesiology is inherently liminal. Leaders navigate tensions between tradition and innovation, global connection and local ownership, institutional stability and apostolic movement. The *shanyrak* in the Foursquare logo captures this vision: a church rooted in Kazakh soil, open to heaven, and centered on Christ.

Foursquare Kazakhstan is not a denominational franchise. It is a contextual church—Spirit-born, Christ-centered, locally rooted, and globally engaged. As such, it offers a compelling witness to how the

40. Thomas Thomasov, Ewald Zelmer, and Alisher Sadik, interview with author, April 17, 2025.

41. Discipleship and Leadership Training is a global leadership formation program of the Global Council of the Foursquare Church.

42. Thomas Thomasov, Ewald Zelmer, and Alisher Sadik, interview with author, April 17, 2025.

gospel takes flesh in a particular place while bearing fruit far beyond it, revealing Christ not as a foreign presence but as Lord of all peoples and cultures.

A CHURCH THAT HAS LEARNED TO BELONG

The development of the Foursquare Church in Kazakhstan reveals a pattern of ecclesial life shaped not by institutional transfer or missionary efficiency, but by patient presence, theological humility, and Spirit-led emergence. In a land marked by imposed change, disrupted trust, and inherited trauma, the church has learned that credibility cannot be claimed; it must be earned through faithfulness over time. What has taken root in Kazakhstan is not a borrowed Christianity but a gospel that has learned to dwell.

This movement has been formed in liminal space—between Islam, Orthodoxy, and secularism, memory and hope, global connection and local ownership. Rather than resolving these tensions, Foursquare leaders have learned to inhabit them, allowing identity to emerge through shared discernment and lived obedience. In this sense, the church's story mirrors Paul's vision in Romans: a community not perfected in advance, but formed through mutual welcome, relational authority, and the slow work of reconciliation across difference.

Measured through the four stages of national church development, Foursquare Kazakhstan has moved from initiation through nurturing and expansion into sending. Yet this movement has not been linear or hurried. Each stage has been held together with the others, ensuring that growth in capacity did not outpace formation in character. Likewise, the four-self principles—self-governing, self-supporting, self-propagating, and self-theologizing—have not been imposed as benchmarks but cultivated as signs of maturing responsibility. What matters most is not advancement through stages, but the church's growing ability to bear the weight of its own life and mission.

The convergence of German and American apostolic partnerships, the leadership of indigenous pastors shaped by suffering and calling, and the commitment to contextual theology have together produced a church that is both rooted and mobile. Symbols such as the *shanyrak* do more than localize identity; they signal a deeper theological truth: Christ does not displace culture but redeems it. The gospel here is not translated merely in language, but in imagination, practice, and belonging.

The inclusion of women in leadership, the formation of leaders through dialogical training, and the emergence of missional networks rather than centralized control all testify to an ecclesiology shaped by the Spirit rather than by fear. In a context where religion has often been regulated, politicized, or instrumentalized, this posture is itself a form of witness.

Foursquare Kazakhstan now stands, not as a mission field but as a mission partner, no longer defined by what it has received but by what it is able to give. From a land once shaped by exile and coercion, a sending church has emerged, prepared to serve neighboring nations with the same humility, adaptability, and relational faithfulness through which it was formed.

The mission of God advances most faithfully when churches are allowed to become themselves. When the gospel is permitted to dwell deeply within a people's history, wounds, and hopes, it gives birth to communities capable of carrying Christ beyond themselves. In Kazakhstan, that work is still unfolding. Yet what has already emerged is unmistakably alive—a church that belongs, and from that belonging, is learning how to be sent.

30

National Church Development in Turkey

Modern-day Turkey occupies a foundational place in the story of Christianity. Situated at the crossroads of empire, culture, and theology, Anatolia functioned as a bridge between East and West in the apostolic and post-apostolic eras. The missionary journeys of Paul, the communities addressed in Revelation, the ecumenical councils of Nicaea and Chalcedon, and the theological witness of the Cappadocian fathers all locate the early formation of Christian mission and doctrine firmly within this land. Turkey was not a peripheral setting for Christianity's beginnings but one of its primary theaters.

This deep Christian inheritance was gradually eclipsed through conquest, Islamization, and centuries of shifting political power. What had once been a center of Christian life came to be widely regarded as resistant to the gospel. Yet in recent decades, Christianity has reemerged in unexpected ways. Small but resilient communities of faith have taken root again, bearing witness within a context marked by historical memory, religious complexity, and social constraint.

The Foursquare Church in Turkey offers a compelling case study of national church development under such conditions. Emerging in the 1990s from a single congregation, it has matured through the four stages of development into an indigenous movement that now sends missionaries beyond its own borders. This growth did not occur through rapid expansion or cultural leverage, but through constraint, patience, and deep formation. It unfolded within Turkey's complex religious landscape, shaped by biblical heritage, the enduring influence of Eastern Orthodox Christianity, and the long shadow of Islam, Ottoman rule, and modern secular nationalism.

Turkish believers today inhabit a liminal space, living between the cultural memory of a Christian past and the lived reality of a predominantly Islamic present. Rather than retreating from this tension or attempting to resolve it prematurely, they have learned to dwell within it. Their witness reflects a resilient, locally rooted expression of the gospel, demonstrating how indigenous leadership, patient formation, and Spirit-led mission can emerge even in environments long assumed to be inhospitable. Turkey's legacy as a cradle of Christian mission is being rearticulated in a new and vital form.

CHRISTIANITY IN MODERN TURKEY

The modern history of Christianity in Turkey cannot be understood apart from the traumatic collapse of the Ottoman world and the rise of Turkish nationalism in the late nineteenth and early twentieth centuries.[1] As the Ottoman Empire weakened, emerging ideologies of Pan-Turkism and ethno-religious homogenization increasingly framed Christian communities as internal threats to national cohesion. What followed was one of the darkest chapters in modern history: a sustained campaign of violence, deportation, and cultural erasure directed against Christian minorities in Anatolia.

Between 1894 and 1924, Armenian, Assyrian, and Greek Christian populations were systematically targeted through massacres, forced marches, starvation, and dispossession.[2] As documented in *The Thirty-Year Genocide*, historians Benny Morris and Dror Ze'evi demonstrate that these atrocities were not isolated episodes of wartime excess but part of an interconnected and prolonged process aimed at the removal of Christian presence from Anatolia.[3] The Armenian Genocide of 1915 stands as the most widely recognized moment within this period, yet it unfolded alongside parallel campaigns against Assyrian and Greek

1. Morris and Ze'evi, *Thirty-Year Genocide*, 15–43; Marlin, *Christian Persecutions in the Middle East*, 65.

2. González, *Story of Christianity*, 2:379.

3. Morris and Ze'evi, *Thirty-Year Genocide*.

communities during the Greco–Turkish War and the formative years of the Turkish Republic.[4]

The consequences were devastating and enduring. Once-vibrant Christian populations were reduced to remnants through death, exile, and forced migration. Churches, schools, monasteries, and cultural institutions were destroyed, confiscated, or repurposed. Survivors carried deep intergenerational trauma, while Christian life was pushed to the margins of public consciousness and national memory. Scholars and advocates have continued to call attention to this largely neglected history, noting that its unresolved legacy still shapes the social, political, and religious realities faced by Christians in Turkey today.[5]

Contemporary Christianity in Turkey reflects this fractured inheritance. The Christian population includes Greek Orthodox, Armenian Apostolic, Greek Catholic and Roman Catholic, and a small but growing Protestant presence, each with distinct histories, ecclesial structures, and degrees of public visibility. These differences complicate any comprehensive demographic analysis. Moreover, the Turkish state does not collect official data on religious affiliation, and religious identity remains a socially sensitive matter. Many Christians choose discretion or invisibility for reasons of safety, employment, and social belonging, further obscuring reliable measurement.

As a result, estimates vary widely. Most place Christians between 0.1 and 2.5 percent of Turkey's population. With more than 86 million citizens, this suggests a range from roughly 80,000 to 2 million Christians. The Joshua Project offers a commonly cited mid-range estimate of approximately 476,000 Christians, or about 0.6 percent of the population.[6] While such figures are imprecise, they nevertheless point to a community that is numerically small and socially vulnerable.

Perhaps more revealing than statistics is social visibility. Özbek and Melahouris note that only about 7 percent of Turks report ever having met a Christian.[7] This figure underscores not only the numerical marginality of the Christian community but also its profound social isolation. For many Turkish believers, faith is lived under the weight of historical memory, national identity, and cultural suspicion, where conversion is often perceived as a betrayal of family, culture, and nation.

4. Morris and Ze'evi, *Thirty-Year Genocide*, 244–62.
5. Gilbert, "Turkey's Christians Face Increasingly Dangerous Persecution."
6. Joshua Project, "Türkiye (Turkey)."
7. Özbek and Melahouris, *Fireflies at Midnight*, 44.

And yet, it is precisely within this constrained and contested space that the contemporary Turkish church bears witness. Its presence is generally quiet rather than public, relational rather than institutional, shaped by suffering, humility, and deep formation rather than by visibility or influence. For missionaries and church leaders, this history demands a posture of reverence rather than strategy, patience rather than speed, and a theology of the cross rather than triumphalism. Christianity in modern Turkey survives, not by cultural power or political protection but by faithfulness. In doing so, it offers a costly yet compelling testimony to the enduring power of the gospel amid loss, marginality, and hope deferred.

FOURSQUARE TURKEY'S FOUR-STAGE DEVELOPMENT

It is within Turkey's complex historical, cultural, and religious landscape that the Foursquare movement has taken root and matured. Since the early 1990s, Foursquare Turkey has progressed through each of the four stages of national church development and now stands as a fully recognized stage-four church. Its journey illustrates how patient formation, indigenous leadership, and translocal partnership can yield a resilient, mission-sending movement even within a highly resistant context. Rather than emerging through rapid expansion or institutional power, Foursquare Turkey developed slowly, shaped by constraint, vulnerability, and discernment.

Stage One: Initiate

The initiating stage of Foursquare Turkey began in the early 1990s with the planting of what was first known as the Independent Turkish Protestant Church of Ankara, later named Kurtuluş.[8] This initial congregation emerged through the efforts of three independent missionaries working alongside a growing core of Turkish believers. During this formative period, a Dutch couple, Sjoerd and Gerdeen Poorta, served the congregation

8. Much of the historical narrative that follows is recounted in İhsan Özbek and Helen Melahouris's *Fireflies at Midnight: A Historical Narrative of Kurtuluş and the Foursquare Work in Turkey*, which offers a firsthand account of the emergence of Kurtuluş Church and the broader Foursquare work in Turkey.

and later became connected to Foursquare when their sending church in the Netherlands joined the movement.

İhsan and Çiğdem Özbek emerged early as key indigenous leaders, serving from 1992, with İhsan elected pastor in 1996. On the day of his appointment, the church adopted the name Kurtuluş, a designation that providentially aligned with the surrounding neighborhood and carried the deeply resonant meaning of "salvation" in the Turkish language.[9] This early stage was marked by proclamation, gathering, and the fragile emergence of local leadership within a context still shaped by historical suspicion toward Christianity.

Connections with Foursquare deepened through invitations to Foursquare Netherlands conferences beginning in 1994, where relational bonds were formed with global leaders and the wider Foursquare family. By 1999, Kurtuluş formally joined Foursquare, marking the transition from isolated initiative to shared apostolic identity. Missionaries from Scotland, the United Kingdom, and FMI supported this stage but always alongside, rather than in place of, growing Turkish leadership.[10]

Stage Two: Nurture

As the church stabilized, attention shifted toward leadership formation and theological grounding. In 2003, the Filipus Ministry Training Program was established in Ankara as a one-year residential initiative integrating classroom instruction, hands-on ministry, and cross-cultural exposure. Filipus became a central mechanism for nurturing leaders during stage two and for preparing the transition into stage three.

Graduates of this season illustrate the fruit of deeply contextual formation: Soner Tufan through the development of Radio Shema; Vedat Özel, a Muslim-background believer whose Bible distribution ministry earned him the nickname "the Bible guy"; and Ibrahim Deveci, who now pastors independently. This stage prioritized depth over speed, focusing on discipleship, theological formation, leadership maturity, and communal unity rather than numerical expansion alone.

9. Özbek and Melahouris, *Fireflies at Midnight*, 90–91.

10. Özbek and Melahouris, *Fireflies at Midnight*, 171–79.

Stage Three: Expand

Expansion in Turkey unfolded under pressure rather than protection. Local leaders and congregations faced persistent threats, social hostility, and periodic violence. The Malatya murders in April 2007—when three Christians, including Turkish converts and a German missionary, were brutally tortured and killed—marked a watershed moment for the wider Christian community.[11] The perpetrators were later apprehended, tried, and convicted, revealing motivations shaped by nationalist sentiment and religious extremism.[12] For Foursquare leaders, including national leader İhsan Özbek, such threats have been enduring realities rather than isolated incidents.

And yet, expansion continued. By December 2023, Foursquare Turkey had grown to forty-nine churches, accompanied by ministries reflecting careful contextual discernment: refugee outreach among Arabic- and Farsi-speaking communities (ARM), ministries serving children with disabilities (Kardelen), and Radio Shema as a regional media voice. Growth during this stage did not signal triumphalism but resilience. The church became increasingly self-propagating and self-organizing while remaining relationally connected to its partners.

Stage Four: Extend

Foursquare Turkey now stands firmly in the sending stage. Beginning in 2019, Turkish believers were commissioned as missionaries to Central Asia, with churches established in Kyrgyzstan and Turkish-speaking fellowships emerging in Georgia and Iran. Exploratory relationships have since extended into Azerbaijan, Moldova, Kuwait, Iraq, Lebanon, and Syria, signaling a movement no longer defined solely by survival but by participation in God's mission beyond its borders.[13]

Alongside cross-border mission, Foursquare Turkey has embodied a theology of compassion through sustained disaster response. In partnership with Foursquare Disaster Relief, the church has served refugees, earthquake victims, and communities affected by regional crises. Mission

11. Blake, "Turkey Christian Missionaries."

12. Yackley, "Turkish Court."

13. Özbek, email message to author, December 28, 2023.

here extends beyond proclamation to embodied solidarity, reflecting a holistic understanding of witness shaped by suffering and service.

MISSIOLOGICAL INTEGRATION

Taken as a whole, the development of Foursquare Turkey reveals how mature Christian witness emerges when theological vision, missional structure, and lived context are held together rather than isolated from one another. The movement's growth cannot be explained by strategy, institutional replication, or external control, but by the sustained interplay of indigenous congregations and translocal mission partnerships, discerned within conditions of cultural constraint, historical trauma, and social marginalization. In Turkey, local churches have remained genuinely local, rooted in language, memory, and relational networks, while apostolic structures have remained genuinely supportive, offering accompaniment, connectivity, and adaptive capacity without displacing local authority. Foursquare Turkey demonstrates how these complementary frameworks—Ralph Winter's categories of modality and sodality, the dynamics of emergence and liminality, the four-self vision of indigenous church maturity, and the four stages of national church development—converge in practice, illuminating how a contextual, resilient, and mission-sending church has taken shape, not through dominance or design but through patient formation, relational trust, and Spirit-led discernment amid risk.

THE TWO STRUCTURES OF GOD'S REDEMPTIVE MISSION: MODALITY, SODALITY, AND EMERGENCE IN TURKEY

Foursquare Turkey illustrates how the two structures of God's redemptive mission, local congregations (modalities) and translocal mission structures (sodalities), can function in complementary rather than competitive ways. From its inception, the movement in Turkey has been shaped by the symbiotic interplay of indigenous congregations and apostolic mission partnerships. Relationships with Foursquare Netherlands, FMI, Foursquare Disaster Relief, and the MENACA Regional Council have contributed, not by imposing external control but by accompanying local leaders through presence, support, and shared discernment.[14]

This partnership has enabled a movement that is both rooted and reaching. Local churches have provided embodied presence, pastoral continuity, and cultural discernment—elements essential for faithfulness in a context marked by historical trauma and social suspicion. Mission agencies, in turn, have supplied apostolic initiative, translocal connectivity, and adaptive capacity, particularly in moments of crisis, expansion, and cross-border mission. Together, these two structures have formed a resilient ecosystem capable of sustaining life within Turkey while extending witness beyond its borders. The result is not imported uniformity but contextual vitality—a gospel movement shaped from within Turkish soil yet connected to the global body of Christ.

The development of Foursquare Turkey as an indigenous, mission-sending church reflects the dynamics described by emergence theory, in which coherence arises through relational networks, shared vulnerability, and adaptive leadership rather than through centralized design. Growth unfolded incrementally, often unpredictably, as local leaders responded faithfully to constraint, risk, and opportunity. What emerged was not the execution of a blueprint but the gradual formation of a living system capable of learning, adapting, and sending.

Liminality provides a further lens for understanding this process. Turkish believers inhabit an in-between space, neither aligned with the dominant religious order nor withdrawn from public life altogether. This liminal identity, shaped by historical rupture and contemporary marginalization, has required the church to relinquish expectations of cultural privilege or institutional power. Yet rather than paralyzing mission, this posture has become fertile ground for innovation, resilience, and faithful witness. Inhabiting liminality has enabled Turkish Christians to discern forms of presence, leadership, and proclamation appropriate to their context, even when visibility carries risk.

Within this liminal and emergent space, the interplay of modality and sodality has proven crucial. Local congregations alone could not have sustained theological formation, leadership development, or cross-border mission under such pressure. Likewise, mission agencies acting independently could not have generated authentic contextual expression

14. Özbek and Melahouris, *Fireflies at Midnight*, bears witness to the many faithful men and women who have contributed to the development of the Foursquare Church in Turkey.

or long-term credibility. Fruitfulness emerged precisely through their cooperation, where authority remained locally rooted and support remained relational rather than directive. This balance prevented dependency on the one hand and isolation on the other, allowing the church to mature with integrity.

Over time, Foursquare Turkey progressed through the four stages of national church development: initiating gospel presence among the unreached, nurturing disciples and leaders through deep formation, expanding through church planting and media outreach under constraint, and extending mission across borders. Today, with forty-nine churches and a growing portfolio of ministries serving Arabic-, Persian-, and Central Asian–speaking communities, Foursquare Turkey has become a shaping influence within the wider MENACA region. Its capacity to send missionaries, respond to humanitarian crises, and accompany neighboring contexts reflects a level of maturity forged through patience rather than power.

Theologically, this journey resonates with Paul's vision in Romans of a Spirit-led community learning to discern faithfulness amid cultural complexity. The church in Turkey has not sought legitimacy through dominance or assimilation but through embodied obedience shaped by suffering, hope, and communal discernment. Foursquare Turkey offers more than a successful case study; it provides a living model of how God's redemptive mission unfolds through the complementary dynamics of modality and sodality, liminality and emergence, to form churches that are at once contextual, resilient, and outward-facing, even in environments marked by resistance and risk.

CONTEXTUALIZING THE GOSPEL IN TURKEY

Contextualization cannot remain a theoretical construct; it must take embodied form in the structures, leadership patterns, and ministries of the local church. In Turkey, where Christian faith is lived under the weight of historical rupture, social marginalization, and religious suspicion, contextualization is not a strategic preference but a theological necessity. Foursquare Turkey offers an example of this embodied approach. From its emergence in the 1990s, the movement prioritized indigenous leadership development and patient formation, most notably through the establishment of the Filipus Ministry Training Center. Alongside this commitment to leadership formation, ministries such as Radio Shema, refugee outreach, and care for children with disabilities demonstrate a holistic expression of the gospel within Turkish society. Here, contextualization is not confined to language or symbolism; it shapes the full life of the church.

Cultural Memory and Local Meaning

Foursquare Turkey has drawn carefully on Turkey's deep Christian heritage, reclaiming Anatolia's memory as a cradle of early Christianity without romanticizing the past or minimizing historical trauma. The naming of the church Kurtuluş ("Salvation") functions as a culturally intelligible and theologically rich contact point, grounding the gospel in the Turkish language and imagination. Such choices demonstrate how biblical meaning can be communicated through forms that resonate deeply within local culture, allowing the gospel to be heard not as a foreign import, but as both ancient and present. In this way, contextualization becomes an act of translation shaped by humility and historical awareness rather than cultural assertion.

Liminality, Trauma, and Formation

Contextualization in Turkey must reckon honestly with history. Centuries of Christian marginalization, nationalist ideology, and Islamic dominance have produced a complex and often painful socioreligious landscape. Foursquare Turkey has not attempted to bypass these realities, nor has it sought to resolve them prematurely. Turkish believers inhabit a liminal space, standing between a suppressed Christian past and a dominant Islamic present. Rather than retreating or capitulating, they have learned to dwell within this tension.

This liminal posture has become a place of formation. It has shaped a church that relinquishes expectations of cultural privilege and instead cultivates resilience, discernment, and hope. Witness in such a context is necessarily modest, relational, and patient, yet no less faithful. By acknowledging historical trauma while bearing courageous testimony in the present, Foursquare Turkey models a form of contextualization that is both realistic about loss and confident in the gospel's power to give life amid constraint.

Local Ownership and Missional Partnership

Healthy contextualization also requires resisting cultural imperialism and dependency. Foursquare Turkey has modeled this through its partnerships with translocal mission structures such as FMI and Foursquare Netherlands. These sodalities have offered training, resources, and relational accompaniment without displacing indigenous leadership or imposing external agendas. Authority, discernment, and theological reflection have remained firmly in Turkish hands.

Such partnership reflects a mature missiology in which local ownership and global connection are held together. Rather than weakening contextual integrity, these relationships have strengthened it, providing support without control and accountability without domination. The result is a genuinely local expression of Foursquare Christianity, globally connected yet locally governed, shaped by mutual trust rather than dependency.

Compassion as Contextual Witness

Contextual mission must also respond to lived realities. In Turkey, this has meant engaging the wounds and vulnerabilities of society through concrete acts of care. Foursquare Turkey's ministries among refugees, people with disabilities, and victims of natural disasters demonstrate a gospel that integrates proclamation and presence. Compassionate action is not treated as ancillary to mission but as integral to it, reflecting a theology in which care for the vulnerable is a faithful expression of the reign of God.

Such responsiveness embodies a missiology that takes seriously the social and physical dimensions of human life. By addressing suffering without instrumentalizing it, the church bears witness to Christ through solidarity, service, and shared humanity.

FAITHFULNESS, MATURITY, AND MISSION

Throughout its development, Foursquare Turkey has maintained fidelity to the core claims of the gospel while adapting its forms and structures to Turkish realities. This balance between theological integrity and cultural attentiveness marks healthy contextualization. The fruit of this faithfulness is visible not only in mature local congregations but also in Turkish disciples now carrying the gospel beyond their own borders, contextualizing it anew in other cultural settings.

Foursquare Turkey's journey embodies with the Four-Stage Model of national church development. From pioneering witness (Stage One) to deep formation and leadership development (Stage Two), to resilient expansion under constraint (Stage Three), and finally to cross-border mission and compassionate service (Stage Four), the movement has matured with discernment and intentionality. Its story demonstrates that contextualization, when rooted in Scripture, shaped by local leadership, attentive to historical and social realities, and sustained through healthy partnership, can produce a resilient and missionally fruitful church.

In a global context where mission increasingly unfolds amid cultural complexity and historical tension, Foursquare Turkey offers a living model of Spirit-led, biblically grounded, and culturally attentive ministry. It provides not a formula to replicate, but a pattern to discern—one that invites churches and mission movements to attend carefully to place, history, and people as they participate faithfully in the mission of God.

MISSION AT THE THRESHOLD

The story of Foursquare Turkey reveals that national church development is primarily a matter of relationships and faithfulness cultivated over time. In a land layered with Christian memory and marked by profound rupture, the reemergence of an indigenous, mission-sending church testifies to the Spirit's quiet persistence. Against a backdrop of persecution, social marginalization, and legal constraint, Turkish believers have learned to inhabit liminality rather than escape it, allowing the gospel to take shape within tension rather than triumph. What has emerged is a contextual church shaped by Scripture, history, suffering, and hope.

Foursquare Turkey's journey through the four stages of national church development demonstrates how patient formation, indigenous leadership, and translocal partnership can converge without collapsing into dependency or control. The movement's embodiment of the four-self principles shows that self-governing, self-supporting, self-propagating, and self-theologizing churches are not abstract ideals, but lived realities forged through trust, discipline, and shared discernment. The complementary interplay of modality and sodality has allowed the church to remain both rooted and reaching—grounded in Turkish soil while extending its witness beyond national borders.

For mission practitioners, Turkey offers a sobering and hopeful lesson. Faithful mission here has required humility rather than visibility, presence rather than power, and endurance rather than immediacy. Growth has not been measured by cultural influence or institutional security, but by depth of formation, resilience under pressure, and willingness to serve beyond one's own survival. Yet it is precisely through these constraints that a mature and faithful witness has taken shape.

Foursquare Turkey is a reminder that the gospel does not depend on cultural dominance to flourish. Instead, it takes root wherever the Spirit forms a people willing to dwell faithfully at the threshold, between memory and hope, loss and promise, rootedness and sending. In such places, the church learns anew that mission is the obedience of a community shaped by the cross and animated by the Spirit, bearing witness to Christ as Lord in the midst of its own story.

The story of Foursquare Turkey is deliberately particular, shaped by a distinct history, cultural pressures, and relational pathways that cannot be replicated elsewhere. Yet precisely in its specificity, the Turkey case illuminates patterns that extend beyond a single national context. The dynamics of patient formation, indigenous leadership, liminality, and translocal partnership observed here are recurring features of national church development in regions marked by historical disruption, religious complexity, and constrained public space.

As the focus now widens beyond Turkey, the question shifts from what happened in one place to what can be discerned across many. The following chapter draws together insights from national church development across Egypt, Romania, Kazakhstan, and Turkey, nations marked by extraordinary diversity yet shaped by common missional pressures such as minority Christian presence, contested identities, and the need for deep formation over rapid expansion.

31

Insights from National Church Development in MENACA and Europe

THE PRECEDING CASE STUDIES tell distinct stories, each shaped by its own history, political realities, and religious landscape. In one setting, churches take shape within Muslim-majority societies marked by regulation, suspicion, and constrained public space. In another, they emerge from the long shadow of Soviet oppression, carrying both the wounds and the adaptive instincts formed under enforced ideological control. Elsewhere, European churches navigate the layered aftershocks of Communism, Orthodoxy, and accelerating secularization. Taken on their own terms, these narratives resist easy comparison. They feel particular, localized, and irreducible.

Yet when these stories are read side by side, a different picture begins to surface. Without collapsing their differences, the cases begin to echo one another. What emerges is a theology of how the Spirit forms faithful, resilient, and indigenous churches amid constraint, complexity, and historical fracture. Growth in these contexts is rarely linear or predictable. It unfolds slowly, through patient formation, contested identity, and hard-won relational trust, rather than through speed, scale, or cultural leverage. The churches that take shape are not uniform in structure or expression, but they share a common posture: faithfulness under pressure and maturity forged through lived obedience.

Importantly, these insights do not flatten difference or erase contextual distinctiveness. On the contrary, they depend upon it. The aim of this synthesis is not to collapse diverse histories into a single story, but to attend carefully to the recurring dynamics through which national church development unfolds across MENACA and Europe today. By holding convergence and divergence together, this chapter seeks to discern patterns without prescribing outcomes, offering interpretive clarity rather than replicable models.

The case studies invite a recalibration of expectations, particularly for mission practitioners, church leaders, and scholars working in a post-Christendom, post-imperial world. The insights that follow are not offered as best practices to be adopted wholesale, but as theological markers that help orient discernment: signs of where the Spirit tends to bring life, how communities are formed under constraint, and what kinds of partnerships and practices sustain indigenous movements over time.

HISTORICAL CONSCIOUSNESS AS MISSIONAL DISCIPLINE

Across all the contexts examined, faithful mission begins with serious attentiveness to history, not as a preliminary survey, but as an ongoing discipline of discernment. In Turkey, Christian witness unfolds in the long shadow of genocide, forced erasure, and the consolidation of Islamic nationalism, where memory itself remains contested and public Christianity is marked by suspicion. In Kazakhstan, the gospel is received through overlapping layers of Eastern Christian memory, Russian imperial expansion, and the deep trauma of Soviet atheism, all of which shape contemporary attitudes toward authority, belief, and institutional religion. In Egypt, Christian witness emerges within an ancient Coptic inheritance that embodies extraordinary resilience, yet operates under Islamic governance and social constraint. In Romania, Orthodoxy's fusion with national identity, the corrosive legacy of Communist repression, and the unresolved wounds of Roma enslavement and exclusion shape every encounter with faith, belonging, and trust.

These histories are not inert background conditions; they are formative forces that continue to structure imagination, fear, hope, and expectation. They shape how authority is perceived, how communities respond to risk, and how the gospel itself is heard, whether as promise, threat, or recovery of what was lost. Mission that ignores these forces risks neglecting patterns of coercion, erasure, or triumphalism that have already inflicted deep harm. By contrast, mission that attends carefully to history learns when to speak, when to listen, and when silence itself is an act of faithfulness.

Historical consciousness functions as a missional discipline. Like Paul addressing the church in Rome, missionaries must learn to exegete not only Scripture but also memory, to discern how past wounds, unresolved trauma, and inherited narratives shape present realities. Paul's gospel does not bypass Israel's history, Rome's power, or the fractures within the community; it speaks directly into them, naming sin, suffering, and hope without denial or despair. Likewise, contextual theology emerges where the gospel speaks truthfully to inherited wounds, disrupted trust, and contested identities, not by overwriting history, but by redeeming it.

Across MENACA and Europe, these case studies demonstrate that national church development is sustained not by historical amnesia, but by historical honesty. Where memory is acknowledged rather than suppressed, communities gain the freedom to imagine a future no longer captive to the past. In such settings, the gospel is heard not as a foreign imposition or ideological threat but as good news capable of naming loss, restoring dignity, and forming new patterns of life marked by reconciliation and hope.

CONTEXTUALIZATION AS THEOLOGICAL FIDELITY

Across the case studies, contextualization consistently emerges not as cultural accommodation or pragmatic adjustment, but as an act of theological obedience.[1] The gospel does not arrive as a disembodied message or a transferable system; it comes as good news that takes flesh within particular social worlds. As with the incarnation itself, the movement of the gospel is always from the universal to the particular, from confession to embodied life. Faithful mission therefore requires more than cultural sensitivity; it demands disciplined attentiveness to how the gospel is heard, lived, and confessed within concrete historical and cultural realities.

In Turkey, contextualization unfolds within honor–shame dynamics where public identity, family loyalty, and social perception carry profound weight. Conversion is never merely personal; it reverberates through kinship networks and communal memory. In Kazakhstan, the gospel encounters a nomadic imagination shaped by movement,

1. Plummer and Terry, *Paul's Missionary Methods*, 170.

resilience, and suspicion of imposed authority, requiring forms of church life that privilege relational trust over institutional control. In Egypt, mission takes shape through dense relational networks marked by hospitality, discretion, and long-term presence, where credibility precedes proclamation. In Romania, decades of totalitarian control and religious compromise have produced deep mistrust of institutions, requiring ecclesial expressions that emphasize authenticity, proximity, and patience rather than visibility or scale. In each context, contextualization emerges as disciplined incarnation, the careful translation of the gospel into forms capable of being received as truthful and trustworthy.

Such contextualization requires holding together theological integrity and cultural intelligibility. The gospel remains one, rooted in the confession of Jesus Christ as Lord, yet it is infinitely translatable without being infinitely malleable. Faithful contextualization neither dilutes the gospel to avoid offense nor rigidly preserves inherited forms that obscure its meaning. Instead, it discerns which elements of Christian life are essential and which are contingent, allowing the substance of the faith to be expressed through local language, symbols, leadership patterns, and communal practices.

Where this balance is maintained, churches mature without losing their distinctiveness or surrendering their confession. Indigenous leadership emerges with confidence rather than dependency. Communities develop practices that resonate deeply with local culture while remaining anchored in Scripture and the historic faith. Contextualization becomes a safeguard of orthodoxy rather than a threat to it. By taking culture seriously, the church protects the gospel from becoming captive to foreign assumptions or colonial patterns, allowing Christ to be confessed, not as an imported authority but as Lord within the lived reality of each people.

Across MENACA and Europe, these case studies affirm that contextualization is not optional to mission, nor is it a concession to modernity. It is the means by which the gospel remains faithful to its own logic: the Word made flesh, dwelling among a particular people, in a particular place, at a particular moment in history.

FORMATION PRECEDES STRUCTURE

Across every context examined, ecclesial life consistently emerges relationally before it becomes institutionally legible. Leaders are formed long before titles are assigned. Communities gather, pray, and practice shared obedience before they recognize themselves as churches. Discipleship precedes governance, and belonging precedes organization. This sequence is not accidental; it reflects the organic way in which Christian community takes shape when the gospel is allowed to generate life from within rather than being imposed from without.

This pattern is especially visible among Roma communities in Romania, where churches have emerged through kinship networks, shared suffering, and trusted leadership rather than formal planning. It appears in Turkey, where home fellowships and relational gatherings provided safe spaces for faith to take root long before institutional structures could be named or protected. In Egypt, emerging networks of believers and leaders are likewise forming through patient relationships and shared practices of prayer, hospitality, and discernment, often without public recognition or formal affiliation. In each case, ecclesial life precedes ecclesial clarity.

This sequence mirrors the New Testament witness. In the early church, communities were formed through proclamation and shared life before offices were formalized and governance structures articulated. Paul's letters address living communities already shaped by the Spirit, not abstract institutions awaiting activation. Leadership emerges as a gift recognized by the community, not as a credential conferred from above. Structure, when it comes, serves life; it does not generate it.

The case studies demonstrate the danger of reversing this order. Structure introduced too early tends to constrain life, fixing forms before relationships have matured and importing expectations before trust has been established. In contexts marked by historical trauma, institutional mistrust, or social vulnerability, premature structure often replicates the very dynamics of control and surveillance that have already wounded communities. By contrast, when structure follows formation, it functions as trellis rather than cage, supporting growth without restricting it.

National church development therefore unfolds at the speed of trust rather than the pace of strategy. Trust is built slowly through shared suffering, faithful presence, and consistent integrity.[2] It cannot be accelerated without cost. Yet where trust is patiently cultivated, communities gain the capacity to sustain leadership, navigate conflict, and extend mission beyond themselves. Formation-first ecclesiology produces churches

2. Plummer and Terry, *Paul's Missionary Methods*, 59; Allen, *Missionary Methods*, 110–11.

that are not only viable, but resilient, capable of maturing into self-governing, self-propagating, and mission-sending communities precisely because their life together has been forged relationally before it was ever formalized.

MODALITY–SODALITY INTERDEPENDENCE

Ralph Winter's modality–sodality paradigm is consistently affirmed across the case studies, not as an abstract framework imposed after the fact, but as an explanatory lens for how healthy mission actually unfolds. National church development flourishes where local congregations (modalities) retain genuine authority, cultural credibility, and responsibility for communal life, while translocal mission structures (sodalities) provide catalytic support through apostolic ministry, theological training, leadership development, relational accountability, and transregional connectivity. When these two structures function in mutual dependence rather than competition, the conditions for sustainable, indigenous movements are created.

In Turkey and Kazakhstan, this interdependence has matured over time and now expresses itself in outward sending. Local churches govern and theologize from within their own contexts, while sodalities such as FMI, regional councils, and Bible institutes extend the church's capacity to train leaders, respond to crisis, and participate in mission beyond national borders. Crucially, these sodalities have not replaced or overridden local authority, but have served it, strengthening what is already emerging rather than redirecting it.

In Egypt and Romania, the relationship between modality and sodality is still being negotiated, yet its necessity is increasingly evident. Early missteps in both contexts reveal the cost of imbalance—where sodalities move too quickly or define outcomes prematurely, dependency and fragility result; where modalities attempt to develop in isolation, leaders lack the training, protection, and translocal perspective needed for long-term resilience. In such settings, the question is not whether sodalities are needed, but how they can function relationally, patiently, and in ways that honor local discernment.

Across all contexts, a consistent pattern emerges. Where modalities and sodalities collaborate relationally rather than hierarchically, indigenous leadership flourishes, trust deepens, and movements mature organically. Where either structure dominates, whether through external control or internal isolation, mission is distorted, producing either dependency or fragmentation. Faithful partnership, therefore, requires humility on both sides: Sodalities must resist the temptation to manage outcomes, and modalities must remain open to accompaniment, correction, and shared mission. When held together in Spirit-led interdependence, these two structures become, not competing systems but complementary expressions of the one mission of God.

LIMINALITY AND EMERGENCE AS NORMATIVE CONDITIONS

Across MENACA and Europe, churches are forming in liminal spaces—between repression and freedom, inherited tradition and rising secularism, social belonging and persistent marginalization. These in-between conditions are not transitional anomalies on the way to stability; they are the normal environment in which contemporary mission now unfolds. Rather than signaling failure or immaturity, liminality has become a defining context for ecclesial life in regions shaped by historical rupture, political volatility, and cultural fragmentation.

In such settings, the church cannot rely on inherited privilege, institutional authority, or cultural alignment to secure its place. Identity, legitimacy, and continuity must be discerned rather than assumed. Liminality strips away illusions of control and exposes the church to vulnerability, yet it also creates space for attentiveness, innovation, and dependence on the Spirit. Within these thresholds, communities learn to listen more carefully, hold identity more humbly, and practice faith with greater intentionality. What appears fragile from the outside often proves resilient from within.

It is precisely within these liminal conditions that new ecclesial forms emerge, often from the margins rather than the center. Roma-led churches in Romania arise through kinship networks and shared suffering rather than formal planning. Diaspora-shaped ministries transform displacement into intercultural mission, reframing loss as vocation. Trauma-informed communities in contexts such as Kazakhstan, Romania, and Egypt embody a gospel that names pain honestly while cultivating hope patiently. In each case, ecclesial life emerges through shared vulnerability, trusted relationships, and lived obedience rather than through institutional control or centralized design.

Here, emergence theory provides language for what strategy alone cannot explain. Coherence develops over time through relational density, adaptive leadership, and mutual trust rather than through linear planning or top-down implementation. Leadership arises organically as communities recognize gifts already at work among them. Structure follows life, adjusting as needed to sustain what the Spirit is bringing forth. What emerges is not disorder, but a different kind of order, one that is responsive rather than rigid, relational rather than managerial.

Taken together, these case studies suggest that liminality and emergence are not temporary conditions to be resolved, but enduring features of mission in a post-Christendom, post-imperial world. The church is increasingly called to live at the threshold, bearing witness without dominance and forming community without certainty of outcome. In such spaces, faithfulness is measured less by control or predictability than by attentiveness to the Spirit's work unfolding quietly over time. Where the church embraces liminality rather than resisting it, emergence becomes not a threat to mission, but one of its most generative gifts.

INCLUSION AS MISSIONAL OBEDIENCE

A striking convergence across the case studies is the centrality of inclusion—particularly the intentional empowerment of women and the full recognition of historically marginalized peoples as leaders, theologians, and agents of mission. Where women are affirmed and authorized to lead, teach, and govern, movements gain depth, resilience, and intergenerational sustainability. Where Roma leaders are entrusted with genuine authority rather than treated merely as recipients of ministry or objects of compassion, ecclesial life multiplies with remarkable vitality. In these contexts, inclusion is not an added feature of mission; it is one of its defining marks.

These patterns are not driven by sociological trends or external pressures, but by theological conviction. Pentecost itself establishes inclusion as a foundational expression of the Spirit's work, as the outpouring of the Spirit disrupts inherited hierarchies and authorizes sons and daughters alike to speak, lead, and bear witness (Acts 2). This same Spirit continues to call forth gifts from the margins, not as exceptions to the rule but as integral participants in God's redemptive mission. To restrict leadership on the basis of gender, ethnicity, or social status is more than unjust; it is a failure to recognize the Spirit's activity already at work within the body of Christ.

The case studies reveal that inclusion functions as a missional accelerant precisely because it aligns authority with calling. In Kazakhstan, where four of the thirty-five Foursquare churches are led by women and nearly a third of Bible Institute students are female, gender inclusion is framed not as cultural accommodation but as obedience to the Spirit. As one leader succinctly put it, "If we limit women, we limit the gospel." In Romania, the emergence of Roma-led churches challenges inherited ecclesial hierarchies and exposes the limits of inclusion without empowerment. In Turkey and Egypt, where visibility carries risk, inclusive leadership fosters shared responsibility and resilience, ensuring that mission does not depend on a narrow circle of authorized actors.

At stake here is not representation alone, but ecclesial integrity. Churches that welcome marginalized peoples without releasing them to govern, teach, and send ultimately reinforce dependency rather than dignity. By contrast, movements that entrust leadership to those historically excluded embody the gospel's reconciling logic, in which belonging precedes respectability and vocation precedes status. Such practices reflect not accommodation to modern sensibilities, but obedience to the Spirit who forms a people reconciled across gender, ethnicity, and social division.

Inclusion is not ancillary to mission, nor is it a strategy for growth. It is a test of faithfulness. Where inclusion is embraced as missional obedience, the church bears witness to the kingdom of God as a present reality, a community in which the gifts of the Spirit are recognized wherever they appear and entrusted for the sake of God's mission in the world.

TOWARD A HOLISTIC VISION OF NATIONAL CHURCH DEVELOPMENT

Taken together, these insights reveal that national church development depends far less on the exportation of models than on the cultivation of conditions in which ecclesial life can emerge, mature, and be released for mission. Across MENACA and Europe, faithful movements arise where history is honored rather than ignored, where formation is prioritized over visibility, where leadership emerges from within the community, where structures remain adaptive and responsive to life, and where partnership is practiced with humility rather than control. These conditions cannot be engineered through strategy alone; they must be patiently nurtured through discernment, trust, and long-term presence.

This holistic vision challenges inherited assumptions about how churches grow and how mission succeeds. In many contexts examined, progress has not followed linear trajectories or measurable benchmarks. Instead, development has been uneven, slow, and often hidden from view. Yet beneath this apparent fragility, the Spirit has been forming communities marked by depth, resilience, and missional readiness. National churches mature not by accelerating through stages, but by dwelling faithfully within them, allowing each season to do its formative work.

Across MENACA and Europe, the Spirit is forming churches through patient obedience at the margins of social and political influence. These churches learn to live without the protections of cultural privilege, relying instead on relational trust, shared vulnerability, and theological clarity forged under pressure. In such settings, faithfulness is measured less by numerical growth or public recognition than by the capacity to endure, to reconcile, and to send.

Crucially, this vision affirms that maturity does not require uniformity. The goal of national church development is not the replication of inherited ecclesial forms, but the emergence of churches that are fully themselves, rooted in their own histories, languages, and social realities; reconciled in communities that embody the gospel across lines of division; and released for mission beyond their own survival. When churches reach this stage of maturity, they are no longer defined primarily by what they have received, but by what they are able to give.

This holistic vision also reframes the task of mission agencies, sending churches, and global partnerships. Their role is not to manage outcomes or impose timelines, but to accompany emerging movements with patience, theological depth, and trust in the Spirit's work. Where such accompaniment is practiced, national churches gain the freedom to discern their own callings, develop their own leaders, and participate fully in the mission of God among the nations.

National church development is not a technical process but a spiritual journey, one that unfolds through obedience, suffering, hope, and shared discernment. The case studies across MENACA and Europe offer, not a blueprint to replicate but a vision to inhabit: a church formed by the

Spirit, faithful in context, and prepared to bear witness from the margins to the ends of the earth.

DISCERNMENT AT THE EDGES OF THE CHURCH

The insights drawn from national church development across MENACA and Europe converge around a shared recognition: faithful mission in the present moment requires discernment rather than duplication. The Spirit is not reproducing identical ecclesial forms across cultures but cultivating distinctive communities shaped by history, constraint, and local agency. What unites these movements is not uniformity of structure or speed of growth but a common orientation toward faithfulness forged under pressure.

Across these contexts, the church is learning again how to live without cultural privilege, institutional certainty, or guaranteed outcomes. History must be honored rather than bypassed. Formation must precede structure. Leadership must emerge from within communities rather than be imposed upon them. Partnerships must be relational rather than transactional. Liminality must be inhabited rather than resolved. Inclusion must be embraced as obedience rather than concession. Together, these dynamics reveal a missiology shaped less by mastery and more by trust in the Spirit's patient work.

What emerges from this comparative study is a posture to be cultivated. National church development flourishes where the church attends carefully to place, memory, and people, where it listens before it speaks, accompanies before it directs, and releases before it controls. In such settings, the gospel takes embodied form in communities reconciled across difference and released for mission beyond their own survival.

These churches are being formed at the edges—edges of power, visibility, and predictability. Yet it is precisely there that the Spirit is giving shape to resilient, indigenous, and mission-sending movements. Their witness suggests that the future of global mission will not be secured by reclaiming dominance or refining technique, but by learning again how to be the church in humility, courage, and hope.

A LEGACY RECLAIMED: THE SPIRIT OF THE FOURSQUARE GOSPEL

This vision is not new. It is woven into the spiritual DNA of the Foursquare movement from its beginning. After the death of her husband, Aimee Semple McPherson returned to the United States as a twenty-year-old widow and single mother. Yet she never lost the missionary fire that had shaped her life and ministry. Her life and ministry embodied the synergy between local church and apostolic mission that continues to guide Foursquare today as a gathered church and a sent people. Writing in October 1927, she declared,

> Angelus Temple is opening one of the mightiest missionary enterprises that has ever been started. Nothing short of establishing missionaries and mission stations in every land and among every kindred, tribe, and tongue, will satisfy these earnest, enthusiastic, and consecrated followers of the Foursquare Gospel. "The field is the world," is their motto, and "Around the world with the Foursquare Gospel" is their slogan. The spirit of the Foursquare Gospel is that of a true pioneer.[3]

At the time, such words may have sounded like evangelistic hyperbole. Yet a century later, history has borne witness to their substance. What began as a single church with a global vision has become a global church with a single vision to disciples of all nations.

The pioneer spirit McPherson named has not faded; it has taken flesh in indigenous leadership, contextual theology, and translocal partnership. The field remains the world, but the workers are no longer merely sent *to* the nations. They are rising *from* the nations, rooted in their own soil, bound together in shared mission, and sent as one.

The insights gathered in this book point toward a deeper question beneath questions of strategy and structure: *What kind of church is the gospel forming for the sake of God's mission today?* To answer this question requires theological synthesis and vocational clarity.

The final chapter returns explicitly to Paul's Letter to the Romans as the interpretive center of this study. From the beginning, Romans has functioned as a missional script, shaping how partnership is imagined, how formation is understood, and how participation in the mission of God is lived. What the case studies have revealed in practice, Romans

3. Van Cleave, *Vine and the Branches*, 10.

now names theologically: a Spirit-formed community learning to live as both gathered and sent, rooted in place yet reaching outward, faithful within local constraints while oriented toward the nations.

The final chapter draws these threads together into a constructive vision for the church at a moment of profound global transition. It asks how the church might move from fragmented support toward genuine co-laboring, from institutional maintenance toward apostolic imagination, and from inherited assumptions toward Spirit-led obedience. In returning to Romans, the argument comes full circle, not to offer a new strategy, but to recover a vocation. The invitation is not simply to understand the mission of God more clearly, but to become more fully the people God is forming for that mission.

32

Becoming Who We Are

THIS BOOK BEGAN WITH a deceptively simple question: *How can Paul's Letter to the Romans inform the development of transformative and mutually beneficial partnerships between churches and missions that advance the mission of God?* Over the course of this study, it has become clear that this question is not finally about strategy, structure, or efficiency. It is a question about the identity and vocation of the church itself.

Romans reforms the church in such a way that mission becomes inevitable. Paul writes as an apostle shaped by a missional horizon. The gospel he proclaims is meant to be embodied, forming a reconciled, Spirit-led community capable of participating together in God's redemptive purposes among the nations. Theology in Romans is vocational rather than abstract. The church is called to live out the gospel in order to get out the gospel.

Throughout this study, biblical exegesis, organizational theory, and contextual missiology have been brought into sustained conversation. Across diverse settings—Turkey, Kazakhstan, Egypt, Romania, and the wider regions of Europe and the Middle East—distinct histories, political realities, and religious landscapes were examined. Each context revealed its own constellation of pressures: state regulation, religious marginalization, post-Communist fracture, diaspora displacement, and the lingering weight of imperial and colonial memory. Yet when these narratives are read together, a shared pattern emerges. The church becomes most faithful, resilient, and generative, not when it retreats into preservation or accelerates toward expansion but when it learns again to inhabit its calling as a people both gathered and sent.

These dynamics are not theoretical. They are visible in the lived experience of churches and mission partnerships across these regions. In contexts marked by constraint rather than cultural dominance, communities have learned to prioritize formation, relational trust, and local leadership development. In post-Communist and post-Christendom settings, churches have been forced to reckon with inherited ecclesial forms while discerning new expressions of witness amid generational and social transition. In each case, fruitfulness is measured less by speed or scale than by the capacity of local believers to govern themselves faithfully, interpret the gospel within their own cultural worlds, and extend that gospel beyond themselves.

One of the central insights to surface repeatedly is the necessity of *creative tension* within the life of the church. Mission does not flourish in the absence of tension, but in its proper calibration. When the church neglects its gathered life, mission becomes thin, disconnected, and unsustainable. When it neglects its sent vocation, faithfulness collapses into maintenance. The problem is not that these tensions exist, but that they are too often denied, overcorrected, or structurally misaligned.

This tension becomes especially visible in the relationship between local churches and translocal mission movements. The case studies demonstrate that mature ecclesial life does not arise from choosing one over the other but from cultivating their interdependence. Where rooted communities and apostolic initiatives learn to co-labor rather than compete, the church becomes both deeply formed and dynamically sent. This is a recovery of the apostolic pattern evident in Paul's own ministry and embedded within the architecture of Romans itself.

Several of the partnerships examined in this study offer concrete illustrations of this reality. In recent years, intentional efforts to foster closer collaboration between local and regional churches and global mission leaders have created spaces of shared learning and mutual transformation. These partnerships did not emerge primarily as funding mechanisms or strategic alignments, but as relational commitments shaped by sustained presence, listening, and trust. As local church leaders engaged the lived realities of global mission contexts, mission ceased to function as an abstract obligation and became a shared vocation. At the same time, missionaries and national leaders encountered not distant benefactors but companions whose own faith and ecclesial imagination were being reshaped through participation in God's work beyond their immediate context.

These partnerships revealed both the fragility and the promise of ecclesial co-laboring. They exposed inherited assumptions about control, ownership, and success while also demonstrating how shared mission can re-form identity. When churches and mission movements remained relationally connected over time, both were changed. Local congregations discovered that their own formation deepened through global engagement, while mission leaders found renewed grounding through sustained partnership with sending communities. In this mutual exchange, the church began to function less as a collection of discrete entities and more as a shared body participating together in God's mission.

Romans functions throughout this study, not only as theological foundation but as a *missional script*. Paul presents the gospel as God's decisive action in history: God's righteousness revealed, Christ's reconciling work accomplished, and the Spirit poured out to form a people drawn from every nation. God is the primary actor, Christ is the climactic revelation, and the Spirit directs the ongoing performance in and through the church. Paul's exhortations in Romans do not simply call for moral improvement or institutional alignment. They summon the church to step into this drama through embodied obedience, mutual service, and shared mission.

Faith, in Romans, becomes a form of participation. The fractured churches of Rome are summoned to become a Spirit-formed ensemble capable of bearing witness together across ethnic, cultural, economic, and social divides. Unity is not pursued for its own sake, nor enforced through uniformity. It is cultivated for the sake of the gospel's credibility and reach. A reconciled church becomes the means by which the reconciling God is made known.

When viewed through the lenses of liminality and emergence, the present moment of the global church appears, not as decline but as reconfiguration. New expressions of mission are emerging, not at the center of inherited institutional power but in the spaces between structures, cultures, and traditions. These liminal spaces, often marked by uncertainty, mobility, and relational dependence, have proven to be fertile ground for the Spirit's work. Across Europe and the Middle East, diaspora communities, marginalized leaders, and post-institutional networks are forming resilient expressions of church life shaped more by trust than control, more by shared discernment than centralized authority.

Across the case studies, the developmental rhythms of church life become visible. Movements mature as local believers assume responsibility for leadership, theological reflection, material sustainability, and outward witness. Fruitfulness is measured, not primarily by numerical expansion but by the capacity of communities to endure pressure, sustain unity across difference, and release leaders for mission beyond themselves. In this way, the church becomes not only indigenous but missionary.

Taken together, these insights point toward a necessary reorientation of the church's missional imagination. Cultural compromise is not overcome by retreat, nor by internal reform alone, but by renewed participation in the mission of God. New frontiers, be they geographic, cultural, and generational, cannot be engaged by isolated congregations or disconnected agencies but only through reciprocal partnerships marked by humility, shared risk, and mutual dependence. Liminal spaces must be embraced rather than feared, and emergent missional practices must be patiently integrated into the church's common life if they are to bear lasting fruit.

At the heart of this reorientation lies a shift from *support* to *co-laboring*. Mission is not sustained by occasional generosity but by shared life, shared discernment, and shared obedience. When churches and apostolic movements recognize one another, not as competitors or consumers but as companions in God's work, the church rediscovers its vocation. This is Paul's hope for Rome: a community rooted in the gospel, formed by the Spirit, shaped by the Scriptures, and released together for the sake of the nations.

What Paul envisioned for the Roman churches is being rehearsed again in our time. The invitation has not changed. The church is still called to step into the drama of God's redemptive work, to trust the Spirit's leading, and to participate with humility, courage, and joy in the mission of God among the nations. Romans does not simply describe what the church believes. It summons the church to become what it already is in Christ.

A brief prayer attributed to Søren Kierkegaard reads, "Today, with God's help, I shall become myself." I offer this work in that same hope. Today, with God's help, may the church become itself, not a collection of competing structures or isolated ministries but a Spirit-formed people, bound together across cultures and contexts, faithful in place and bold in witness. To become ourselves in this way is not self-assertion but obedience. It is to take our place in the ongoing story of God's mission, trusting that the same Spirit who formed the church in Rome is still at work, forming, sending, and sustaining a people through whom Christ is made known among the nations.

Bibliography

Ábel, František. "The Role of Israel Concerning the Gentiles in the Context of Romans 11:25–27." *Journal of Jewish and Christian Studies* 7 (2020) 26–53.

Achim, Viorel. *The Roma in Romanian History*. Budapest: Central European University Press, 2004.

Allen, Roland. *Missionary Methods: St. Paul's or Ours?* Grand Rapids: Eerdmans, 1962.

Allworth, Edward, et al. "Kazakhstan." *Encyclopaedia Britannica*, Apr. 6, 2026. https://www.britannica.com/place/Kazakhstan.

Altaweel, Mark, and Andrea Squitieri. "The Spread of Common Languages." Chapter 9 in *Revolutionizing a World: From Small States to Universalism in the Pre-Islamic Near East*, 231–39. London: UCL, 2018. https://doi.org/10.2307/j.ctt21c4td4.13.

Amstutz, John L. *Disciples of All Nations: Continuous Mission Until He Comes*. Los Angeles: Foursquare Missions International, 2009.

Anderson, Allan Heaton. *An Introduction to Pentecostalism: Global Charismatic Christianity*. New York: Cambridge University Press, 2013.

Anderson, Ray S. *The Soul of Ministry: Forming Leaders for God's People*. Louisville: Westminster John Knox, 1997.

Andreescu, Gabriel, and Liviu Andreescu. "Church and State in Post-Communist Romania: Priorities on the Research Agenda." *Journal for the Study of Religions and Ideologies* 8 (Winter 2009) 19–45. https://www.researchgate.net/publication/49614199.

Arichea, Daniel C., and Eugene Albert Nida. *A Handbook on Paul's Letter to the Galatians*. UBS Handbook Series. New York: United Bible Societies, 1976.

Arndt, William, et al. *A Greek-English Lexicon of the New Testament and Other Early Christian Literature*. Chicago: University of Chicago Press, 2000.

Athanasius of Alexandria. *Athanasius: On the Incarnation of the Word of God*. Translated by T. Herbert Bindley. 2nd rev. ed. London: The Religious Tract Society, 1903.

Baker, Mark D., and J. Ross Wagner, "The Righteousness of God and Hurricane Mitch: Reading Romans in Hurricane-Devastated Honduras." In *Navigating Romans Through Cultures: Challenging Readings by Charting a New Course*, ed. Khiok-khng (K. K.) Yeo, 108–11. London: T&T Clark, 2004.

Balz, Horst Robert, and Gerhard Schneider. *Exegetical Dictionary of the New Testament*. Vol. 1. Grand Rapids: Eerdmans, 2002.

Barclay, William. *The Letter to the Romans. The New Daily Study Bible*. Louisville: Westminster John Knox, 2017.

Barran, Michael. "Pauline Mission as Salvific Intentionality." In *Paul as Missionary: Identity, Activity, Theology, and Practice*, edited by Trevor J. Burke and Brian S. Rosner, 234–46. New York: Bloomsbury T&T Clark, 2011.

Barrett, Lois Y., et al. *Missional Church: A Vision for the Sending of the Church in North America*. Grand Rapids: Eerdmans, 1998.

Bartchy, S. Scott. "Slavery: New Testament." In *The Anchor Yale Bible Dictionary*, edited by David Noel Freedman, 6:65–66. New York: Doubleday, 1992.

Barth, Karl. *Church Dogmatics*. 4/3.1: *The Doctrine of Reconciliation*. Edited by G. W. Bromiley and T. F. Torrance. Translated by Geoffrey W. Bromiley. Edinburgh: T&T Clark, 1961.

———. *The Epistle to the Romans*. Translated by Edwyn C. Hoskyns. Oxford: Oxford University Press, 1933.

Barth, Markus. *Ephesians: Introduction, Translation, and Commentary on Chapters 4–6*. Anchor Yale Bible 34A. New Haven: Yale University Press, 2008.

Beker, J. Christiaan. *Paul the Apostle: The Triumph of God in Life and Thought*. Philadelphia: Fortress, 1980.

Bertram, Georg, and Karl Ludwig Schmidt. "Ἔθνος, Ἐθνικός." In *Theological Dictionary of the New Testament*, edited by Gerhard Kittel and Gerhard Friedrich and translated by Geoffrey W. Bromiley, 2:364–72. Grand Rapids: Eerdmans, 1964–1976.

Betz, Hans Dieter. "Hellenism." In *The Anchor Yale Bible Dictionary*, edited by David Noel Freedman, 3:127–35. New York: Doubleday, 1992.

Bevans, Stephen B. *Models of Contextual Theology*. Rev. and expanded ed. Maryknoll, NY: Orbis, 2002.

Blake, Daniel. "Turkey Christian Missionaries Horrifically Tortured Before Killings." Christian Today, Apr. 26, 2007. https://www.christiantoday.com/news/turkey-christian-missionaries-horrifically-tortured-before-killings.

Blumhofer, Edith Waldvogel. *Aimee Semple McPherson: Everybody's Sister*. Grand Rapids: Eerdmans, 1993.

Bosch, David J. *Transforming Mission: Paradigm Shifts in Theology of Mission*. Maryknoll, NY: Orbis, 2011.

Brannan, Rick, et al., eds. *The Lexham English Septuagint*. Bellingham, WA: Lexham, 2012. Digital ed.

Bray, Gerald, ed. *Romans*. Ancient Christian Commentary on Scripture 6. 2nd ed. Downers Grove, IL: InterVarsity, 1998.

Britannica Editors. "Aral Sea." *Encyclopaedia Britannica*, Mar. 19, 2025. https://www.britannica.com/place/Aral-Sea.

———. "Battle of Actium." *Encyclopaedia Britannica*, April 30, 2024. https://www.britannica.com/event/Battle-of-Actium-ancient-Roman-history.

———. "Central Asia." *Encyclopaedia Britannica*, Mar. 28, 2026. https://www.britannica.com/place/Central-Asia.

———. "Middle East." *Encyclopaedia Britannica*, Apr. 8, 2026. https://www.britannica.com/place/Middle-East.

———. "Optimates and Populares." *Encyclopaedia Britannica*, Dec. 13, 2016. https://www.britannica.com/topic/Optimates-and-Populares.

Broughton, T. Robert S. "The Romanization of Spain: The Problem and the Evidence." *Proceedings of the American Philosophical Society* 103 (1959) 645–51.

Brownlee, Jason. *Violence Against Copts in Egypt*. Carnegie Endowment for International Peace, Nov. 1, 2013. http://www.jstor.com/stable/resrep13083.

Bruce, F. F. *The Spreading Flame: The Rise and Progress of Christianity from Its First Beginnings to the Conversion of the English*. Grand Rapids: Eerdmans, 1995.

Brueggemann, Walter. *A Commentary on Jeremiah: Exile and Homecoming*. Grand Rapids: Eerdmans, 1998.

———. *Isaiah 40–66*. Edited by Patrick D. Miller and David L. Bartlett. Westminster Bible Companion. Louisville: Westminster John Knox, 1998.

———. *The Prophetic Imagination*. Minneapolis: Fortress, 2018.

———. *Theology of the Old Testament: Testimony, Dispute, Advocacy*. Minneapolis: Fortress, 2005.

Bryan, Christopher. *A Preface to Romans: Notes on the Epistle in Its Literary and Cultural Setting*. New York: Oxford University Press, 2000.

Bultmann, Rudolf. *Jesus Christ and Mythology*. New York: Charles Scribner's Sons, 1958.

———. *New Testament and Mythology and Other Basic Writings*. Edited by Schubert M. Ogden. Minneapolis: Fortress, 1984.

Burton, Keith August. "By Any Means Necessary, All Israel Will Be Saved." In *Scripture, Cultures, and Criticism: Interpretive Steps and Critical Issues Raised by Robert Jewett*, edited by K. K. Yeo, 246–59. Eugene, OR: Pickwick, 2022.

Cahn, Claude, and Elspeth Guild. *Recent Migration of Roma in Europe*. Strasbourg: Council of Europe Commissioner for Human Rights, 2010.

Calvert, Nancy L. "Abraham." In *Dictionary of Paul and His Letters*, edited by Gerald F. Hawthorne et al., 1–9. Downers Grove, IL: InterVarsity, 1993.

Calvin, John. *Epistles of Paul to the Romans and Thessalonians*. Translated by R. MacKenzie. Calvin's New Testament Commentaries. Grand Rapids: Eerdmans, 1965.

Camp, Bruce K. "A Theological Examination of the Two-Structure Theory." *Missiology: An International Review* 23 (1995) 197–209.

Campbell, Douglas A. *The Deliverance of God: An Apocalyptic Rereading of Justification in Paul*. Grand Rapids: Eerdmans, 2009.

Carroll R., M. Daniel. *Christians at the Border: Immigration, the Church, and the Bible*. Grand Rapids: Baker Academic, 2008.

Carroll, Scott T. "Tacitus (Person)." In *The Anchor Yale Bible Dictionary*, edited by David Noel Freedman, 6:306. New York: Doubleday, 1992.

Carson, D. A., and Douglas J. Moo. *An Introduction to the New Testament*. Grand Rapids, MI: Zondervan Academic, 2005.

Carson, Timothy, et al. *Crossing Thresholds: A Practical Theology of Liminality*. Cambridge: Lutterworth, 2021.

Chapman, Colin. "Christians in the Middle East—Past, Present and Future." Transformation 29 (2012) 91–110. https://www.jstor.org/stable/10.2307/90008076.

———. "The Spread and Development of Islam." In *Encountering the World of Islam*, edited by Keith E. Swartley, 50–62. Atlanta: Authentic, 2008.

Chapman, Mark D. *Anglican Theology*. New York: Bloomsbury, 2012.

Chaves, Mark. "Denominations as Dual Structures: An Organizational Analysis." *Sociology of Religion* 54 (1993) 147–69.

Chia, Edmund Kee-Fook. *Asian Christianity and Theology: Inculturation, Interreligious Dialogue, Integral Liberation*. Milton Park, UK: Routledge, 2021.

Cho, Youngmo. *Spirit and Kingdom in the Writings of Luke and Paul: An Attempt to Reconcile These Concepts*. Milton Keynes: Paternoster, 2005.

Cho, Youngmo, and Hyung Dae Park. *Acts: A New Covenant Commentary*. Vol. 2. New Covenant Commentary Series. Edited by Michael F. Bird and Craig Keener. Eugene, OR: Cascade, 2019.

Chrysostom, John. *Treatise on the Priesthood*. In vol. 9 of *The Nicene and Post-Nicene Fathers* (*NPNF*), Series 1. Edited by Philip Schaff. 1886–1889. 14 vols. Repr., Peabody, MA: Hendrickson, 1999.

Ciampa, Roy E. "Paul's Theology of the Gospel." In *Paul as Missionary: Identity, Activity, Theology, and Practice*, edited by Trevor J. Burke and Brian S. Rosner, 169–89. London: T&T Clark, 2011.

Ciobanu, Ruxandra Oana. "Diverging or Converging Communities? Stages of International Migration from Rural Romania." In *Mobility in Transition: Migration Patterns After EU Enlargement*, edited by Birgit Glorius et al., 65–84. Amsterdam: Amsterdam University Press, 2013.

Clark, Colin, and Margaret Greenfields. *Here to Stay: The Gypsies and Travellers of Britain*. Hatfield: University of Hertfordshire Press, 2006.

Clark, Victoria. *Why Angels Fall: A Journey Through Orthodox Europe from Byzantium to Kosovo*. New York: St. Martin's, 2000.

Clayton, Philip. *Mind and Emergence: From Quantum to Consciousness*. Oxford: Oxford University Press, 2004.

Clayton, Philip, and Paul Davies, eds. *The Re-Emergence of Emergence: The Emergentist Hypothesis from Science to Religion*. Oxford: Oxford University Press, 2006.

Clowney, Edmund P. "A Biblical Theology of Prayer." In *Teach Us to Pray: Prayer in the Bible and the World*, edited by D. A. Carson, 136–75. Eugene, OR: Wipf & Stock, 2002.

Cole, Daniel M. I. *Isaiah's Servant in Paul: The Hermeneutics and Ethics of Paul's Use of Isaiah 49–54*. Tübingen: Mohr Siebeck, 2021.

Colenso, John William. *St. Paul's Epistle to the Romans: Newly Translated and Explained from a Missionary Point of View*. New York: Appleton, 1863.

Congress of Leaders of World and Traditional Religions. "About the Congress." https://religions-congress.org/en/page/o-sezde.

Conn, Harvie M., and Manuel Ortiz. *Urban Ministry: The Kingdom, the City, and the People of God*. Downers Grove, IL: InterVarsity, 2001.

Cooley, Alison E. *Res Gestae Divi Augusti: Text, Translation, and Commentary*. Cambridge: Cambridge University Press, 2009.

Corradini, Antonella, and Timothy O'Connor, eds. *Emergence in Science and Philosophy*. New York: Routledge, 2010.

Council of Europe. "Estimates on Roma Population in European Countries." Publications, July 2, 2012. https://rm.coe.int/CoERMPublicCommonSearchServices/DisplayDCTMContent?documentId=09000016800088ea9.

———. "Roma History Factsheets." Roma and Travellers. https://www.coe.int/en/web/roma-and-travellers/roma-history-factsheets.

Cranfield, C. E. B. *Romans: A Shorter Commentary*. Grand Rapids: Eerdmans, 2018.

Crisler, Channing L. *An Intertextual Commentary on Romans*. 4 vols. Eugene, OR: Pickwick, 2021–2026.

———. *Reading Romans as Lament*. Eugene, OR: Pickwick, 2016.

Croasmun, Matthew. *The Emergence of Sin: The Cosmic Tyrant in Romans*. New York: Oxford University Press, 2017.

Croft, Darin A. *Horned Armadillos and Rafting Monkeys: The Fascinating Fossil Mammals of South America*. Bloomington: Indiana University Press, 2016.

Crowe, David M. *A History of the Gypsies of Eastern Europe and Russia*. 2nd ed. New York: Palgrave Macmillan, 2007.

Cummings, Sally N. *Kazakhstan: Power and the Elite*. London: I. B. Tauris, 2005.

———. *Understanding Central Asia: Politics and Contested Transformations*. London: Routledge, 2012.

Dahl, Nils A. *Studies in Paul: Theology for the Early Christian Mission*. Minneapolis: Augsburg, 1977.

Daube, David. "Onesimos." *The Harvard Theological Review* 79 (1986) 40–43. http://www.jstor.org/stable/1509399.

Davies, J. "Theodicy." In *Dictionary of the Old Testament: Wisdom, Poetry & Writings*, edited by Tremper Longman III and Peter Enns, 808–17. Downers Grove, IL: InterVarsity, 2008.

Davis, Mark A. *Invasion Biology*. Oxford: Oxford University Press, 2009.

Deissmann, Adolf. *Light from the Ancient East: The New Testament Illustrated by Recently Discovered Texts of the Graeco-Roman World*. Translated by Lionel R. M. Strachan. London: Hodder & Stoughton, 1910.

deSilva, David A. *An Introduction to the New Testament: Contexts, Methods and Ministry Formation*. Downers Grove, IL: InterVarsity, 2004.

———. *Honor, Patronage, Kinship, and Purity: Unlocking New Testament Culture*. Rev. and expanded ed. Downers Grove, IL: IVP Academic, 2022.

Dinkler, Erich. "Existentialist Interpretation of the New Testament." *The Journal of Religion* 32 (1952) 87–96. http://www.jstor.org/stable/1197359.

Dittenberger, Wilhelm, ed. *Orientis Graeci Inscriptiones Selectae*. 2 vols. 1903–1905. Reprint, Hildesheim: Olms, 1960.

Donfried, Karl P. *The Romans Debate*. 2nd rev. and expanded ed. Grand Rapids: Baker Academic, 2011.

Douglas, Alex P. "A Call to Law: The Septuagint of Isaiah 8 and Gentile Law Observance." *Journal of Biblical Literature* 137 (2018) 87–104. http://www.jstor.org/stable/10.15699/jbl.1371.2018.344664.

Downs, David J. *The Offering of the Gentiles: Paul's Collection for Jerusalem in Its Chronological, Cultural, and Cultic Contexts*. Grand Rapids: Eerdmans, 2008.

Droge, A. J. "Apologetics, NT." In *The Anchor Yale Bible Dictionary*, edited by David Noel Freedman, 1:305–7. New York: Doubleday, 1992.

DuBose, Francis M. *God Who Sends: A Fresh Quest for Biblical Mission*. Nashville: Broadman, 1983.

Dunn, James D. G. "The New Perspective on Paul." *Bulletin of the John Rylands Library, Manchester* 65 (1983) 95–122. https://jstor.org/stable/community.28212203.

———. "Paul's Conversion—A Light to the Disputes." Chapter 16 in *The New Perspective on Paul: Collected Essays*, edited by J. D. G. Dunn. Wissenschaftliche Untersuchungen zum Neuen Testament 185. Tübingen: Mohr Siebeck, 2005.

———. *Romans 1–8*. Word Biblical Commentary 38A Dallas: Word, 1988.

———. *Romans 9–16*. Word Biblical Commentary 38B Dallas: Word, 1988.

———. *The Theology of Paul the Apostle*. New York: T&T Clark, 2003.

Dunne, Michele. "The Limits of Authoritarian Resilience: Egypt After the Arab Spring." *Journal of Democracy* 24 (2013) 34–48.

Dupont, Jean. *2025 MENACA Field Guide*. Independently published, 2025.

Echo Park Evangelistic Association. "About EPEA." 2024 https://www.echoparkevangelisticassociation.org/about---epea.

Edwards, Jonathan. *The Works of Jonathan Edwards*. Vol. 2. Edinburgh: Banner of Truth, 1974.

Ehrensperger, Kathy, and R. Ward Holder, eds. *Reformation Readings of Romans*. London: T&T Clark, 2008.

Eisenbaum, Pamela. *Paul Was Not a Christian: The Original Message of a Misunderstood Apostle*. New York: HarperOne, 2010.

Ellingworth, Paul. *The Epistle to the Hebrews: A Commentary on the Greek Text*. The New International Greek Testament Commentary. Grand Rapids: Eerdmans; Paternoster, 1993.

Elliott, Neil. *Paul Against the Nations: Soundings in Romans*. Eugene, OR: Cascade, 2023.

Elwell, Walter A., and Barry J. Beitzel. "Egypt, Egyptians." In *Baker Encyclopedia of the Bible*, edited by Walter A. Elwell, 662–75. Grand Rapids: Baker. 1988.

———. "Tarshish (Place)." In *Baker Encyclopedia of the Bible*, edited by Walter A. Elwell, 2036–37. Grand Rapids: Baker, 1988.

Enns, Peter. *Inspiration and Incarnation: Evangelicals and the Problem of the Old Testament*. 2nd ed. Grand Rapids: Baker Academic, 2015.

Epstein, Daniel Mark. *Sister Aimee: The Life of Aimee Semple McPherson*. New York: Houghton Mifflin Harcourt, 1994.

Ericksen, Robert P. *Complicity in the Holocaust: Churches and Universities in Nazi Germany*. New York: Cambridge University Press, 2012.

———. *Theologians Under Hitler: Gerhard Kittel, Paul Althaus, and Emanuel Hirsch*. New Haven: Yale University Press, 1985.

Escarfuller, Juan. "Repudiating Assimilation in Reading Romans 9–11." In *Navigating Romans Through Cultures: Challenging Readings by Charting a New Course*, edited by Khiok-Khng (K. K.) Yeo, 57–75. London: T&T Clark, 2004.

Esler, Philip F. *Conflict and Identity in Romans: The Social Setting of Paul's Letter*. Minneapolis: Fortress, 2003.

European Commission. *EU Roma Strategic Framework for Equality, Inclusion and Participation for 2020–2030*. Brussels: European Commission, 2020. https://commission.europa.eu/system/files/2021-01/eu_roma_strategic_framework_for_equality_inclusion_and_participation_for_2020_-_2030_0.pdf.

———. *Eurostat Regional Yearbook 2023*. Luxembourg: Publications Office of European Commission, 2023. https://ec.europa.eu/eurostat/web/products-flagship-publications/w/ks-ha-23-001.

———. *A New EU Roma Strategic Framework: Factscheet—October 2020*. Brussels: European Commission, 2020.

Eusebius. *Church History*. In vol. 1 of *The Nicene and Post-Nicene Fathers* (*NPNF*), Series 2. Edited by Philip Schaff and Henry Wace. 1886–1900. 14 vols. Repr., Peabody, MA: Hendrickson, 1999.

Ferguson, A. R. "The Origin and Development of the Kiwifruit Industry." In *Kiwifruit: Science and Management*, edited by I. J. Warrington and G. C. Weston, 15–29. Auckland: Ray Richards, 1990.

Finger, Reta H. *Paul and the Roman House Churches: A Simulation*. Eugene, OR: Wipf & Stock, 2006.

Fitzmyer, Joseph A. *Romans: A New Translation with Introduction and Commentary*. Anchor Yale Bible 33. New Haven: Yale University Press, 2008.

Flemming, Dean E. *Contextualization in the New Testament: Patterns for Theology and Mission*. Downers Grove, IL: InterVarsity, 2005.

The Foursquare Church. "The Foursquare Global Distinctives." https://www.foursquare.org/about/beliefs/#global-distinctives.

———. "History." https://www.foursquare.org/about/history/.

———. "Our Mission and Approach." https://www.foursquare.org/about/mission/.

———. "Presidential Job Description." https://foursquare-leader.s3.amazonaws.com/events/election/Cabinet_President_Job_Description.pdf.

———. "Shared Mission: Global Distinctives." Foursquare Resources, Oct. 11, 2020. https://resources.foursquare.org/shared_mission_global_distinctives_part_6/.

———. "Up-to-Date Information on the Five Stakes." Foursquare Resources, Jan. 21, 2015. https://resources.foursquare.org/up_to_date_information_on_the_five_stakes/.

———. "What We Believe." https://www.foursquare.org/about/beliefs/.

Foursquare Missions International. *Regional Strategy Document: MENACA + Europe*. Internal publication, 2022.

Frankfurter, David. *Christianizing Egypt: Syncretism and Local Worlds in Late Antiquity*. Princeton: Princeton University Press, 2018.

Freedman, David Noel, ed. *The Anchor Yale Bible Dictionary*. 6 vols. New York: Doubleday, 1992.

Freedom House. *Freedom in the World 2023*. Washington, DC: Freedom House, 2023. https://freedomhouse.org/sites/default/files/2023-03/FIW_World_2023_DigtalPDF.pdf.

Friedrich, Gerhard. "Εὐαγγελίζομαι, Εὐαγγέλιον, Προευαγγελίζομαι, Εὐαγγελιστής." In *Theological Dictionary of the New Testament*, edited by Gerhard Kittel and Gerhard Friedrich and translated by Geoffrey W. Bromiley, 2:707–37. Grand Rapids: Eerdmans, 1964–1976.

Frier, Bruce W. *Landlords and Tenants in Imperial Rome*. Princeton: Princeton University Press, 1980.

Frost, Michael, and Alan Hirsch. *The Shaping of Things to Come: Innovation and Mission for the 21st-Century Church*. Grand Rapids: Baker, 2013.

Gabra, Gawdat, and Hany N. Takla, eds. *Christianity and Monasticism in Alexandria and the Egyptian Deserts*. Cairo: American University in Cairo Press, 2020.

Gaca, Kathy L., and L. L. Welborn, eds. *Early Patristic Readings of Romans*. New York: Bloomsbury Academic, 2006.

Gaventa, Beverly Roberts, ed. *Apocalyptic Paul: Cosmos and Anthropos in Romans 5–8*. Waco, TX: Baylor University Press, 2019.

———. "The Mission of God in Paul's Letter to the Romans." In *Paul as Missionary: Identity, Activity, Theology, and Practice*, edited by Trevor J. Burke and Brian S. Rosner, 65–75. New York: Bloomsbury T&T Clark, 2011.

———. *Our Mother Saint Paul*. Louisville: Westminster John Knox, 2007.

Gibson, Richard J. "Paul the Missionary, in Priestly Service." In *Paul as Missionary: Identity, Activity, Theology, and Practice*, edited by Trevor J. Burke and Brian S. Rosner, 51–62. New York: Bloomsbury T&T Clark, 2011.

Gilbert, Lela. "Turkey's Christians Face Increasingly Dangerous Persecution." *Newsweek*, Apr. 13, 2021. https://www.newsweek.com/turkeys-christians-face-increasingly-dangerous-persecution-opinion-1583041.

Gillman, Florence Morgan. "Tertius (Person)." In *The Anchor Yale Bible Dictionary*, edited by David Noel Freedman, 6:389. New York: Doubleday, 1992.

Giordano, Christian, and Andrea Boscoboinik. "The Roma 'Problem': Ethnicisation or Social Marginalisation?" In *Social Inclusion and Cultural Identity of Roma Communities in South-Eastern Europe*, edited by Gabriela Mirescu, 11–18. Basel: Swisspeace, 2011. http://www.jstor.com/stable/resrep11110.6.

Gladigow, Burkhard. "Roman Religion." In *The Anchor Yale Bible Dictionary*, edited by David Noel Freedman, 5:810–1163. New York: Doubleday, 1992.

Goheen, Michael W. *A Light to the Nations: The Missional Church and the Biblical Story.* Grand Rapids: Baker Academic, 2011.

Goheen, Michael W., and Timothy M. Sheridan. *Becoming a Missionary Church: Lesslie Newbigin and Contemporary Church Movements.* Grand Rapids: Baker Academic, 2022.

Goldingay, John. *Isaiah for Everyone.* Old Testament for Everyone. Louisville: Westminster John Knox, 2015.

———. *Israel's Faith.* Vol. 2 of *Old Testament Theology.* Dower's Grove, IL: IVP Academic, 2006.

———. *Israel's Gospel.* Vol. 1 of *Old Testament Theology.* Downers Grove, IL: IVP Academic, 2003.

———. *Israel's Life.* Vol. 3 of *Old Testament Theology.* Downers Grove, IL: InterVarsity, 2009.

Goldstein, Jeffrey. "Emergence as a Construct: History and Issues." *Emergence* (1999) 49–72.

González, Justo L. *Out of Every Tribe and Nation: Christian Theology at the Ethnic Roundtable.* Nashville: Abingdon, 1992.

———. *The Story of Christianity. Volume 1: The Early Church to the Dawn of the Reformation.* New York. HarperOne. 2010.

———. *The Story of Christianity. Volume 2: The Reformation to the Present Day.* New York. HarperOne. 2010.

Gorman, Michael J., and Nijay K. Gupta. *Cruciformity: Paul's Narrative Spirituality of the Cross.* Grand Rapids: Eerdmans, 2021.

Green, Bernard. *Christianity in Ancient Rome: The First Three Centuries.* New York: T&T Clark, 2010.

Greenlee, David, et al. "Exploring the Intersection of Community Development, the Least Reached and Emerging, Vibrant Churches." *Transformation* 37 (2020) 105–118.

Greenman, Jeffrey P., and Gene L. Green, eds. *Global Theology in Evangelical Perspective: Exploring the Contextual Nature of Theology and Mission.* Downers Grove, IL: IVP Academic, 2012.

Greenman, Jeffrey P., and Timothy Larsen, eds. *Reading Romans Through the Centuries: From the Early Church to Karl Barth.* Grand Rapids: Brazos, 2005.

Gregory of Nyssa. *Gregory of Nyssa Against Eunomius.* In vol. 5 of *The Nicene and Post-Nicene Fathers* (*NPNF*), Series 2. Edited by Philip Schaff and Henry Wace. 1886–1900. 14 vols. Repr., Peabody, MA: Hendrickson, 1999.

Grenholm, Cristina, and Daniel Patte, eds. *Gender, Tradition, and Romans: Shared Ground, Uncertain Borders.* London: T&T Clark International, 2005.

Guastello, Stephen J. *Managing Emergent Phenomena: Nonlinear Dynamics in Work Organizations.* Mahwah, NJ: Lawrence Erlbaum Associates, 2002.

Guder, Darrell L., ed. *Missional Church: A Vision for the Sending of the Church in North America.* Grand Rapids: Eerdmans, 1998.

Hall, John F. "Rome (Place)." In *The Anchor Yale Bible Dictionary*, edited by David Noel Freedman, 5:826–38. New York: Doubleday, 1992.

Hammersley, Martyn. *What Is Qualitative Research?* London: Bloomsbury Academic, 2013.

Hancock, Ian. *We Are the Romani People.* Hatfield: University of Hertfordshire Press, 2002.

Handy, Lowell K. "Tarshish." In *Lexham Bible Dictionary*, edited by John D. Barry et al. Bellingham, WA: Lexham, 2016. Digital ed.

Harrill, J. Albert. "The Use of the New Testament in the American Slave Controversy: A Case History in the Hermeneutical Tension Between Biblical Criticism and Christian Moral Debate." *Religion and American Culture: A Journal of Interpretation* 10 (2000) 149–86. https://doi.org/10.2307/1123945.

Harris, R. Laird. "698 חסד." In *Theological Wordbook of the Old Testament*, edited by R. Laird Harris et al., 1:305–7. Chicago: Moody, 1999.

Hart, David Bentley. *The Hidden and the Manifest: Essays in Theology and Metaphysics.* Grand Rapids: Eerdmans, 2017.

———. *Tradition and Apocalypse: An Essay on the Future of Christian Belief.* Grand Rapids: Baker Academic, 2022.

Harvey, John D. *Romans: Exegetical Guide to the Greek New Testament.* Edited by Andreas J. Köstenberger and Robert W. Yarbrough. Nashville: B&H Academic, 2017.

Hattar, Kinda. "CPI 2023 for Middle East & North Africa: Dysfunctional Approach to Fighting Corruption Undermines Progress." Transparency International, Jan. 30, 2024. https://www.transparency.org/en/news/cpi-2023-middle-east-north-africa-dysfunctional-approach-fighting-corruption.

Havea, Jione, ed. *Mission and Context.* Lanham, MD: Fortress Academic, 2020.

Hays, Richard B. *Echoes of Scripture in the Letters of Paul.* New Haven: Yale University Press, 1993.

Heifetz, Ronald A., and Marty Linsky. *Leadership on the Line: Staying Alive Through the Dangers of Leading.* Boston: Harvard Business Review, 2002.

Heilig, Christoph. "Roman Context." Chapter 4 in *Hidden Criticism? The Methodology and Plausibility of the Search for a Counter-Imperial Subtext in Paul.* Tübingen: Mohr Siebeck, 2015.

Heschel, Abraham Joshua. *God in Search of Man: A Philosophy of Judaism.* New York: Farrar, Straus and Giroux, 1955.

———. *The Prophets.* New York: Harper & Row, 1962.

———. *The Sabbath: Its Meaning for Modern Man.* New York: Farrar, Straus and Giroux, 1951.

Heschel, Susannah. *The Aryan Jesus: Christian Theologians and the Bible in Nazi Germany.* Princeton: Princeton University Press, 2008.

Hiebert, Paul G. *Anthropological Insights for Missionaries.* Grand Rapids: Baker, 2006.

Hiebert, Paul G., and Eloise Hiebert Meneses. *Incarnational Ministry: Planting Churches in Band, Tribal, Peasant, and Urban Societies*. Grand Rapids: Baker, 1995.

Hinnebusch, Raymond, and Anoushiravan Ehteshami, eds. *The Foreign Policies of Middle East States*. 2nd ed. Boulder: Lynne Rienner, 2014.

Hirsch, Alan. *The Forgotten Ways: Reactivating Apostolic Movements*. Grand Rapids: Brazos, 2006.

Hitchins, Keith. *A Concise History of Romania*. Cambridge: Cambridge University Press, 2014.

———. *Rumania, 1866–1947*. Oxford: Clarendon, 1994.

Hofstede, Geert. "Business Cultures." *UNESCO Courier* 47 (1994) 12–16.

Holland, Tom. *Contours of Pauline Theology: A Radical New Survey of the Influences on Paul's Biblical Writings*. Fearn, Scotland: Christian Focus, 2004.

Honey, J. G., et al. "Camelidae." In *Evolution of Tertiary Mammals of North America*, edited by C. M. Janis et al., 439–62. Cambridge: Cambridge University Press, 1998.

Horváth, István, and Remus Gabriel Anghel. *Migration and Development in Romania: A Case Study*. Cluj-Napoca: ISPMN, 2009.

Howard, George. "Romans 3:21–31 and the Inclusion of the Gentiles." *The Harvard Theological Review* 63 (1970) 223–33. http://www.jstor.org/stable/1509026.

———. *Paul: Crisis in Galatia*. Cambridge: Cambridge University Press, 1979.

Hultgren, Arlund J. "Paul's Christology and His Mission to the Gentiles." In *Paul as Missionary: Identity, Activity, Theology, and Practice*, edited by Trevor J. Burke and Brian S. Rosner, 115–27. New York: Bloomsbury T&T Clark, 2011.

Human Rights Watch. *World Report 2025: Events of 2024*. New York: Human Rights Watch, 2025. https://www.hrw.org/sites/default/files/media_2025/01/World%20Report%202025.pdf.

Irenaeus. *Against Heresies*. In vol. 1 of *The Ante-Nicene Fathers* (*ANF*). Edited by Alexander Roberts and James Donaldson. 1885–1887. 10 vols. Repr., Peabody, MA: Hendrickson, 1999.

Institutul Național de Statistică (INS). "Recensământul Populației și Locuințelor 2021—Date Provizorii." https://www.recensamantromania.ro.

International Christian Church. "Middle East." May 13, 2025. https://www.persecution.org/countries/egypt/.

Issa, Islam. *Alexandria: The City that Changed the World*. New York: Pegasus, 2024.

Jandt, F. E. *An Introduction to Intercultural Communication: Identities in a Global Community*. Thousand Oaks, CA: SAGE, 2018.

Jeffers, James S. *Conflict at Rome: Social Order and Hierarchy in Early Christianity*. Minneapolis: Fortress, 1991.

———. *The Greco-Roman World of the New Testament*. Downers Grove, IL: InterVarsity, 1999.

Jenkins, Philip. *The Lost History of Christianity: The Thousand-Year Golden Age of the Church in the Middle East, Africa, and Asia—and How It Died*. New York: HarperOne, 2009.

———. *The Next Christendom*. New York: Oxford University Press, 2011.

Jennings, Willie James. *Acts*. Belief: A Theological Commentary on the Bible. Louisville: Westminster John Knox, 2017.

———. *The Christian Imagination: Theology and the Origins of Race*. New Haven: Yale University Press, 2010.

Jensen, Erik. *Barbarians in the Greek and Roman World*. Indianapolis: Hackett, 2018.

Jensen, Henrik Jeldtoft. *Complexity Science: The Study of Emergence*. Cambridge: Cambridge University Press, 2023.

Jersak, Bradley. *A More Christlike God: A More Beautiful Gospel*. Pasadena, CA: Plain Truth Ministries, 2015.

———. *Out of the Embers: Faith after the Great Deconstruction*. New Kensington, PA: Whitaker House, 2022.

Jevons, Frank Byron. "Hellenism and Christianity." *The Harvard Theological Review* 1 (1908) 169–88. http://www.jstor.org/stable/1506959.

Jewett, Robert, and Roy David Kotansky. *Romans: A Commentary*. Edited by Eldon Jay Epp. Hermeneia: A Critical and Historical Commentary on the Bible. Minneapolis: Fortress, 2006.

Jewett, Robert. *Romans: A Short Commentary*. Minneapolis: Fortress, 2013.

Jobes, Karen H., and Moisés Silva. *Invitation to the Septuagint*. Grand Rapids: Baker Academic, 2000.

Johnson, Luke Timothy. *The Apostle Paul*. Chantilly, VA: The Teaching Company, 2001.

Jones, Donald L. "Roman Imperial Cult." In *The Anchor Yale Bible Dictionary*, edited by David Noel Freedman, 5:806–9. New York: Doubleday, 1992.

Josephus, Flavius. *The Works of Josephus: Complete and Unabridged*. Translated by William Whiston. Peabody, MA: Hendrickson, 1987.

Joshua Project. "Türkiye (Turkey)." https://joshuaproject.net/countries/TU.

Kaldellis, Anthony. *The New Roman Empire: A History of Byzantium*. New York: Oxford University Press, 2023.

Kalkandjieva, Daniela. "A Comparative Analysis on Church–State Relations in Eastern Orthodoxy: Concepts, Models, and Principles." *Journal of Church and State* 53 (2011) 587–614.

Käsemann, Ernst. *Commentary on Romans*. Translated and edited by Geoffrey W. Bromiley. Grand Rapids: Eerdmans, 1980.

———. *On Being a Disciple of the Crucified Nazarene: Unpublished Lectures and Sermons*. Translated by Roy A. Harrisville. Grand Rapids: Eerdmans, 2010.

Kateregga, Badru D., and David W. Shenk. *A Muslim and a Christian in Dialogue*. Scottdale, PA: Herald, 1997.

Kauffman, Stuart. *At Home in the Universe: The Search for the Laws of Self-Organization and Complexity*. New York: Oxford University Press, 1995.

Keifert, Patrick, and Nigel Rooms. *Forming the Missional Church: Creating Deep Cultural Change in Congregations*. Cambridge: Grove, 2014.

Keller, Timothy. *Center Church: Doing Balanced, Gospel-Centered Ministry in Your City*. Grand Rapids: Zondervan, 2012

Keown, Mark J. *Romans and the Mission of God*. Eugene, OR: Wipf & Stock, 2021.

Khalid, Adeeb. *Islam After Communism: Religion and Politics in Central Asia*. Berkeley: University of California Press, 2007.

Kim, Enoch Jinsik. *Mission Strategy in the City: Cultivation of Inter-Ethnic Common Grounds*. Eugene, OR: Pickwick, 2017.

Kim, Seyoon. "Jesus, Sayings Of." In *Dictionary of Paul and His Letters*, edited by Gerald F. Hawthorne et al, 474–92. Downers Grove, IL: InterVarsity, 1993.

———. "Paul as an Eschatological Herald." In *Paul as Missionary: Identity, Activity, Theology, and Practice*, edited by Trevor J. Burke and Brian S. Rosner, 9–24. New York: Bloomsbury T&T Clark, 2011.

Kitchen, K. A., "Egypt, History of." in *The Anchor Yale Bible Dictionary*, ed. David Noel Freedman, 2:321–31. New York: Doubleday. 1992.

Kittel, Gerhard, and Gerhard Friedrich, eds. *Theological Dictionary of the New Testament*. Translated by Geoffrey W. Bromiley. 10 vols. Grand Rapids: Eerdmans, 1964–1976.

Kóczé, Judit, and Hristo Kyuchukov. *Roma in Romania*. Berlin: Friedrich-Ebert-Stiftung, 2017.

Krastev, Ivan. *After Europe*. Philadelphia: University of Pennsylvania Press, 2020.

Kruse, Colin G. *Paul's Letter to the Romans*. Pillar New Testament Commentary. Grand Rapids: Eerdmans, 2012.

Kugler, Chris. "Faith." In *Lexham Theological Wordbook*, edited by Douglas Mangum et al. Lexham Bible Reference Series. Bellingham, WA: Lexham, 2014. Digital ed.

Laederich, Stéphane. "Roma Cultural Identity." In *Social Inclusion and Cultural Identity of Roma Communities in South-Eastern Europe*, edited by Gabriela Mirescu, 19–26. Bern: Swisspeace, 2011.

Lampe, Peter. *From Paul to Valentinus: Christians at Rome in the First Two Centuries*. Translated by M. Steinhauser. Minneapolis: Fortress, 2003.

———. "Herodian (Person)." In *The Anchor Yale Bible Dictionary*, edited by David Noel Freedman, 3:176. New York: Doubleday, 1992.

Lateiner, Donald. "Historiography: Greco-Roman Historiography." In *The Anchor Yale Bible Dictionary*, ed. David Noel Freedman, 3:212–19. New York: Doubleday, 1992.

Law, Timothy Michael. *When God Spoke Greek: The Septuagint and the Making of the Christian Bible*. Oxford: Oxford University Press, 2013.

Leenhardt, Franz J., *The Epistle to the Romans: A Commentary*. Translated by Harold Knight. Cleveland: World, 1961.

Le Glay, Marcel, et al. *A History of Rome*. 4th ed. Malden, MA: Wiley-Blackwell, 2009.

Lendon, J. E. *Empire of Honour: The Art of Government in the Roman World*. Oxford: Clarendon, 1997.

Lincoln, Andrew T. *Ephesians*. Word Biblical Commentary 42. Dallas: Word, 1990.

Lipka, Michael. "Conclusions." Chapter 5 in *Roman Gods: A Conceptual Approach*. Leiden: Brill, 2009. http://www.jstor.org/stable/10.1163/j.ctt1w8h314.10.

Little, Christopher R. *Mission in the Way of Paul: Biblical Mission for the Church in the Twenty-First Century*. New York: Peter Lang, 2005.

Little, Donald, et al. "Egypt." *Encyclopaedia Britannica*, Apr. 6, 2026. https://www.britannica.com/place/Egypt.

Longenecker, Richard N. *Introducing Romans: Critical Issues in Paul's Most Famous Letter*. Grand Rapids: Eerdmans, 2011.

———. *The Epistle to the Romans: A Commentary on the Greek Text*. Edited by I. Howard Marshall and Donald A. Hagner. New International Greek Testament Commentary. Grand Rapids: Eerdmans, 2016.

Longman, Timothy. *Christianity and Genocide in Rwanda*. Cambridge: Cambridge University Press, 2010.

Longman, Tremper, III, and Peter Enns, eds. *Dictionary of the Old Testament: Wisdom, Poetry, and Writings*. Downer's Grove: IVP Academic, 2003.

Lossky, Vladimir. *Orthodox Theology: An Introduction*. Crestwood, NY: St. Vladimir's Seminary Press, 1978.

Luther, Martin. *Commentary on Romans.* Translated by J. Theodore Mueller. Grand Rapids: Kregel, 1982.

MacMullen, Ramsay. *Roman Social Relations, 50 B.C. to A.D. 284.* New Haven: Yale University Press, 1974.

Magda, Ksenija. "Ἐθνῶν ἀπόστολος: A Case for Translating ἔθνη in Romans Consistently as 'Nations.'" *Bogoslovlje* 79 (2020) 5–26.

Majumdar, Samirah. *Government Restrictions on Religion Stayed at Peak Levels Globally in 2022.* Pew Research Center, Dec. 18, 2024. https://www.pewresearch.org/wp-content/uploads/sites/20/2024/12/PR_2024.12.18_restrictions-on-religion-2022_report.pdf.

Marlin, George J. *Christian Persecutions in the Middle East: A 21st Century Tragedy.* South Bend, IN: St. Augustine's, 2015.

Marshall, Howard. *Acts: An Introduction and Commentary.* Tyndale New Testament Commentaries 5. Downers Grove, IL: InterVarsity, 1980.

Martin, Ralph P. "Creed." In *Dictionary of Paul and His Letters*, edited by Gerald F. Hawthorne et al., 190–92. Downers Grove, IL: InterVarsity, 1993.

Marushiakova, Elena, and Veselin Popov. "The Roma—A Nation Without a State? Historical Background and Contemporary Tendencies." *Nationalities Papers* 27 (1999) 201–26.

Mathis, Donny Ray, II. "Romans." The Gospel Coalition, 2023. https://www.thegospelcoalition.org/commentary/romans/.

Matras, Yaron. *Romani: A Linguistic Introduction.* Cambridge: Cambridge University Press, 2005.

McGrath, Alister E. "Cross, Theology of The." In *Dictionary of Paul and His Letters*, edited by Gerald F. Hawthorne et al., 192–97. Downers Grove, IL: InterVarsity, 1993.

———. *Historical Theology: An Introduction to the History of Christian Thought.* Chichester, UK: John Wiley & Sons, 2013.

McKnight, Scot. *Reading Romans Backwards: A Gospel of Peace in the Midst of Empire.* Waco, TX: Baylor University Press, 2019.

McPherson, Aimee Semple. *The Bridal Call.* Oct. 1927.

———. *This Is That: The Experiences, Sermons, and Writings of Aimee Semple McPherson.* Edited by Douglas Harrolf. Published by the editor, 2016.

Meeks, Wayne A. *The First Urban Christians: The Social World of the Apostle Paul.* New Haven: Yale University Press, 2003.

Miranda, José P. *Marx and the Bible: A Critique of the Philosophy of Oppression.* Maryknoll, NY: Orbis, 2004.

Mirescu, Gabriela. "Exclusion, Inclusion, Illusion: Shifting the Perspective on Social Inclusion of Romanian Roma." In *Social Inclusion and Cultural Identity of Roma Communities in South-Eastern Europe*, edited by Gabriela Mirescu, 57–63. Bern: Swisspeace, 2011.

Moffett, Samuel H. *A History of Christianity in Asia. Vol. I: Beginnings to 1500.* 2nd rev. ed. Maryknoll, NY: Orbis, 1998.

Montgomery, James. *New Testament Fire in the Philippines.* N.p.: Church Growth Research in the Philippines, 1972.

Moo, Douglas J. *The Letters to the Colossians and to Philemon.* The Pillar New Testament Commentary. Grand Rapids: Eerdmans, 2008.

Moore, George Foot. "Christian Writers on Judaism." *Harvard Theological Review* 14 (1921) 197–254.

———. *Judaism in the First Centuries of the Christian Era: The Age of the Tannaim*. Vol. 1. Cambridge: Harvard University Press, 1927.

Morris, Benny, and Dror Ze'evi. *The Thirty-Year Genocide*. Cambridge. Harvard University Press. 2019

Morris, Leon. *The Epistle to the Romans*. Pillar New Testament Commentary. Grand Rapids: Eerdmans, 1988.

Moss, Candida. *God's Ghostwriters: Enslaved Christians and the Making of the Bible*. New York: HarperOne, 2024.

Mounce, Robert H. "Preaching, Kerygma." In *Dictionary of Paul and His Letters*, edited by Gerald F. Hawthorne et al., 735–37. Downers Grove, IL: InterVarsity, 1993.

———. *Romans*. The New American Commentary 27. Nashville: Broadman & Holman, 1995.

Murphy-O'Connor, Jerome. *Paul: A Critical Life*. Oxford: Clarendon, 1996.

Nagy, Dorottya. "Theory and Method in Mission Studies/Missiology." In *The Oxford Handbook of Mission Studies*, edited by Kirsteen Kim et al., 56–74. Oxford: Oxford University Press, 2022. https://doi.org/10.1093/oxfordhb/9780198831723.013.3.

Nanos, Mark D. *Reading Romans Within Judaism: Collected Essays of Mark D. Nanos*. Vol. 2. Eugene, OR: Cascade, 2018.

———. *The Mystery of Romans: The Jewish Context of Paul's Letter*. Minneapolis: Fortress, 1996.

Nanos, Mark D., and Magnus Zetterholm. *Paul Within Judaism: Restoring the First-Century Context to the Apostle*. Minneapolis: Fortress, 2015.

Naselli, Andrew David. *Romans: A Concise Guide to the Greatest Letter Ever Written*. Bellingham, WA: Lexham, 2022.

National Institute of Statistics (Romania). RPL 2021. "2021 Population and Housing Census: Population by Ethnicity." https://www.recensamantromania.ro.

National Research Council. *Ecological Indicators for the Nation*. Washington, DC: National Academies Press, 2000.

Newbigin, Lesslie. *The Gospel in a Pluralist Society*. Grand Rapids: Eerdmans, 1989.

———. *The Open Secret: An Introduction to the Theology of Mission*. Rev. ed. Grand Rapids: Eerdmans, 1995.

Nicholls, B. J. "Contextualization." In *New Dictionary of Theology: Historical and Systematic*, edited by Martin Davie et al., 215. Downers Grove, IL: InterVarsity, 2016.

Niebauer, Michael. *Virtuous Persuasion: A Theology of Christian Mission*. Bellingham, WA: Lexham, 2022.

Nieman, James R. "The Theological Work of Denominations." In *Church, Identity, and Change*, edited by David A. Roozen and James R. Nieman, 625–53. Grand Rapids: Eerdmans, 2005.

Noll, Mark A. *The Civil War as a Theological Crisis*. Chapel Hill: University of North Carolina Press, 2006.

Odum, Eugene P. *Ecology and Our Endangered Life-Support Systems*. Sunderland, MA: Sinauer Associates, 1993.

———. *The Old Religion in a New World: The History of North American Christianity*. Grand Rapids: Eerdmans, 2002.

Odum, Eugene P., and Gary W. Barrett. *Fundamentals of Ecology*. 5th ed. Belmont, CA: Thomson Brooks/Cole, 2005.

Nygren, Anders. *Commentary on Romans*. Translated by Carl C. Rasmussen. Philadelphia: Fortress, 1949.

O'Brien, Peter T. *Gospel and Mission in the Writings of Paul*. Grand Rapids: Baker, 1995.

———. *The Letter to the Ephesians*. The Pillar New Testament Commentary. Grand Rapids: Eerdmans, 1999.

O'Connor, Timothy, and Hong Yu Wong. "Emergent Properties." Stanford Encyclopedia of Philosophy Archive. Summer 2015 ed., Jun. 3, 2015. Edited by Edward N. Zalta. https://plato.stanford.edu/archives/sum2015/entries/properties-emergent/.

Oden, Thomas C. *Classic Christianity: A Systematic Theology*. San Francisco: HarperOne, 2009.

———. *Life in the Spirit: Systematic Theology*. Vol. 3. San Francisco: Harper SanFrancisco, 1992.

Olson, Roger E. *The Mosaic of Christian Belief: Twenty Centuries of Unity and Diversity*. 2nd ed. Downers Grove, IL: IVP Academic, 2016.

Omran, Emad Attia Mohamed, and Yuriy Bilan. "Female Labour Force Participation and the Economic Development in Egypt." *European Journal of Interdisciplinary Studies* 14 (2022) 1–12.

Onesti, Karen L., and Manfred T. Brauch. "Righteousness, Righteousness of God." In *Dictionary of Paul and His Letters*, edited by Gerald F. Hawthorne et al., 827–37. Downers Grove, IL: InterVarsity, 1993.

Origen. *On First Principles: A Reader's Edition*. Translated and edited by John Behr. Oxford Early Christian Texts. Oxford: Oxford University Press, 2017.

Osborne, Grant R. "Hermeneutics/Interpreting Paul." In *Dictionary of Paul and His Letters*, edited by Gerald F. Hawthorne et al., 396. Downers Grove, IL: InterVarsity, 1993.

———. *Romans*. The IVP New Testament Commentary Series. Downers Grove, IL: InterVarsity, 2004.

Ott, Craig, et al. *Encountering Theology of Mission: Biblical Foundations, Historical Developments, and Contemporary Issues*. Grand Rapids: Baker Academic, 2010.

Özbek, İhsan, and Helen Melahouris. *Fireflies at Midnight: A Historical Narrative of Kurtuluş and the Foursquare Work in Turkey*. San Antonio, TX: Wineseed, 2023.

Pachuau, Lalsangkima. *God at Work in the World: Theology and Mission in the Global Church*. Grand Rapids: Baker Academic, 2022.

Padgett, Alan G. "Marcion." In *Dictionary of the Later New Testament and Its Developments*, edited by Ralph P. Martin and Peter H. Davids, 705–8. Downers Grove, IL: InterVarsity, 1997.

Pannenberg, Wolfhart. *Systematic Theology*. Vol. 1. Grand Rapids: Eerdmans, 1991.

Pao, David W. *Colossians and Philemon*. Zondervan Exegetical Commentary on the New Testament. Grand Rapids: Zondervan, 2012.

Park, M. Sydney. "What Does Romans 16 Say about the Ministry of Women in the Earliest Church?" In *Paul's Letter to the Romans: Theological Essays*, edited by Douglas J. Moo et al., 357–74. Peabody, MA: Hendrickson Academic, 2023.

Pascu, Gabriel, and Bogdan Doboş. "Roma Communities and Pentecostal Churches in Romania." *Journal of Religion in Europe* 6 (2013) 231–63.

Patrick. *Confession of St. Patrick*. Christian Classics Ethereal Library. https://www.ccel.org/ccel/patrick/confession.pdf.

Patte, Daniel, and Cristina Grenholm, eds. *Romans Through History and Culture.* Harrisburg, PA: Trinity, 2003–2013.

Patte, Daniel, and Eugene TeSelle, eds. *Engaging Augustine on Romans: Self, Context, and Theology in Interpretation.* Harrisburg, PA: Trinity, 2002.

Paul, Shalom M. *Isaiah 40–66: Translation and Commentary.* Eerdmans Critical Commentary. Grand Rapids: Eerdmans, 2012.

Penna, Romano. "Judaism: Judaism in Rome." In *The Anchor Yale Bible Dictionary*, edited by David Noel Freedman, 3:1074. New York: Doubleday, 1992.

Peters, George W. *A Biblical Theology of Missions.* Chicago: Moody, 1984.

Peters, Greg. *The Story of Monasticism: Retrieving an Ancient Tradition for Contemporary Spirituality.* Grand Rapids: Baker, 2015.

Piper, John. *The Future of Justification: A Response to N. T. Wright.* Wheaton, IL: Crossway, 2007.

Pitre, Brant, et al. *Paul, a New Covenant Jew.* Grand Rapids: Eerdmans, 2019.

Plummer, Robert L. and John Mark Terry, eds. *Paul's Missionary Methods: In His Time and Ours.* Downers Grove, IL: IVP Academic. 2012.

Pollard, Justin, and Howard Reid. *The Rise and Fall of Alexandria: Birthplace of the Modern Mind.* New York: Viking, 2006.

Porter, Stanley E. *The Letter to the Romans: A Linguistic and Literary Commentary.* Sheffield: Sheffield Phoenix, 2015.

Porter, Stanley E., and Christopher D. Stanley, eds. *As It Is Written: Studying Paul's Use of Scripture.* Symposium Series 50. Atlanta: Society of Biblical Literature, 2008.

Punt, Jeremy. "Paul, Hermeneutics and the Scriptures of Israel." Neotestamentica 30 (1996) 377. https://www.jstor.org/stable/43048273.

Quell, Gottfried, and Ethelbert Stauffer. "Ἀγαπάω, Ἀγάπη, Ἀγαπητός." In *Theological Dictionary of the New Testament*, edited by Gerhard Kittel and Gerhard Friedrich and translated by Geoffrey W. Bromiley, 1:21–55. Grand Rapids: Eerdmans, 1964–1976.

Rector, Lallene J. "Shame and Honor Systems in the Book of Romans: A Psychological Analysis of the Struggle for Superiority Within and Between the Roman Tenement and House Churches." In *Scripture, Cultures, and Criticism: Interpretive Steps and Critical Issues Raised by Robert Jewett*, edited by K. K. Yeo, 117–29. Contrapuntal Readings of the Bible in World Christianity 9. Eugene, OR: Pickwick, 2022.

Rengstorf, Karl Heinrich. "Ἀποστέλλω (πέμπω), Ἐξαποστέλλω, Ἀπόστολος, Ψευδαπόστολος, Ἀποστολή." In *Theological Dictionary of the New Testament*, edited by Gerhard Kittel and Gerhard Friedrich and translated by Geoffrey W. Bromiley, 1:398–447. Grand Rapids: Eerdmans, 1964–1976.

Reymond, Robert L. *Paul: Missionary Theologian.* Tain, UK: Mentor, 2006.

Richardson, John S. *The Romans in Spain.* Oxford: Blackwell, 1996.

Rohoziński, Jerzy. "Religious Revival and Its Limitations in the Postwar Soviet Union: The Case of Northern Kazakhstan." *Studia Religiologica* 57 (2024) 51–71.

Roma at a Glance. N.p.: Roma Initiative Office, 2021.

Romanides, John S. *The Ancestral Sin.* Ridgewood, NJ: Zephyr, 2002.

Romocea, Cristian G. "Church–State Relations in Post-1989 Romania." *Journal of Church and State* 53 (2011) 243–77.

Roper, Jeff. *Following Wisdom, Leading Wisely: Proverbs as Ancient Wisdom for Today's Leader.* Eugene, OR: Wipf and Stock, 2024.

Ropes, James Hardy. "'Righteousness' and 'The Righteousness of God' in the Old Testament and in St. Paul." *Journal of Biblical Literature* 22 (1903) 211–27. https://www.jstor.org/stable/3259199.

Rosen-Zvi, Ishay, and Adi Ophir. "Paul and the Invention of the Gentiles." *The Jewish Quarterly Review* 105 (Winter 2015) 1–41.

Rosner, Brian S. "The Glory of God in Paul's Missionary Theology and Practice." In *Paul as Missionary: Identity, Activity, Theology, and Practice*, edited by Trevor J. Burke and Brian S. Rosner, 158–68. New York: Bloomsbury T&T Clark, 2011.

Rosscup, James E. *An Exposition on Prayer in the Bible: Igniting the Fuel to Flame Our Communication with God*. 4 vols. Bellingham, WA: Lexham, 2008.

Royster, Dmitri. *St. Paul's Epistle to the Romans*. Crestwood, NY: St. Vladimir's Seminary Press, 2008.

Ruffin, M. Holt, and Daniel C. Waugh, eds. *Civil Society in Central Asia*. Seattle: University of Washington Press, 1999.

Ruthven, Malise. *Islam in the World*. 3rd ed. New York: Oxford University Press, 2006.

Rybarczyk, Edmund J. *Beyond Salvation: Eastern Orthodoxy and Classical Pentecostalism on Becoming Like Christ*. Milton Keynes, UK: Paternoster, 2006.

Sacks, Jonathan. *Morality: Restoring the Common Good in Divided Times*. New York: Basic, 2020.

———. *To Heal a Fractured World: The Ethics of Responsibility*. New York: Schocken, 2007.

Saleh, Alam, and Hendrik Kraetzschmar. "Politicized Identities, Securitized Politics: Sunni–Shi'a Politics in Egypt." *Middle East Journal* 69 (2015) 545–62. http://www.jstor.org/stable/43698287.

Saller, Richard P. "Culture and Religion." *Encyclopaedia Britannica*, Mar. 25, 2026. https://www.britannica.com/place/ancient-Rome/Culture-and-religion.

Sanders, E. P. *Paul and Palestinian Judaism: A Comparison of Patterns of Religion*. 40th Anniversary Edition. Minneapolis: Fortress, 2017.

Sandnes, Karl Olav. "Prophet-Like Apostle: A Note on the 'Radical New Perspective' in Pauline Studies." *Biblica* 96 (2015) 550–64. https://www.jstor.org/stable/43922787.

Sanneh, Lamin. *Translating the Message: The Missionary Impact on Culture*. 2nd ed. Maryknoll, NY: Orbis, 2009.

Schnabel, Eckhard J. *Early Christian Mission*. 2 vols. Downers Grove, IL: InterVarsity, 2004.

———. *Paul the Missionary: Realities, Strategies, and Methods*. Downers Grove, IL: IVP Academic, 2008.

Schreiner, Thomas R. "Justification: The Saving Righteousness of God in Christ." *Journal of the Evangelical Theological Society* 54 (2011) 19–34. https://etsjets.org/wp-content/uploads/2011/08/files_JETS-PDFs_54_54-1_JETS_54-1_19-34_Schreiner.pdf.

———. *Romans*. Baker Exegetical Commentary on the New Testament 6. Grand Rapids: Baker, 1998.

Schubert, Paul. *The Form and Function of the Pauline Thanksgivings*. Berlin: Töpelmann, 1939.

Seifrid, Mark A. *Christ, Our Righteousness: Paul's Theology of Justification*. Downers Grove, IL: InterVarsity, 2000.

Shaw, Mark, and Wanjiru M. Gitau. *The Kingdom of God in Africa: A History of African Christianity*. Carlisle, UK: Langham, 2020.

Shedd, W. G. T., *A Critical and Doctrinal Commentary upon the Epistle of St. Paul to the Romans*. New York: Scribner, Armstrong, and Co., 1879.

Shohe, Zakal. "The Hermeneutic of Love, Honor, and Hospitality: Redefining Relationships in Romans 12–13." In *Scripture, Cultures, and Criticism: Interpretive Steps and Critical Issues Raised by Robert Jewett*, edited by K. K. Yeo, 231–50. Contrapuntal Readings of the Bible in World Christianity 9. Eugene, OR: Pickwick, 2022.

Silva, Moisés, ed. *New International Dictionary of New Testament Theology and Exegesis*. Grand Rapids: Zondervan, 2014.

Smartley, Keith, ed. *Encountering the World of Islam*. Atlanta: Authentic, 2008.

Smith, Charles Gordon, et al. "Egypt." *Encyclopaedia Britannica*, Mar. 18, 2026. https://www.britannica.com/place/Egypt.

Sprinkle, Preston M. "The Old Perspective on the New Perspective: A Review of Some 'Pre-Sanders' Thinkers." *Themelios* 30 (2005) 21–31.

Sproul, R. C. *The Gospel of God: An Exposition of Romans*. Great Britain: Christian Focus, 1994.

Stan, Lavinia, and Lucian Turcescu. *Religion and Politics in Post-Communist Romania*. Oxford: Oxford University Press, 2007.

Stanley, Christopher D. *Paul and the Language of Scripture: Citation Technique in the Pauline Epistles and Contemporary Literature*. Cambridge: Cambridge University Press, 1992.

Stark, Rodney. *The Rise of Christianity: A Sociologist Considers History*. Princeton: Princeton University Press, 1996.

Stendahl, Krister. "The Apostle Paul and the Introspective Conscience of the West." *Harvard Theological Review* 56 (1963) 199–215. http://www.jstor.org/stable/1508631.

———. *Paul Among Jews and Gentiles and Other Essays*. Philadelphia: Fortress, 1976.

Stenschke, Christoph W. "Paul's Jewish Gospel and the Claims of Rome in Paul's Epistle to the Romans." *Neotestamentica* 46 (2012) 338–78.

Stuhlmacher, Peter. *Paul's Letter to the Romans: A Commentary*. Translated by Scott J. Hafemann. Louisville, KY: Westminster John Knox, 1994.

Stults, Donald Le Roy. *Grasping Truth and Reality: Lesslie Newbigin's Theology of Mission to the Western World*. Eugene, OR: Wipf & Stock, 2008.

Sutton, Matthew Avery. *Aimee Semple McPherson and the Resurrection of Christian America*. Cambridge: Harvard University Press, 2001.

Tacitus, Cornelius. *The Annals and The Histories*. New York: Random House, 2003.

Tarazi, Paul Nadim. *The Chrysostom Bible. Romans: A Commentary*. Crestwood, NY: St. Vladimir's Seminary Press, 2010.

Teeter, Emily. *Religion and Ritual in Ancient Egypt*. New York: Cambridge University, 2011.

Tennent, Timothy C. *Invitation to World Missions: A Trinitarian Missiology for the Twenty-first Century*. Grand Rapids: Kregel, 2010.

The Modern Geopolitical State and the Future of National Church Development in the Foursquare Movement. Internal FMI Proposal, 2023.

Thomassen, Bjørn. *Liminality and the Modern: Living Through the In-Between*. London: Routledge, 2014.

Thompson, James W. "Paul as Missionary Pastor." In *Paul as Missionary: Identity, Activity, Theology, and Practice*, edited by Trevor J. Burke and Brian S. Rosner, 25–36. New York: Bloomsbury T&T Clark, 2011.

Thompson, Jason. *A History of Egypt: From Earliest Times to the Present*. New York: Anchor, 2008.

Timmins, Will N. "Why Paul Wrote Romans: Putting the Pieces Together." *Themelios* 43 (2018) https://www.thegospelcoalition.org/themelios/article/why-paul-wrote-romans-putting-the-pieces-together/.

Turner, Geoffrey. "Paul and the Old Testament—His Legacy and Ours." *New Blackfriars* 91 (2010) 128–41. https://www.jstor.org/stable/43251378.

Turner, Victor. *The Ritual Process: Structure and Anti-Structure*. Ithaca, NY: Cornell University Press, 1977.

Turner, Victor, and Edith Turner. *Image and Pilgrimage in Christian Culture*. New York: Columbia University Press, 1995.

Twiss, Richard. *Rescuing the Gospel from the Cowboys: A Native American Expression of the Jesus Way*. Downers Grove, IL: InterVarsity, 2015.

Tyson, Joseph B. "'Works of Law' in Galatians." *Journal of Biblical Literature* 92 (1973) 423–31. https://doi.org/10.2307/3263582.

UNHCR. "Refugee Context in Egypt." https://www.unhcr.org/eg/refugee-context-egypt.

United Nations Statistics Division. *Composition of Macro Geographical (Continental) Regions, Geographical Sub-Regions, and Selected Economic and Other Groupings*. https://unstats.un.org/unsd/methodology/m49/.

US Census Bureau. "Arizona." QuickFacts. https://www.census.gov/quickfacts/fact/table/AZ/PST045224.

———. "California." QuickFacts. https://www.census.gov/quickfacts/fact/table/CA/PST045224.

———. "Nevada." QuickFacts. https://www.census.gov/quickfacts/fact/table/NV/PST045224.

———. "Utah." QuickFacts. https://www.census.gov/quickfacts/fact/table/UT/PST045224.

US Commission on International Religious Freedom (USCIRF). *2025 Annual Report*. Washington, DC: USCIRF, 2025.

Vail, Ted. "Foursquare Missiology: Reproducible, Empowering, and Relational." *Pentecostal Education: A Journal of the World Alliance for Pentecostal Theological Education* 8 (Fall 2023) 155–68.

Van Cleave, Nathaniel M. *The Vine and the Branches: A History of the International Church of the Foursquare Gospel*. Lake Mary, FL: Creation House, 2014.

Van Engen, Charles E. *God's Missionary People: Rethinking the Purpose of the Local Church*. Grand Rapids: Baker, 1991.

Van Gelder, Craig, and Dwight J. Zscheile. *The Missional Church in Perspective: Mapping Trends and Shaping the Conversation*. Grand Rapids: Baker Academic, 2011.

Van Gennep, Arnold. *The Rites of Passage*. Translated by Monika B. Vizedom and Gabrielle L. Caffee. Chicago: University of Chicago Press, 1960.

Ventura, Luca. "Poorest Countries in the World 2025." *Global Finance Magazine*, Sept. 11, 2025. https://gfmag.com/data/economic-data/poorest-country-in-the-world/.

Verdery, Katherine. *National Ideology Under Socialism: Identity and Cultural Politics in Ceausescu's Romania*. Berkeley: University of California Press, 1991.

Verkuyl, Johannes. *Contemporary Missiology: An Introduction*. Grand Rapids: Eerdmans. 1978.

Viguera, Maria J., et al. "Romanization of Spain." *Encyclopaedia Britannica*, Mar. 22, 2026. https://www.britannica.com/place/Spain/Romanization.

Volf, Miroslav. *Exclusion and Embrace: A Theological Exploration of Identity, Otherness, and Reconciliation*. Rev. and updated ed. Nashville: Abingdon, 2019.

———. *A Public Faith: How Followers of Christ Should Serve the Common Good*. Grand Rapids: Brazos, 2011.

Wagner, J. Ross. *Heralds of the Good News: Isaiah and Paul in Concert in the Letter to the Romans*. Boston: Brill, 2003.

Walls, Andrew F. *The Missionary Movement in Christian History: Studies in the Transmission of Faith*. Maryknoll, NY: Orbis, 1996.

Walton, John H., and J. Harvey Walton. *The Lost World of the Torah: Law as Covenant and Wisdom in Ancient Context*. Downers Grove, IL: IVP Academic, 2019.

Warrington, Keith. *Pentecostal Theology: A Theology of Encounter*. New York: T&T Clark, 2008.

Wells, Colin M. "Roman Empire." In *The Anchor Yale Bible Dictionary*, edited by David Noel Freedman, 5:801–6. New York: Doubleday, 1992.

Wenham, David. *Paul: Follower of Jesus or Founder of Christianity?* Grand Rapids: Eerdmans, 1995.

Wheatley, Margaret J. *Leadership and the New Science: Discovering Order in a Chaotic World*. 3rd ed. San Francisco: Berrett-Koehler, 2006.

"Why Did Christianity Conquer the Roman Empire?" *The Biblical World* 22 (1903) 478. http://www.jstor.org/stable/3140817.

Wilkins, Michael J. "Christian." In *The Anchor Yale Bible Dictionary*, edited by David Noel Freedman, 1:925–26. New York: Doubleday, 1992.

Windley, Brian Frederick, et al. "Europe." *Encyclopaedia Britannica*, Apr. 7, 2026. https://www.britannica.com/place/Europe.

Winter, Ralph D. "The Two Structures of God's Redemptive Mission." *Missiology: An International Review* 2 (1974) 121–33.

Witherington, Ben, III, and Darlene Hyatt. *Paul's Letter to the Romans: A Socio-Rhetorical Commentary*. Grand Rapids: Eerdmans, 2004.

World Bank Group. "Romania." https://www.worldbank.org/en/country/romania.

Worldometer. "Northern Africa Population." https://www.worldometers.info/world-population/northern-africa-population/.

World Tourism Organization (UNWTO). *Tourism Highlights 2024 Edition*. Madrid: UNWTO, 2024.

Wright, Christopher J. H. *The Mission of God: Unlocking the Bible's Grand Narrative*. Downers Grove, IL: IVP Academic, 2018.

Wright, N. T. "A New Tübingen School? Ernst Käsemann and His Commentary on Romans." Themelios 7 (1982) https://www.thegospelcoalition.org/themelios/article/a-new-tubingen-school-ernst-kasemann-and-his-commentary-on-romans/.

———. *Paul and the Faithfulness of God*. Christian Origins and the Question of God 4. Minneapolis: Fortress, 2013.

Wuellner, Wilhelm. "Paul's Rhetoric of Argumentation in Romans: An Alternative to the Donfried–Karris Debate over Romans." *The Catholic Biblical Quarterly* 38 (1976) 330–51.

Yackley, Ayla Jean. "Turkish Court Jails 5 Men for Life over Murder of Christians." *Business Insider*, Sept. 28, 2016. https://www.businessinsider.com/turkish-court-jails-5-men-for-life-over-murder-of-christians-2016-9.

Yemelianova, Galina M. "Islam, National Identity and Politics in Contemporary Kazakhstan." *Asian Ethnicity* 15 (2014) 286–301.

Yeo, K. K., ed. *From Rome to Beijing: Symposia on Robert Jewett's Commentary on Romans*. Lincoln, NE: Kairos Studies, 2013.

———. *Scripture, Cultures, and Criticism: Interpretive Steps and Critical Issues Raised by Robert Jewett*. Contrapuntal Readings of the Bible in World Christianity 9. Eugene, OR: Pickwick, 2022.

Yong, Amos. *The Missiological Spirit: Christian Mission Theology in the Third Millennium Global Context*. Eugene, OR: Cascade, 2014.

Zespri Kiwifruit. "What Is the Origin of Kiwifruit?" https://www.zespri.com/en-UK/blogdetail/what-is-the-origin-of-kiwifruit.

www.ingramcontent.com/pod-product-compliance
Lightning Source LLC
LaVergne TN
LVHW020519100826
845148LV00010B/1284